TIBERIUS AND THE CHARISMA OF AUGUSTUS

The historian Tacitus began his *Annals* with the death of Augustus. He considered this date, not Actium, to be the pivotal moment in the crystallization of "rule by one man." This book considers the role played by Augustus' successor, Tiberius, in preserving the system created by the ultimate victor of Rome's civil wars. Drawing upon the work of sociologists and political scientists, it uses the lens of the routinization of charisma to demonstrate how Tiberius' reverence for Augustus and preservation of his policies enacted lasting political change. Tiberius' encouragement of the cult of Divus Augustus and his own refusal of divine honors carry over into other aspects of his reign, where Tiberius recedes into the background, permanently withdrawing from Rome. The charisma of Augustus protected his family, the *domus Augusta*, and the entire empire, even after his death. This enshrined the position of Augustus as a permanent institution, the principate.

REBECCA EDWARDS is a former Associate Professor of Classics at Wright State University.

TIBERIUS AND THE CHARISMA OF AUGUSTUS

The Principate Enshrined

REBECCA EDWARDS

CAMBRIDGE
UNIVERSITY PRESS

CAMBRIDGE
UNIVERSITY PRESS

Shaftesbury Road, Cambridge CB2 8EA, United Kingdom

One Liberty Plaza, 20th Floor, New York, NY 10006, USA

477 Williamstown Road, Port Melbourne, VIC 3207, Australia

314–321, 3rd Floor, Plot 3, Splendor Forum, Jasola District Centre, New Delhi – 110025, India

103 Penang Road, #05-06/07, Visioncrest Commercial, Singapore 238467

Cambridge University Press is part of Cambridge University Press & Assessment, a department of the University of Cambridge.

We share the University's mission to contribute to society through the pursuit of education, learning and research at the highest international levels of excellence.

www.cambridge.org
Information on this title: www.cambridge.org/9781009476676

DOI: 10.1017/9781009476713

First published 2025

A catalogue record for this publication is available from the British Library

A Cataloging-in-Publication data record for this book is available from the Library of Congress

ISBN 978-1-009-47667-6 Hardback

Contents

List of Figures and Tables   *page* vi
Acknowledgements   vii
Abbreviations   ix

   Introduction   I

1 Augustan Charisma and Its Transfer   7

2 Tiberius and the Imperial Cult   36

3 Charismatic Precedents   66

4 The Power of Images of Augustus in the Age of Tiberius   98

5 Charismatic Images of Augustus in Tiberian Authors   135

6 *Maiestas* and the Protection of Augustan Charisma   166

   Conclusions   207

Bibliography   210
Index   238

v

Figures and Tables

Figures

4.1 Divus Augustus Pater *aes*   *page* 100
4.2 Tiberius, Copenhagen 623/IN 1445   118
4.3 Augustus, Louvre MA 1280   119
4.4 Augustus of Prima Porta   120
4.5 Tiberius, Copenhagen 624/IN 1750   121
4.6 Tiberius, Chiaramonti   122
4.7 Augustus, Louvre MA 1246   124
4.8 Tiberius Cup, Triumph Scene   126
4.9 The Sword of Tiberius   127
4.10 The Gemma Augustea   129
4.11 The Grand Camée   130
4.12 Livia and Tiberius   132
4.13 Livia and Augustus   133

Tables

4.1 Portraits of Tiberius as identified by Boschung,
Pollini, and Hertel   *page* 117

Acknowledgements

The concept for this book originated twenty years ago in my dissertation at Indiana University, under the direction of Eleanor Leach. I wish she could have lived to see the final product. I received valuable advice from the other members of my committee, Jim Franklin, Betty Rose Nagle, and Julie Van Voorhis. After defending my dissertation, I shelved the project and turned to work on Tacitus. Ultimately, I found myself returning to the idea that Tacitus found so paradoxical: how could a man who seemed so "Republican" be responsible for making the principate a permanent institution?

I began work on this book in earnest thanks to a year-long research leave granted by Wright State University. I would like to thank my colleagues for their support, especially my fellow Classicists, Bruce Laforse and Jeannie Marchand, and my former department chair, Ava Chamberlain, whose advice on the publishing process has been much appreciated. I would like to thank the American Academy in Rome. I began my dissertation while attending the Academy's Classical Summer School. I began the monograph as a Visiting Scholar. I would like to thank the librarians at Cal Poly San Luis Obispo for securing the materials necessary to complete this work.

On a personal level, I want to thank my parents, Craig and Sue Edwards, for constantly asking how the book was coming along. I wish to thank my brother, Matt, and his family for listening to me ramble about the writing process. Kris Young has been a constant cheerleader in this endeavor, while reminding me to have fun every once in a while. Thanks to Fred and Carol Astaire for giving me a soft place to land. And last, but certainly not least, *maximas gratias* to my partner, John Astaire.

All translations are my own unless otherwise indicated. The following translations are cited throughout the text:

Basore, John. 1935. *Seneca. Moral Essays, Vol. III: De Beneficiis.* Loeb Classical Library. Cambridge, MA: Harvard University Press.

Cary, Earnest. 1914–1927. *Cassius Dio. Roman History.* 9 vols. Loeb Classical Library. Cambridge, MA: Harvard University Press.

Colson, F. H. 1962. *Philo. On the Embassy to Gaius.* Loeb Classical Library. Cambridge, MA: Harvard University Press.

Feldman, Louis. 1965. *Josephus. Jewish Antiquities, Vol. VIII: Books 18–19.* Loeb Classical Library. Cambridge, MA: Harvard University Press.

Jones, Horace. 1917–1932. *Strabo. Geography.* 8 vols. Loeb Classical Library. Cambridge, MA: Harvard University Press.

Ker, Walter. 1963. *Cicero. Philippics.* Loeb Classical Library. Cambridge, MA: Harvard University Press.

Perry, Ben. 1965. *Babrius, Phaedrus. Fables.* Loeb Classical Library. Cambridge, MA: Harvard University Press.

Russell, Donald. 2002. *Quintilian. The Orator's Education, Vol. IV: Books 9–10.* Loeb Classical Library. Cambridge, MA: Harvard University Press.

Rolfe, J. C. 1914. *Suetonius. Lives of the Caesars, Vol. I: Julius, Augustus, Tiberius, Gaius Caligula.* Loeb Classical Library. Cambridge, MA: Harvard University Press.

Sherk, Robert. 1988. *The Roman Empire: Augustus to Hadrian.* Cambridge: Cambridge University Press.

Warner, Rex. 1976. *Plutarch. The Fall of the Roman Republic: Marius, Sulla, Crassus, Pompey, Caesar, Cicero.* London: Penguin.

White, Horace. 1913. *Appian. Roman History, Vol. IV: The Civil Wars, Books 3.27–5.* Loeb Classical Library. Cambridge, MA: Harvard University Press.

Abbreviations

Abbreviations of ancient authors follow those used by the *Oxford Classical Dictionary*. Periodicals are cited according to *L'année philologique*. Frequently cited modern works are abbreviated as follows:

AE   *L'année épigraphique*
BMCRE   Mattingly, H. 1965. *Coins of the Roman Empire in the British Museum. Vol. 1: Augustus to Vitellius.* London: Trustees of the British Museum.
CBN   Giard, Jean-Baptiste. 1976. *Catalogue de la Bibliothèque Nationale de France, Catalogue des Monnaies de l'Empire Romain, I Auguste.* Paris: Bibliothèque Nationale de France.
CIL   *Corpus Inscriptionum Latinarum*
Inscr. It. Degrassi, A. 1963. *Inscriptiones Italiae XIII.2: Fasti anni Numani et Iuliani.* Rome: Istituto Poligrafico dello Stato.
E.-J.²   Ehrenberg, V. and A. H. M. Jones. 1976. *Documents Illustrating the Reigns of Augustus and Tiberius.* 2nd ed. Oxford: Oxford University Press.
FiE   *Forschungen in Ephesos*
FRH   Cornell, T. J., ed. 2013. *Fragments of the Roman Historians.* 3 vols. Oxford: Oxford University Press.
IvE   *Die Inschriften von Ephesos*
ILS   *Inscriptiones Latinae Selectae*
IRT   *Inscriptions of Roman Tripolitania*
LSJ   Liddell, H., R. Scott, and H. S. Jones. 1968. *Greek–English Lexicon.* Oxford: Oxford University Press.
OCD   *The Oxford Classical Dictionary*, online ed.
OLD   *The Oxford Latin Dictionary*
P. Oxy.   *Papyri from Oxyrhynchus*

RIC   Sutherland, C. H. V. and R. A. G. Carson. 1984. *Roman Imperial Coinage. Vol. 1: 39 BC to AD 69.* 2nd ed. London: Spink.

RIT   *Die römischen Inschriften von Tarraco*

RPC   Burnett, A., M. Amandry, and P. P. Ripollès. 1992. *Roman Provincial Coinage. Vol. 1: from the death of Caesar to the death of Vitellius (44 BC–AD 69).* London: British Museum Press.

RRC   Crawford, M. 1975. *Roman Republican Coinage.* 2 vols. Cambridge: Cambridge University Press.

SEG   *Supplementum Epigraphicum Graecum*

Introduction

On August 19, AD 14, after a long and relatively peaceful reign, Augustus died just a few weeks shy of his seventy-seventh birthday.[1] His adopted sons – his grandsons by his disgraced daughter Julia – had died over a decade prior. After their deaths, he had adopted his stepson, Tiberius, having compelled Tiberius to adopt his own nephew and Augustus' great-nephew, Germanicus. As the series of military despots and civil wars which preceded the rule of Augustus had proven, the security of Rome rested upon a smooth transition between Augustus and his successor. According to Velleius Paterculus (2.124), an eyewitness to the transition of power, there was great fear on the part of the Senate and great concern among the people that Tiberius might not step into the position left vacant by Augustus. Due to the length of Augustus' reign, many may not have lived through the chaos of the civil wars themselves, but the cultural memory of those years was still strong enough to generate fear. What if Tiberius had actually refused? Tacitus (*Ann.* 1.13) states that Augustus in his last days had considered four men besides Tiberius as *capax imperii*. Germanicus was not one of them. Furthermore, neither Germanicus nor anyone else held the proconsular *imperium* and *tribunicia potestas* conferred upon Tiberius during the last years of Augustus' reign. At the time of Augustus' death, only Tiberius held powers even remotely close to those wielded by Augustus.

In the end, Tiberius not only succeeded Augustus but ruled for twenty-three years without any major challenge to his position. It would take a century before another ruler lasted more than twenty years, when Hadrian succeeded the charismatic Trajan in 117 and ruled until his death (by natural causes) in 138. Of Tiberius' immediate successors, Caligula was assassinated by his own guard, Claudius was murdered (allegedly) by his wife/niece Agrippina, and Nero was overthrown by a military rebellion and

---

[1] All dates are AD unless otherwise indicated.

the condemnation of the Senate. The demise of the Julio-Claudian line led to a civil war that ultimately gave birth to a new dynasty. Yet throughout all the turmoil which threatened various principes, the idea of a principate survived.

The matter of Augustus' immediate successor is vitally important in examining the formation and duration of the Roman principate. Had Augustus been succeeded by another military despot intent on wiping out his reforms, he would have stood in a long line of late Republican figures who possessed power and charisma, a concept to which we shall return shortly, but whose revolutionary reforms had no lasting effect on the nature of government. In order for the power and charisma amassed by Augustus during his lengthy reign to outlive him, it was necessary that his successor adopt the same policies and promote the same ideology. In other words, the true test of the power of the principate was not the reign of Augustus but that of Tiberius.

In this book, I argue that the key to Tiberius' success was the charismatic image of his divine predecessor, Augustus. That his contemporaries recognized this can be seen in the exchange between Tiberius and the conspirator Clemens, a former slave of Agrippa Postumus. Clemens, impersonating his deceased master, gathered a not insignificant following of those who rallied around "Agrippa" as the only other living son of Augustus. According to Tacitus, Clemens amassed supporters of all classes. The conspiracy likely involved plans to win over the armies, the linchpin for imperial power.[2] In both Tacitus' and Dio's account, Clemens was quietly arrested and brought before Tiberius. Tiberius pointedly asked Clemens how he came to be Agrippa. Clemens retorted, "In the same way in which you became Caesar" (quomodo tu Caesar, Tac. Ann. 2.40.3; οὗτος ὡς καὶ σὺ Καῖσαρ, Dio 57.16.4). Clemens' taunt is both insulting and insightful. By perpetuating the myth that Augustus continued to watch over his family and the empire, Tiberius was able to preserve the Augustan system. That said, Tiberius never claimed to be Augustus any more than Peter claimed to be Jesus. Tiberius' reverence for Augustus and his recognition that the status Augustus created, while imperfect, had ended civil wars, played a critical role in shaping the early principate.

---

[2] Cogitore (2002: 180) demonstrates that while neither author directly refers to the actions of Clemens as a conspiracy, the information in Tac. Ann. 2.39–40 and Dio 57.16.3–4 indicates that there was a very real plot. Suetonius (Tib. 25) connects the threat of Clemens directly to Tiberius' hesitation in accepting power. We will discuss this matter further in Chapter 1. The plot of Clemens and its possible ties to the trial of Libo will be explored in Chapter 6.

Despite the reputation acquired by Tiberius for *dissimulatio*, I believe Tiberius was sincere in his desire to honor Augustus and preserve the stability he had brought to the state. Given the hostility projected by later writers, it is hard to imagine a genuine bond between Augustus and Tiberius. And yet, Tiberius' father had died when he was nine (Suet. *Tib.* 6). Tiberius gave games in memory of his father and grandfather, paid for by Augustus and Livia (Suet. *Tib.* 7). This indicates that Augustus was his guardian after his father's death. Tiberius rode next to Marcellus in Augustus' Actian triumph (Suet. *Tib.* 6). Suetonius (*Tib.* 7) implies that Augustus led him to the forum to receive his *toga virilis*. Although Augustus did not adopt Tiberius until he was a middle-aged man, in many ways Augustus was the only father Tiberius had ever known. In contrast to the apparently warm relationship between the two found in letters recorded by Suetonius is the statement that Augustus adopted Tiberius not only due to the pressure put upon him by his wife but also so that he might look better by comparison (Suet. *Tib.* 21; cf. Tac. *Ann.* 1.10.7, Dio 56.45.3). Despite these assertions, Suetonius concludes by mentioning that when Augustus adopted Tiberius, he swore that he was doing it for the sake of the republic (*rei publicae causa*).

Whatever his motive, in adopting Tiberius and compelling the Senate to award him extraordinary powers, Augustus paved the way for Tiberius to inherit his position and preserve the vast majority of his policies. Tiberius' adherence to the policies of Augustus crystallized the form of the principate which would remain more or less intact for centuries. As Geiger (2018: 86) points out, aside from a brief "intermezzo at the time of Trajan," Augustus, not Julius Caesar, was seen as the first emperor. The principate only survived the death of Augustus because of his successor's professed adherence to Augustus' *facta dictaque*, as well as Tiberius' consistent promotion of Augustus and other members of the Julio-Claudian family in public venues. But things could have taken a different turn.

Indeed, the institutionalization of the position of Augustus could have played out quite differently had he been succeeded by the beloved and charismatic Germanicus. In the historical sources, Germanicus is presented as a "Republican" like his father Drusus (Tac. *Ann.* 1.33.2; Suet. *Tib.* 50).[3]

---

[3] Pelling argues that Germanicus as portrayed by Tacitus is out of place in the Augustan principate. He compares the views of the people at their respective funerals: "the poles of comparison are here, not of Germanicus and Tiberius, but Germanicus and Augustus. Or better, the whole world of Germanicus and the world of the principate: for so much of Tiberius is already there in Augustus" (1993: 78).

But as many scholars have noted, Germanicus' conduct in the field and during his tour of the East resembles more closely the Antonian conception of a Hellenistic monarchy than the Augustan facade of a "restored Republic."[4] Pani, who makes the strongest case, points out that in his decrees to the Alexandrians, Germanicus failed to mention the Senate, focusing instead on amplifying the honors for Augustus, Tiberius, and Livia and downplaying those to himself.[5] Likewise, as Augustus had forbidden any senator to enter Egypt without his permission, even if he had some sort of *maius imperium*, Germanicus' failure to consult Tiberius regarding his tour of Egypt was a serious diplomatic mistake.[6]

Aside from Germanicus' alleged ineptitude, there is also his significant personal charisma. As this book will argue, Tiberius, lacking personal charisma himself, was forced to rely upon the charisma of others, most notably Augustus, in preserving the power of the "house of Augustus," the *domus divina/domus Augusta*.[7] However, Germanicus, by most accounts, possessed personal charisma of his own which would have allowed him to make revolutionary changes to the Augustan system, for better or worse. It seems unfair to speculate on what kind of princeps Germanicus would have been based on the reigns of Caligula, Claudius, and Nero, but all three were related by blood not just to Augustus but to Germanicus as well. Out of the three, only Claudius seems to have drawn heavily on the precedents of Augustus (and Tiberius), and he alone is mentioned alongside them in the *lex de imperio Vespasiani*, a document which attempts to define the powers of those laying claim to the position of princeps after the civil wars of 69.[8]

Using Max Weber's concepts regarding charismatic leadership and the ways in which it can instigate lasting political and social change, I demonstrate that by frequently promoting the image of Augustus and relying heavily on Augustan precedents, Tiberius "routinized" the charismatic position created by his predecessor. In the context of Roman history, Weber's ideas concerning charismatic leadership have thus far only been applied to identifying charismatic leaders and studying the imperial cult.

---

[4] See especially Borzsák 1970, Rutland 1987: 158, Pani 1987, and Schmitzer 2000: 272.

[5] Pani 1987: 4–5, referring to *P. Oxy.* 2435 and E.-J.[2] 320.

[6] On Germanicus in Egypt, see Weingärtner 1969 and Hennig 1972.

[7] We will discuss the terminology of *domus divina/Augusta* in Chapter 2.

[8] For an overview of the *lex de imperio Vespasiani*, see Tuori's entry in the *OCD* and Crawford 1996: 1.549–53. Detailed scholarship on various aspects of the document can be found in the volume *La Lex de imperio Vespasiani e la Roma dei Flavi* (Capogrossi Colognesi and Tassi Scandone 2009).

I believe it is equally important to pursue the political implications of Tiberius' persistent appeal to the charisma of Divus Augustus.[9]

Christoph Hatscher's analysis of this phenomenon, *Charisma und Res Publica*, ends the line of truly charismatic leaders with Julius Caesar (2000: 75). But the political reforms which Julius Caesar tried to implement were too shocking to the traditional system to effect any lasting change; those of Augustus endured for centuries after his death. Fears (1977: 132) ascribed charisma to every Roman emperor, conceiving the princeps in terms of the Hellenistic ruler cult. Fears seems to have overlooked the difference between charisma that has been routinized into a formal position and pure charisma in the Weberian sense. Pure charisma is a rare and revolutionary quality which can be transferred to others and used to institutionalize reforms. At the opposite end of the spectrum from Fears, Veyne (1990: 306) denied charismatic authority to any Roman emperor.[10] Veyne's approach fails to consider the evolution of the unique position Augustus forged over so many years. Octavian/Augustus used his own personal charisma, combined with the critical circumstances of the times, to bring about an irreversible change in Roman government. While he may have inherited the charismatic popularity of Julius Caesar, to deny Augustus' personal charisma is to deny, to use Syme's (1939) term, the "Roman Revolution."

Edward Shils, expounding on Weber, states regarding revolutionary charismatic movements that they are usually unsuccessful when they attempt to overthrow traditional systems, but "Less often, the movement is successful, and the result is a charismatic order or at least an order in which a charismatic overlay covers the more tenacious routines of the older institutional system" (1975: 132). This is precisely what occurred under Augustus' so-called *res publica restituta*.[11] It is sometimes asserted that, unlike Augustus, Tiberius was a true "Republican," and that, although they misfired, his attempts to return power to the Senate were sincere.[12] However, this too could be seen as an imitation of Augustus, who claimed

---

[9] Cooley does cite the importance of Tiberius presenting himself as "somewhat imbued with at least some of Augustus' special status" (2019: 85). However, her focus is on the terminology of *principatus* and *paterna statio*, ideas to which we will return in Chapter 1.

[10] Cf. Flaig 2019 [1992]: 65.

[11] On the problematic nature of this term, see especially Judge 2019 and the criticisms of Lindholmer 2020.

[12] See especially Schrömbges 1986.

he restored laws and rights to the Roman people.[13] Many members of the
Senate had benefitted from the Augustan system and were all too willing to
follow Tiberius' lead.[14] Nevertheless, while the charisma of Augustus was
overlaid on traditional Roman institutions, his personal charisma compelled allegiance to his family from all facets of Roman society and ensured
the succession of his adopted son (Tiberius), great-grandson (Caligula),
great-nephew (Claudius), and great-great-grandson (Nero).

   In this book, we will examine the various aspects of the routinization of
Augustan charisma in the reign of Tiberius. We will begin (Chapter 1)
with a discussion of the modern theories of charismatic leadership and its
revolutionary qualities, followed by an analysis of the succession from the
charismatic Augustus to his noncharismatic successor. We will then
(Chapter 2) examine the imperial cult, a key instrument in the routinization of Augustan charisma and one to which Weber's ideas about charisma
have already been applied by Price (1984) and Ando (2000), among
others. In Chapter 3, we will look closely at the implications of the
statement Tacitus reports Tiberius as having made, that he followed the
words and deeds of Augustus as if they were law (*qui omnia facta dictaque
eius vice legis observem*, *Ann.* 4.37).[15] In Chapter 4, we will examine, with a
nod to Zanker's *The Power of Images in the Age of Augustus* (1988), the
power of images of Augustus in the age of Tiberius. In Chapter 5, we will
look at the way in which authors of the Tiberian era interpreted signals
from the *domus Augusta* and the Senate. Finally, in Chapter 6, we will
address the most problematic aspect of Tiberius' principate, the rise of
trials for *maiestas* (and related charges of treason) and their connection to
the instability of the *domus divina/Augusta*. Tiberius' tacit endorsement,
despite his own reservations, of the succession of Caligula is perhaps a
more telling sign of his reverence for Augustan charisma than any other
aspect of his reign.[16] By ensuring his successor would come from the line
of Divus Augustus, Tiberius cemented Augustus' image as the savior of
Rome and guaranteed that his system would endure.

[13] See Rich and Williams 1999 for an aureus of Octavian with the legend LEGES ET IVRA P.R.
RESTITVIT. Cf. Abdy and Harling 2005. For a nuanced discussion of how this evidence relates to
the problematic idea of *res publica restituta*, see Cowan 2019.
[14] On the Senate as protector of the image of Divus Augustus in the *Senatus Consultum de Pisone*, see
Cowan 2009a: 470–5.
[15] On Tacitus' tendency to blame Tiberius for all the evils of the Augustan system, see Griffin
1985 and Cowan 2009b. Cowan in particular points out Tiberius' selectivity regarding which
precedents he claims to follow in Tacitus' narrative.
[16] See especially Tac. *Ann.* 6.46.

CHAPTER I

Augustan Charisma and Its Transfer

Max Weber on Charismatic Leadership

The concept of charisma has made its way into multiple treatments of the imperial cult in the twentieth and twenty-first centuries, starting with Taeger's *Charisma. Studien zur Geschichte des Antiken Herrscherskultes* (1957) and continuing up to Boschung's brief 2015 article, "Divus Augustus. Das Charisma des Herrschers und seine postume Beglaubigung."[1] Ironically, neither of these scholars actually attempt to define categorically how the worship of Augustus, both in his own lifetime and afterwards, fits into Weber's theories of charismatic leadership. Indeed, while the term "charisma" is frequently bandied about in Classical scholarship, few have actually addressed the difficulties in trying to apply Weber's concept of charisma and charismatic leadership to Augustus. Hatscher (2000) attempted to explain how Weber's concept of charismatic leadership could be applied to multiple leaders at the end of the Republic. In particular, he focused on Sulla and Julius Caesar as leaders who fit his criteria, eschewing Octavian/Augustus as a charismatic leader. Despite his effort, his treatment was excoriated by Flaig (2004) and gently refuted by David (2002).[2]

In 2006, Lendon offered a more thorough refutation of the general application of Weber's concept of "legitimate authority" (*legitime Herrschaft*) to ancient Rome. He asserted (2006: 57) that Classicists have too casually sampled from Weber's theories without truly understanding them and that Augustus' charisma was not hereditary. This argument was particularly aimed at Ando (2000: xii), who claimed that Augustus was a charismatic leader but did not follow up on the process which transferred that personal charisma to the office of the principate. Lendon highlighted

---

[1] We will discuss the role played by charisma in the imperial cult in the next chapter.
[2] See also Gotter 2008: 175 n. 12. Hatscher (2000: 24–37) does provide an overview of the study of charisma in the ancient world, with a focus primarily on German scholarship. For other analyses of recent scholarship on charisma in imperial Rome, see Sommer 2011 and Kahlos 2020.

the difficulties inherent in applying charisma to the principate since Weber's works "display a considerable degree of confusion and internal contradiction" (2006: 54). Indeed, the three types of Weberian authority (*Herrschaft*) – rational/legal, traditional, and charismatic – do not exist in isolation from each other. One would be hard pressed to apply any of these terms exclusively to any system of government used by the Romans. The last of these is especially problematic. While the terms legal and traditional are somewhat grounded in tangible and definable realities, charisma is a term borrowed from the often intangible and indefinable world of religious experience.

To complicate matters even further, Weber himself never fully defined the process of routinization, nor did he always distinguish charismatic leadership from his two other forms of legitimate *Herrschaft*. Thus, Ando theorizes, "With these cautions in mind, we may begin with the hypotheses that the Senate understood the emperor's rule to be based on rational grounds, that the army stressed the traditional nature of his power, and that the population of the provinces viewed him as a charismatic figure in Weber's sense" (2000: 25). Ando applies this blanket statement towards all emperors, not just Augustus. But claiming all emperors to be charismatic simply by virtue of their office undermines Weber's definition of charisma as "extraordinary" (*außeralltäglich*) and revolutionary. Moreover, Ando does not explain what he means when he says that the Senate understood the princeps to have authority based on rational/legal grounds. While the emperor could hold the consulship, he often did not. The foundational basis of his unique legal authority, the *tribunicia potestas*, ran contrary to the intentions of the Republican office of Plebeian Tribune (especially considering Augustus was a patrician).[3] Augustus' election as Pontifex Maximus occurred after he had already secured power through other means. Thus, unlike Republican magistrates who had to canvass for office, the princeps held offices by virtue of being princeps.

Likewise, there is nothing inherently traditional in the authority of the princeps among the army. The princeps commanded the armies through legates and members of his own family but rarely led troops himself after becoming princeps. No one would dispute that Octavian/Augustus seized power through military means.[4] But, as we shall see, his hold over the army was not through their traditional obedience to their commanders but

---

[3] On Octavius'/Augustus' patrician status, see Toher 2017: 226.

[4] As Syme emphasized in 1939, and as Börm and Havener (2012) reiterate, Octavian came to power as a military dictator. Regardless of any legal basis for his power, his victory in civil war overshadowed his entire reign.

rather their belief in his charismatic ability to ensure victory. Weber (1968: 1125) himself recognized this, citing the eventual ability of the army to proclaim their commander as emperor. Flaig (2019 [1992]; 2011: 72) has argued that much of the emperor's power derived from *consensus* or an "Akzeptanz-System," requiring the support of the army, the Senate, and the plebs.[5] Charisma is a two-way street. Charisma must be recognized by the leader's followers.[6] However, the leader must also be able to manipulate his followers in order to secure his position.

Thus, we turn to the charismatic basis for the princeps' power. The term charisma was originally used by Rudolf Sohm (1892 and 1923) to describe the hierarchy of the early church. Weber extended its application to contrast with the other two forms of legitimate *Herrschaft*.[7] While Weber was able to define (to a certain degree) the basis of legal/rational and traditional leadership, the origin of charisma in Paul's letters as a "divine favor" bestowed by God creates difficulties. Complicating matters further, Weber treated charisma differently in different contexts. In delineating the three pure types of legitimate rule, Weber described the charismatic as "resting on devotion to the exceptional sanctity, heroism or exemplary character of an individual or person, and of the normative patterns or order revealed or ordained by him (charismatic authority)" (1968: 215). Weber expands the religious aspect of charisma to include "heroism" (*Heldenkraft*) and "extraordinariness" (*Vorbildlichkeit*). In his treatment of the "routinization" (*Veralltäglichung*) of charisma, Weber elaborates:

> Charismatic rulership in the typical sense described above always results from unusual, especially political or economic situations, or from extraordinary psychic, particularly religious states, or from both together. It arises from collective excitement produced by extraordinary events and from surrender to heroism of any kind. This alone is sufficient to warrant the conclusion that the faith of the leader himself and of his disciples in his charisma – be it of a prophetic or any other kind – is undiminished, consistent and effective only *in statu nascendi*, just as is true of the faithful devotion to him and his mission on the part of those to whom he considers himself sent. (1968: 1121)

---

[5] Flaig first introduced the concept of *consensus* in his 1992 book *Den Kaiser Herausfordern*, which has since been revised in a second edition (2019). See also Cooley 2019: 81.

[6] For studies on the relationships between charismatic leaders and their followers, see Willner 1984 and Madsen and Snow 1991.

[7] On Weber's debt to Sohm and other theologians for the concept of charisma, see Adair-Toteff 2020: 7–9.

When the crisis eases and the charismatic authority becomes routinized, it ceases to be purely charismatic and turns into an institution. This is precisely what happened with the principate. But I would argue, contrary to Weber's own perceptions of the principate, that the process was not finalized by Augustus but rather by Tiberius.

Weber himself was certainly familiar with the history of the Roman world, especially the late Republic. His relationship with Theodor Mommsen is described in varying degrees of warmth.[8] But as Furedi points out, "The one person who did not have much of a conversation with Augustus was Max Weber" (2013: 91). Weber said little about Augustus or the Roman principate in his main treatment of legitimate *Herrschaft* in *Wirtschaft und Gesellschaft* (*Economy and Society*). Weber observed that the legitimacy of the Roman emperor did not stem from any *lex de imperio* but from "acclamation by the army of a victorious hero" (*Heeresakklamation des siegreichischen Helden*). He did not take this point any further and immediately moved on to the nature of succession. The Roman emperor could name his successor in a legal sense only as a *paterfamilias* could name his primary heir. This was how most peaceful successions did take place, including that from Augustus to Tiberius. However, Weber did not mention that Augustus was also responsible for making sure that Tiberius had the necessary legal powers to ensure his succession not only to the role of *paterfamilias* of the *domus Augusta* but also as princeps of the state. Without discussing the process, Weber (2005: 495–6) stated that eventually charisma was transferred to the position of princeps. Weber (2005: 497) acknowledged that Augustus was careful in observing Roman aristocratic sensitivity by distinguishing his power from the Hellenistic monarchy threatened by Caesar but went no further in exploring the transition from Republic to principate. Nevertheless, he laid the foundations for later explorations of the nature of charisma and its routinization.

Charisma and *Auctoritas*

In order to utilize Max Weber's conception of charisma with respect to Augustus and the principate, we must examine the theory in its socio-logical context. Roger Eatwell (2006) identifies particular aspects of Weber's ideas of charismatic leadership in his studies of the Fascist and Nazi movements which led to World War II. I believe these can also be

---

[8] On the connection between Mommsen and Weber, see Momigliano 1982: 29 and Nippel 2007.

applied to the early principate.[9] After all, Syme was partially inspired to write his critical analysis of Augustus' rise to power and the institutionalization of the principate, *The Roman Revolution* (1939), by the rise of totalitarian governments in Europe in the 1930s.[10] By using Eatwell's criteria, we can answer the fundamental question: was Augustus a charismatic leader in the Weberian sense? Eatwell specifies four traits useful in identifying a charismatic leader: 1) missionary vision; 2) symbiotic hierarchy; 3) Manichean demonization; and 4) personal presence. All of these markers can be found in Augustus' rise to and consolidation of sole supreme power.

First, Eatwell specifies: "Charismatic leaders may at times make compromises. . . However, ultimately true charismatics are driven by some form of mission. . . This sense of mission is often linked to a foundation myth" (2006: 144). While we can never truly know how Octavian felt at the time of Caesar's death, later authors and the considerably older Augustus all assert that Octavian's rise to power stemmed from a desire to avenge his father and to restore the Republic. Cicero, an eyewitness to the aftermath of Caesar's assassination, believed that he could compel Octavian to align his interests with those of the *boni* seeking to restore the oligarchic Republic, as opposed to Mark Antony, who seemed to have stepped into the dictator's shoes. D. Brutus claimed that Cicero considered Octavian "a young man to be praised, honored, and then eliminated" (*laudandum adulescentem, ornandum, tollendum*, Cic. *Ad Fam.* 11.20.1).[11] Later authors anecdotally ascribe to Cicero an awareness of Octavian's future greatness. Plutarch maintains that Cicero was inclined to help the young Octavian not only because of his hatred of Antony and affection for Octavian's stepfather, Marcius Philippus, but also because of a prophetic dream:

> Cicero had a dream in which someone invited the sons of the senators to the Capitol because Jupiter was going to appoint one of them to be the ruler of Rome. The citizens came running up eagerly and posted themselves round the temple, and the boys in their purple-bordered togas took their places in silence. Suddenly, the doors opened and one by one the boys rose up and walked round past the god, who inspected each of them in turn. All, to their sorrow, were dismissed until this young Caesar came into the god's

---

[9] For similar criteria for determining what constitutes a charismatic leader, see Trice and Beyer 1986: 118–19.
[10] See Birley's introduction to Syme's correspondence (2020: 15–22) for Syme's connections in Nazi Germany and Vivas García 2017 for the influence of Levi's portrayal of Octavian as a "capoparte" on *The Roman Revolution*.
[11] Cicero manipulates the double entendre of *tollendum*, which can also mean "to be raised up."

presence. Then the god stretched out his hand and said: "Romans, you shall
have an end of civil wars, when this boy becomes your ruler." (Plut. *Cic.* 44,
Penguin trans. Warner; cf. Suet. *Aug.* 94.9; Dio 45.2; Tert. *De Anim.* 46.7)

Even more auspiciously, Octavian had been born in Cicero's consulship.
Suetonius (*Aug.* 94) also cites harbingers of Octavian's future greatness,
although many of these may be later interpolations or fabrications.
Regardless of the origin of these stories, the fact remains that such
prophecies of future greatness were circulating after Augustus came to
power and were given credence.

The second of Eatwell's criteria for identifying a charismatic leader
Augustus also did everything he could to enhance this charismatic
image. In addition to accepting divine honors indirectly while refusing
them outright, he engaged in certain behaviors which might make him
seem more than human. Suetonius (*Aug.* 79.1) relates the story of a Gallic
chief who was especially moved by Augustus' countenance (*vultus*), which
was so tranquil and serene that the Gaul abandoned plans to throw him off
a cliff. Suetonius adds that Augustus had clear and shining eyes (*oculos
habuit claros ac nitidos*), from which he wished it to be thought that there
was in them something of a divine strength (*quiddam divini vigoris*), and
he was pleased if, whenever he looked at anyone very closely, that person
lowered his face as if before the glow of the sun (*ad fulgorem solis vultum
summitteret, Aug.* 79.2). Augustus promoted his charismatic image with
actions which seemed to be favored by the gods themselves, beginning
with the vengeance visited upon Caesar's assassins and culminating in his
achievement of peace. Augustus himself later delineated his own motiv-
ations in the *Res Gestae*, completed shortly before his death. He justified
his *pietas* in avenging his father and, more importantly, foregrounded his
role in ending a nearly hundred-year cycle of civil wars. Much has been
written on the *Saeculum Augustum*, and we need not rehash it here (see
especially Zanker 1988, Chapter 5). Needless to say, both Augustus and
his contemporaries believed that he had been divinely sent to bring peace
to the Roman world.

The second of Eatwell's criteria for identifying a charismatic leader
centers on what he terms "symbiotic hierarchy." As he observes,
"Charismatics can at times also portray themselves as ordinary men, merely
obeying the wishes of the people" (2006: 145). Augustus portrayed himself
as *civilis princeps*.[12] According to Suetonius (*Aug.* 73, 76–7, 86–7), his
mannerisms, behavior, conversational speech, and even his diet created the

---

[12] On this self-presentation, see especially Wallace-Hadrill 1982.

image of a humble man who lived no differently from other Romans.[13] Although the reality is far more complicated, for our purposes, image is more important than reality.

Octavian's/Augustus' desire to portray himself as a man of the people was guided by the nature of the conflict through which he came to power and closely connected to the third specification for charismatic leadership – demonization of the enemy. Octavian benefited greatly from vilifying Antony's alliance with Cleopatra. According to the *Res Gestae* (*RG* 25), *tota Italia* swore an oath to support Octavian as he headed east to destroy the Egyptian queen. Horace's famous ode (*Car.* 1.37) celebrating the victory at Actium indicates the perception of Cleopatra in contemporary Rome. After the fall of Antony and Cleopatra, Augustus was able to use other foreign conflicts to add to his glory. The *Res Gestae* is peppered with names of subject kings and peoples. More importantly, in 27 BC Augustus did return several provinces to the Roman people but retained any provinces with substantial numbers of troops. This allowed him to claim military victories fought, if not by himself, then by generals fighting under his auspices.[14]

Finally, Eatwell acknowledges that the charismatic leader must possess that certain *je ne sais quoi* which modern popular culture identifies with the term "charisma." According to Suetonius (*Aug.* 79.1), Augustus' personal appearance was pleasing and his manner graceful but not artificial. Extant statues of Augustus, most famously that found at Livia's villa at Prima Porta, project such a charismatic bearing regardless of Augustus' actual appearance. Beyond his personal appearance was his meteoric rise to power at a young age and his ability to create *consensus*. Writing considerably later, Tacitus and Dio claim to report the mood at Augustus' funeral. While Tacitus reports the negatives as well as the positives, Dio has Tiberius deliver a eulogy in which Augustus is portrayed as superhuman. But both agree that it was Octavian's/Augustus' ability to adapt to any political situation which was the key to his success (see esp. Tac. *Ann.* 1.2, 1.9; Dio 56.39). It was not for nothing that his first signet ring bore the sign of a sphinx (Pliny, *HN* 37.10; Dio 51.3.6). Pliny further adds that the

---

[13] Wiseman (2019) argues that Augustus was a populist leader fighting against the corrupt oligarchs of the late Republic. His approach is criticized by Lipps 2020. For a recent survey of the many diverse views of Augustus' motives, see Goodman's review (2018) of twelve books published to celebrate the bimillennium of Augustus' death.

[14] The most obvious consequence was the monopolization of the triumph and the denial of *spolia opima* to Crassus. See Hickson 1991. On the distinction of returning the provinces to the *populus Romanus* to be ruled by former elected magistrates, see Millar 1989.

sphinx was replaced by the image of Alexander the Great, another charismatic figure; Dio states that it was an image of Augustus himself. This then became the seal for all later emperors.[15]

Thus, Augustus fits all four of the criteria which Eatwell uses to examine the charismatic qualities of autocratic leaders in the era prior to World War II, especially Mussolini (who expressed sincere admiration for the first princeps).[16] Eatwell further examines four conditions under which a charismatic leader can rise to power. The first of these, and the one emphasized originally by Weber, is a moment of national crisis.[17] By any reckoning, in the aftermath of Caesar's murder, the Roman constitution, whatever that entailed, was undergoing the ultimate crisis of identity. As Cicero observed (*Att.* 14.12), the liberators had failed to accomplish their goal because they only did half of what was needed: they had not assassinated Mark Antony. Chaos engulfed the Roman world in the years 44–42 BC, leading to Cicero's own death. The solution to restoring stability was supposedly an emergency coalition of three men with a stake in Caesar's legacy – *triumviri rei publicae constituendae*. Ultimately, the other two made tactical errors which allowed Octavian to emerge as victor. But in order to shed the mantle of triumvir and institute a new era of peace and prosperity, Octavian entered the Senate in January of 27 BC and relinquished his powers (which had already expired).[18] He emerged even stronger, confirmed in his position as *primus inter pares* and dubbed Augustus.

Eatwell further observes, "the rise of charismatic leaders requires some form of historical-cultural legitimation" (2006: 149). In many ways, Augustus was successful because he grafted his charismatic leadership onto pre-existing institutions. Augustus' revival of ancient cults and rejection of extraordinary honors erased any fears that Julius Caesar's heir and namesake would follow in his adoptive father's footsteps. By refusing the

---

[15] Except, supposedly, Galba, who used an ancestral image of a "dog looking out of a ship's prow" (Dio 51.3.7). On Augustus' rings, see Simpson 2005a. Simpson argues that Dio is anachronistic in stating that subsequent emperors used Augustus' ring as a seal and dates the change to the reign of Vespasian.

[16] For the restorations of the Mausoleum of Augustus and the Ara Pacis under Mussolini, see Arthurs 2012: 68–74. For the massive exposition in 1937–8 celebrating the bimillennial anniversary of Augustus' birth, the Mostra Augustea della Romanità, see Arthurs 2012: 91–124.

[17] Madsen and Snow (1991:12–23, 36–44) provide a study of how crises in general allow the rise of a charismatic leader, focusing on the career of Juan Perón in Argentina.

[18] Vervaet (2009) argues convincingly that although the term of the triumvirate had expired (as had the power of the other two triumvirs), Octavian held onto those powers until he formally resigned his position. For an alternative explanation, see Roddaz 2003.

position of dictator, even in its traditional iteration as an emergency office limited to six months, Augustus made a strong statement about the ways in which he would wield power. Indeed, the only innovation which Augustus introduced to strengthen his position was *tribunicia potestas*. Unable to hold the office of Tribune of the Plebs without having himself adopted out of the Iulii Caesares, Augustus needed a way to set himself apart from other senators and, more importantly, to interpose his veto without coming across as a tyrant.[19] The sacrosanctity which came with the position also played into his image as a divine savior.

According to Eatwell's third situational criterion, "charismatic leaders are more likely to emerge when political parties are weak or held in contempt" (2006: 150). While Rome did not have political parties in the modern sense, it certainly had its share of factions. The much-discussed Optimates and Populares were not the only voices in the political arena of the late Republic, but they were the loudest. The death of Caesar left Antony to assume the mantle of the Populares; and yet, it did not suit him. The elimination of Brutus and Cassius left Sextus Pompey as the last "Pompeian," but he was unable to capitalize on this reputation. Octavian was able to appeal to both sides, winning over Cicero, at least somewhat, then ultimately rousing the Caesarian party to avenge Caesar's death. By playing both sides against the middle, Augustus was able ultimately to achieve Cicero's dream of a *consensus ordinum*. As Tacitus observed (*Ann.* 1.2), Augustus took control of a world worn out by war and factionalism.

The final situational construct laid out by Eatwell is a societal loss of faith in religious, social, and political institutions. Following the psychological studies of Friedländer (1978), Eatwell asserts, "there are certain historical conditions, such as the waning of religion, in which people in large numbers become 'charisma hungry'" (2006: 151). The loss of faith in institutions leads to varying degrees of fear. This fear then drives people to look for a savior. A charismatic leader "helps give people a sense that politics is not pointless – that the leader can change things, whilst at the same time remaining responsive to the followers' needs" (2006: 151).[20] As mentioned earlier, *tota Italia* swore an oath to Octavian before Actium. In 2 BC, the *populus Romanus* (along with the Senate and the *equites*) designated Augustus as *pater patriae*, which he considered, according to

---

[19] On the evolution of *tribunicia potestas*, see Brennan's article in the *OCD*.
[20] See also Madsen and Snow 1991: 9–23.

Suetonius (*Aug.* 58), the crowning honor of his illustrious career.[21] This is confirmed by the fact that the acclamation as *pater patriae* is the last item featured in the *Res Gestae* (35). Augustus' image as a divine savior throughout his lifetime paved the way for his posthumous deification and the routinization of his charisma.

Some would argue that Augustus inherited the charisma of Julius Caesar and later established his leadership on a traditional and legal basis.[22] Yes, Octavian's adoption accelerated his rise to power, and, yes, Augustus cloaked his power in Republican institutions. But that does not preclude him from having manipulated his public image to become a charismatic leader in his own right. Augustus was consciously involved in a revival of outdated or long extinct religious institutions as well as conjuring up the memory of heroes of early Rome (see esp. Zanker 1988: 101–139). The very choice of the name Augustus (as opposed to the proposed alternative of Romulus) was designed to recall Ennius' famous line:

> It has been 700 years, more or less,
> since famous Rome was founded by august augury.
>
> septingenti sunt paulo plus aut minus anni,
> augusto augurio postquam incluta condita Roma est. (*Ann.* 245 M)

The name was also intended to evoke imagery associated with the verb *augeo*, as displayed by the prevalent agricultural and bucolic motifs in Augustan monuments like the Ara Pacis.[23] Augustus recognized the charismatic power his name would hold for his successor. Upon his adoption, Tiberius became Ti. Iulius Caesar. But when the opportunity arose for him to earn his own unique honorific based on his many triumphs or even the cognomen "Pius" to demonstrate his loyalty to his adoptive father, Augustus interjected, insisting that Tiberius would assume *his* cognomen upon his death (Suet. *Tib.* 17.2). Augustus recognized the charismatic power of the name and its ability to help Tiberius succeed to his adoptive father's unique position.

Tiberius' inconsistency in using the name after his ascension demonstrates the charismatic power of the cognomen. Cowan (2009a: 476–7) explains this inconsistency by reasoning that Tiberius, trying to differentiate himself from his predecessor, faced pressure from his peers to imitate

---

[21] As Cooley observes (2009: 272–3), Augustus inserts the *equites* into the traditional formula of SPQR. On the term *pater patriae*, see especially Alföldi 1971.

[22] Hatscher (2000: 221) denies Octavian any personal charisma. Yet Julius Caesar also began his career by manipulating the charismatic image of his uncle Marius (Suet. *Iul.* 1, 11).

[23] See Zanker 1988: 172–83.

Augustus. Two of the most notable instances where Tiberius does use the name are in the letter to Gytheion and the *Senatus Consultum de Cn. Pisone Patre* (*SCPP*). The letter to Gytheion, to be discussed in Chapter 2, is addressed to a Greek polis. In the letter, Tiberius refuses divine honors for himself. The *SCPP*, as we shall discuss in Chapter 4, is a document drafted in the aftermath of the chaos surrounding the death of Germanicus. The document was meant to be published throughout the empire. At least the first of these instances lines up loosely with the assertions of Suetonius (*Tib.* 26) and Dio (57.8.2) that Tiberius only used the cognomen "Augustus" in correspondence with foreign leaders.[24] Tiberius used the name Augustus in order to borrow charisma from his predecessor when addressing cities which expected him to have divine qualities, or, in the case of the *SCPP*, when he needed to display authority throughout the empire in the wake of a major shock to the *domus Augusta*.

The name Augustus is closely connected to the noun *auctoritas*.[25] One of the challenges in analyzing the early principate involves the term *auctoritas* and the use of that *auctoritas* to create *consensus*. Both of these words, used by Augustus himself in the *Res Gestae*, have connections to ideas of pure charismatic leadership.[26] Egon Flaig (2019 [1992], 2015), building on a somewhat neglected article by Hans Instinsky (1940), has underscored the importance of *consensus* in the rule of any princeps.[27] *Consensus* was negotiated by a carefully crafted dialogue originating from Octavian's military power and his desire as Augustus to cloak his charismatic rule with Republican titles. *Consensus, auctoritas,* and charisma are not mutually exclusive. Indeed, by the primary principle of Weber's definition of charismatic rule – that the ruled obey the ruler because of their belief in his charismatic authority – *consensus* is a necessary prerequisite for determining a ruler to be charismatic.

Other scholars have tried to foreground the idea of *auctoritas* with respect to Augustus' unique position. In his book on authority as a sociological construct, Furedi (2013: 91) conflates Weber's idea of charismatic authority with the Roman concept of *auctoritas*. He (2013: 92) then rejects the idea that *auctoritas* is essential to a discussion of charismatic leadership. He cites Galinsky's (1996: 80; cf. Galinsky 2015)

[24] See Scott 1932 for other examples in letters to cities in the Greek East.
[25] By way of comparison, Cowan (2018: 415 n. 29) points out, "*auctoritas* is not attributed to Julius Caesar in Velleius' text."
[26] On *consensus* in the *Res Gestae*, see Cooley 2009: 258.
[27] Grenade (1961) also discusses the importance of *consensus*.

contention that "[Augustus'] leadership was not simply 'charismatic' but was defined in terms of traditional virtues." Galinsky, however, places the emphasis on "simply." As stated above, charisma and *auctoritas* are not mutually exclusive.[28] Adair-Toteff (2005) observes that Weber himself had trouble integrating the complex Roman idea of *auctoritas* into his theories of legitimate rule, often conflating *Herrschaft* with *Autorität*.[29] Despite his dismissal of *auctoritas* as a complement of Augustus' charisma, Furedi adds in a footnote, "Augustus' principate can lay a claim to be associated with all three of Weber's ideal types of legitimate domination" (2013: 92 n. 103).

The discussion of charisma and *auctoritas* is complicated by Augustus' declaration at *Res Gestae* 34 that he had no more *potestas* than his fellow magistrates but exceeded them in *auctoritas*. Rowe proposes that Augustus was using the term *auctoritas* specifically to refer to his position as *princeps senatus*. He believes Augustus was stressing the fact that he had colleagues as princeps, especially in his shared magistracies (2013: 12).[30] Galinsky (2015: 244) rejects Rowe's argument, demonstrating that Augustus' *auctoritas* existed before his leadership of the Senate and extended beyond any influence he may have had with that body. Augustus' *auctoritas* was a manifestation of his charisma.[31] Parsi (1963: 25–6) points out that Tiberius seemed to refuse any claims to personal *auctoritas*, citing Suetonius' report (*Tib.* 27) that Tiberius preferred to be known not as the *auctor* of a particular proposition in the Senate but as *suasor*. Yet while Parsi (1963: 23) argues that Tiberius' refusal to claim *auctoritas* was a denial that he had inherited Augustus' charisma, in fact it was quite the opposite. Tiberius had inherited Augustus' charisma but had manifestly refused to claim any for himself. Indeed, *auctoritas* was not a hallmark of later emperors. While emperors certainly had *auctoritas*, once Tiberius had used Augustus' charisma and *auctoritas* to institutionalize the principate, the person holding the position of princeps had a rational/legal basis for his authority.

---

[28] Cf. Lobur 2008: 61.

[29] ". . . in the same part of the *Wirtschaft und Gesellschaft* Weber writes of *Herrschaft* and immediately adds 'Autorität' ('authority') (1976: 122). And in *Politik als Beruf* he coupled *Herrschaft* and *Autorität* in his discussion of 'charismatische Herrschaft' (1992: 160). Thus, 'domination' may be perfectly acceptable for both traditional and legal *Herrschaft*; however, because the charismatic person does not, and cannot, resort to compulsion, 'authority' seems a better choice for charismatic *Herrschaft*" (Adair-Toteff 2005: 191–2).

[30] Rowe (2021) returns to the notion of collegiality in Augustus' vision of his position, to be discussed below in the context of the senatorial debates following Augustus' death.

[31] See Stahl 2008: 31.

Recusatio, Cunctatio, or *Impudentissimus Mimus?*
Tiberius Accepts His Burden

While scholars in religious studies and political science have made case studies of the routinization of charisma, the most detailed and seminal work on the phenomenon has been done in the field of organizational leadership.[32] In their book on *Charismatic Leadership in Organizations,* Conger and Kanungo (1998: 28) lamented, "We know almost nothing about the routinization of charismatic leadership." Trice and Beyer (1986: 134–5) laid the groundwork for analyses of routinization by examining leadership transitions in nonprofit organizations. In a study focusing on Alcoholics Anonymous and the National Council on Alcoholism, they distinguished key aspects necessary for the routinization of charisma after the death or resignation of the charismatic leader:

(1) "the development of an administrative apparatus, that stands apart from the charismatic, to cope with the ongoing operating needs generated by putting the charismatic's program into practice."

(2) "the transformation and transference of the charisma to others in the organization by means of rites, ceremonials, and symbols."

(3) "the incorporation of the charismatic's message and mission into the written and oral traditions of the organization."

(4) "the selection of a successor who resembles the charismatic sufficiently to be like a 'reincarnation'."

(5) "the degree to which the organization (or other collectivity) continues to express, to work toward, and to cohere around the charismatic message and mission of the founder (or reformer)."

All of these factors in the routinization of charisma will be discussed in what follows. In particular, the prescription laid out under Rubric 2 can be seen in the institution and propagation of the cult of Divus Augustus, as we will examine in Chapter 2. Those found in Rubrics 1 and 5 will be discussed in Chapter 3 on Tiberius' continuation of Augustus' policies. Our discussion of Tiberian authors in Chapter 5 and the section in Chapter 4 on Tiberian inscriptions fulfills the requirements for Rubric 3.

---

[32] For studies on the application of the theory of routinization of charisma to Catholicism and Islam, respectively, see Gresham 2003 and Brockopp 2020. Hoffmann (2009) looks at both hereditary charisma and the use of legal/traditional institutions in the routinization of the charisma of Fidel Castro. Madsen and Snow (1991) examine the legacy of Juan Perón in Argentina.

But Weber himself (1968: 246–9) noted that the most important factor for the routinization of charisma was that laid out by Rubric 4, the choice of successor. He believed that one of the following mechanisms could be used:

(a) a new charismatic leader could be sought.
(b) the new leader could be revealed through divine signs.
(c) the charismatic leader could designate his own successor, who would be recognized by his followers.
(d) a charismatically qualified administrative staff could designate a successor.
(e) charisma could be passed on through heredity (*Erbscharisma*).
(f) charisma could be passed through a specific office with a ritual inauguration.

While Weber treated these as separate circumstances, in the succession of Tiberius we can see elements of each. The predictions of Tiberius' future greatness (Suet. *Tib.* 14) which suggest (a) and (b) were likely injected retroactively after Tiberius' rise to power. The stronger factors are (c) and (e). Augustus designated Tiberius as his political heir (c) by granting him *tribunicia potestas* and *imperium* supposedly equal to his own (we will discuss this further below). He made him his familial heir (e) by formally adopting him as his son. Finally, the Senate confirmed Tiberius' position as Augustus' political successor, demonstrating aspects of (d) and (f). This process not only passed Augustus' charisma on to his successor Tiberius (as well as the other members of the *domus divina/Augusta*) but also began the transfer of Augustan charisma from his own unique *statio* to the lasting institution of the principate.[33]

As we shall see, one of the key components of Tiberius' ability to "routinize the charisma" of Augustus was his own lack of personal charisma and his excessive reliance upon that of his predecessor. In their study on the routinization of the position of a charismatic business leader in a consortium known as SEMATECH (Semiconductor Manufacturing Technology), Beyer and Browning (1999) note that one of the reasons why the charismatic image of the original CEO remained so influential was

---

[33] In her article on "Charismatic leadership in ancient Rome" for *The Routledge International Handbook of Charisma*, Kahlos (2020: 71) cites my dissertation (Edwards 2003) for the routinization of the principate through Tiberius. On the importance of the term *statio* (as opposed to *principatus*) in the formation of understanding Augustus' position, see especially Cooley 2019.

his successor's lack of charisma.[34] Conger and Kanungo (1998: 29–30) observed the same phenomenon in similar transitions, most notably those following Steve Jobs, Lee Iacocca, and Walt Disney. The enshrinement of the charisma of a corporate leader is more likely when "a charismatic leader is replaced by a more managerially oriented individual" (1998: 29). Although there are certain authors (especially Velleius) who portray Tiberius as somewhat charismatic, after he became princeps Tiberius' reclusive nature and inability to communicate with the Senate made him increasingly unpopular.[35] Thus, Tiberius was forced to perpetuate the charismatic image of Augustus both by claiming that Divus Augustus continued to watch over his family and by promoting the more charismatic members of Augustus' bloodline, especially Germanicus. Due to this lack of personal charisma, Tiberius "routinized" the charisma of Augustus into the institution of the principate.

The principate was institutionalized not just by Tiberius assuming his father's *statio* but also by his ruling as if he were still guided by Augustus. Indeed, Lyasse (2008: 96–105) points to multiple examples, some of which will be discussed in later chapters, where Tiberius himself (assuming his words are reported somewhat accurately) reiterates his own inferiority in comparison with the divine mind of Augustus. That is to say, while Augustus had plenty of time to prepare for the inevitable, his choice of Tiberius proved to be more prescient than even he could have foreseen. Had Augustus been succeeded by someone with personal charisma, that person could have radically altered the nascent principate. Or abolished it altogether in favor of a "Hellenistic monarchy," as was purported to be the goal of Caesar and Antony. Nevertheless, while the transition from Augustus to Tiberius may have been peaceful, it was not without challenges. It was, after all, the first time such a transfer of power had ever taken place.

In his discussion of the ways in which Suetonius frames narratives of succession from one emperor to the other, Osgood (2013) notes the lack of agreement regarding the transition from Augustus to Tiberius in both ancient and modern sources. He specifically mentions the arguments of Syme and Gruen, who stand at opposite ends of the spectrum regarding any succession policy which may or may not have been orchestrated by

---

[34] "Noyce's successor, Bill Spencer, had a different interpersonal style that was less emotionally engaging and more rational than Noyce's. However, he made a point of announcing when he became CEO that he intended to carry Noyce's vision forward" (Beyer and Browning 1999: 516).

[35] In his analysis of Velleius, Lobur (2008: 102) uses a subheading, "Tiberius: The Rise of a Charismatic Leader."

Augustus. Syme (1939: 341) argued that throughout his career as sole ruler Augustus had carefully delineated a dynastic policy favoring members of his own family. Even with his adoption of Tiberius, Augustus ensured the principate would return to his own bloodline through Tiberius' adoption of Germanicus, Augustus' great-nephew, who was also married to Augustus' granddaughter Agrippina. Gruen (2005: 38–42) counters that Augustus had notoriously not named a successor when he was gravely ill in 23 BC and had continued to avoid any suggestions that he was hand-picking someone to succeed to his position. As Osgood observes, there are many other opinions between these two extremes. "But there is a simple explanation for this debate: from start to finish, nothing about 'succession' was ever made explicit by Augustus, or the Senate and People – there were no edicts, no decrees, no laws about the succession to Augustus" (2013: 25).

After Actium, Octavian faced a serious dilemma. Once he had defeated Antony and Cleopatra, he no longer needed the extraordinary powers assumed after the expiration of the triumvirate. The example of Caesar was undoubtedly foremost in his mind. Upon his return to Rome, Octavian began a series of negotiations in late 28 BC, formalized in two meetings of the Senate in January of 27 BC. At the first meeting, he laid aside his powers, which were then, for the most part, returned to him by the Senate. At the second, he was recognized with the charismatic cognomen "Augustus." And, as Rich (2012: 78) demonstrates, the renewal of those powers in 18 and 8 BC consolidated Augustus' legitimacy while still preserving the charade that he would lay down power once it was no longer necessary. The renewal of Augustus' powers had taken place through senatorial procedure, but there were further steps which increased Augustus' *auctoritas*. The last of these steps, and the one Augustus claims in the *Res Gestae* (35) to have cherished the most, was the acclamation as *pater patriae* by all classes of Roman society in 2 BC. From his victory at Actium until his death in 14, Augustus had almost forty-five years to define his position.[36] He also had time to ensure that after his death his *statio* would be filled by a hand-picked successor. After the disappointing deaths of Marcellus, Agrippa, Lucius, and Gaius, that hand-picked successor could only be Tiberius.

From his youth, Tiberius had been promoted by Augustus through various offices and honors. He rode alongside Augustus' beloved nephew

---

[36] On the impossibility of reducing the formation of the principate to one particular phase of the career of Octavian/Augustus, see Hurlet 2015: 70–85.

Marcellus in the Actian triumph (Suet. *Tib.* 6). When Agrippa died, Augustus chose Tiberius to replace Agrippa (who had replaced Marcellus) as his daughter's husband. Augustus' adoption of his grandsons indicated that the future of the regime lay with Gaius and Lucius, not Tiberius; "cruel fate" had other plans. We may never know why Tiberius left Rome in 6 BC and took up an extended residency on Rhodes.[37] Regardless of why he went, or even why he was allowed to return, by AD 4 Tiberius was the only member of the *domus Augusta* (besides perhaps Germanicus) whom Augustus trusted to preserve the system of government developed over his long career.

By the death of Augustus, Tiberius had been granted extraordinary powers, control over armies and provinces, and a position in the Senate that seemed to be equal or only slightly inferior to that of Augustus. But those powers had been granted through the advocacy of Augustus. It was not clear what would happen to some of those powers when Augustus died. And yet, Tiberius could not give up the powers granted to him by Augustus (and, nominally, the Senate) without seeming to be an *impudentissimus mimus* (Suet. *Tib.* 24.1). There was no template for a peaceful transition of power. If we believe Tacitus (*Ann.* 1.7), Tiberius immediately sent out messages to the armies and only hesitated to act as princeps in the Senate.[38]

Despite confusion in the subsequent senatorial debates about Tiberius' new position, an oath of loyalty to Tiberius and the *domus Augusta* was administered, first to the consuls and then to other members of Roman society (Tac. *Ann.* 1.7.2). While we cannot know the exact nature of that particular oath, we do have evidence of oaths in the provinces which may reflect the language of the original from Rome. González (1988: 120) believes that an oath of loyalty to Augustus' heirs Gaius and Lucius discovered in Baetica was merely one in a series of such oaths, serving as a forerunner to a later oath of allegiance to Tiberius. Weinstock goes even further to assert that the oath of allegiance to Tiberius discovered in

---

[37] Bellemore (2007) argues rather persuasively that Tiberius did not retreat to Rhodes in order to make a (failed) power play but rather to retire from public life. She also argues that despite tension between them, relations between Tiberius and Augustus remained respectful. Southern (2014: 286–8) goes so far as to suggest that Tiberius was actually working "undercover" for Augustus, supplying information about the situation in the East and keeping a distant eye on Gaius.

[38] An intriguing new document discovered in Spain and recently published by Caballos Rufino (2021) seems connected to an oath of obedience to Tiberius with a promise of a donative. I thank the anonymous reviewer for bringing it to my attention.

Cyprus was authored by Augustus.[39] He specifies (1962: 315–6) two factors in the oath which deviate from the formula found in other known loyalty oaths. The first is the emphasis on obedience (*hupakousesthai, peitharchēsein*). The second is the injunction to honor the emperor in a religious sense (*sebasesthai*). Another document from Messene which expresses provincial allegiance to Tiberius in the immediate aftermath of the death of Augustus is even more striking.[40] Throughout the document, Augustus is consistently mentioned before Tiberius, despite the awareness by the provincials that "the god is no longer manifest to us" (38). Provincial magistrates understood the importance of the deification of Augustus in Tiberius' assumption of his father's *statio*.

According to Tacitus (*Ann.* 1.72.1), while Tiberius may have allowed an oath of loyalty to himself and his family, most likely because such an oath was originally Augustus' idea, Tiberius refused to allow the Senate to swear on his *acta*. Tacitus links this with Tiberius' refusal to accept the honorific title *pater patriae*, insisting that Tiberius never relented on either matter (cf. Suet. *Tib.* 26.2). While refusing an oath on his own *acta*, Tiberius compelled the Senate to swear upon the *acta* of his predecessor. In 25, Tiberius removed Apidius Merula from the Senate because he had not sworn on the *acta* of Augustus (Tac. *Ann.* 4.42.3). While Tiberius understood the need to accept honors and overtures of loyalty to himself and the *domus divina*/*domus Augusta*, he also understood that if he accepted excessive honors such as the title of *pater patriae* and an oath of loyalty to his *acta*, he would diminish the image of Augustus and, to a certain degree, undermine the power derived from the charisma of his predecessor.

Although Tiberius was Augustus' adopted son and legal heir, had sent orders to the armies, and had received oaths of loyalty from the provinces, like Augustus, he needed the Senate to formally recognize his *statio*. Tiberius was attempting the first peaceful succession of power from one princeps to another. That the Senate would accept his assumption of Augustus' *statio* seems a foregone conclusion, but there was no blueprint for how that process would play out. Augustus had taken decades to negotiate his power with the Senate. Tiberius had to consolidate his position within a few weeks. Our most detailed sources for the debates

---

[39] The oath was first published by Mitford 1960. Mitford points out a lacuna in front of Tiberius' name: "That Tiberius on his accession refused the title *Imperator* is well known. Manifestly the drafter of our oath, drawing it up on Tiberius' succession in AD 14, was aware of this refusal, uncertain of its permanence or sincerity. And this uncertainty gives us effectively the date of our inscription" (1960: 79).

[40] Harrison 2012.

in the Senate following Augustus' death, Tacitus and Dio, fail to agree. Other ancient sources like Velleius and Suetonius further complicate matters in their brevity. For the purposes of this discussion, we will focus on two specific issues: what powers did Tiberius have and did any of them expire with Augustus' death? and why did Tiberius hesitate in accepting power?

The first of these questions can be dispensed with fairly quickly. The most important power necessary for Tiberius to assert his control over the Senate was *tribunicia potestas*. This power granted the holder, among other things, the right to summon the Senate. As mentioned above, Augustus had this bestowed upon himself so that he could wield the powers of a Plebeian Tribune without actually being one. He later had the Senate give *tribunicia potestas* to his trusted *adiutor* Agrippa. After Agrippa's death, Augustus relied increasingly upon Tiberius. Thus, Tiberius was granted *tribunicia potestas* in 6 BC for a five-year period (Suet. *Tib.* 9.3; Dio 55.9.4).[41] That tenure expired while Tiberius was living in virtual exile on Rhodes. After his adoption by Augustus in AD 4, Tiberius was again granted *tribunicia potestas*, according to Dio (55.13.2) for ten years, although Suetonius (*Tib.* 16.1) states that it was for five. The contemporary historian Velleius (2.103.3) gives no term limit and adds that Tiberius protested against it (*recusante*). Tiberius continued to hold *tribunicia potestas* for the rest of Augustus' life, either through renewal of the grants (if Suetonius is correct) or through the duration of the ten-year term reported in Dio. And yet, Tiberius' *tribunicia potestas* was publicly renewed in 13 (Dio 56.28.1). As Swan (2004: 294) argues, since the previous grant had not yet expired, Augustus was preparing for his approaching death by solidifying Tiberius' position. Dio mentions in the same passage that Augustus reluctantly accepted a (now formulaic) renewal of his own powers and requested that, on account of his age, he should be allowed to meet with a *consilium* of senators rather than with the entire Senate. At this point, Tiberius' *tribunicia potestas* was likely without a term limit, renewed annually as Augustus' had been.[42]

If the *tribunicia potestas* which Tiberius held did not expire upon the death of Augustus and was used to summon the Senate after his death, what of the *imperium* necessary to control the army? In 27 BC, when

---

[41] On the motives for Augustus' promotion of Tiberius at this particular time (as opposed to the occasion of his marriage to Julia in 11 BC), see Swan 2004: 85.

[42] Lacey (1979: 33 n. 38) believes that this then became an "Augustan precedent" for designating unequivocally one's successor; thus, when *tribunicia potestas* was granted to Drusus in 22, there was no mention of a term limit.

Octavian returned power to the Senate, it was not merely as simple as laying aside his position as triumvir (regardless of whether or not he still called himself a triumvir, he had not yet formally renounced those powers). He still held the consulship until 23 BC, so he had the *imperium* of that magistracy. A bigger issue was his control over the provinces. Thus, when he gave up his powers beyond those of the consulship, the Senate returned to him, indefinitely, *imperium pro consulare* over all the provinces which had a strong military presence.[43] Most likely, when Augustus had the Senate renew Tiberius' *tribunicia potestas* in 13, he also had them grant Tiberius *imperium pro consulare* over the provinces under the control of the princeps.[44] In 6, Augustus had associated Tiberius in the foundation of a fund specifically intended to pay for the retirement of veterans, the *aerarium militare* (Dio 55.25.1–3).[45] In fact, instead of accepting contributions from other aristocrats, Augustus instituted an unpopular tax to supplement the fund. This monopolized the control of the army for Augustus and his family.

The paramount question still remains, if Tiberius held powers equivalent to those of Augustus upon the latter's death, what exactly was being negotiated in those Senate meetings which took place in September of 14? And why did Tiberius hesitate, if indeed he did hesitate, to accept Augustus' *statio*? The most common explanations for Tiberius' hesitation are laid out by Flaig (2007; cf. 2019: 236–45). The first, that Tiberius' powers had expired upon the death of Augustus, has already been dismissed. Likewise, the second explanation, that Tiberius did not have all of the same powers as Augustus. Indefinite *tribunicia potestas* gave Tiberius power over the Senate, and whatever *imperium* he held was surely greater than that of any other magistrate. The other three explanations require further discussion. The first of these, that Tacitus, Suetonius, and Dio are correct in attributing fear of the mutinies, especially in Germania, as a reason for Tiberius' hesitation, will be dealt with in the next section.

---

[43] The arrangement is obscured by the inventiveness of Dio and the brevity of *Res Gestae* 34. For a good overview, see Turpin 1994. As for the later conception of *maius imperium*, Pani (2001: 258) notes that the first known use of the phrase refers to the awarding of extra powers in the provinces given to Germanicus. We have no evidence of the term ever having been used by Augustus to describe his own power or that of any of his assistants.

[44] See Swan 2004: 294 (citing Vell. 2.121.1 and Suet. *Tib.* 21.1), Hurlet 1997: 158 and 2015: 147–8, Ferrary 2003: 424, and Rich 2012: 81. Castritius (2015: 451) argues that Tiberius' *imperium proconsulare maius*, having been granted at the same time that Augustus received a renewal of his powers, was nullified by the latter's death. None of our ancient sources gives any indication that the Senate or, more importantly, the army believed this to be the case.

[45] On the reform of the military as part of Augustus' consolidation of support for the succession of Tiberius, see Dalla Rosa 2018.

Subsequently, we will address the two interrelated explanations that Tiberius was clarifying his relationship with the Senate, or, as Flaig believes, was re-enacting a "rite of passage," akin to Augustus' so-called *recusatio imperii* of 27 BC.[46]

In order to understand the role played by the mutinies in the events which followed the death of Augustus, we must untangle the problematic timeline laid out by our sources.[47] There are several independently confirmed dates which serve as guidelines for the chronology of events. We know from various *fasti* (E.-J.[2] 50), as well as Suetonius (*Aug.* 100), that Augustus died on August 19, 14. We also know that Augustus was deified on September 17 (E.-J.[2] 52). Tacitus indicates (*Ann.* 1.10.8–11.1) that Tiberius did not engage in formal debate about his *statio* until after the deification of Augustus was ordained. So, Tiberius accepted his position as princeps (or at least ceased to refuse it) no earlier than September 17. We know from astrological tables that the eclipse used by Drusus and Junius Blaesus to quell the Pannonian mutiny can be dated to September 27. Otherwise, the chronology is rather unclear.

Sage (1982/3) offers the most convincing reconstruction of the sequence of events following Augustus' death.[48] He believes that the mutinies began smoldering among the Pannonian and Rhine legions in early September, a few days after the death of Augustus had been announced.[49] News of the mutinies was likely spreading in Rome before the meeting of the Senate on September 17. Again, we know that the mutiny in Pannonia was not resolved until September 27 and was considered serious enough for Tiberius to send Drusus with a detachment of the Praetorian Guard led by Sejanus. However, the mutiny among the legions in Germania seemed to have been initially resolved by the promises of Germanicus. "News of Germanicus' success could have arrived by the 14th or 15th of the month" (Sage 1982/3: 305). Despite Germanicus' ill-conceived attempt to

---

[46] In his study of the history of *recusatio imperii* under the late Republic and early empire, Huttner (2004) spends little time on Tiberius. While Huttner (2004: 147) sees Tiberius' behavior as influenced by what Augustus had done in 27 BC, he also believes Tiberius was sincere in trying to give more power to the Senate.

[47] For a comparative analysis of Dio, Tacitus, Suetonius, and Velleius on the events of August–October of 14, see Appendix II of Mallan (2020: 356–63).

[48] See also Mallan 2020: 362–3. Wellesley (1967) argues that Tiberius assumed power as early as September 3, immediately after the funeral of Augustus, condensing the debate from a few weeks to a few days. His timeline has generally been rejected.

[49] For a reading of Tacitus' account of the mutinies which focuses especially on the language of madness and disease, see Woodman 2006. For a comparison of the mutinies as narrated by Tacitus, Suetonius, and Dio, see Malloch 2004.

conciliate the soldiers, the mutiny among the Rhine legions was not over. The arrival of an embassy from the Senate served to unmask Germanicus' ruse. Eventually, according to the historical sources, the threat to send away Agrippina and Caligula, the darling of the legions, brought the soldiers to heel.[50]

The real question, then, involves Tiberius' perception of a threat from Germanicus. All the sources agree that Germanicus himself remained loyal to Tiberius (and the implied wishes of Augustus). But Tacitus suggests (*Ann.* 1.7.6) that there were supporters of Germanicus (perhaps even his own wife) whose devotion conjured up the fear (or hope) that Germanicus might not want to wait his turn. Velleius claims that the soldiers sought a new commander, a new *status*, and a new form of government (*novum ducem, novum statum, novam quaerebant rem publicam*, 2.125.1).[51] He does not clarify what that *nova res publica* would have entailed but indicates civil war and the overthrow of the Augustan system. Woodman (1998: 57) believes that this may indeed have been a genuine concern of Tiberius, who made sure to grant Germanicus *maius imperium*.[52] Even if Germanicus had decided to make a power play, the loyalty of the Praetorian Guard and Tiberius' presence in Rome would have given Tiberius the upper hand.

The notion that the soldiers in Germania seriously intended to oust Tiberius in favor of Germanicus, believing that he would improve their conditions, is a fiction fashioned by the writers of the later reigns of Caligula and Claudius.[53] The reasons for the mutiny in Germania were the same as those for the mutiny in Pannonia: extension of service time in the later years of Augustus, abuse by centurions and other middle officers, and resentment of the high pay afforded to the Praetorian Guard while

---

[50] Dio (57.5) states that Germanicus secretly sent away his wife and son. They were discovered and held hostage by the mutinous soldiers, who then, for no particular reason, had a "change of heart" (*metabolēn*). Tacitus (*Ann.* 1.40–4) makes a direct connection between Germanicus' decision to send away his family and the repentance of the soldiers. Suetonius (*Cal.* 9) reports the tradition that Caligula was the key. Brice sees the move less as a sign of Germanicus' using the charisma of his family and more as a threat: "Tacitus' emotional narrative aside, the departure of the innocents provided an open sign for the troops that their commander had resolved to employ violence within the camp" (2015: 116).

[51] Velleius attributes revolutionary ideas to soldiers involved in both mutinies, not just the one in Germania. For this passage in the context of Velleius' narrative, see Woodman 1977: 228–9.

[52] Flach (1973: 559) argues that the fear of Germanicus played no role in Tiberius' delay in accepting power.

[53] Sawiński (2018: 209) expresses serious doubts that these troops were indeed fiercely loyal to Germanicus.

wages for legionaries remained stagnant.[54] The dramatic nature of the mutinies was exacerbated by the troops recently conscripted in Rome and sent to these areas in the aftermath of the Pannonian revolt and the Varian disaster (Tac. *Ann.* 1.31.4; cf. Dio 56.23, 57.5.4). Despite the persistent attempts to portray Germanicus as one who (like his father Drusus) might have "restored the Republic," Germanicus' confidence in his personal charisma (and that of his wife) would indicate the opposite. His first solution to the mutiny in Germania was to threaten suicide. When that failed (spectacularly) after a soldier offered him a sharper sword, Germanicus used his wife and son (the future emperor Caligula) as bargaining chips. Subsequently, Germanicus unleashed slaughter by allowing those troops he deemed loyal to himself to "discipline" the ringleaders of the mutiny (Tac. *Ann.* 1.49). He then led his men on an unprovoked genocidal attack against the Marsi (Tac. *Ann.* 1.50).

While many scholars question the extent to which Tiberius allowed fear of a challenge from Germanicus to delay his consolidation of power, Pettinger (2012) claims, relying heavily on Suetonius (*Tib.* 25.1), that not only was Tiberius afraid of Germanicus, but he was also concerned about possible uprisings led by Clemens, the slave posing as Agrippa Postumus, and the conspiracy of Libo. Both the arrest of Clemens and the trial of Libo are firmly set by Tacitus in the year 16, two years after the accession debate.[55] If the murder of Agrippa took place shortly after the death of Augustus on August 19, it would be difficult to imagine a slave posing as him making his way to the legions and stirring up trouble before the senatorial debate of September 17.[56] While Pettinger is perhaps correct in connecting all these figures to a larger problem within the *domus Augusta*, especially among the legions of Germania, there is no evidence in our other sources that Tiberius was aware of any movement by Clemens at this time, nor that Libo had amassed a following to challenge Tiberius. Even more unlikely is the notion that Libo, Clemens, and Germanicus were all part of a larger movement to "restore the Republic."[57] This is

---

[54] Regardless of the other details surrounding the mutinies, as Tacitus (*Ann.* 1.31.4) states: *venisse tempus quo veterani maturam missionem, iuvenes largiora stipendia, cuncti modum miseriarum exposcerent saevitiamque centurionum ulciscerentur.*

[55] "That Libo and Clemens were factors in Tiberius' hesitation seems impossible" (Sage 1982/3: 299).

[56] The debate over who was responsible for the death of Agrippa rages on. I am inclined to agree with Seager, "That the decision to liquidate Agrippa had been taken by Augustus cannot be doubted" (2005: 41). We will discuss the affairs of Libo and Clemens in greater detail in Chapter 6.

[57] For criticisms of Pettinger's arguments that Libo was aiming to "restore the Republic," see Strunk 2012 and Levick 2013a. In her analysis of conspiracies against Tiberius, Cogitore (2002: 47–85) believes none of them had such goals.

merely wishful thinking on the part of later historians, as well as a desire to set up Germanicus as a foil for Tiberius, who was portrayed as becoming increasingly tyrannical after the death of his adopted son.

If we discard the idea that Tiberius was afraid of a challenge to his supremacy, we are then left with the explanations for his hesitation to accept Augustus' *statio* which have occupied modern historians: either he was badly re-enacting Augustus' so-called *recusatio imperii* from 27 BC, or he was trying to allow the Senate some say in how his government would be formed. Given, however, that Augustus himself had cloaked his power in Republican offices and had renegotiated his role in the state after laying down his position as triumvir, these two explanations cannot be taken as incompatible. As for the first explanation, Flaig (2007), who has consistently argued that the principate was based on negotiations of *consensus* between various facets of society, believes that in refusing exceptional powers Tiberius was engaging in a "performative act" which he traces back to previous politicians, especially Pompey. Flaig (2007: 80 n. 16) rejects any comparisons with Augustus' so-called *recusatio imperii* of 27 BC. But Augustus himself was renouncing the emergency powers granted during the triumvirate and distancing himself from the illegal positions held by Julius Caesar, thus falling in line more closely with the actions of Pompey than those of his adoptive father. Moreover, even if their situations were not entirely the same, Tiberius' desire to receive from the Senate a formal confirmation of powers which he already held and his proposal to share the burden of government with others bear too many resemblances to accounts of Augustus' actions in 27 BC to be ignored.[58] Whether or not Tiberius was sincere (and I believe he was) in beginning his reign by negotiating with the Senate, he sent a clear message that his principate should merely be seen as a continuation of that of Augustus. This was not a ritual that was later adopted by other emperors. We have no evidence of any such *recusatio* among any of the other Julio-Claudians or even among those who succeeded them.[59]

Augustus' negotiations with the Senate in January of 27 BC resulted in him being recognized as *primus inter pares*. This highlighted his extraordinary *auctoritas*. But at that point he was still holding the consulship. As already discussed, when he discontinued holding that office in 23 BC,

[58] Huttner 2004: 130. Cf. Flaig 2007: 98–9.

[59] Jakobson and Cotton (1985) argue that there was a ten-day delay between when Caligula was first acclaimed emperor and when he formally accepted power in the Senate. They claim that Caligula initially refused power, thus enacting his own *recusatio imperii*. Scheid (1992: 233) points out that the *Acta Arvalia* indicate otherwise.

he was granted *tribunicia potestas.* A decade later he became Pontifex Maximus. And a decade after that, he was hailed as *pater patriae.* Although Tiberius condensed into a few weeks the consolidation of powers which Augustus had accumulated over years, he did preserve the illusion that the Senate had the right to grant those powers. Even if he held *imperium* and *tribunicia potestas* upon Augustus' death, Tiberius did not become Pontifex Maximus until March of 15.[60] Although the senatorial debates following the death of Augustus may cause confusion for those who would like to pinpoint a *dies imperii,* Tiberius was acknowledging that Augustus consistently renegotiated his role in government.[61]

Ironically, part of the confusion regarding Tiberius' role after Augustus' death may have been caused by Augustus himself. According to Dio, in addition to the documents mentioned by Suetonius (his will, instructions for his funeral, and an account of the empire), Augustus left behind a set of directives (*entolas kai episkēpseis*) for Tiberius and the people. These included restrictions on freeing slaves and creating new citizens, intended to preserve Augustus' ideal of creating Roman citizens the old-fashioned way. Another included the prohibition, mentioned by Tacitus (*Ann.* 1.11.4), against expanding the borders of the empire. But the most problematic, and the most important in the context of the succession debate, is the following: "He exhorted them to trust the public business to all who had ability both to understand and to act, and never to let it depend on any one person; in this way no one would set his mind on a tyranny, nor would the State, on the other hand, go to ruin if one man fell" (Dio [Xiph.] 56.33.4; Loeb trans. Cary).[62] Considering that upon Augustus' death Tiberius had at least some, if not all, of the same powers as Augustus, what exactly did these instructions mean?

While Ober (1982) believes that all of the advice detailed by Dio was actually the result of Tiberius trying to attribute his own ideas to Augustus, at least the first two, limiting citizenship and the manumission of slaves, were right in line with Augustus' own professed policies.[63] We will deal with the prohibition on expanding the empire in Chapter 3, but this too

---

[60] Pasco-Pranger (2006: 209) observes that while July was the traditional month for the election of the Pontifex Maximus, after Augustus the precedent ensured that future elections would take place in March. Cf. Hurlet 1997: 161 n. 423.

[61] Parsi-Magdelain 1978: 397. Cf. Barrandon, Suspène, and Gaffiero 2010: 167.

[62] τά τε κοινὰ πᾶσι τοῖς δυναμένοις καὶ εἰδέναι καὶ πράττειν ἐπιτρέπειν, καὶ ἐς μηδένα ἕνα ἀναρτᾶν αὐτὰ παρήνεσέ σφισιν, ὅπως μήτε τυραννίδος τις ἐπιθυμήσῃ, μήτ' αὖ πταίσαντος ἐκείνου τὸ δημόσιον σφαλῇ,

[63] Brunt (1984: 425) shows some skepticism for this argument without overtly naming Ober. Cf. Rich 2003: 334 n. 27. For Augustus' attitudes towards citizenship and manumission, see Suet. *Aug.* 40.3.

was probably in line with Augustus' wishes at the time. Thus, the recommendation for sharing of power may have been genuinely Augustan, reflecting a desire for Tiberius to share power with Germanicus, and perhaps Drusus, in the same way Augustus had with Tiberius.[64] Tiberius certainly seems to have believed in the sentiment that the empire should not be entrusted to one man (or perhaps even one family), pronouncing to the masses who lamented the death of Germanicus that rulers were mortal, but the republic was eternal (*principes mortales, rem publicam aeternam*, Tac. *Ann.* 3.6.3). Mallan notes that in 27 BC, even though Augustus had taken control of the militarized provinces, which were to be governed by his appointed legates, he left the rest to be governed by former magistrates and designated Rome and parts of Italy as under jurisdiction of the urban prefect. "If this is correct, then Tiberius' plan of AD 14 may have been simply a reiteration of Augustus' plan of 27 BC, designed to maintain the status quo" (2020: 109). Unfortunately, the Senate did not understand what either Augustus or Tiberius intended.[65]

Although Dio attributes the suggestion of shared power to mandates left by Augustus, he makes no mention of that mandate when Tiberius subsequently proposes such a division (57.2.4). Tacitus' version of the senatorial debates omits any mention that Augustus had suggested the division of powers. Once Tiberius had ensured the deification of Augustus, the Senate pleaded with him to clarify his own position:

> And he discussed various things about the magnitude of the empire and his own modesty; that only the mind of Divus Augustus was capable of such a great burden: that he had learned from his own experience, having been called by Augustus to undertake part of his cares, how arduous, how subject to fortune was the burden of ruling over everything. Thus, in a state supported by so many illustrious men, they should not surrender everything to one man: more men would more easily carry out the duties of the republic by sharing the labor.

> et ille varie disserebat de magnitudine imperii, sua modestia. solam divi Augusti mentem tantae molis capacem: se in partem curarum ab illo vocatum experiendo didicisse quam arduum, quam subiectum fortunae regendi cuncta onus. proinde in civitate tot inlustribus viris subnixa non

---

[64] See Brunt 1984: 425 and Bellemore 2013: 86.

[65] Judge (2019) argues that Augustus had believed in the importance of promoting "friendly competition." Ultimately, he failed. Tiberius likewise intended to share power but was thwarted by the Senate (2019: 67). Rowe (2021) contends that the central issue of the accession debate was not whether Tiberius would take control but whether he would share power with others.

ad unum omnia deferrent: plures facilius munia rei publicae sociatis laboribus exsecuturos. (*Ann.* 1.11.1)

Woodman analyzes the two most likely interpretations by members of the Senate. Either "he was proposing a variation on the arrangement which obtained under Augustus" (1998: 48) or Tiberius was suggesting a complete withdrawal from power. If, as Tacitus implies, Tiberius' speech left open the possibility of his immediate retirement from politics, it is understandable that the Senate completely panicked. Even if this was not Tiberius' intention, his suggestion left the senators in an awkward position. Those, like Asinius Gallus, who questioned the nature of the proposal merely provoked Tiberius' exasperation.[66] Gallus attempted to save face with an argument that he was trying to get Tiberius to admit the empire could not be divided. Even more tellingly, Gallus immediately followed this assertion by praising Augustus (*addidit laudem de Augusto*) and highlighting Tiberius' service under his predecessor (Tac. *Ann.* 1.12.3). While Tiberius advertised his insecurity at taking up the burden that Augustus had once shouldered, his peers in the Senate recognized the charismatic power inherited by Tiberius as Augustus' designated successor.

This assumes that Tiberius was genuinely trying to renegotiate the position of princeps. However, the other most common explanation, that mentioned above as being championed by Flaig (2007), is that Tiberius was engaging in a "ritual of *consensus*." Such an argument is supported by Velleius' account. Velleius, who would likely have been present at the debate as a *candidatus Caesaris* for the praetorship, glosses over all the details. Instead, he focuses on the danger had Tiberius refused to step into the position intended for him by Augustus. The *maiestas* of Tiberius was critical to preserving peace (2.124.1). While Tacitus and Dio may have had the hindsight of multiple transfers of power, some peaceful, others not, Velleius was witnessing the first transition in what would later be known as the principate.[67] He makes no mention of any division of powers, although he does highlight in the subsequent narrative the roles played by Germanicus, Drusus, and Sejanus as *adiutores*.[68]

---

[66] Bellemore (2013: 88) proposes that Gallus as Drusus' stepfather and a kinsman of Germanicus "was in a good position to know their weaknesses." His line of questioning was thus intended to thwart any attempt by Tiberius to share power with them.

[67] On the term *principatus* in Velleius, see Cooley 2019: 73–9. Cooley observes that Velleius' term for the unique position held by Augustus, *statio*, implied military protection: "The whole idea of *statio* fits nicely with descriptions of the *princeps* as protector and savior of the *res publica*" (2019: 78).

[68] Strabo (6.4.2) also mentions that Germanicus and Drusus were assisting Tiberius.

Ultimately, Velleius (2.124.2) paints a picture of a reluctant Tiberius being forced to accept power:

> Nevertheless, there was one sort of struggle for the whole state, for the Senate and the people fighting with Caesar that he should succeed to the *statio* of his father, and of Caesar that he should be permitted rather to live as an equal citizen rather than an eminent princeps. Finally, he was won over more by reason than the honor, since he saw that whatever he did not undertake to protect would surely perish; and with regard to this one man alone, it happened that he refused the principate almost longer than others had fought with arms to seize it.

> Una tamen veluti luctatio civitatis fuit, pugnantis cum Caesare senatus populique Romani, ut stationi paternae succederet, illius, ut potius aequalem civem quam eminentem liceret agere principem. Tandem magis ratione quam honore victus est, cum quicquid tuendum non suscepisset, periturum videret, solique huic contigit paene diutius recusare principatum quam, ut occuparent eum, alii armis pugnaverant.[69]

Tacitus also indicates that Tiberius did not so much accept the principate as cease to refuse it (*Ann.* 1.13.5). Chronologically and ideologically, Velleius and Tacitus represent very different historiographical perspectives on Tiberius. But both agree that the primary result of the senatorial debates, whatever the intention of Tiberius, was the acknowledgement that Tiberius now held the position vacated by Augustus.

Tacitus criticizes Tiberius for hesitating before the Senate when he had already given commands to the army, stating that he was leaving room for the distinction that he seemed to have been called and chosen by the state rather than to have crept in through his mother's manipulation of the elderly Augustus: *dabat et famae, ut vocatus electusque potius a re publica videretur quam per uxorium ambitum et senili adoptione inrepsisse* (*Ann.* 1.7.7). While Tacitus qualifies the participles *vocatus* and *electus* with *ut*, "Tiberius' desire to appear called to office in his own right not only may have been the correct one, but also may have been the *official* explanation for his delay" (Sage 1982/3: 314; his italics). Like Augustus, Tiberius had been granted extraordinary power by virtue of his relationship to a charismatic adoptive father. And like Augustus, Tiberius felt the need to secure those powers by appearing to refuse them, only to have them confirmed by

---

[69] On Velleius' use of *statio* as possibly reflecting Tiberius' own language, see Matthews 2010: 70, who points out that the word is used in the *Senatus Consultum de Cn. Pisone* (128–9). See also Woodman 1977: 222.

the Senate. Tiberius was forced to accept a power which he hoped one day to set aside, as Augustus had supposedly wished as well (Sen. *Brev.* 10.4.2).

Conclusions

Although Max Weber did not analyze the career of Augustus and the origins of the Roman principate in great detail, he did provide a framework for understanding the position of princeps. Despite arguments to the contrary, Augustus was a charismatic ruler. He capitalized on the chaos of the civil wars and secured sole power through military means. He then used religious, social, and legal imagery to consolidate his power through a period of over forty years. His *auctoritas* was a manifestation of his charisma. Both his personal charisma and his political *auctoritas* allowed him to create not only a new conception of the *res publica* but also a new dynasty. The true test of revolutionary change is the transfer of the charismatic power that created it. Tiberius' lack of personal charisma proved key in the routinization of the *statio* of Augustus into the legal structure of the principate. In his negotiations with the Senate, regardless of his intent, he secured permanently the position of one man as *primus inter pares* or princeps. His obligation to preserve the system created by Augustus ultimately led him to rely heavily upon the charismatic image of his predecessor. As we shall see, this both preserved the principate as a new form of government and created problems for the second princeps, who struggled to live up to the idealized image of Divus Augustus that he himself had been so instrumental in creating.

CHAPTER 2

Tiberius and the Imperial Cult

Augustus and the Cult of Divus Iulius

The imperial cult served as an important and conspicuous instrument for the routinization of Augustus' charisma. Before we can address Tiberius' promotion of the worship of Divus Augustus, however, we must establish a basis for comparison with Augustus' treatment of Divus Iulius. No one would dispute that the deification of Julius Caesar was of critical importance to the position of the young Octavian. While perhaps he would have been able to galvanize Caesar's troops even if Caesar had not been made a god, the institution of the cult of Divus Iulius made Octavian's path to power significantly easier. Indeed, Julius Caesar himself was a charismatic leader. Nevertheless, his power was consolidated through an illegal and despotic dictatorship, a dictatorship so akin to monarchy that it prompted his assassination.

Caesar's charisma as a military leader and popular politician was transferred to Octavian through his testamentary adoption. C. Octavius became C. Julius Caesar. But even more importantly, he became *divi filius*. While Octavian may have agitated strongly for Caesar's deification, the foundation had already been laid by Caesar himself.[1] Moreover, Octavian was not solely responsible for implementing the cult of Divus Iulius. Despite his initial resistance to Caesar's post-mortem deification, Antony took full advantage of his position as Caesar's *flamen*, especially in consolidating power in the eastern part of the empire.[2] While Dio states (51.20.6–9) that Octavian instituted a cult of Caesar and Dea Roma for the provinces of

---

[1] For the debate over divine honors granted to Caesar before his death, see especially Weinstock 1971: 270–317 and Koortbojian 2013: 21–4.

[2] Regarding Antony's tardiness in enforcing the laws passed to deify Caesar upon his death, see Gesche 1968: 70–8. For his support of divine honors for the living Caesar, see Ferriès 2012: 68–9. On the point that Antony was as much Caesar's heir (in a political sense) as Octavian, see Schmid 2005: 46–7.

Asia and Bithynia in 29 BC, evidence exists of an earlier date for such a cult in Ephesus. Kirbihler and Zabrana posit that worship of Julius Caesar existed in the Artemision as early as 40/39 BC.[3] An inscription there records the name Marcus Antonius, along with the word *hieromnēmonēa*, which Kirbihler and Zabrana (2014: 114) consider parallel to the Latin *flamonium* or *flaminatus*. They see this inscription from Ephesus as a translation of a resolution concerning the deification of Caesar initially passed in Rome. They conclude that even if Antony did not initiate the cult himself, he at least supported the initiative of the locals.[4]

Another problem stems from Dio's comments that after Actium, Octavian/Augustus allowed Roman citizens in Asia and Bithynia to worship Divus Iulius (alongside Roma) but permitted only Hellenes to worship himself (51.20.6–7).[5] Whittaker (1996: 94) questions Dio's veracity, especially in connecting the worship of Divus Iulius with the goddess Roma. She adds that Octavian may not have been responsible for initiating the cult of Divus Iulius in the East. As mentioned above, there is evidence for a shrine of some sort to Divus Iulius at Ephesus which predates the edict recorded by Dio. Instead, it seems more likely that Octavian was responsible for linking the cults of Divus Iulius and Roma for the first time. This in turn would benefit Octavian in establishing supremacy in the East after Actium. If the impetus for worship of Divus Iulius in Asia, specifically at Ephesus, came from Antony or the locals (or both), a victorious Octavian was merely reshaping and expanding the pre-existing cult for his own purposes. Regardless, by the first decade BC the shrine of Divus Iulius at Ephesus was overshadowed by an adjacent Augusteum.

More important than the origins of the cult of Divus Iulius is the subsequent attitude of Augustus once he had shed his image as a boy relying on nothing more than a name.[6] As time passed, C. Julius Caesar became increasingly divorced from Divus Iulius. Thus, Caesar was separated into two images: the great military general and the abstract divine father of Octavian/Augustus. While White (1988) argues that the diminution of Caesar has been exaggerated, the general consensus continues to

---

[3] *FiE* 4, 3, 24 = *IvE* 4324; discussed by Kirbihler and Zabrana 2014: 114–16. See also Price (1984: 254 [Catalog 27]), who dates the shrine to 29 BC based on Dio.

[4] Kirbihler and Zabrana add (2014: 124 n. 105) that Antony could have laid the groundwork during visits to Ephesus in 41, 39/38, and 33/32 BC.

[5] As Whittaker points out, although Dio fails to mention the worship of the goddess Roma in connection with worship of Octavian/Augustus, "these temples are, however, known from other sources, and it is certain that the goddess Roma was also included in the dedication" (1996: 93–4).

[6] Cicero (*Phil.* 13.24), quoting Antony: "*qui omnia nomini debes.*"

favor the original opinion of Syme (1959: 58) that Caesar was "neutral-ized" in Augustan imagery.[7] Even Toher (2009), who refutes Syme's arguments as well as his process of argumentation, comes to the inevitable conclusion that portrayals of Caesar were subordinated to the needs of the regime.[8]

Nevertheless, Divus Iulius did not completely disappear from the public sphere during the reign of Augustus. As Sumi (2011) demonstrates, the Temple of Divus Iulius was an important venue for the promotion of the *domus Augusta* under Augustus, especially in the context of funerals for members of the imperial family.[9] He highlights the transfer of elections from the large porch in front of the Republican Temple of Castor (before the fire of 14 BC) to the new rostra attached to the Temple of Divus Iulius. The Temple of Divus Iulius was prominently located in the Roman Forum and was later connected to the restored Temple of Castor by the Parthian Arch. But it was only one part of a larger complex of buildings meant to enhance the *domus Augusta*. Indeed, before the completion of his own posthumous temple, Augustus was worshipped as a new deity not in the temple of his divine father but in that of his divine ancestor Mars Ultor, whose temple dominated the forum built by Augustus to mirror (and outshine) the Forum of Julius Caesar.

Augustus also manipulated the image of the so-called "star of Caesar," the comet which appeared during games celebrated in Caesar's honor in 44 BC.[10] Upon its appearance, it was hailed as a star carrying Caesar's spirit back to the heavens. Yet, as time passed, it became more and more associated with the beginning of a new *saeculum*. Pliny the Elder (*HN* 2.93–4) explains that Augustus connected the "star of Caesar" more closely with his own ascent to power than his father's deification:

> A comet is worshipped in only one place in the entire world – a temple at
> Rome. This comet was considered fortunate for Divus Augustus by his own
> reckoning, since it appeared at the beginning of games which he was
> producing for Venus Genetrix, not long after the death of his father

[7] Ramage (1985) presents the strongest defense of Syme. White mentions Ramage only in a footnote and does not engage with his article.

[8] Cf. Levick 2009a: 209.

[9] See also Phillips 2011. Weinstock downplays the significance of this structure, "The Temple of Divus Iulius was the only temple in Rome which had a Rostra, the importance of which was in turn enhanced by this connection; it was used, naturally, at the funerals of the family, but also on other occasions. But however singular it was, it hardly had any extraordinary or even religious significance" (1971: 400–1).

[10] On this comet, see especially Ramsey and Licht 1997. On the "star of Caesar" on coins, see Weisser 2016: 177–81.

Caesar, in a *collegium* instituted by him. For with these words, he proclaimed his joy: 'On the very days of my games a comet (long-haired star) was visible for seven days in the northern part of the sky. It arose at the eleventh hour of the day, was clear, and was visible from every land. The common people believed that this star signified the soul of Caesar received among the *numina* of the immortal gods, and for this reason that symbol was added to the portrait of the head of Caesar which we dedicated in the forum soon after.' He said these things in public: but inwardly he rejoiced because he believed that the comet had been born for him and that he had been born in it; and, if we are speaking truthfully, it was beneficial for the entire world.[11]

The shift of emphasis away from Divus Iulius to *divi filius* can be seen in public imagery. Hekster (2015: 45–6) observes this especially on coinage once Octavian became Augustus.[12] The same is also true for statuary groups: "Out of fifty-one dynastic groups from Italy, assembled by Rose [1997], only one, a Tiberian group from Herculaneum, includes a statue of Julius Caesar... By contrast, out of the thirty-nine Italian groups that are post-Augustan, sixteen include statues of Augustus" (2015: 171).[13] Moreover, "The Arval Brothers ... never sacrificed to Divus Julius; when they worshipped the list of *Divi*, it began with Divus Augustus, and this was presumably general for all the other colleges of state priesthoods too" (Gradel 2002: 263). Priests of Julius Caesar are rarely noticed after his first *flamen*, Mark Antony. The only epigraphic evidence for a priest of Divus Iulius outside of Italy is in Africa (*CIL* VIII 7986 = *ILS* 6862). Inscriptions record four priests within Italy outside of Rome. Two of those inscriptions come from the same town, Brixia (*CIL* V 4384; *CIL* V 4459).[14] Laird (2015: 121) notes that the meeting place for the Augustales in Herculaneum contained images of Divus Iulius and Divus Augustus, but the inscriptions on the bases for the now lost statues made no familial connection between the two. Thus, the perception at the municipal level

---

[11] *Cometes in uno totius orbis loco colitur in templo Romae, admodum faustus divo Augusto iudicatus ab ipso, qui incipiente eo apparuit ludis quos faciebat Veneri Genetrici non multo post obitum patris Caesaris in collegio ab eo instituto. namque his verbis id gaudium prodit: "Iis ipsis ludorum meorum diebus sidus crinitum per septem dies in regione caeli quae sub septentrionibus est conspectum est. id oriebatur circa undecimam horam diei clarumque et omnibus e terris conspicuum fuit. eo sidere significari volgus credidit Caesaris animam inter deorum immortalium numina receptam, quo nomine id insigne simulacro capitis eius, quod mox in foro consecravimus, adiectum est." haec ille in publicum: interiore gaudio sibi illum natum seque in eo nasci interpretatus est; et, si verum fatemur, salutare id terris fuit.*

[12] See also Gesche 1978: 382 and Balty 2012.

[13] On the lack of statue groups including Caesar under later Julio-Claudians, see Zanker 2009: 311.

[14] McIntyre 2016: 75. The other two are *AE* 1975 353 from Fermo and *CIL* IX 2598 in Teruentum.

by the end of the reign of Augustus was that Divus Iulius was more a prototype for Divus Augustus than the founder of a divine line.[15]

Aside from serving as a precedent for Augustus' impending deification, Caesar features minimally in the works of Ovid, a witness (if from a distance) to the end of Augustus' reign. Ovid's *Fasti* covers in its surviving portions the first six months of the year. During this time period in the extant official calendars of the Roman year, as Herbert-Brown notes, Caesar had three *feriae* in his honor – his victories in Spain and at Alexandria (March 17), his defeat of King Juba at Thapsus (April 6), and his birthday (July 12). Only one is mentioned by Ovid. Under his treatment of the Megalensian games in April, Ovid reports an exchange with a veteran who was at Thapsus in 46 BC. The veteran stresses that he fought against Juba with Caesar as his general (*dux mihi Caesar erat*, 4.381). No mention is made of the divine Caesar. Indeed, as Herbert-Brown (1994: 115) observes, a Caesarian veteran spending a day dedicated to Julius Caesar at the Megalensia demonstrates that the meaning of this particular day has been overshadowed by Augustus' games. Ovid's marginalization of Julius Caesar continues throughout the *Fasti*. In recounting the deification of Romulus, Ovid quips that Mars had made his son a god while Caesar had been made a god by his son (*caelestem fecit te pater, ille patrem*, 2.144). Caesar is deified not because of his earthly deeds but in spite of them. This forms a stark contrast to the accounts of Augustus' divinization, earned by bringing peace and prosperity to Rome after years of civil war.[16] That Divus Iulius was exalted as a god specifically with reference to the actions of Augustus foregrounds the *pietas* of Augustus towards his adoptive father and not the actions which earned Caesar a place in the heavens.

Finally, Julius Caesar is never mentioned by name in the *Res Gestae*; he is "my parent" (2) and "my father" (10.1). Augustus calls himself *divi filius* without specifically mentioning which *divus*. Although in general Augustus avoids names (aside from those of magistrates) in the *Res Gestae*, by contrast, Tiberius is named as Augustus' son (*RG* 8.9); also, at

---

[15] Laird (2015: 121 (n. 38 attributes the suggestion to a conversation with Alain Gowing)) hypothesizes that one reason for the inclusion of Divus Iulius in this setting may be a concentration of Caesar's veterans in the area. Laird also points out that there is only one other group dated to the Tiberian era which includes Divus Iulius, echoing the sentiments of Rose (1997: 23): "this shift may reflect the official rhetoric of the Julio-Claudian emperors, particularly that of Tiberius, who never featured portraits of Julius Caesar on coinage, as well as a new emphasis on living members of the imperial household" (2015: 121 n. 81).

[16] See also the two versions of Caesar's apotheosis at *Met.* 15.745–51 and *Fasti* 3.697–710.

RG 30, Augustus specifies that Tiberius was his stepson (*qui tum erat privignus*) when he was fighting in Pannonia from 12–9 BC. Thus, while the charisma of Divus Iulius played an important role in Octavian's rise to power, once he changed his name to validate his own personal charisma, Augustus had a much more ambiguous relationship with Caesar, separating the divine father from the problematic tyrant.

Even more so than it had been for Divus Iulius, the path to immortality was well laid out for Augustus. There is no need here to examine in detail the oblique semi-divine honors granted to Augustus before his death, especially involving the worship of his *genius* and/or *numen*.[17] As for the worship of the actual person of Augustus, we return again to the passage in Dio concerning Octavian's edict in 29 BC that Divus Iulius could be worshipped by all the inhabitants of Asia, but worship of himself was limited to non-Romans. Dio adds the problematic assertion: "For in the capital itself and in Italy generally no emperor, however worthy of renown he has been, has dared to do this; still, even there various divine honors are bestowed after their death upon such emperors as have ruled uprightly, and, in fact, shrines are built to them" (51.20.8; Loeb trans. Cary).[18] This only pertains to official deification by the Senate and enshrinement among the gods of the state. Unofficially, little effort was made to clamp down on private and municipal awards of divine honors to Augustus. After Naulochus, Appian (*BC* 5.132.1) states that the local cities enshrined Octavian among their gods. Tacitus, albeit in the context of those criticizing Augustus at his funeral, states that no honors were left to the gods since he wished to be cultivated by temples and with divine images through *flamines* and other priests (*nihil deorum honoribus relictum cum se templis et effigie numinum per flamines et sacerdotes coli vellet, Ann.* 1.10). Suetonius (*Aug.* 52) diplomatically states that Augustus refused divine honors in Rome. Reading between the lines, Mellor concludes, "this certainly implies that the cult existed in other parts of Italy" (1981: 983–4 n. 197).[19] At the

---

[17] For discussions of the cult of his *genius* as a compromise for divine worship of the living Augustus, first extensively developed by Taylor (1931: 181–204), see especially Fishwick 1990a: 375–87; contra Gradel 2002: 162–97. On the whole, I agree with Fishwick (2005: 246–9), who points out in response to Gradel that the *genius* can be worshiped divinely as a *numen* (as can any divine quality or deity), but that the two are not the same thing.

[18] ἐν γάρ τοι τῷ ἄστει αὐτῷ τῇ τε ἄλλῃ Ἰταλίᾳ οὐκ ἔστιν ὅστις τῶν καὶ ἐφ' ὁποσονοῦν λόγου τινὸς ἀξίων ἐτόλμησε τοῦτο ποιῆσαι· μεταλλάξασι μέντοι κἀνταῦθα τοῖς ὀρθῶς αὐταρχήσασιν ἄλλαι τε ἰσόθεοι τιμαὶ δίδονται καὶ δὴ καὶ ἡρῷα ποιεῖται. On the shrines in Asia at Pergamum and in Bithynia at Nicomedia, see Burrell 2004: 17–22, 147–50. Burrell (2004: 17–8) believes Dio's comments are drawn from some sort of official decree originally in Latin.

[19] On municipal priests of Augustus attested during his lifetime, most notably on the document honoring Gaius at Pisa and the *Tabula Hebana*, see Arnaldi 2008.

death of Augustus, there was a clear infrastructure for his deification and worship. But there was no guarantee that the worship of Augustus would endure once Tiberius had established his own power.

Tiberius and the Cult of Divus Augustus Pater

By the end of the reign of Augustus, the worship of Divus Iulius had been marginalized. This trend would continue throughout the reign of Tiberius until he became little more than a cipher. Tiberius would not allow the worship of Divus Augustus to fall into the same decline. He helped lay the foundations for the cult of Augustus even before his death, dedicating an altar of some sort, most likely to his *numen*, or divine aspect. The primary evidence for this altar comes from the *Fasti Praenestini* for January 17:

> The priests, [augurs, quindecimvirs for performing rituals,] and septemvirs of sacred feasts sacrifice victims to [the *numen* of Augustus at the altar] which Tiberius Caesar dedicated.

> Holiday [by *senatus consultum* because on this day Tiberius Caesar] dedicated [an altar] to his father [Divus] Augustus.

> Pontifices, a[ugures, xvviri s(acris) f(aciundis), vii]vir(i) epulonum victumas in/m[ola]nt n[umini Augusti ad aram q]uam dedicavit Ti. Caesar.

> Fe[riae ex s(enatus) c(onsulto), q]u[od eo die Ti. Caesar aram divo] Aug(usto) patri dedicavit.

The fragmentary inscription makes it impossible to know for sure if it was an altar to the *numen* of Augustus, but it is clear that Tiberius did dedicate something to his adoptive father.[20] The conjecture that it was an altar to the *numen* of Augustus is based on the evidence for such altars in the provinces.[21] Because of the lack of certainty in reconstructing the missing letters in the *Fasti Praenestini*, Gradel contends, "The *ara numinis Augusti* in Rome is a ghost of modern scholarship" (2002: 238).[22] However,

---

[20] Degrassi accepts Mommsen's emendation with the caveat, "N[umini] Mommsen, quod probandum esse videtur, licet quis vestigium primae litterae ad M pertinere existimare possit," *Inscr. It.* XIII.2 p. 115.

[21] Narbo, *CIL* XII 4333 = *ILS* 112; Forum Clodii, *CIL* XI 3303. On the Augusteum and the dedication of an altar to *numen Augustum* at Forum Clodii, see Gasperini 2008: 97–8. While the shrine to Augustus predated his death, the *terminus ante quem* for the *ara* to the *numen Augustum* is 18 (Gasperini 2008: 119). Fishwick (2005: 242) cites a dedication to the *numen* of Augustus at Leptis Magna (*IRT* 324a). There are also inscriptions at Forum Sempronii (*numini Augusto*), see Marengo 2008: 154; and at Tarraco (*numen Augusti*) (*RIT* 48), see Garriguet 2002: 148.

[22] By contrast, Severy (2003: 195–6) assumes without question the existence of an altar dedicated by Tiberius to Augustus' *numen*.

Fishwick (2005: 237–245) has persuasively argued it is more likely that an Ara Numinis Augusti in Rome influenced the provinces than that separate dedications to the *numen* of Augustus were set up in civic centers in Narbo, Forum Clodii, and Leptis Magna. To reinforce the family connection between Tiberius and Augustus, the date of the dedication for the presumed Ara Numinis Augusti (or whatever monument was commemorated in the *Fasti Praenestini*) was the anniversary of Augustus' marriage to Livia, January 17 (*Inscr. It.* XIII.2 401).

While Augustus was not directly worshipped during his own lifetime in Rome itself, this official dedication served as a forerunner to his later deification. Fishwick observes that the cult of the *numen* of the living Augustus was unique:

> The cult of the Numen Augusti, on the other hand, first appears at the very end of Augustus' life and is attested in a small number of instances under Tiberius but then seems to drop out of sight until re-emerging in the Antonine period and, much more abundantly, under the Severi and later. The obvious reason for this is that none of Augustus' immediate successors possessed the prestige and charisma to justify a cult that came close to outright deification in life (Fishwick 1990a: 611; cf. Fishwick 1994: 138).

The *numen* of Augustus continued its protective influence over his family and the Roman people even after his death. In the *Senatus Consultum de Cn. Pisone Patre* (*SCPP*), among Piso's many crimes against the state are his insults to the *numen* of Augustus (45–8 and 68–70).[23] There is no comparable cult of the *numen* of Tiberius. Both before and after his death, the *numen* of Augustus ensured the security of the Roman world.

Tiberius was also closely bound to the worship of Augustus' *providentia* through Augustus' adoption of Tiberius and Tiberius' adoption of Germanicus. Whether the Ara Providentiae was built by Augustus or Tiberius (or, more likely, both), it was advertised on coins at moments of dynastic importance, leaving little doubt that the *providentia* in question involved the choice of successor.[24] The location of the altar in the Campus Martius, probably opposite the Ara Pacis, made a clear statement that this

---

[23] We will discuss these lines in greater detail in Chapter 4.

[24] On Tiberius as the first to promote this virtue, see Schmid 2005: 262. As Trillmich (1988: 492) points out, the monument and the coins on which it was featured (e.g., *BMCRE* I 146 = *RIC* I[2] 80) could also have wider meaning. Tiberius was celebrated for his own *providentia* in an inscription from Interamna dated to 32 (*CIL* XI 4170): *Providentiae Ti. Caesaris Augusti nati ad aeternitatem Romani nominis*. On the connection between *providentia* and *aeternitas*, see Charlesworth 1936: 110. On Tiberius' *providentia* as a general, see Velleius 2.115.5.

monument celebrated the *domus Augusta*.[25] The Ara Providentiae is mentioned in the *SCPP* (82–4) as being a site where Piso's name had been inscribed on a statue of Germanicus, so it must predate the ugliness surrounding the latter's death in 19.[26] Cox (2005: 253) argues that since the *Res Gestae* includes an event from May of 14 (the *lustrum* closing the census conducted by Tiberius and Augustus (*RG* 8.4)) and does not mention the altar, the Ara Providentiae could not have been built before Augustus' death. While she may be correct that the altar was not completed by then, construction could certainly have been underway. The Ara Pacis took three and a half years to complete.[27]

Barrandon, Suspène, and Gaffiero (2010) have used chemical analysis to date the earliest issues of coins featuring the Ara Providentiae to 15. They connect such coins to the dedication of the altar, which they believe took place on June 26, the anniversary of Augustus' adoption of Tiberius.[28] While it would make sense for Tiberius to advertise the *providentia* of Augustus early in his reign, he celebrated the altar on coins as late as 37.[29] According to the acts of the Fratres Arvales (*CIL* VI 2028 = *AE* 1983 95), in 38 a sacrifice was made at this altar on June 26, indicating the site's continued importance in the reign of Germanicus' son, Tiberius' grandson, and Augustus' great-grandson, Caligula. Moreover, the date chosen for Tiberius' adoption exemplifies Augustus' *providentia*. June 26 was not only the date the adoption was formalized (*Fasti Amit.*) but also the Summer Solstice under the Julian Calendar (*CIL* I[2] p. 221; Ovid, *Fast.* 6.785–90).[30] Schmid (2005: 266–7) suggests that the choice of this day,

---

[25] On the position of the Ara Providentiae as opposite the Ara Pacis, see Eck et al. 1996: 199–200.

[26] Fishwick (2010; cf. 2017: 184–91) connects an altar at Emerita to the Ara Providentiae. He believes that Fulcinius Trio as magistrate under Tiberius was responsible for beginning the construction of a copy of the Ara Providentiae, but that after it was begun the locals incorporated Agrippa, the patron of the colony, undercutting Tiberius, who was dead by the time the altar was completed (2017: 212–3). Saquete (2005: 291) disagrees, citing coins from Emerita featuring Divus Augustus Pater and Tiberius which advertise *providentia* (*RPC* I 28, 34–6, 45–6). He (2005: 292; cf. 304) sees the possible Altar of Providentia at Emerita as having been instigated by Fulcinius Trio after he witnessed the importance of that virtue to the succession policy undermined by the death of Germanicus. As one of the prosecutors of Piso (Tac. *Ann.* 3.11), Trio would have been cognizant of the significance of the monument.

[27] The Ara Pacis was inaugurated on July 30, 13 BC (*Fasti Amit.*) and consecrated on January 31, 9 BC (*Fasti Praen.*, Ovid, *Fasti* 1.709–24).

[28] Lyasse (2008: 93) dates the altar to immediately following the death of Augustus.

[29] On coins bearing the Ara Providentiae (*RIC* I[2] 81) as being issued in 15/16, 22/23, and 34–7, see Barrandon, Suspène, and Gaffiero 2010: 159.

[30] Much has been made of Ovid's failure in the *Fasti* to mention Tiberius' adoption. As Littlewood has observed, following Herbert-Brown (1994: 229–33), "Since 26 June was not marked as a public holiday in any of the official *Fasti*, Ovid was not obliged to celebrate it in his calendar poem" (2006: xx; cf. 226–7). The adoption is, however, noted in *Fasti Amiternini*, as cited above. Syme (1978a) believes that Ovid's *Fasti* was written before Tiberius' adoption had taken place.

being the longest with respect to daylight, celebrated the bringing of light and order to the world through the *pax Augusta*. Schrömbges (1986: 38–9) ties the date of the adoption to Augustus' worship of Apollo and the Ludi Saeculares. The date was perhaps also chosen to downplay "cruel fate," as it was the date upon which Augustus had adopted his grandsons Gaius and Lucius in 17 BC.[31] Velleius gives the date of Tiberius' adoption as June 27. If this is correct, it ties the adoption to the cult of Jupiter Stator, a cult associated from Rome's earliest beginnings with the stability of the state. In his letters to Tiberius as recorded by Suetonius (*Tib.* 21.4–7), Augustus considers Tiberius to be the savior of the Roman people through his various military successes. At any rate, beginning with Tiberius' adoption, celebrations of events in the *domus Augusta* often coincided with dates already significant in the Augustan calendar.[32] The anniversary of Tiberius' adoption continued to be celebrated annually, even after his death, a consistent reminder of Augustus' *providentia*.

Tiberius had played an important role in promoting Augustus' divine qualities during the latter's reign; he also understood the importance of enshrining his father as a god of the state. In the weeks following the death of Augustus, Tiberius' first act in the Senate was to guarantee that Augustus was given the funeral he desired. His second was to ensure that Augustus was deified (on September 17, *Inscr. It.* XIII.2 510). As discussed above, the foundation for Augustus' deification had long been prepared. And, as mentioned in Chapter 1, he had left instructions for his funeral which no doubt indicated the ritual by which he would be celebrated as divine.[33] But none of that would matter if he were not welcomed into the official state pantheon by the Senate, or if the worship of the living Tiberius eclipsed that of the new Divus Augustus. While Tiberius faced none of the resistance Octavian had met with in his attempt to deify Julius Caesar, the trend towards excessive honors for Tiberius threatened to undermine the charismatic divinity of Augustus. Thus, when in the midst of the discussion of Augustus' funeral Valerius Messalla suggested that an oath to Tiberius be renewed annually, Tiberius shut him down.

---

[31] On the coincidence of the two adoption dates, see Cox 2005: 252. Schmid (2005: 265) hypothesizes that Tiberius himself may have chosen the date.

[32] Schrömbges (1986: 36–7) notes that the date of the dedication of the Temple of Concordia coincided with the anniversary of Augustus' receiving his sacred cognomen (January 16) (more on this below). He adds the coincidence of Tiberius' Illyrian triumph and the second battle of Philippi (October 23).

[33] On the route of Augustus' funeral as possibly imitating that of a triumph, see Zanker 2004: 40–1.

Tacitus (*Ann.* 1.10.8) indicates that Augustus' deification was a simple formality, easily passed by the Senate after Augustus' funeral.[34] But in the next sentence, the senators are shown directing their prayers (*preces*) to Tiberius, not the new *divus*. Tacitus (*Ann.* 1.11.1) reports in indirect speech that Tiberius immediately deflected such honor away from himself and towards Augustus by stating that only the mind of Divus Augustus was capable of ruling the empire. Given that the exchange took place in the Senate, Tacitus is likely reporting something very close to what Tiberius actually said.[35] Dio includes a funeral oration supposedly given by Tiberius. In it, he compares Augustus to Romulus and Hercules (56.36) and concludes:

> It was for all this, therefore, that you, with good reason, made him your leader and a father of the people, that you honored him with many marks of esteem and with ever so many consulships, and that you finally made him a demigod and declared him to be immortal. Hence it is fitting also that we should not mourn for him, but that, while we now at last give his body back to Nature, we should glorify his spirit, as that of a god, forever. (56.41.9; Loeb trans. Cary)

While this speech is more the work of Dio than Tiberius, it reflects some of the genuine reverence which Tiberius showed for Augustus both before and after his death.[36] It also highlights the idea that in order to continue to shoulder the burden of the empire, a burden which could only truly be managed by Augustus (as Tacitus has Tiberius state), Tiberius would rule under the guidance of the new god.

Although Augustus may have drawn up the blueprint for his own posthumous worship, Tiberius was instrumental in its implementation. Dio is very specific in attributing the primary impetus for the deification of Augustus to Tiberius:

> A shrine voted by the Senate and built by Livia and Tiberius was erected to the dead emperor in Rome, and others in many different places, some of the communities voluntarily building them and others unwillingly... Such were the decrees passed in memory of Augustus, nominally by the Senate, but actually by Tiberius and Livia. For when some men proposed one thing and some another, the Senate decreed that Tiberius should receive suggestions in writing from its members and then select whichever he chose. (56.46.3; 47.1; Loeb trans. Cary)

---

[34] On the ritual for deifying emperors, see Price 1987 and Gradel 2002: 260–324.

[35] On Tacitus' citation of Tiberian speech, see especially Miller 1968 and Wharton 1997. Cf. Suet. *Tib.* 23, who omits details about the Senate meetings yet does state that Tiberius was overcome by grief.

[36] On Tiberius' speech in Dio, see Swan 2004: 325–6.

Dio gives some credit to Livia, saying she took part in the selection of honors. Nevertheless, she would not have been able to make proposals before the Senate.[37] Tiberius may have had a considerably easier time deifying Augustus than Octavian had enacting the divine honors granted to Caesar before his death, but he also made sure that the honors granted to Divus Augustus eclipsed those of Divus Iulius. Lyasse (2008: 78–84) notes that while Julius Caesar, Jupiter, Mars, and Quirinus all had *flamines*, the creation of the new priesthood of Sodales Augustales was unique.[38] The precedent dated all the way back to Titus Tatius. This *collegium* of priests, made up primarily of members of the imperial family and their inner circle, was soon to play an integral role in the cult of not only Divus Augustus but the entire *domus Augusta*.

Tiberius was criticized for his failure to complete the Temple of Divus Augustus (Suet. *Tib.* 47.1). But the fact that it was dedicated in 37 by his successor Caligula suggests that only Tiberius' failure to return to Rome prevented its dedication. It also indicates that it took at least twelve years to build, assuming it was not completed by the time Tiberius left Rome for good in 26.[39] Although it may have seemed to others that Tiberius did not care about the temple he had vowed to his deified father, a more likely explanation is that he cared too much. We know Tiberius personally selected artwork for the temple (Pliny, *HN* 35.40.131).[40] As he did with the Temple of Concordia and that of Castor, both of which he refurbished under Augustus, Tiberius took his time to make sure that the Temple of Divus Augustus was grand enough for its divine inhabitant.

In addition to building the Temple of Augustus in Rome, Tiberius was responsible for promoting the worship of the Julian *gens* at Bovillae.[41] According to Suetonius (*Aug.* 99), Augustus' body was brought from Nola to Bovillae, where it was prepared for its funeral cortège to Rome. Tacitus

---

[37] However, as Lyasse (2008: 71) points out, by bribing a certain Numerius (Dio 56.46.2) to swear that he had seen the spirit of Augustus ascending to the heavens, Livia associated his deification with that of Romulus, bypassing the more problematic deification of Caesar. Cf. Suet. *Aug.* 100.4.

[38] See also Taylor 1929: 91–2, who adds that Livia's position as *flaminica* was also unique.

[39] The Temple of Mars Ultor was vowed in 42 BC and dedicated, still unfinished, in 2 BC. The Temple of Divus Iulius was dedicated in 29 BC, thirteen years after it had been begun in 42 BC. Likewise, the restorations of the Temple of Ceres and the Temple of Flora in the Forum Boarium, destroyed by a fire, were begun in 31 BC. The buildings were dedicated by Tiberius in 17. See Haselberger 2007: 183.

[40] Suetonius mentions (*Tib.* 74) a particularly grand statue of Apollo acquired to decorate the library of the temple signaling to Tiberius that he could not dedicate the temple himself. On the temple, see Hänlein-Schäfer 1985: 113–78.

[41] Weinstock 1971: 5–7. On the problematic evidence for a "shrine to the Julii" at Bovillae predating the one erected by Tiberius, see Badian 2009: 14–15.

(*Ann.* 2.41) tells us that at the end of 16 Tiberius dedicated a *sacrarium* to the Julian *gens* and an *effigies* to Divus Augustus at Bovillae.[42] Excavations have turned up a previous affiliation of the Julian *gens* with Bovillae, an altar to Vediovis Pater dedicated by the GENTEILES IVLIEI.[43] Bovillae had ties to Alba Longa, a city supposedly founded by the ancestor of the Julian *gens*, Aeneas' son Iulus. Iulus may have been associated with or assimilated to Vediovis, who also has connections to Apollo.[44] Other than that, there do not seem to be any strong ties between the Julii and Bovillae until the time of Augustus. As Badian notes, the connection of the Julian *gens* to Bovillae was tenuous and only became prominent after the death of Augustus, primarily because "Augustus and Tiberius, of course, had a special interest in 'proving' their Julian descent" (2009: 15).[45] Circus games were added, or, if they had originated under Augustus, expanded.[46] They continued into the reign of Nero, who, celebrating the birth of his daughter by Poppaea in 63, honored Antium by instituting circus games modeled on those at Bovillae dedicated to the *gens Iulia* (Tac. *Ann.* 15.23). The Sodales Augustales were responsible for ceremonies honoring Augustus and his Julian ancestors in Bovillae.[47] Tiberius also built smaller shrines to Divus Augustus in the house where Augustus died at Nola (Dio 56.46.3) and on the Palatine (Suet. *Tib.* 51; Tac. *Ann.* 4.52).[48]

At the sites mentioned above, Tiberius promoted the worship of Augustus either in or around Rome. This sent a clear message to the provinces. Tacitus (*Ann.* 1.78) records that shortly after the death of Augustus an embassy from Hispania Tarraconensis solicited the right to build a temple to Divus Augustus. An altar to Augustus already existed in Tarraco (Quint. *Inst.* 6.3.77); a temple would enhance the honor of the

---

[42] As Doboşi states (1935: 359), Tacitus is our only evidence for this *sacrarium*. There is no reason, however, to doubt his testimony, and a statue of Augustus in the guise of Jupiter has been found at the site (Doboşi 1935: 365). Balty (2007: 65) believes that a statue of Augustus in the Torlonia Collection belongs "sans doute" to Tiberius' restoration of the shrine.

[43] Doboşi 1935: 266–73.

[44] Doboşi 1935: 273. See Aulus Gellius 5.12 for the similar iconography of Vediovis and Apollo, albeit with a mistaken interpretation.

[45] Tiberius also undertook to rebuild the Temple of Venus at Eryx but does not seem to have fulfilled that vow (Tac. *Ann.* 4.43.4; cf. Suet. *Claud.* 25.5).

[46] The evidence for *ludi* instituted by Augustus is derived from one fragmentary inscription (*CIL* XIV 2417) and assumed by Badian 2009: 15. See also Weinstock 1957: 147.

[47] Weinstock 1971: 7, based on fragments of the *Fasti* found at Bovillae, esp. *CIL* XIV 2388–91. On the distinction between the Sodales Augustales as opposed to the local Augustales in various regions outside of Rome, see Linderski 2007: 179–83. See also Wohlmayr 2013: 212, who concludes that the circus at Bovillae was most likely built during Tiberius' reign.

[48] On the distinction between the *sacrarium* built into the imperial complex on the Palatine and the Temple of Divus Augustus, see Fishwick 1992: 245–55.

new Divus.[49] More importantly, this grant would be seen as an *exemplum* for all the provinces. Fishwick argues that when the example was followed by Augusta Emerita the initiative may have actually come from the governor at that time, Fulcinius Trio, who "owed his career and advancement to Tiberius" (2017: 65). Fulcinius encouraged the builders of the temple to model it after the Temple of Concordia in Rome, much as temples at Tarraco, Corduba, and in the Municipal Forum at Emerita were modeled on the Temple of Mars Ultor. While Fishwick (2017: 65) sees the similarity between the Temple of Divus Augustus at Emerita and the Temple of Concordia, refurbished by Tiberius, as evidence that Fulcinius was emphasizing the primacy of Tiberius, the temple was dedicated to Divus Augustus.[50] Saquete (2005: 282) dates Trio's governorship of Lusitania as subsequent to his role in the trial of Piso in 20. That would leave a five-year time difference between the grant of the temple in nearby Tarraco and the initiative of the neighboring province to build its own temple. On the other hand, contrary to Fishwick's conjecture, it is entirely possible that the leading citizens of Emerita took it upon themselves to build the temple without any prodding from their governor. There was already a temple to Augustus and Roma in the forum at Emerita.[51] As a compromise, Saquete (2005: 303–4) posits that the temple had already been planned by the locals, but that Fulcinius Trio suggested modeling the temple on that of Concordia in Rome.

Coins issued under Tiberius display the temples at Tarraco and Emerita, signaling their importance in provincial iconography. The coins from Tarraco feature either a seated figure of Divus Augustus with the legend DEO AVGVSTO (*RPC* 1 221–4) or the head of Augustus with a radiate crown and the legend DIVVS AVGVSTVS PATER (*RPC* 1 218–20).[52] These images, along with other issues featuring an octostyle temple with the legend C V T T AETERNITATIS AVGVSTAE (*RPC* 1 224, 226), demonstrate the desire of provincials to prove their reverence for Divus

[49] On municipal worship of Augustus in Spain during his own lifetime, see Ramage 1998: 482–90.

[50] On problematic evidence, Fishwick, following Saquete (2005: 293–9), asserts that a pair of statues, one of Tiberius and one of Concordia, flanked the entrance to the temple (2017: 70–84). For a relief said to be from southern Spain featuring Tiberius with a figure who may be Concordia standing before some sort of local *genius*, see Pollini 2012: 97–101. Pollini dates the relief somewhere between 14–31.

[51] On the temple to the imperial cult in Emerita, see Nogales Bassarate 2007. On the imperial cult in Emerita in general, see Saquete and Álvarez Martínez 2007.

[52] We will examine the iconography of DIVVS AVGVSTVS PATER on Tiberian coins more closely in Chapter 4.

Augustus during the reign of Tiberius.[53] Fishwick (1987: 1.151) argues that the epithet "Augustae" was understood to be personally associated with Augustus himself. The *aeternitas* celebrated on these coins was not just some generic idea but a reminder that the peace and prosperity initiated by Divus Augustus would continue under his heirs.[54] Saquete (2005: 293) observes that in addition to the coins from Emerita depicting Divus Augustus Pater on the obverse with the temple and the legend AETERNITATI AVGVSTAE (*RPC* 1 29) on the reverse, coins with the same reverse feature Tiberius as Pontifex Maximus (*RPC* 1 47–8), suggesting that Tiberius played some role in the promotion of that temple.

In conjunction with encouraging temples to Divus Augustus, Tiberius punished those who did not honor his divine father. Both Dio ([Xiph.] 57.24.6) and Tacitus (*Ann.* 4.36) mention that Tiberius revoked privileges from the state of Cyzicus because it had vowed a shrine to Augustus but failed to complete it. Apidius Merula was removed from the Senate for not swearing to uphold the *acta* of Divus Augustus (Tac. *Ann.* 4.42.3). And while Suetonius' account (*Tib.* 58) of the treason trials under Tiberius is extremely murky, at the end of his list of minor offenses which were punished excessively he includes the odd example of a man who perished for allowing an honor to be decreed to him in the colony where he lived on the same day on which honors had been decreed for Augustus. We do not know the details of this case, although Tacitus (*Ann.* 6.18.2) narrates an attack against descendants of Theophanes because their ancestor, a supporter of Pompey, had been accorded divine honors in Achaea.[55] In all three of these episodes, Tiberius was a motivating force in punishing slights to the divinity of Augustus.

Alongside the new priesthood of the Sodales Augustales, Tiberius instituted the flaminate of Augustus. Modeled ostensibly on the flaminate of Divus Iulius, the flaminate of Augustus had much in common as well with the *flamen Dialis*, enjoying certain benefits without being bound by the same restrictions. While it is highly likely that Augustus himself made the original selection of Germanicus as his first *flamen*, Tiberius fulfilled the

---

[53] As Garriguet (2002: 163) points out, even if the temple at Tarraco had not yet been completed at the time, Emerita followed its example and issued coins featuring a temple to *aeternitas Augusta*. He also posits (2002: 166–7) that the temple to Divus Augustus was a temple for the entire province of Hispania Ulterior.

[54] Schmitzer (2000: 297) notes that Tiberius is also closely connected with the *aeternitas* of the *pax Augusta* by Velleius Paterculus (2.103.4–5).

[55] This may have been related to a ban issued just before the fall of Sejanus on offering sacrifices to human beings (Dio 58.8.4).

investiture. More importantly, when Germanicus died, Tiberius chose his own son Drusus as successor in the priesthood. As the *flamen* of Augustus was supposed to be chosen only from members of the Julian line, this reinforced Drusus' position as a grandson of Augustus through his father's adoption. Upon Drusus' death, the priesthood passed to Nero, son of Germanicus.[56] Thus, under Tiberius the flaminate of Augustus was not simply a priesthood honoring his predecessor; it was also the mark of his intended successor. By contrast, after the death of Mark Antony, the flaminate of Divus Iulius passed to Sextus Appuleius, the husband of the elder Octavia, Augustus' half-sister.[57] In the reign of Claudius, the *flamen* of Divus Augustus absorbed the duties of the cult of Divus Iulius.

There can be no doubt that the deification of Augustus was necessary for the consolidation of power by members of his family. Nevertheless, Tiberius seems to have been sincere in his personal worship of Augustus. Tacitus (*Ann.* 4.52) reports that Agrippina, upset over the prosecution of her cousin, Claudia Pulchra, confronted Tiberius. She found him sacrificing to his father. Although Divus Augustus had a shrine in the Temple of Mars Ultor while his own temple was being built, the intimacy of the ensuing conversation suggests that it took place in a private setting. Thus, twelve years after the death of Augustus, Tiberius was discovered by chance (*forte*) offering sacrifices to his predecessor. We know the passage refers to Augustus and not Tiberius' natural father because Agrippina immediately rebukes Tiberius for worshipping Augustus as a god while persecuting the true descendants of his divine blood, herself and her sons.

Intriguingly, Agrippina specifically states, at least according to Tacitus, that Claudia Pulchra was being attacked because she had chosen Agrippina *ad cultum*. This, as well as the previous statement, indicates that Agrippina felt that she herself was worthy of divine cult.[58] Certainly, living members of the *domus Augusta* were given divine honors in the East, but the idea of Agrippina, or anyone else living, being worshipped in Rome was bordering on blasphemy, at least in the view of Tiberius. This sentiment, rather than the complaint regarding the prosecution of her cousin, was what provoked

---

[56] *CIL* VI 40373 = *ILS* 183. See Lyasse 2008: 86.

[57] Weinstock 1971: 308. For the proposition that the *flamen Iulialis* after Antony was actually the son of Sex. Appuleius, see Pollini 1986: 456–8. Hoffman Lewis (1955: 77; cf. 37) does not commit ("either Augustus' brother-in-law or his nephew").

[58] Martin and Woodman (1989: 217) translate in their note, "that she had chosen to devote herself to Ag," and point to *OLD* 10a for *cultus*, which reads, "The worship or veneration (of a deity)." Cf. Tac. *Ann.* 4.68.1, where Titius Sabinus is attacked *ob amicitiam Germanici*, to which Tacitus adds *neque enim omiserat coniugem liberosque eius percolere*, and *OLD* 3 for *percolo*.

the *raram vocem* from Tiberius (in Greek, no less), paraphrased by Tacitus as saying that she should not consider herself to be wounded simply because she was not ruling (*Ann.* 4.52.3; cf. Suet. *Tib.* 53.1). Tiberius understood that what Augustus had achieved in ending the civil wars and establishing orderly government was worthy of divine honors. The other members of the *domus Augusta* derived their charisma solely from him.

Velleius Paterculus, who could be considered to have had insight into Tiberius' regime, corroborates Tiberius' reverence for his adoptive father. He asserts that Tiberius "sanctified his father not by edict but by worship; he did not just call him a god but made him one" (*sacravit parentem suum Caesar non imperio, sed religione, non appellavit eum, sed fecit deum*, 2.126.1). And despite the later problems which arose from the *maiestas* laws (to be discussed in Chapter 6), when pressed to indict a man who had committed perjury after swearing to Divus Augustus, Tiberius treated Divus Augustus as if he were a true god in the Roman pantheon: "The oath must be judged as if he had perjured by Jove: the injuries of the gods are a concern for the gods" (*Ius iurandum perinde aestimandum quam si Iovem fefellisset: deorum iniurias dis curae*, Tac. *Ann.* 1.73).

The precedent for deifying one's adoptive father had been firmly set by Octavian/Augustus. But Tiberius' continuous promotion of Divus Augustus distinguished his policy from that of his predecessor. After reinventing himself as Augustus, the first princeps no longer owed everything to (another man's) name. Divus Iulius continued to play an important role in promoting the *domus divina*, but, aside from the temple in Rome itself, the cult of Divus Iulius ceased to be actively fostered. A new precedent had been set by Tiberius in his honors for Divus Augustus as well as in his attitude towards honors for himself.

Tiberius' Refusal of Divine Honors

While Augustus may have been subtle in his acceptance and refusal of divine honors during his own lifetime, his deification was inevitable. Tiberius, on the other hand, seems to have scrupulously avoided any indication that he was divine other than through his parentage. Naturally, Tiberius had no control over private dedications which honored him as divine or semi-divine. Thus, we will not concern ourselves with dedications to Tiberius which were beyond his control.[59] As with

---

[59] On priests of Tiberius in Italy, Paci points out that at least some of the inscriptions recording priests date to after his death (2008: 210; with reference to an inscription from Asculum recording *sexviri*

Augustus, we are only interested here in official honors awarded at Rome and by the provinces.

The best evidence for Tiberius' repudiation of divine honors comes from a passage of Tacitus regarding a proposed temple in Hispania Ulterior and a letter from Tiberius to the Laconian city of Gytheion. According to Tacitus (*Ann.* 4.37–8), in 25 the province of Hispania Ulterior sent an embassy to the Senate asking to build a temple to Tiberius and his mother, modeled on a temple which had been granted to Asia two years earlier (*Ann.* 4.15). Tacitus has Tiberius reject the offer, using *oratio recta*:

> I know, senators, that my constancy has been found wanting by many, since I did not object to the cities of Asia recently seeking the same thing. Therefore, I will lay out at the same time a defense of my previous silence and what I have decided for the future. Since Divus Augustus, whose deeds and pronouncements, all of them, I observe as if they were law, did not prohibit a temple to be built to himself and the city of Rome at Pergamum, I followed his agreeable example all the more readily, especially since the worship of the Senate was added to my cult. But although to have done this once may have earned some pardon, to be consecrated in imitation of *numina* throughout the provinces would be self-seeking and arrogant. And honor for Augustus would vanish if it were made common with indiscriminate flattery. I call you as witnesses, senators, and I wish posterity to remember, that I am mortal, and that I perform the duties of a man, and I have enough if I should fulfill my role as princeps. They will pay more than enough tribute to my memory who believe that I was worthy of my ancestors, provident of your affairs, constant in dangers, and not afraid to cause offense for the sake of the public good. These will be my temples in your hearts, these the most beautiful statues and the ones which will endure. For those which are constructed from stone, if the judgment of posterity should turn to hatred, are spurned as sepulchers. Thus, I pray to our allies, citizens, and the gods themselves, that the gods grant me a calm mind, understanding of both human and divine law, until the end of my life, and that my fellow citizens, whenever I should die, might honor my deeds and the fame of my name with praise and kind memories.

> scio, patres conscripti, constantiam meam a plerisque desideratam quod Asiae civitatibus nuper idem istud petentibus non sim adversatus. ergo et prioris silentii defensionem et quid in futurum statuerim simul aperiam. cum divus Augustus sibi atque urbi Romae templum apud Pergamum sisti non prohibuisset, qui omnia facta dictaque eius vice legis observem,

---

Tiberiales). Paci also notes (2008: 214) that only two inscriptions in Italy regarding priests of Tiberius date after 20, indicating that as Tiberius' policy became more widely known, communities refrained from giving him divine honors.

placitum iam exemplum promptius secutus sum quia cultui meo veneratio senatus adiungebatur. ceterum ut semel recepisse veniam habuerit, ita per omnis provincias effigie numinum sacrari ambitiosum, superbum; et vanescet Augusti honor si promiscis adulationibus vulgatur. Ego me, patres conscripti, mortalem esse et hominum officia fungi satisque habere si locum principem impleam et vos testor et meminisse posteros volo; qui satis superque memoriae meae tribuent, ut maioribus meis dignum, rerum vestrarum providum, constantem in periculis, offensionum pro utilitate publica non pavidum credant. haec mihi in animis vestris templa, hae pulcherrimae effigies et mansurae. nam quae saxo struuntur, si iudicium posterorum in odium vertit, pro sepulchris spernuntur. proinde socios civis et deos ipsos precor, hos ut mihi ad finem usque vitae quietam et intellegentem humani divinique iuris mentem duint, illos ut, quandoque concessero, cum laude et bonis recordationibus facta atque famam nominis mei prosequantur.

After Tacitus records Tiberius' diplomatic response, he then summarizes alleged criticism Tiberius received for such a refusal, especially since he had already granted the province of Asia the right to build a temple to himself, his mother, and the Senate. Even though Tacitus reports that Augustus was criticized at his funeral for accepting divine honors, here Tiberius is criticized for the opposite.[60]

There are two reasons for Tiberius' refusal. The first is that while the people of Asia had included Livia and the Senate in their request, the people of Spain were asking to build a temple to Tiberius alone.[61] Indeed, oversight of the temple in Asia was handed over to the Senate. In images of the temple on coinage minted under Caligula, Tiberius is depicted as a priest in the temple on the reverse; Livia and the Senate are advertised on the obverse (*RPC* I 2469; Price 1984: 258 (catalog 45)). Moreover, the provinces of Asia were motivated to request the temple to Tiberius, Livia, and the Senate because of the role each had played, especially the Senate, in the punishment of the corrupt governors C. Silanus and Lucilius Capito (Tac. *Ann.* 3.66–9; 4.15).[62] The Senate presided over the debate as to where the temple should be located, ultimately selecting Smyrna (*Ann.* 4.55–6). In addition to honoring the Senate, Tiberius may have been more

---

[60] On the criticism of Tiberius for refusing divine honors, see Pelling 2010: 369 and Levene 2012: 72.

[61] Pelling (2010: 368 n. 5) observes, crediting O'Gorman, that Baetica was a province governed by senatorial appointment, which would make dropping the Senate from the temple even more embarrassing for Tiberius.

[62] Burrell 2004: 38. Cf. McIntyre 2016: 35. Certain cities were also particularly thankful to Tiberius for his financial assistance after an earthquake in 17 (Suet. *Tib.* 48; Tac. *Ann.* 2.47). For a list of sources on the earthquake, see Goodyear 1981: 336.

likely to allow a temple to be dedicated to himself and Livia because the request was made in 23, when he was trying to boost the image of the *domus Augusta* after the deaths of Germanicus and Drusus.[63] To celebrate the new temple, Nero, the eldest son of Germanicus, gave a speech of thanks before the Senate.

In the second part of his refusal to allow Hispania Ulterior to build a temple to himself, Tiberius expresses concern about the dilution of the cult of his predecessor. Tiberius had already encouraged the building of temples to Divus Augustus in Spain. He believed that any temple dedicated solely to himself would diminish the cult of Augustus, something he assiduously refused to do. This can be seen even more clearly in a letter written by Tiberius to the Laconian city of Gytheion. While the passage from Tacitus may or may not report Tiberius' actual response to Hispania Ulterior, the inscription from Gytheion gives us direct evidence of Tiberius' attitude towards divine honors for himself. We can also see his dedicated promotion of the cult of Augustus and his circumspect position on honors for other members of the *domus Augusta*. He was not being "Republican" in refusing divine honors for himself. He had no problem promoting the cult of his dead father. And although he denied deification for his mother upon her death, he allowed certain sacred honors to his deceased sons Germanicus and Drusus, as we shall see in Chapter 4. In his responses, Tiberius consistently deflected divine honors away from himself and towards the more charismatic and ideologically important members of the family.

The inscription from Gytheion can be dated to the early part of Tiberius' principate. Tiberius refers to himself as Pontifex Maximus, a title he accepted on March 10, 15 (*Fast. Praen.*). Germanicus is mentioned as though he were still alive, providing a *terminus ante quem* of 19. An early dating seems preferable, as the ephors of Gytheion were likely trying to appeal to the new princeps by equating him with his predecessor and by referring to him as *pater patriae*, a title he explicitly refused.[64] Tiberius' response reads as follows:

> [Letter of Tiber]ius. *vv* | [Tiberius Caesar,] son of the [god Aug]ustus, Augustus, pontifex maximus, holding the tribunician power | [for the sixteenth time (AD 15),] to the Gytheion ephors and the city, greetings.

---

[63] Schrömbges (1986: 230) believes this was done to help Drusus' side of the family, but Tacitus' narrative indicates that Germanicus' sons benefitted as well.

[64] Suet. *Tib.* 26.2, 67.2; Tac. *Ann.* 1.72.1, 2.87.2; Dio 57.8.1, 58.12.8, 58.22.1. On the refusal of *pater patriae* by other principes who later accepted the title, see Stevenson 2007: 122.

When he was sent by you | [to] me and my mother as an envoy, Decimus Turranius Nikanor || *delivered* your letter to me, to which had been attached the items voted into law | [by] you to show your piety for my father and your esteem for us. | [For] these things I praise you and believe it fitting that in general all me|n and in particular your city should hold in reserve – because of the great size of the | benefits of my father to all the world – the honors that are appropriate for gods; || I myself am content with more moderate honors, as befit men. My mo|ther will give you her answer, when she learns from you what decision you have made about the honors for her. (Trans. Sherk 1988: 57)

[Τιβέριος Καῖσαρ θεοῦ Σεβ]αστοῦ υἱὸ[ς Σ]εβαστὸς ἀρχιερεὺς δημαρχικῆς ἐξουσίας/[τὸ ἑκκαιδέκατο]ν/Γυθεατῶν ἐφόροις καὶ τῇ πόλει, χαίρειν. ὁ πεμφθεὶς ὑφ᾽ ὑμῶν [πρός τ]ε ἐμὲ καὶ τὴν ἐμὴν μητέρα πρεσβευτὴς Δέκμος Τυρράνιος Νεικάνωρ//[ἀνέδ]ωκέν μοι τὴν ὑμετέραν ἐπιστολὴν ᾗ προσεγέγραπτο τὰ νομοθετηθέν/[τα ὑφ᾽ ὑ]μῶν εἰς εὐσέβειαν μὲν τοῦ ἐμοῦ πατρὸς τιμὴν δὲ τὴν ἡμετέραν./[ἐ]φ᾽ οἷς ὑμᾶς ἐπαινῶν προσήκειν ὑπ(ο)λαμβάνω<ι> καὶ κοινῇ πάντας ἀνθρώ/πους καὶ ἰδίᾳ τὴν ὑμετέραν πόλιν ἐξαιρέτους φυλάσσειν τῶι μεγέθει τῶν τοῦ ἐμοῦ πατρὸς εἰς ἅπαντα τὸν κόσμον εὐεργεσιῶν τὰς θεοῖς πρεπούσας// τιμάς, αὐτὸς δὲ ἀρκοῦμαι ταῖς μετριωτέραις τε καὶ ἀνθρωπείοις· ἡ μέντοι ἐμὴ μή/τηρ τόθ᾽ ὑμῖν ἀποκρινεῖται ὅταν αἴσθηται παρ᾽ ὑμῶν ἣν ἔχετε περὶ τῶν εἰς αὐτὴν τιμῶν/κρίσιν. (E.-J.² 102 = *SEG* XI.922–3)

Tiberius thanks the citizens for their piety (*eusebeia*) towards his father and the honor (*timē*) shown towards himself. His refusal is somewhat formulaic and may have been based on similar responses given by Augustus to curb excessive honors.[65] Significantly, he then adds that divine honors should be reserved for his father in return for the deeds of good will (*euergesiōn*) Augustus had performed and that he is satisfied with honors which are more moderate and suitable for men. Excessive honors to the living princeps would diminish the glory of the one who had recently joined the gods.

Tiberius allows Livia to make her own response, which has not been preserved. A dedication to Livia in the form of Tyche on a statue base found in the same complex would indicate that she did accept worship under this guise. That Tiberius wished to restrict the honor shown to his mother provided a great deal of ammunition for scandalmongers and later historians (e.g., Tac. *Ann.* 1.14). But Tiberius' policy for his mother followed the policy he held for himself. As she was still alive, she could not truly receive divine honors. That he refused to deify her after her death

---

[65] On this formula, see Charlesworth 1939.

would indicate that he did not seek to be deified himself. Moreover, he would not diminish the honors shown to Augustus by granting them to a woman, even his own mother.

Domus Augusta/Domus Divina

Despite his refusal of divine honors for himself, Tiberius recognized the importance of perpetuating the image that Augustus' divine charisma lived on in the family which would provide his successors, the *domus divina* or *domus Augusta*.[66] The term *domus* had been used to refer to the family of Augustus as early as 2 BC, when Augustus was granted the title *pater patriae*.[67] According to Suetonius (*Aug.* 58), Messalla led the acclamation, wishing good fortune not just to Augustus himself but also to his *domus* ("*quod bonum*," inquit, "*faustumque sit tibi domuique tuae, Caesar Auguste!*").[68] The specific phrase *domus Augusta* appears in a passage of Ovid's *Epistulae ex Ponto* (2.2.74) dated to 13. A dedication from Lucus Feroniae (*AE* 1978 295) dated to the year 33 provides a firm *terminus ante quem* for the use of the term *domus divina*. Even during Augustus' own lifetime, the family of Augustus was subsumed into worship and reverence for the princeps, especially once the cult of Augustus and Roma became standard in the eastern part of the empire. Over time, the meaning of the term evolved from "the house of Augustus" to "the august house," and eventually, after the deification of the patriarch, "the house of the divine."[69] The word *domus* was used as opposed to *familia* or *gens* because the *domus* came to include descendants of Augustus outside of the Julian *gens*, even outside of his immediate family. As Corbier (2001: 166–7) illustrates, by the early years of Tiberius' principate the *domus Augusta* had crystallized into a specific unit, extending beyond members of the Julian and Claudian *gentes* to anyone related by birth, marriage, or adoption to

---

[66] While Cogitore attempts to distinguish the two, claiming that *domus divina* is more honorific while *domus Augusta* is more political, she admits that the relationship between the two terms is murky (2002: 163).

[67] As Moreau (2009: 38) remarks, the prayers made by Augustus for the welfare of himself and his family at the Ludi Saeculares (*CIL* vi 32323 = *ILS* 5050) do not fall into the same category as prayers made for Augustus and his *domus* by others. In asking the gods to be propitious to himself and his family, Augustus was emulating Republican precedents.

[68] On other evidence for use of the term *domus* in the reign of Augustus, see Hurlet 2015: 133.

[69] On this evolution, see Moreau 2009: 36. For early indications that the *domus Augusta* was subsumed into the divinity of Augustus, including Ovid's shrine to the *sacra domus* (*Ex Ponto* 2.8), see Corbier 2001: 181–2. For more on Ovid's poems honoring the house of Augustus, see Chapter 5.

Augustus.[70] Moreover, the members of the *domus Augusta* were heirs to the charisma of their divine founder.

The Sodales Augustales, initially created to foster the worship of Augustus, were also responsible for offering vows on behalf of other members of the imperial family. When Livia fell ill in 22, the Senate decreed various honors, including supplications to the gods and games to be produced by the pontifices, augurs, quindecimvirs, septemvirs, and Sodales Augustales. L. Apronius proposed that the Fetials should preside over the games as well. Tiberius rejected this, stating that the Fetials had never played such a role and reminding the Senate that the Sodales Augustales had been created precisely to fulfill vows on behalf of the *domus Augusta* (Tac. *Ann.* 3.64). The Sodales Augustales also made sacrifices on behalf of the *manes* of deceased members of the family (*Tabula Siarensis* 1b, 1–5).[71] Their status continued to grow throughout the reign of Tiberius.[72]

The celebration of Divus Augustus and the *domus Augusta* was a key part of consolidating Augustus' charisma. It was fueled by Tiberius' refusal of divine honors, as discussed in the previous section. The process of diverting divine honors away from himself and towards other members of his household actually began before Tiberius became princeps. In addition to dedicating the presumed altar to the *numen* of Augustus and the altar to his *providentia*, Tiberius was also responsible for refurbishing the Temple of Castor and the Temple of Concordia. In both these instances he restored the temples not only in his own name but also that of his brother Drusus. Tiberius vowed to refurbish the Temple of Concordia in 7 BC, only two years after Drusus had died. By the time Tiberius dedicated the temple on January 16, 10 (Ovid, *Fasti* 1.64-8; Dio 56.25; cf. Suet. *Tib.* 20, where the year is given as 12), Drusus had been dead for almost nineteen years.[73] During that time, Tiberius had taken extra care decorating the temple despite spending many years away from Rome. After his adoption, Tiberius would have wanted to highlight the concord in the *domus*. "Augusta" was added as an epithet to Concordia, and Tiberius preserved the name of his brother (and his adopted son Germanicus' father) Drusus in the dedication.

---

[70] Cf. Gibson 2013: 10. On the significance of determining who was or was not in the *domus* and how various configurations led to conflict within the *domus*, see Cogitore 2002: 161–75.
[71] Swan 2004: 351–2 and Corbier 2001: 181.   [72] Hoffman Lewis 1955: 155.
[73] On the decoration of the Temple of Concordia and the dynastic significance of the statuary groups, see Bravi 1998 and Kellum 2000.

Likewise, Tiberius took advantage of the opportunity to restore the Temple of Castor.[74] In this case, as far as we know, he had not made some vow shortly after his brother's death which he was bound to fulfill. Fifteen years had passed between Drusus' death and the dedication of the Temple of Castor in 6. Nevertheless, the association with two devoted brothers, one having died young, made Tiberius' restoration of the Temple of Castor all too appropriate. According to Dio (55.1.5), two young men were reportedly seen in Drusus' camp right before he died, connecting his premature death (and Tiberius' attendant devotion) more directly to the Dioscuri.[75] The Temple of Castor would remind people of the *pietas* Tiberius had displayed in rushing to his brother's deathbed (Val. Max. 5.5.3). It was in Tiberius' best interests to continue to promote the image of his deceased (and charismatic) brother.[76] Indeed, Augustus had ensured that *imagines* of the Julii were present at Drusus' funeral even though Drusus had never been adopted into the Julian *gens*. Moreover, Drusus was buried in the Mausoleum of Augustus, not an ancestral tomb of the Claudii Nerones. Champlin (2011) posits that Drusus' later prominence was an attempt to supplant the importance of the Julian line with the Claudian. He makes too much of Dio's claim (55.27.3–4) that Tiberius inscribed his name on the Temple of Castor with the agnomen "Claudianus." Dio quickly adds that Tiberius called himself Claudianus because of his adoption by Augustus. Champlin believes Tiberius was trying to advertise his Claudian blood and connect himself to his brother. This is certainly true but does not supersede Tiberius' pride in his adoption by Augustus.[77] Moreover, as Champlin concedes (2011: 85), if we discount Dio, there is no concrete epigraphic evidence for Tiberius ever styling himself as Claudianus.[78]

Fragments thought to bear an inscription from the Temple of Castor (*CIL* vi 40339; *AE* 1992: 55, inscr. 159) have provided more questions

---

[74] On the archaeological remains, see Sande and Zahle 1988 and Nilson et al. 2009. Champlin 2011: 83 argues against the standard theory that the temples Tiberius restored had been destroyed by fire.

[75] Champlin 2011 provides a thorough analysis of Tiberius and Drusus being portrayed as Pollux and Castor (with an emphasis on that order). See also Sumi 2009: 174–9.

[76] An arch in the city wall around Saepinum (*CIL* ix 2443 = *ILS* 147 = E.-J.² 79) indicates Tiberius built the wall in his and his brother's name before his adoption by Augustus but after his return to Rome. For problems with dating the inscription, see Bernecker 1976 and Stylow 1977. *CIL* vi 40337 records an inscription discovered at San Paolo Fuori le Mura in the name of Ti. Caesar Aug. [f.] and Nero Claudius Germ[anicus]. Without context, it is impossible to say from where the inscription came, but it may have been connected with Tiberius' restoration of the Temple of Concordia.

[77] Cf. Gartrell 2021: 166–7.   [78] Cf. Alföldy 1992: 54. See also Swan 2004: 186.

than answers.[79] Alföldy (1992) proposed that the names and titles of Tiberius and Drusus were placed side by side, with Tiberius on the left and Drusus on the right. The fact that only thirteen letters remain of an inscription that may have contained over two hundred letters leaves his interpretation subject to reservations. Nevertheless, the reconstruction of the inscription does suggest that the dedication referred to the building as that of Pollux and Castor, not the usual Castor and Pollux. The epigraphic evidence is seconded by Suetonius' reversal of the usual names in his description of Tiberius' dedication (*dedicavit et Concordiae aedem, item Pollucis et Castoris suo fratrisque nomine de manubiis, Tib.* 20).[80] The reversal of the normal order of the Dioscuri and the placement, if Alföldy is correct, of the names and titles of the two brothers side by side on the facade indicates that Tiberius considered his deceased brother as his equal. It would also have associated Tiberius with Pollux and Drusus with Castor, emphasizing Tiberius' divine parentage through adoption. By reviving the image of his long-deceased brother, Tiberius used the identification with the Dioscuri to remind viewers of the role played by the two brothers in defending Rome, as well as their (or at least Pollux's) divine parentage from Jupiter, with whom Augustus had long been associated.[81]

The imagery of the Dioscuri had already been used in conjunction with Gaius and Lucius, the adopted sons/grandsons of Augustus.[82] However, those connections were more oblique than the obvious association created by Tiberius' dedication of the Temple of Castor. In the next generation Germanicus and Drusus were also associated with the Dioscuri.[83] Drusus the Younger earned the nickname "Castor" after a run-in with Sejanus.[84] His association with his charismatic brother Germanicus would further promote the interests of Tiberius in convincing Rome that the entire dynasty was blessed by the gods, especially Divus Augustus. Drusus' twin sons, born shortly after the death of Germanicus (Tac. *Ann.* 2.84), offered a natural comparison to the "heavenly twins." Even after the death of one in early childhood, the other was still referred to as Tiberius Gemellus ("the Twin").

---

[79] For a brief overview, see Champlin 2011: 87 n. 41 and Gartrell 2021: 166–71.

[80] As Alföldy (1992: 49 n. 37) notes, the same inversion is found in Propertius (3.14.17).

[81] Ironic, considering the rumor that Augustus was Drusus' biological father (Suet. *Claud.* 1.1). On Augustus as Jupiter, see Fears 1981a: 56–69.

[82] On the connection of pairs of imperial heirs to Castor and Pollux, see Gartrell 2021: 145–93. Cf. Suspène 2001: 112–3. Champlin (2011: 99) categorically refutes any association involving Gaius and Lucius.

[83] Cf. Severy 2003: 195.   [84] On this nickname, see Scott 1930 and Mallan 2020: 206.

In the years following the adoptions, Tiberius' dedication of the Temple of (Pollux and) Castor, followed by that of the Temple of Concordia Augusta, would have reinforced the image of a harmonious transition from Augustus to Tiberius and then, one day, to Germanicus. They also associated Tiberius more closely with his beloved brother and his charismatic nephew/adopted son Germanicus, who was married to Augustus' granddaughter Agrippina the Elder. By tying himself both to his adoptive father Augustus and his charismatic (although not deified) brother Drusus, Tiberius was compensating for his lack of personal charisma.[85] The overall effect was a strong message that Divus Augustus continued to watch over his *domus* and the state. It is surely no accident that the Senate met at the Temple of Concordia to vote for the execution of Sejanus (Dio 58.11.4).[86] The Senate had met in the same temple to condemn the Catilinarian conspirators in December of 63 BC (Cic. *Cat.* 3.21; Sall. *BC* 46.5, 49.4; Plut. *Cic.* 19.1). Sejanus' attacks on the sons of Germanicus (and thus grandsons of Tiberius by adoption and of Drusus the Elder by birth) threatened the state just as the conspiracy of Catiline had done years earlier.[87]

Tiberius' restorations were part of a larger reconfiguration of the Roman Forum advertising Augustus and his family members. Both temples were dedicated in January, an important month for the promotion of the *domus Augusta*. The presumed altar to the *numen* of Augustus was dedicated on January 17, 6. The date was the wedding anniversary of Augustus and Livia. Tiberius' dedication of the Temple of Castor on January 27 (*Fast. Praen.*; *Inscr. It.* XIII.2 p. 117) in the same year that he dedicated the altar would have driven home the message that Augustus' charismatic *numen* protected his family, especially Tiberius and Germanicus. The dedication of the Temple of Concordia on January 16, 10 coincided with the anniversary of Augustus' assumption of his quasi-divine cognomen (*Fast. Praen.* = *Inscr. It.* XIII.2 p. 115).[88] Sumi (2009: 184) discerns that this

---

[85] Suspène (2001: 112) also sees this as part of a larger movement to thwart attempts to use the image of Agrippa to promote the interests of Agrippa Postumus.

[86] In addition to its connections to Concordia Augusta, the temple was also conveniently located near the Tullianum, where Sejanus would be executed (Talbert 1984: 119).

[87] On a literary note, Tacitus' description of Sejanus (*Ann.* 4.1) borrows much from Sallust's description of Catiline. See Martin and Woodman 1989: 84–5.

[88] See also Cooley (2009: 261) on *Res Gestae* 34.2. As Pasco-Pranger (2006: 197) points out, the anniversary of the original dedication of the Temple of Concordia was July 22, so January 16 "was actively chosen" to coincide with the anniversary of Augustus receiving his honorary cognomen "and just preceding the anniversary of Livia and Augustus' marriage." Cf. Littlewood 2006: 30. Contra Levick (1978a: 217). Ovid (*Fasti* 1.587–90) curiously associates the assumption of the name Augustus with January 13. For a possible explanation, see Herbert-Brown 1994: 200–1.

portended a smooth transition from Augustus to the man who would inherit his charismatic cognomen.[89]

With regard to Livia's role in this transfer of power, the last two couplets of Ovid's entry in the *Fasti* on the Temple of Concordia have generated debate. Ovid hails Tiberius as *dux venerande* and continues: "You offered spoils from a conquered race | and built a temple to the goddess whom you yourself worship. | Your mother established this goddess as well both by her deeds and by an altar; | she alone has been found worthy of the bed of mighty Jove" (*inde triumphatae libasti munera gentis | templaque fecisti, quam colis ipse, deae. | hanc tua constituit genetrix et rebus et ara, | sola toro magni digna reperta Iovis, Fasti* 1.647–50). In Book 6, Ovid celebrates the dedication of a shrine to Concordia in the Porticus Liviae: "You also, Concordia, Livia honored with a magnificent shrine | which she herself offered to her dear husband" (*Te quoque magnifica, Concordia, dedicat aede | Livia, quam caro praestitit ipsa viro, Fasti* 6.637–8). The context makes it clear that Ovid is referring to a shrine Livia built and dedicated in honor of her husband.[90] Presuming that the first book of the *Fasti* was revised after Ovid's exile, one must wonder if Ovid rewrote the passage regarding Tiberius' dedication of the Temple to Concordia after he had written the lines from Book 6 addressed to Livia.[91] The addition of Livia to the Tiberian passage, if it is an addition, indicates Ovid's perception from exile of the need to emphasize concord in the imperial household.[92]

The dedications to the Dioscuri and Concordia are both celebrated in the Pseudo-Ovidian *Consolatio ad Liviam*, dated to the Julio-Claudian era.[93] Following an exhortation that Germania will pay for the death of Drusus, the poet exclaims "Consider also the sons of Leda, brothers, concordant stars, | and the temples conspicuous in the Roman Forum" (*Adice Ledaeos, concordia sidera, fratres | templaque Romano conspicienda foro*, 283–4).[94] Even years after their dedications, the Temple of

---

[89] On the importance of Concordia in imagery promoting the succession of Tiberius, see Mlasowsky 1996: 315–20.

[90] The unresolvable debate over the nature of Livia's *aedes* is discussed by Richardson 1978, Flory 1984, and Simpson 1991.

[91] Fantham (1985: 262) expands upon the theory that Ovid rewrote various parts of the *Fasti* to celebrate Concordia as Tiberius came to power. On the passage in Book 1, see Green 2004: 291–9.

[92] Farrell 2013: 67–8. The connection of Livia, Tiberius, and Concordia seems to have influenced the *aedificium Eumachiae* at Pompeii, which contains a cryptoporticus dedicated to Concordia Augusta and Pietas (*CIL* x 813). Richardson (1988: 197) dates the building to no earlier than 2/3, when Eumachia's husband was duovir. See also Franklin 2001: 33.

[93] For ongoing debate on the date, see Schoonhoven 1992. His dating is refuted by Gradel 2002: 269 n. 13.

[94] On this passage, see Schoonhaven 1992: 16–18.

Concordia and the Temple of Castor were associated with the portrayal of Tiberius and Drusus as the Dioscuri. The ultimate manifestation of brotherly *concordia*, while perhaps based on genuine affection, became an important image throughout the reign of Tiberius, linking Tiberius more closely to his charismatic adoptive father and the descendants of his brother's line.

Concordia had previously been associated with the resolution of internal struggles in the late Republic.[95] Julius Caesar had used the idea of *concordia nova* in his iconography.[96] Likewise, after the death of Julius Caesar, Antony convened the Senate in the Temple of Concordia, according to Cicero (*Phil.* 2.7–8, 5.7), transforming the temple into a prison. In the early years of the triumvirate, Concordia was stressed as the goddess protecting a tenuous alliance. Coins issued by Octavian advertised this triumviral *concordia* (*RRC* 529.4a, 4b). In the aftermath of Actium, *concordia* became more problematic as Augustus consolidated his power over the state. Concordia, however, did re-emerge in 11 BC, when Augustus melted down statues of himself and erected a statue of Concordia along with statues of Janus, Salus, and Pax (Ovid, *Fasti* 3.881; Dio 54.35.2). In that year, Augustus compelled Tiberius to marry the recently widowed Julia. Thus began the transformation of Concordia from a representation of harmony within the state to one of stability within the *domus Augusta*.

Despite the careful planning and messaging of Augustus, as we have seen in Chapter 1, Tiberius' accession to his father's *statio* was not without its difficulties. In 16, Libo was put on trial for a conspiracy involving attacks on members of the imperial family. We shall discuss these proceedings further in Chapter 6. Let us note here that after the death of Libo, offerings were made to Jove, Mars, and Concordia (Tac. *Ann.* 2.32). Jupiter and Mars were featured prominently in the iconography of the reign of Augustus. The inclusion of Concordia alongside these two deities, while not extraordinary, is significant. Dio (57.15.5) adds that these offerings were made on behalf of Tiberius, Augustus, and Divus Iulius. In addition to the testimony of the historians, epigraphic evidence has preserved some vows made on the behalf of Tiberius in this temple. Pekáry (1966–67) has argued that these vows were made to Tiberius in celebration of his survival of the conspiracy of Sejanus. Levick (1978a) disputes these claims and asserts that the dedications are those mentioned by

---

[95] For a thorough treatment of Concordia in imperial ideology, see Lobur 2008.
[96] See Weinstock 1971: 260–6.

Tacitus after the conspiracy of Libo. The date of the dedications is not as significant as the fact that, in the wake of a conspiracy against Tiberius and other members of the *domus Augusta*, dedications were made in the Temple of Concordia.

While *concordia* was not the only Tiberian virtue, it was the only virtue awarded its own temple. Moreover, aside from an issue of *dupondii* in 22/23 featuring a round temple which could be a shrine to Divus Augustus, it is the only temple which appears on Tiberian coinage.[97] It does not appear until 34, the twentieth anniversary of Tiberius' accession.[98] As Pekáry (1966-67: 106) observes, unlike other coins advertising Tiberian virtues, this sestertius depicts the temple but does not bear the title and image of Concordia. Grant (1950: 43) notes that the issuance of a coin celebrating Concordia at this time coincides not only with the twentieth anniversary of Tiberius' assumption of his father's *statio* but also the fiftieth anniversary of the Ludi Saeculares (assuming the coins to Concordia were commissioned in 33). Along with these coins a series was issued depicting Divus Augustus Pater flanked by eagles and thunderbolts.[99] Just as the imagery of Concordia was used to reassure everyone that the transition after the death of Augustus would be peaceful, these coins were issued when Tiberius' days were numbered and his popularity was at an all-time low, especially after the downfall of Sejanus and the financial crisis of 33. This virtue was undoubtedly chosen to remind the Romans that Tiberius had been adopted by Augustus, who wanted to be succeeded in his *statio* by someone from his own *domus*. In addition to advertising harmony in the *domus Augusta*, the issues featuring the Temple of Concordia would also remind their audience of Tiberius' devotion to his brother Drusus, the co-dedicator of the temple. This would support the peaceful succession of Caligula, the great-grandson of Augustus and the grandson of Drusus.

Conclusions

Weber borrowed the idea of charismatic leadership from Sohm's analysis of the early church hierarchy. Thus, previous scholars have used the

---

[97] The round temple (*BMCRE* I 142; *RIC* I² 74) is flanked by a lamb and a calf, the typical sacrifices made to the deified Augustus according to Prudentius (*C. Symm.* 1.245–248). The temple has also been identified as the shrine to Vesta on the Palatine, based especially on the depiction of the Vestals on the Sorrento base. See Ryberg 1955: 49 and Fishwick 1990b.

[98] *BMCRE* I 16, 132, 133, 134; *RIC* I² 55, 61, 67. For the identification of the temple as that of Concordia, see *BMCRE* I.cxxxviii.

[99] *BMCRE* I 154–60; *RIC* I² 82–3.

imperial cult as an entry point for discussing the charismatic nature of the principate. The imperial cult was central to the routinization of Augustan charisma. Unlike Octavian/Augustus, who began to overshadow his deified father as he consolidated his own power, Tiberius consistently propagated the cult of Divus Augustus throughout his reign. He also promoted the charismatic images of other members of the *domus Augusta*, especially his brother Drusus and Drusus' son (and his own by adoption) Germanicus. More importantly, he refused any divine honors for himself. He fostered the idea that Divus Augustus was continuing to watch over his family and the state. This assured all orders of Roman society that a princeps from the *domus Augusta* would preserve stability. While the imperial cult consolidated the position of Augustus from a religious perspective, other steps were necessary from a legal and social perspective. Tiberius not only had to show that Divus Augustus was a god. He had to prove that he was worthy to have been made one.

CHAPTER 3

Charismatic Precedents

One of the more famous Tiberian utterances found in Tacitus is his claim, when declining a temple to himself in Spain, that he was closely observing Augustan precedent. We have discussed this passage in the previous chapter in the context of Tiberius' refusal of divine honors. Here I would like to focus on Tiberius' rationale for this action, as well as others we will explore further in this chapter:

> Since Divus Augustus, whose deeds and pronouncements, all of them, I observe as if they were law, did not prohibit a temple to be built to himself and the city of Rome at Pergamum, I followed his agreeable example all the more readily, especially since the worship of the Senate was added to my cult. But although to have done this once may have earned some pardon, to be consecrated in imitation of *numina* throughout the provinces would be self-seeking and arrogant. And honor for Augustus would vanish if it were made common with indiscriminate flattery. (Tac. *Ann.* 4.37)

> cum divus Augustus sibi atque urbi Romae templum apud Pergamum sisti non prohibuisset, qui omnia facta dictaque eius vice legis observem, placitum iam exemplum promptius secutus sum quia cultui meo veneratio senatus adiungebatur. ceterum ut semel recepisse veniam habuerit, ita per omnis provincias effigie numinum sacrari ambitiosum, superbum; et vanescet Augusti honor si promiscis adulationibus vulgatur.

Two intermingling threads run throughout this passage: the respect which Tiberius holds for Augustus, to the extent that his refusal of divine honors is justified by the desire to enhance the worship of Augustus (or at least not to detract from it), and a more general declaration on the part of Tiberius that he observes *all* the actions and words of Augustus as a kind of law.[1]

---

[1] Cf. Tac. *Ann.* 1.77.4, where Tiberius refuses to overrule an Augustan injunction against whipping *histriones*: *neque fas Tiberio infringere dicta eius*. See also *Ann.* 1.14, 2.59, 3.24, 3.29, 3.68, and 3.71. Cowan (2009b: 199) has shown that in Tacitus' narrative Tiberius presents himself as the chief interpreter of Augustus' *facta dictaque*.

66

As we shall see, Tiberius did not always follow the precedent of Augustus. When Tiberius did deviate from Augustan practice, he did so to promote the *domus Augusta* and to stabilize the Augustan system.

As discussed in the previous chapter, the young Octavian relied heavily on the image of the newly deified Caesar in the early part of his career. However, Antony, having control over Julius Caesar's papers after his assassination, became the chief arbiter of what Caesar would have wanted, often, as Cicero snipes, using Caesar's name to implement his own will.[2] Moreover, as Octavian began to reshape himself into Augustus, he increasingly distanced himself from the acts of Julius Caesar. Augustus, as far as we know, invoked a precedent set by Caesar just once and only as an unfavorable comparison. In the midst of an economic crisis in 6, Augustus instituted a 5 percent tax on inheritances. The tax exempted inheritances by immediate family and the poor (Dio 55.25.5). The tax was extremely unpopular, and when the people expressed their discontent, Augustus justified the tax as one which Caesar had intended to institute, claiming he had found it in "notes left by Caesar" (*Kaisaros hupomnēmasi*). Levick (2009a: 213) believes that Augustus may have been invoking Caesar because he was suffering from comparison with him at a time when military setbacks and famine had damaged the princeps' public image. Tiberius, by contrast, invoked Augustan precedent throughout his reign. Indeed, we can see a general pattern in Tiberius' political use of Augustus. As was the case in his attitude towards divine honors, Tiberius seems reluctant to thrust himself into the spotlight. Instead, he either scrupulously continued to follow Augustan precedents, often making sure to give credit to his predecessor, or he carefully explained his reasons when he deviated from those precedents. All of this lent a charismatic air to the *acta* of Divus Augustus, *acta* upon which the Senate were compelled to swear an oath annually.

Tiberius and the Senate

The most telling piece of information regarding Tiberius' relationship with the Senate and his desire to cast his reign as a continuation of that of Augustus is his rejection of honors which could have been considered excessive, including his refusal to allow the Senate to swear an oath by his acts. This in and of itself would not seem too extraordinary, especially in the early reign of Tiberius when, by all accounts, he was a *civilis princeps*

---

[2] On Cicero's *Philippics* and the matter of Caesar's papers, see Ramsey 1994.

(or at least seemed to be). What is more striking is the compulsion that the senators swear an oath to uphold the acts of Augustus, an oath which Tiberius himself observed. Tiberius' insistence upon an oath to preserve the acts of Augustus displays his awareness, already seen in the debates following the death of Augustus, that Augustus had created something unique, something that must be preserved. Not only was Augustus divine, but his acts were divinely ordained as well. The charisma of Augustus became routinized in the political sphere as it had been enshrined in the imperial cult.

Tiberius' respect for the acts of Augustus can be contrasted with his portrayal of himself as a mere mortal. Unfortunately, years of complaisance under Julius Caesar and Augustus had left the Senate unable to function without a superhuman princeps. It was not Tiberius' fault that he ended up repeatedly leaving the Senate house proclaiming that the senators were "men prepared for slavery" (*o homines ad servitutem paratos*, Tac. *Ann.* 3.65). But their subservience was his problem as he tried to navigate his role as the presumed *princeps senatus*. Tiberius, like Augustus, gave the impression that he took meetings of the Senate seriously, penalizing senators for nonattendance according to his predecessor's policy.[3] However, despite his best efforts, his very presence (or absence) could influence the outcome of senatorial debates.

Tiberius is often given more credit than he deserves for attempting to restore dignity to the Senate. As Brunt (1984: 435) points out, much of our knowledge of senatorial debates during the reigns of Augustus and Tiberius is skewed by the sources, especially Tacitus, who, despite his promise (*Ann.* 3.24), never wrote a history of the reign of Augustus. As we know from the *Senatus Consultum* from Larinum (discussed below) and the *Tabula Hebana* (discussed in Chapter 4), during the reign of Tiberius the Senate frequently met at or near the Temple of Apollo on the Palatine, as they did towards the end of Augustus' reign.[4] This building was adjacent to the homes of both Augustus and Tiberius. After Tiberius moved to Capri, his communication with the Senate was limited to correspondence, using in particular the Praetorian Prefect as an intermediary. Thus, even if Tiberius seems to have wanted the Senate to take more initiative, his continuation of Augustan practices, combined with his own

---

[3] On Tiberius' regulation of the Senate, see Talbert 1984: 138–41.

[4] See Thompson 1981, Bonnefond-Coudry 1989: 179–82, Corbier 1992: 893–8, Palombi 1993, and Wiseman 2019: 135–9. We will discuss in the next chapter the meetings on the Palatine in 19 to vote honors to Germanicus. Dio (58.9) specifies that the Senate was meeting on the Palatine when Tiberius' letter criticizing Sejanus was read.

premature retirement, destroyed any independence the body may have retained.

One of the main reforms attributed to Tiberius which granted more power to the Senate was the transfer of elections from the people to the Senate. Even this Brunt (1984: 429) would attribute to Augustus.[5] As Woodman (1977: 227) notes in his commentary on Velleius 2.124.3, there had been several messy elections under Augustus, especially in the turbulent later years. Thus, Augustus not only left Tiberius a slate of preferred candidates but also instructions for the reform of elections.[6] Hollard (2010: 178–9) believes that the change in elections under Tiberius was not as radical as Tacitus suggests. Indeed, the process of transforming the role of the people in the elections had already begun in 8. She draws upon a statement made by Dio, that Augustus "had the year before personally appointed all who were to hold office, because there were factional outbreaks, and in this and the following years he merely posted a bulletin recommending to the plebs and to the people those whom he favoured" (55.34.2; Loeb trans. Cary). This added to *nominatio* by the princeps the favor of *commendatio*, ensuring that those chosen by the emperor would be automatically approved in the *comitia*.

So why does Tacitus assert that a radical change took place in the first elections for the praetorship held after the death of Augustus? Tiberius' deferral to the Senate in the election of praetors for this particular year may have been intended as a temporary expedient to stave off potential violence in the wake of the death of Augustus. Nevertheless, instead of an original policy created by Tiberius, this transfer of elections was just another step in a long evolutionary process giving more power to the Senate and leaving the urban plebs with a ritualistic role in affirming candidates already chosen.[7] This process had already begun a few years earlier with the provisions restated in the later *lex Valeria Cornelia*, setting up certain centuries which would vote before anyone else. By 5, five centuries each had been delegated in honor of the recently deceased Lucius and Gaius Caesar. After the deaths of Germanicus and Drusus, ten more were added. In completing the transfer of the elections which had already begun under Augustus and approving the addition of honorary centuries for his own

---

[5] Dettenhofer (2002) argues that moving elections to the Senate greatly reduced the need for candidates to spend money on campaigns and diminished the desire for former magistrates to govern provinces (2002: 355). This argument is refuted by Hurlet 2006: 113 n. 378.

[6] For the view that Augustus merely left Tiberius a list of preferred candidates, see Lacey 1963: 170.

[7] Caligula attempted to transfer elections back to the plebs but was forced to return to the system implemented by Tiberius (Dio 59.9 and 59.20; Suet. *Cal.* 16.2).

dead sons, Tiberius was continuing the same practices Augustus had followed in elections during the last years of his reign.

Likewise, under Tiberius the Senate preserved the Augustan ban on *nobiles* performing on stage and in the arena. The *Senatus Consultum* from Larinum, dated by the names of the consuls to 19, reinforced past enactments.[8] Dio, our main source for the previous measures, states that in 38 BC, "an act was... passed prohibiting any senator from fighting as a gladiator" (48.43.2; Loeb trans. Cary). In 22 BC, a policy banning senators from the stage was extended to descendants of senators, *equites*, and women of the upper classes (Dio 54.2.5). However, as Levick (1983: 107) observes, the ban fell into abeyance and the Senate was compelled to act in 11. Again, Dio is our main source:

> Three senators, as before, transacted business with embassies, and the knights – a fact which may cause surprise – were allowed to fight as gladiators. The reason for this was that some were making light of the disfranchisement imposed as the penalty for such conduct. For inasmuch as there proved to be no use in forbidding it, and the guilty seemed to require a greater punishment, or else because it seemed possible that they might even be turned aside from this course, they were granted permission to take part in such contests. In this way they incurred death instead of disfranchisement; for they fought just as much as ever, especially since their contests were eagerly witnessed, so that even Augustus used to watch them in company with the praetors who superintended the contests. (56.25.7–8; Loeb trans. Cary)

Dio implies that Augustus allowed senators and knights to fight in gladiatorial contests because he understood the deception used to get around the earlier laws and believed that the threat of death in the ring was punishment enough for those willing to circumvent those laws. According to Dio (57.14.3), during games given by his son Drusus in 15, Tiberius, following the precedent set in 11, allowed a gladiatorial combat between two knights. However, after one knight had killed the other, Tiberius prohibited him from fighting again as a gladiator. Tiberius, unlike Augustus (according to Dio's account), refused to watch the combat. Like Augustus, however, Tiberius believed in the promotion of the senatorial and equestrian classes.

---

[8] For images of the *tabula* on which the *senatus consultum* was inscribed, as well as overlays of all the various proposed emendations, see Stelluti 1997. This volume includes excerpts, translated into Italian, from major works on the *senatus consultum*, most notably from Levick (1983), Lebek (1990 and 1991), and McGinn (1992). Ricci (2006: 17–48) also details the various proposed readings, emendations, and additions.

Thus, in 19 several measures were passed which were intended to restore the *dignitas* of the nobility. While the *Senatus Consultum* from Larinum contradicts the exceptions supposedly allowed in 11, it reinforces the policies recounted for 38 and 22 BC. The primary difference is that the *Senatus Consultum* from Larinum focuses on the use of *fraus* to circumvent previous laws.[9] In the same year, Tacitus records a similar measure being taken against women of the senatorial and equestrian classes using loopholes to get around the *lex Iulia de adulteriis coercendis* (*Ann.* 2.85; cf. Suet. *Tib.* 35). A woman named Vistilia, born from a family of senatorial rank, was indicted for trying to circumvent the laws against adultery by declaring herself as a prostitute to the aediles. Her husband was also accused of pandering (*lenocinium*) for not denouncing her. Although her husband, Titidius Labeo, was spared after pointing out that the sixty-day window for such a denunciation had not yet closed, Vistilia was exiled to the island of Seriphos.

Some have attempted to graft the law which Tacitus states arose in response to Vistilia's case onto the missing parts of the *tabula* containing the *Senatus Consultum* from Larinum. However, they were likely two separate laws passed in connection with each other.[10] One reason the measures are so closely connected is that Suetonius mentions both of these prohibitions in the same paragraph (*Tib.* 35.2):

> Shameful women, so that they might be removed from the rights and dignity of matrons in order to avoid the penalties of the laws, began to register with a pimp; and anyone most profligate from the youth of either order, so as not to be bound by the decree of the Senate regarding theatrical and gladiatorial productions, willingly accepted designation as dishonored; all of them, male and female, lest there should be any refuge for anyone from such deceit, he punished with exile.

> feminae famosae, ut ad evitandas legum poenas iure ac dignitate matronali exsolverentur, lenocinium profiteri coeperant, et ex iuventute utriusque ordinis profligatissimus quisque, quominus in opera scaenae harenaeque edenda senatus consulto teneretur, famosi iudicii notam sponte subibant; eos easque omnes, ne quod refugium in tali fraude cuiquam esset, exilio adfecit.

Suetonius has no interest in chronology; from Tacitus and the *Senatus Consultum* from Larinum we know that both of these measures were

---

[9] See Ricci 2006: 75; cf. 110–13.

[10] See Lebek 1990: 40. McGinn (1992: 292) notes that the *Senatus Consultum* from Larinum must have been passed in the first six months of 19 and likely preceded the case of Vistilia. Levick (1983: 114) argues the opposite, claiming precedence for Vistilia's case. Both agree that the measures are connected by their intent if not by the *Senatus Consultum* from Larinum

actually passed in the same year. Suetonius attributes all the agency to Tiberius. This is natural as he is writing a biography. However, as Lebek (1991: 57) points out, Tacitus makes it clear that the initiative to punish Vistilia came from the Senate. The *Senatus Consultum* from Larinum demonstrates that the Senate was also primarily responsible for the actions taken against members of the upper classes appearing on stage or in the arena. That said, for Tiberius to ensure that these reforms were enforced, he would have needed the support of the Senate since the reforms were intended to curb the improper behavior of members of that order. Either way, both the Senate and Tiberius acted together to preserve the Augustan precedent.

Economic Stability

As stated above, Tiberius was notorious for claiming to follow Augustus' policies. In doing so, he professed reverence for his predecessor's divine wisdom. The only time, as far as we know, that Tiberius claimed to have surpassed Augustus was in exasperation over alleged negligence in the grain supply. Tacitus reports that, in the midst of a spike in grain prices in Rome in 32, sedition broke out, particularly in the theater. Tiberius wrote to the Senate and magistrates, rebuking them for not controlling the situation, and added how much more grain than Augustus he had procured (*Ann.* 4.13.1).[11] If Tiberius allowed himself just this once to contrast himself favorably to Augustus, it pales in comparison with the number of times in which he endured criticism for his supposed lack of concern for the Roman economy.

It would be easy, based upon Suetonius' figure (*Cal.* 37) for the large amount of money left by Tiberius upon his death (2.7 billion sesterces), to accuse him of stinginess. Rodewald (1976: 71) has long since explained this away, demonstrating that the lack of inflow from new imperial conquests towards the end of Augustus' reign led to a need for Augustus and Tiberius to spend less. We will discuss the lack of conquests during Tiberius' reign in the next section. Regardless of the reasons, Tiberius was the first ruler faced with a need to normalize the imperial system without expanding it.[12] Revenues from the provinces had to be balanced against

---

[11] As Bollinger (1969: 56) comments, his tone is very similar to that expressed by Augustus when people complained about the price of wine. According to Suet. (*Aug.* 42.1), Augustus responded to their complaints by pointing out that thanks to his son-in-law Agrippa, who built several aqueducts, "people would not suffer thirst" (*satis provisum a genero suo Agrippa perductis pluribus aquis, ne homines sitirent*).

[12] Goodyear (1981: 177) suggests that the expeditions of Germanicus played a role in the financial difficulties of Tiberius' early reign.

the expenses of the capital. Undoubtedly, especially in comparison with his successors', Tiberius' economic policies were conservative. Given his experiences in the later years of Augustus, especially the grain shortages and foreign disasters, Tiberius can be seen as preparing for the worst rather than spending liberally in better times.

Despite his fiscal conservatism, Tiberius was capable of *liberalitas*.[13] Tacitus famously criticizes Tiberius for his negligence in paying the legacies left to various members of society by Augustus. Analyzing the figures cited by Tacitus (*Ann.* 1.8.2), Suetonius (*Aug.* 101.2), and Dio (57.14.3), Goodyear (1972: 145) argues that, in fact, Tiberius may have distributed money in addition to that already designated by Augustus. Rogers contends that while Tiberius was often accused of stinginess, he was actually fairly generous in his *beneficia*. If one extrapolates from Rogers' figures (1943: 19), Tiberius' known benefactions total roughly $337 million.[14] This does not include his loans in 33. However, unlike Augustus, who added to the *Res Gestae* an account of all his benefactions, Tiberius claimed no such credit.

In the reign of Tiberius, bread was a necessity without which the imperial system would collapse; circuses were an opportunity for the unruly to protest. Although Dio (57.11.5) states that in the early part of his reign Tiberius attended the games regularly, the second princeps earned notoriety for his failure to give games. Nevertheless, under Tiberius the traditional games operated regularly.[15] That there were fewer extraordinary games than there had been under Augustus was to be expected, especially since the dynastic needs of the family had significantly changed. Once Germanicus and Drusus had died, the image of the *domus Augusta* became increasingly complex. When the children of Germanicus were favored as successors to Tiberius, Nero and Drusus were thrust into the spotlight prematurely by their mother Agrippina. The matter was further complicated by Tiberius' withdrawal from Rome in 26. Without the princeps (or

[13] For a table depicting the *liberalitas* of Tiberius including *congiaria*, donatives, and interest-free loans, see Wolters 1999: 240; cf. 246. Wolters also points out that the *liberalitas* of Gaius in the first year of his reign was largely funded by money left behind by Tiberius.

[14] Rogers gives a total of $19 million in 1943. I have converted the value for October 2023 using the US inflation calculator (www.usinflationcalculator.com/).

[15] "The *Fasti Antiates Ministrorum Domus Augustae* [*Inscr. It.* XIII.2 p. 206] give some evidence for the level of the state grant made towards three festivals within the period AD 23 to 37: 380,000 HS for the *Ludi Apollinares* (1 day of circus races + 7 days of theatrical performances); 760,000 HS for the *Ludi Romani* (5 days circus + 7 days theater + 2 days feast + 2 days horse trials); and 600,000 HS for the *Ludi Plebeii* (3 days circus + 7 days theater + 2 days feasts + 2 days horse trials). In addition, the token sum of 10,000 HS was granted for the *Ludi Augustales*" (Talbert 1984: 61).

another member of the *domus*) to serve as patron for the games, the magistrates put them on without any additional fanfare.

Tiberius certainly earned *invidia* after the disaster at Fidenae in 27, for which Tacitus (*Ann.* 4.62; cf. Suet. *Tib.* 40) holds Tiberius responsible. A freedman named Atilius, intending to make a quick and tidy profit, built an amphitheater which was inherently unstable. However, as Chamberland has observed, aside from being produced by a freedman, Atilius' games may not have been so different from other games given throughout Italy: "Possibly other men produced shows near Rome with the same aim of profit-making in mind, but our sources are silent because no disaster occurred" (2007: 147). Despite Tacitus' sardonic comments placing the blame on Tiberius, disaster relief was quickly dispensed after the collapse of the amphitheater. While Tacitus (*Ann.* 4.63) attributes the relief to the *nobiles*, Suetonius (*Tib.* 40) states that upon hearing of the disaster Tiberius immediately crossed to the mainland to offer his support. The Senate passed a decree regulating such games in the future.

Tacitus again disparages Tiberius in the succeeding chapter, which deals with another calamity, a fire on the Caelian hill. According to Tacitus, the people attributed the disaster to Tiberius' absence from Rome. Tiberius, however, immediately began dispensing funds for relief. Tacitus uses the occasion of Tiberius' generosity to show the Senate's subservience. The Senate passed a decree thanking Tiberius. But instead of stopping there, the Senate proceeded to propose changing the name of the Mons Caelius to the Mons Augustus (*Ann.* 4.64; cf. Suet. *Tib.* 48.1). Apparently, a statue of Tiberius in the home of a senator named Junius had survived the fire. The proposal to change the name to Augustus signals that as far as the Senate was concerned, Tiberius had taken over the *statio* of the first princeps. It was also a reminder of the charismatic power of the name Augustus.

Tiberius, well-known for his failure to build, did restore the Theater of Pompey after a fire in 21 (Tac. *Ann.* 3.72; Vell. 2.130; Sen. *Ad Marc.* 22.4).[16] Tiberius also provided relief after a fire on the Aventine in 36 which destroyed part of the circus (Tac. *Ann.* 6.45). Tiberius' distribution of 100 million sesterces would have been used to rebuild houses and *insulae* as well as the damaged circus. Tiberius made sure that the money was properly distributed by setting up a commission including the

---

[16] On Tiberius' failure to fund new buildings, see Thornton and Thornton 1989: 46–51. For Tiberian restoration of older buildings, see Tac. *Ann.* 2.49, Dio 57.10, and Vell. 2.130. On Pompey's Theater, see Packer 2010.

husbands of his granddaughters and Publius Petronius, who was nomin-
ated by the consuls. As Tiberius' granddaughters (the daughters of
Germanicus) were also the great-granddaughters of Augustus (through
their mother Agrippina), their husbands' role in distributing funds would
have linked the *liberalitas* inextricably to the *domus Augusta*. Tiberius also
exhibited generosity to his subjects outside of Rome. His financial support
for the cities of Asia which were struck by an earthquake was rewarded
with a colossal statue.[17] The act of *liberalitas* was also celebrated on coins
issued with the legend CIVITATIBVS ASIAE RESTITVTIS (*BMCRE* 1
70–73). This was, according to Suetonius (*Tib.* 48.2), the only time that
Tiberius gave any sort of relief to the provinces.

The most famous episode regarding Tiberius' fiscal policy, and one that
has generated much speculation about the money supply, interest rates,
and land prices during the time period, is an economic crisis which took
place in the year 33. Tacitus is our best source for the episode, but his
account is muddled by personal commentary on lending as a source of
income for a respectable Roman.[18] We have already mentioned above a
spike in grain prices in the previous year. Tacitus does not connect the two
events, but they may be related. In Tacitus' account (*Ann.* 6.16–7),
predatory accusers brought forth prosecutions under an obsolete
Caesarian law.[19] Tacitus seems sympathetic to the idea, if not the agency,
of prosecuting those who had abused laws of usury. The presiding praetor
recognized how many senators were vulnerable to prosecution and referred
the matter to the Senate. The Senate appealed to Tiberius, who instituted
an eighteen-month moratorium for everyone to arrange their affairs in
compliance with the law.[20] This triggered a shortage of liquid capital
(*inopia rei nummariae*). Tacitus claims the problem was exacerbated by
the large amount of money locked in the treasury from land confiscation.
The Senate directed every creditor to invest two-thirds of his capital in
Italian land. Creditors then called in all their loans. Debtors were afraid of

[17] For sources on the earthquake, including Tac. *Ann.* 2.47, Pliny, *HN* 2.200, and Suet. *Tib.* 48.2, see
Goodyear 1981: 336. For a more precise breakdown of Tiberius' subvention, see Alpers 1995:
85–7.
[18] Dio (58.16.2) states in his narrative for 31 that a tax of 0.5 percent was raised to 1 percent. This
would appear to be clawback of the tax remission after the annexation of Cappadocia (Tac. *Ann.*
2.42). Mallan believes Dio is mistaken: "It is likely that it was in 32 or 33 in response to the
financial crisis of those years" (2020: 310).
[19] For an analysis of what exactly Caesar's law entailed and when it would have originated, see
Frederiksen 1966.
[20] Dio (58.21) claims it was Tiberius himself who reactivated Caesar's law although he does not
explain why. Dio's account is focused on the suicide of Tiberius' friend Nerva, who supposedly
starved himself to death in protest of Tiberius' policy.

infamia. Usurers hoarded money to buy land. Land prices then fell. Tiberius stepped in, providing 100 million sesterces for no-interest loans. Private creditors began to lend again. The law fell back into abeyance.

Ultimately, this incident caused no long-term damage to the Roman economy, and Tiberius' response was the same as Augustus' actions when credit was tight. According to Suetonius, the inflow of money into Rome after the capture of Alexandria led to a fall in interest rates and a rise in land prices. Subsequently, "whenever there was an excess of funds from the property of those who had been condemned, he loaned it without interest for fixed periods to any who could give security for double the amount" (*qui cavere in duplum possent, Aug.* 41; Loeb trans. Rolfe). Tacitus (*Ann.* 6.17.3) states that Tiberius extended loans under the same terms: *si debitor populo in duplum praediis cavisset*. Notably, the terms of Tiberius' loans included securities in property (*praediis*). Suetonius does not specifically mention land in terms of the deposit borrowers were required to give under Augustus, although it is possibly implied. The decline in land ownership by senators became such a problem that Trajan promoted a measure compelling candidates for office to own land in Italy (Pliny, *Ep.* 6.19).[21] Moreover, Tiberius' willingness to allow delators to prosecute senators under Caesar's law may have been prompted by the grain shortage in the previous year. Bellen (1976: 220) directly connects the two, claiming a failure in crops throughout the empire would have led Tiberius to devise some plan whereby senators would be compelled to own more land in Italy. The manner in which the plan was implemented was disastrous. Nevertheless, Tiberius' loans solved the crisis. They also likely spurred more senators to invest in Italian land, at least in the short term.

Tacitus' comment that the crisis was tied to a shortage of coin has driven many to argue, most notably Tenney Frank (1935), that Tiberius inadvertently created the problem by hoarding money.[22] Rodewald's 1976 monograph, *Money in the Age of Tiberius*, offered reasoned arguments against Frank's assertions which have been, for the most part, cautiously accepted

---

[21] On the notion that land ownership was intrinsic to the concept of nobility, see Tchernia 2016: 187.

[22] Thornton and Thornton argue that the crisis was at least partly Keynesian in nature, caused by Tiberius' lack of investment in public building, yet they also admit the possibility that "In the pure money case the crisis was a simple cash squeeze caused by the event suggested in the ancient sources – the sudden decision to enforce an old law requiring cash backing for real estate loans" (1990: 660). Elliott (2015: 274–6) demonstrates the many problems involved in Thornton and Thornton's earlier study on building projects under the Julio-Claudians (1989), a study which the authors use to support their analysis of the crisis of 33.

by later scholars.[23] We have no hard evidence that there was a shortage of coin in circulation under Tiberius. The fact that creditors called for payment of debts in full and then subsequently sat on their cash while land prices fell, knowing that they had eighteen months to buy land – that is what led to the *inopia rei nummariae*, not a pre-existing shortage of coin. Rodewald has even argued that under Tiberius more coins were minted annually than during parts of Augustus' reign. Using data from coin hoards, he concludes, "under Tiberius the average annual output of silver coins was not much smaller than it had been in the time of Augustus, and that the average annual output of gold coins was perhaps somewhat larger" (1976: 11). Naturally, some of the money produced in Rome and in the mints of the West was siphoned out of Italy through overseas trade and pay for soldiers.[24] Even so, a decrease in the ready supply of money due to trade and military spending was not the primary cause of the crisis.

In the economic crisis of 33, many were faced not only with a shortfall of financial capital but also with a devastating loss of social capital (Tac. *Ann.* 6.17.3).[25] The interest-free loans supplied by Tiberius would only have been available to those who already owned enough property to provide security for those loans, particularly senators. This was not the only time Tiberius helped senators out of financial difficulties. In comparison with Augustus, Tiberius received a reputation for stinginess in this respect.[26] Tacitus (*Ann.* 2.37–8; cf. Suet. *Tib.* 47) prefaces the story of Hortalus, grandson of the famous orator Hortensius, by stating that Tiberius did help some senators to keep their rank. While Suetonius implies that Tiberius' treatment of Hortalus was the norm, Tacitus considered it unusual. However, the circumstances must be examined. Tiberius was being petitioned in the Senate to give more money to a man who had already been given a large sum by Augustus. Moreover, Tiberius' response, "Divus Augustus gave you the money, Hortalus, but not as a result of having been accosted, nor by some law that it should

---

[23] Although, as Elliott (2015) remarks, Rodewald's arguments have been largely ignored by nonspecialists, who often choose to interpret the crisis of 33 in light of modern economic crises.
[24] Tchernia (2016: 186) believes that it was around this time that trade routes with India began to develop more quickly. Rodewald (1976: 51) does not think that trade with India was a contributing factor to the financial crisis of 33.
[25] See Elliott 2015: 279.
[26] Dio is more generous than Tacitus or Suetonius. While offering no specifics, he says, "He enriched numerous senators who were poor and, on that account, no longer wished to be members of the Senate; yet he did not do this indiscriminately, but actually expunged the names of some for licentiousness and of others for poverty when they could give no satisfactory reason for it" (57.10.3–4; Loeb trans. Cary).

always be given" (*dedit tibi, Hortale, divus Augustus pecuniam, sed non conpellatus, nec ea lege, ut semper daretur*), indicates that he was especially irritated by being compelled to give Hortalus money solely because Augustus had done so. Recognizing Tiberius' devotion to his deified predecessor, Hortalus had chosen to make an appeal that he knew Tiberius would not be able to resist. And indeed, after dressing Hortalus down for the manner in which he had approached the princeps, Tiberius did end up giving him money. Tiberius' reluctance to throw good money after bad seems to be justified, for Tacitus finishes his account by telling us that the house of Hortensius continued to decline into poverty.[27] According to Valerius Maximus (3.5.4), a grandson of Hortensius "lived his life more abjectly and obscenely than any whore." Shackleton-Bailey, in his notes to the Loeb translation (2000: 293 n. 8), identifies this man as: "Son (or possibly brother) of the orator's grandson M. Hortalus who was rebuffed in the Senate by Tiberius in AD 16." Even if this identification is not exact, it would still indicate that the dissipation of this family was more likely due to their own moral failings than Augustus' encouragement to breed.

Moreover, as Cooley (2009: 278) remarks, Augustus' acts of generosity seem to be limited to a few specific time periods after he had raised the financial requirements for senatorial membership, during which he infused cash into the pockets of senators who fell short. Tacitus (*Ann.* 2.48.3) acknowledges that Tiberius relieved the honest poverty of the innocent but refused to help those in debt due to their own vices, either removing them from the Senate or allowing them to bow out gracefully.[28] Tacitus had previously mentioned (*Ann.* 1.75.2–4) instances where Tiberius stepped in to help senators financially. When Aurelius Pius complained about damage to his property from the construction of a road and aqueduct, the praetors in charge of the *aerarium* were reluctant to compensate him. Tiberius reimbursed Aurelius himself. In the same passage, Tacitus tells us that Tiberius made a gift of 200,000 sesterces to Propertius Celer, who had fallen below the senatorial census requirement. Others, like Hortalus, were required to plead their case before the Senate. As we have seen, this could cause some embarrassment, leading Tacitus to claim that many senators silently slipped into poverty.

---

[27] For an overview of the degeneracy of the Hortensii in the late Republic and early principate, see Goodyear 1981: 300–3.

[28] Tacitus lists five senators in particular removed from the Senate for their ignoble lack of funds. For criticism of the way in which Tiberius heard such requests for financial help, see Seneca, *De Ben.* 2.7–8; cf. *Ep.* 122.10.

Tacitus does praise Tiberius' habit of refusing bequests left to him by people with whom he was not close, in particular passing on a legacy from the intestate Aemilia Musa to her kinsman Aemilius Lepidus when legally it should have passed to the state.[29] He also gave over his share of an inheritance upon finding out that Marcus Servilius had received it in an earlier version of the will. As Tacitus states (*Ann.* 2.48.2), he accepted no bequest unless he had earned it by his friendship. In this too, Tiberius was imitating Augustus. Suetonius (*Aug.* 66.4) tells us that Augustus refused legacies from strangers and gave those from acquaintances to the deceased's children. However, he did accept bequests from friends.

The final aspect of the Tiberian economy which must be addressed, and one which Tacitus attributes as a cause of the financial crisis in 33, is the confiscation of property from those condemned of certain crimes. Tacitus' implication that the property was hoarded by Tiberius is somewhat undermined by his statement that Sejanus' property was transferred from the *aerarium* to the *fiscus* (*Ann.* 6.2).[30] Tiberius transferred the property out of the *aerarium* and into his *fiscus* presumably because Sejanus' wealth had originally been a personal gift. However, transfers between the treasury of the state and the princeps' property had actually been going on for quite some time. Augustus himself made donations to the *aerarium* whenever there was a shortfall and boasts in the *Res Gestae* of the many *beneficia* paid from his personal funds. The gradual blurring of the lines between the *aerarium*, the princeps' personal *patrimonium*, and the *fisci* of individual provinces ultimately led to the princeps and his administrators taking control over the entire budget of the empire.[31] As for the confiscations themselves being a factor in any shortage of land or currency, Tchernia (2016: 183) notes that the uptick in confiscation of the property of those condemned actually began well before the crisis; our only reason for connecting the two is Tacitus' personal opinion.

Perhaps the most notorious case of property confiscation concerns Sextus Marius, "the richest man in Spain." He was prosecuted shortly after the financial crisis nominally on charges of incest but actually, according to Tacitus, because of the magnitude of his wealth (*Ann.* 6.19.1; cf. Dio 58.22.1–4). Tacitus states that Tiberius set aside for

---

[29] According to Dio (58.16.2), after the fall of Sejanus, Tiberius began accepting all bequests.

[30] On the meaning of Tacitus' comment that there was no difference between the two treasuries, see Alpers 1995: 71–81.

[31] See Brunt 1966. Alpers (1995: 29–45; 89–91) demonstrates clearly that the term *fiscus* as applied to the princeps' "privy purse" is anachronistic for the time of Augustus and Tiberius. However, imperial procurators did collect money for the provincial *fisci*. See also Wolters 2003: 156.

himself Marius' gold and copper mines even though they had been made public property (*publicarentur*). Tacitus paints Tiberius as a greedy tyrant intent on recouping the losses of his recent *liberalitas*. Naturally, the reality is far more complicated. Champlin (2015: 293–4) asserts that Marius was convicted of *maiestas*, perhaps as part of the purge of the followers of Sejanus in that year. As for Tacitus' statement that Tiberius appropriated the mines for himself, Brunt (1966: 82) has reasonably argued that Tacitus misrepresents Tiberius' decision to use his own men to run the mines as opposed to turning them over to the provincial governor.[32]

Nevertheless, all our sources depict a rather large contrast between Tiberius' alleged stinginess and the generosity of which Augustus boasts in his *Res Gestae*. Why, if Tiberius claimed to follow Augustan precedents as if they were law, was his distribution of *beneficia* so different from that of his predecessor? First, Augustus, due to the legacies in his will and the financial pressures which arose towards the end of his reign, had left the imperial treasury rather drained.[33] Second, Tiberius consistently made comparisons between himself and Augustus in which he claimed his inferiority. His own natural reluctance to enjoy the spotlight, combined with his reverence for Augustus, led Tiberius to ensure economic (and thus political) stability without advertising his own personal benefactions.

The *Pax Augusta*

Tacitus' assessment of Tiberius as unconcerned with extending the boundaries of the empire (*princeps proferendi imperi incuriosus, Ann.* 4.32.2), combined with the mandate supposedly left by Augustus to consolidate the empire within its current limits (*consilium coercendi intra terminos imperii, Ann.* 1.11), prejudice our opinion of Tiberian policies in the provinces and abroad, especially in contrast with the early career of Octavian/Augustus. For many years, Tacitus' statement was accepted as evidence that Augustus had altered his formerly expansionist foreign policy in the later years of his reign, particularly following the notorious disaster inflicted upon Varus and his legions.[34] Ober (1982) even argued that this document might have been written by Tiberius himself, using Augustus' sanction to justify his own policies. Regardless, Tiberius portrayed himself

---

[32] Cf. Hirt 2010: 85, who refutes Suetonius' dubious claim at *Tib.* 49.2 that Tiberius cancelled private and civic mining rights (*ius metallorum ac vectigalium*) as "an untenable exaggeration."

[33] See Champlin 1989: 160.

[34] The acceptance of a shift in late-Augustan foreign policy is rather commonplace; see especially Levick 1999 [1976]: 143 and Seager 2005: 174.

as continuing the policies of Augustus, policies which Tiberius would have been instrumental in shaping throughout his adult life.

Tiberius spent the vast majority of his career before becoming princeps securing the *pax Augusta*. He saw service at both ends of the empire in diplomatic missions to Armenia and Parthia and military campaigns in Raetia, Pannonia, and Germania. After the death of Agrippa, Tiberius was Augustus' most trusted and successful general. This made Tiberius' retreat to Rhodes in 6 BC especially troubling for Augustus, particularly because his adopted sons and presumed heirs, Gaius and Lucius, were not yet capable of taking command. In the end, Lucius died in Massilia without having accomplished anything great. Gaius, although achieving diplomatic success in Parthia, was wounded during a revolt in Armenia. Dio ([Zon.] 55.10a.8; cf. Vell. 2.102.2–3) reports that subsequently Gaius wrote to Augustus to announce his formal retirement from public life, to which a panicked Augustus agreed. Gaius died in Syria while attempting to return to Italy. And so, Augustus was forced to make peace with Tiberius and adopt him as his heir. Soon, Tiberius, now joined by his own adopted son Germanicus, was back in the field.

Subsequent to the annexation of Egypt, Octavian/Augustus spent significantly less time on campaign. The conquest of Spain was conducted mostly by Agrippa and other generals, although Augustus himself did visit the front. After returning to Rome with great fanfare (celebrated by the dedication of the Altar of Fortuna Redux in 19 BC), Augustus seldom left Italy. He delegated the campaigning to others.[35] Tiberius was thus imitating Augustus, whose last tour as a commander in the field was at age 36, by not going abroad on military campaigns after becoming princeps. Augustus had reached a point where a military setback would do more harm to his reputation than a victory would do good. Moreover, Augustus wanted to offer opportunities for younger members of the *domus Augusta* to earn laurels. These are the same reasons Tiberius gave when explaining why he did not personally visit the mutinying troops (Tac. *Ann.* 1.57) or directly address the rebellion in Gaul by Sacrovir and Florus (Tac. *Ann.* 3.47). Like his predecessor, Tiberius entrusted his campaigns to others and used diplomacy when possible. More importantly, both before and after

[35] As both Barnes (1974: 21) and Rich (2009: 156, 159) point out, after the conquest of Spain, Augustus never personally commanded troops in the field. Velleius (2.39.3), when listing territories conquered by Augustus, includes only Spain and Egypt. Tiberius is credited with conquering Illyricum, Dalmatia, Raetia, Vindelicia, Noricum, Pannonia, and the Scordisci, as well as annexing Cappadocia as princeps.

becoming princeps, Tiberius claimed his success under the auspices of
Victoria Augusti.[36]

Throughout the latter part of Augustus' reign, Tiberius' advice as the
leading general in problematic areas of the empire would have been
instrumental in guiding policy. Velleius Paterculus served in the military
under Tiberius in several campaigns. Most prominent among the qualities
for which Velleius praises Tiberius as a commander is his unwillingness to
risk his men's lives for an easy victory. At 2.97.4, Velleius, summarizing
Tiberius' campaigns in Germania after the death of Drusus, states that
Tiberius conducted them through *virtus* and *fortuna*. More importantly,
he won victories without any loss of the army entrusted to him. Velleius
foregrounds Tiberius' concern for his troops again at 2.114.1–2, where the
commander used his own personal resources to tend to the sick.
He highlights Tiberius' valuing the safety of his men over personal glory
at 2.115.5 and 2.120.2 (cf. 2.107.3).

Tiberius' conservative approach is often contrasted with Augustus'
claims in the *Res Gestae* to have conquered pretty much the entire world
as it was known to the Romans, in particular Germania up to the Elbe.
Again, Velleius' comments as an officer fighting under Tiberius are
instructive.[37] At least twice (2.113.2, 2.120.2) Velleius indicates that
Tiberius in the field acted against the instructions or intentions of
Augustus, once in returning extra troops levied by Augustus to help with
the rebellion in Illyricum and then in exceeding Augustus' orders by
penetrating more deeply into Germania than originally planned.[38]
According to Velleius (2.120.2), after the slaughter of Varus in 9,
Tiberius crossed the Rhine and "made war against the enemy which his
father and his country were content merely to keep at bay" (*ultro Rhenum
cum exercitu transgreditur <et> arma infert hosti quae arcuisse pater et patria
contenti erant*).[39] This implies that Augustus' primary concern in
Germania was to secure the territory along the Rhine, perhaps as far as
the Weser.[40] In fact, the first action Velleius reports in Tiberius' campaign

---

[36] See especially Gagé 1930 and Lyasse 2008: 116–25.
[37] In his commentary on Velleius, Woodman (1977: 153–4) argues against the traditional belief that
Augustus had a firm plan to make Germania into a province bordered in the west by the Rhine and
the east by the Elbe.
[38] Suetonius (*Tib.* 16) states that during the rebellion in Illyricum, Tiberius persevered in his attacks
despite having been recalled.
[39] Woodman (1977: 206–7) inserts the "*et*" in his text to show that the two clauses are connected.
[40] Eck sees this as being particularly based around the altar at *oppidum Ubiorum* (2011: 20).

to stabilize the area is not in Germania but Gaul (*mittitur ad Germaniam, Gallias confirmat*, 2.120.1).

The responsibility for the policy of consolidating the empire within its boundaries (*consilium coercendi intra terminos imperii*) was likely shared between Augustus and Tiberius. In the earlier part of his reign, Augustus perhaps had every intention of subduing all Germania up to the Elbe and the Ocean (the North Sea). But after Drusus' death, Tiberius' withdrawal to Rhodes, the deaths of Gaius and Lucius, the revolts in Illyricum, and the slaughter of Varus' legions in Germania, Augustus became more conservative in his approach to the region.[41] While to some degree this can be attributed to the influence of Tiberius after his adoption, it also stems from Roman ignorance of the region, its geography, and the nature of the tribes who traveled through it. It had taken Rome over two hundred years to gain control of the entire Iberian Peninsula, and that area was bordered by Roman Gaul and the sea.[42] It is no wonder that Germania, which bordered territories never conquered by the Romans, would prove so difficult to master.[43]

Before the Varian disaster, both Drusus the Elder and Tiberius had spent many years campaigning in Germania. Yet despite Velleius' often misinterpreted claim, Germania had not been consolidated as a province up to the Elbe. The emphasis in the famous quote regarding Tiberius' success in Germania after taking over the campaign from his deceased brother Drusus – *sic perdomuit eam, ut in formam paene stipendiariae redigeret provinciae* (2.97.4) – should be on the *paene*. Although L. Domitius Ahenobarbus, husband of Augustus' niece Antonia Maior, supposedly constructed an altar along the Elbe (Tac. *Ann.* 4.44.2; Dio [Zon.] 55.10a.2), there is no evidence of permanent military settlements beyond the Weser.[44] Dio (56.18.1) complicates matters further by stating that the Romans had begun to build civilian settlements (*poleis*) in Germania. Recent excavations at Waldgirmes have proven him correct.[45] Even so, Waldgirmes is on the western side of the Weser. While Augustus

---

[41] Kehne (2002: 315) doubts any serious claim to the Elbe as a border in 6, pointing out the lack of troops stationed beyond the Weser.

[42] For an overview of Augustus' consolidation of troublesome Spain, see Gruen 1990: 399–401.

[43] As Brunt states in his assessment of Agrippa's map in the Porticus Vipsania: "Agrippa himself evidently had no notion of the size of the land-mass east of the Rhine" (1963: 175)

[44] For the argument that the river which Domitius crossed was the Saale, not the Elbe, see Rives 1999: 297 and Swan 2004: 123–4.

[45] See von Schnurbein 2003.

may have portrayed Germania as a pacified Roman province up to the Elbe, the reality was much different.[46]

Not only did the terrain of Germania pose problems for consolidating the region, but the nature of the Germanic tribes made the idea of quickly and easily creating a province extremely unrealistic. Germanic (and Gallic) tribes were constantly on the move, especially late in the reign of Augustus.[47] These migrations threatened any parts of Germania to which the Romans might lay claim as well as the supposedly secure province of Gaul, the recently conquered Alpine provinces, and Illyricum. The massive uprising in Illyricum in the midst of Roman preparations for an invasion of Germania was a clear sign that pacified provinces could never be taken for granted. Indeed, Wells (1972: 238) argues that it was not so much the Varian disaster as the toll taken by quelling the uprising in Illyricum which ultimately halted Roman expansion in northeastern Europe. Moreover, as Cooley (2009: 221) observes, in the *Res Gestae* Augustus differentiates Germania from the *provinciae* of Gallia and Hispania and only claims to have brought peace to Germania up to the Elbe (*Gallias et Hispanias provincias, item Germaniam qua includit Oceanus a Gadibus ad ostium Albis fluminis pacavi, RG* 26.2).[48]

Ultimately, as Tacitus (*Ann.* 1.3.6) recognized, troops were sent to Germania after the Varian disaster not to secure the area as a province but rather to avenge Varus and rehabilitate the reputation of the Roman army. While saving face through the recovery of standards lost by Varus' legions was politically important, Augustus and Tiberius surely recognized the difficulty in engaging in extensive military action, especially after the rebellion in Illyricum. Nevertheless, military glory was the cornerstone of

---

[46] Timpe (2008) has pointed out that the Romans' ignorance of the terrain of Germania near the Elbe would have made it difficult for Augustus to create any sort of definite plan of consolidation. Strabo (7.1.4) asserts regarding the tribes along the Elbe, "they would have been better known if Augustus had permitted his generals to cross the Elbe to pursue those who had withdrawn there": κἂν πλείω δὲ γνώριμα ὑπῆρξεν, εἰ ἐπέτρεπε τοῖς στρατηγοῖς ὁ Σεβαστὸς διαβαίνειν τὸν Ἄλβιν μετιοῦσι τοὺς ἐκεῖσε ἀπανισταμένους. He later adds (7.2.4), "those areas beyond the Elbe that are along the Ocean are entirely unknown to us": τὰ δὲ πέραν τοῦ Ἄλβιος τὰ πρὸς τῷ ὠκεανῷ παντάπασιν ἄγνωστα ἡμῖν ἐστιν. Compare the epic description of the areas visited by men shipwrecked during Germanicus' attempt to bring ships around the North Sea given by Albinovanus Pedo and quoted at Seneca, *Suas.* 1.15.

[47] On problems with the identification of tribes and the tracing of their movements, see Rives 1999: 227–9.

[48] The Greek reads: Γαλατίαν καὶ Ἰσπανίας, ὁμοίως δὲ καὶ Γερμανίαν καθὼς Ὠκεανὸς περικλείει ἀπ(ὸ) Γαδε(ίρων) μέχρι στόματος Ἄλβιος ποταμο(ῦ ἐν) εἰρήνῃ κατέστεσα, omitting the Greek word for *provincias*, ἐπαρχίας.

the charismatic image of the *domus Augusta*.[49] As in the case of the return of the standards captured by the Parthians, military and diplomatic successes could be parlayed into propaganda portraying the submission of a menacing foreign threat, propaganda which would promote not just the reigning *imperator* but also his potential heirs. Despite the realities of Germanicus' campaigns in Germania, just as Tiberius had been granted a triumph for a war which was obviously not completed (Dio 55.6.5, 55.8.2; cf. Suet. *Tib.* 9.2, Vell. 2.97.4, Ovid, *Fasti* 1.647), so too was Germanicus awarded a triumph (Tac. *Ann.* 2.41; Strabo 7.1.4) even though Arminius was still at large.[50] Tacitus reports that Germanicus triumphed over the Cherusci, Chatti, Angrivarii, and whatever other nations inhabit the territory up to the Elbe (*Germanicus Caesar . . . triumphavit de Cheruscis Chattisque et Angrivariis quaeque aliae nationes usque ad Albim colunt, Ann.* 2.41).[51] Thus, as in the *Res Gestae*, the Elbe retained its importance as the boundary for Roman propaganda.

We turn, then, to the supposed abandonment of Germania and the recall of Germanicus.[52] Tacitus (*Ann.* 2.26), prejudiced by the belief that a jealous Tiberius desired to send Germanicus away from his beloved troops and the campaign where he was most likely to earn glory, indicates support for Germanicus' claim that one more year would have allowed him to finish off the Germani.[53] After a season of campaigning with mixed results, Germanicus erected a trophy dedicated to Mars, Jupiter, and Augustus because the nations between the Rhine and Elbe had been subdued (*debellatis inter Rhenum Albimque nationibus*, Tac. *Ann.* 2.22). Despite this claim of victory, Germanicus wanted to pursue further campaigns, campaigns which Tiberius knew would be Pyrrhic. In achieving his great victories, Germanicus had suffered heavy losses. Those losses were

---

[49] On the prominence of the Rhine armies in promoting members of the *domus Augusta*, see Kehne 2002: 318–20. Cf. the sentiments of Strabo regarding the treachery of the Cherusci against Varus, "But they all paid the penalty, and afforded the younger Germanicus a most brilliant triumph" (7.1.4; Loeb trans. Jones).

[50] On the dynastic connotations of the triumph, which featured Germanicus' children joining their father in his chariot, see McWilliam 2010. The triumph is mentioned in the *fasti Amiternini* and the *fasti Ostienses* for May 26, 17.

[51] According to the *Tabula Siarensis* (IIa 9–13), Germanicus conquered the Germani (*Germanis bello superatis*) and chased them from Gaul.

[52] Eck (2009: 188) believes the Varian disaster did not alter Augustus' plans for Germania and places the blame for its abandonment squarely on the shoulders of Tiberius. In a later work (2018), he contends that the *consilium coercendi intra terminos imperii* included the recovery of Germania. Telschow (1975: 164–6) sees a definite defensive shift in the military actions of Tiberius and Germanicus in 11 and 12.

[53] Telschow (1975: 154–7) argues that Tacitus' account was overly influenced by Domitian's restraint of Agricola.

supplemented with exactions from neighboring Gaul and may have played a role in the rebellion of Sacrovir and Florus a few years later.[54]

If not for the report of the *consilium coercendi intra terminos imperii*, our perception of Tiberius' foreign policy might not be so different from our perception of Augustus' foreign policy in the second half of his reign. After the acquisition of Egypt and the consolidation of Spain, Augustus reacted to situations in ways which saved face for the Roman state (and his own image as a charismatic *imperator*). Moreover, Augustus had significantly reduced the number of legions after Actium. Brunt (1963: 171) notes that after the civil wars, the willingness of Italians to join the army declined, so much so that Augustus had trouble conscripting troops in the wake of the Pannonian revolt and the Varian disaster. Despite the smaller size of the army, Augustus established a military treasury in 6 to address the rising costs of keeping professional troops under arms (Dio 55.24.9–25). The legions in Pannonia and on the Rhine mutinied over their pay and length of service upon the death of Augustus.[55] Resources were clearly stretched to their limits.

Given the limitations of manpower and the shortage of members of the *domus Augusta* to lead troops in the field, as was the case for Tiberius later, Augustus preferred to resolve conflicts by diplomacy rather than open warfare. Telschow (1975: 166) argues that Augustus recognized the wisdom of treating the tribes across the Rhine in the same way he had treated eastern kings.[56] Thus, following Augustus' precedent, once Germanicus had punished the Germani and recovered some of the standards lost by Varus' legions, Tiberius turned to diplomatic measures, sending Drusus to stir up discontent against the powerful leader of the Marcomanni, Maroboduus (Tac. *Ann.* 2.62–3).[57] As Tacitus (*Ann.*

---

[54] See Koestermann (1963: 495) on Tac. *Ann.* 3.40.1.

[55] On the financial considerations limiting further military action and causing the mutinies, see Eich 2009.

[56] Strabo observes regarding the Cimbri, "they sent as a present to Augustus the most sacred kettle in their country, with a plea for his friendship and for an amnesty of their earlier offences, and when their petition was granted, they set sail for home" (7.2.1; Loeb trans. Jones). One can imagine similar gifts from other Germanic tribes, although they are not specified by Strabo.

[57] Cf. Velleius 2.108.2, who states that Maroboduus had a *certum imperium vimque regiam*. Strabo, writing after the victory of Germanicus, specifies Boihaemum as "the domain of Maroboduus, the place whither he caused to migrate not only several other peoples, but in particular the Marcomanni, his fellow-tribesmen; for after his return from Rome, this man, who before had been only a private citizen, was placed in charge of the affairs of state, for, as a youth he had been at Rome and had enjoyed the favor of Augustus, and on his return he took rulership and acquired, in addition to the peoples aforementioned, the Lugii (a large tribe), the Zumi, the Butones, the Mugilones, the Sibini, and also the Semnones, a large tribe of the Suevi themselves" (7.1.3; Loeb trans. Jones). On Maroboduus' domains and allied tribes, see Dobiáš 1960: 157.

2.64.1) states, confirming Velleius' assertions that Tiberius preferred victories which did not endanger his men, "Tiberius was happier, since he had confirmed peace through wisdom rather than if he had made war through battles." By forcing the Germani to side with either Arminius or Maroboduus, Tiberius exploited the tribal nature of the peoples living between the Rhine and the Elbe. Tiberius brought about the downfall of Maroboduus and his pawn against Maroboduus, Catualda.[58] Shortly afterwards (Tac. *Ann.* 2.88), the Germani, in particular the Chatti, turned against their supposed liberator Arminius, asking Tiberius to send poison to be used against him. Tiberius refused to get involved. Not much later, Arminius, aiming at sole power, was killed by the treachery of his countrymen. Thus, with no loss of soldiers, Tiberius had destroyed the two greatest enemies of Rome in Germania, Maroboduus and Arminius.[59]

While Tiberius may have scored a diplomatic coup by ousting Maroboduus from power and reducing the threat from the Marcomanni and their allies, he also suffered embarrassment when the Frisii rebelled. Tacitus claims that the jealous Tiberius did not want to entrust the war to anyone, nor did the Senate care about the "outposts of the empire" (*imperii extrema*). This is understandable. In 28, Germanicus and Drusus were dead. Nero, the son of Germanicus, was perhaps old enough to lead an expedition, but his mother, Agrippina, had made sure that Tiberius would never trust him with any army, especially one in Germania. The Frisii were merely an allied kingdom paying tribute in oxhides for military use.[60] The administrator who provoked the rebellion is described as *e primipilaribus* (Tac. *Ann.* 4.72). As the generals on the scene had already mismanaged their response, allowing heavy casualties, Tiberius saw little point in further military action. Although, according to Tacitus (*Ann.* 4.74), "The Frisian name became famous among the Germani," it did little to inspire other uprisings in Tiberius' reign. Tiberius was efficient in dealing with problems that arose in other parts of the empire, most notably in Africa with Tacfarinas and in Gaul under Florus and Sacrovir.[61] In the

---

[58] After being invited to Italy by Tiberius, Maroboduus lived a further eighteen years at Ravenna; Catualda, driven out of Germania by the Hermunduiri, found refuge at Forum Julium. The remains of the kingdom of Maroboduus were placed under the rule of Vannius, king of the Quadi (Tac. *Ann.* 2.63).

[59] The consequences extended further: "During the remainder of Tiberius's principate this resulted in the creation of a chain of clients from Lower Germany to the middle Danube" (Luttwak 2016: 21).

[60] On the history of Rome's alliance with the Frisii, see Rives 1999: 260–2.

[61] On the rebellion of Tacfarinas and its possible causes, see Vanacker 2015. Bellemore (2003: 284) argues that Tacitus exaggerated the Gallic rebellion and compressed the timeline to denigrate

West, Tiberius maintained the *pax Augusta* with limited military action and no substantial loss of territory.

Tiberius' strategies in the East also clearly reflect Augustan precedents. Despite Germanicus' protests about being sent to the East, Tiberius himself had been recalled from Germania to deal with problems in Armenia in 6 BC (Dio [Xiph. and Zon.] 55.9). Augustus had previously sent him to Armenia in 20 BC to place a Roman-backed king on the throne. The pressure Rome's influence in Armenia put on the Parthians facilitated the return of the standards taken from Crassus and Antony's generals.[62] After Tiberius' withdrawal to Rhodes, Gaius was sent to the East in his first steps as Augustus' presumed successor. Tiberius' motives in sending Germanicus east were only called into question because of Germanicus' premature death and the insinuations of later historians.[63] Tiberius took advantage of the situation in Asia Minor to ease economic strains in Rome. Following the precedent set by Augustus in his annexation of the kingdom of Amyntas (Dio 53.26.3), Tiberius annexed the kingdoms of Cappadocia and Commagene (and possibly Cilicia), turning them into Roman provinces (Tac. *Ann.* 2.42, 2.56).[64] This allowed for a reduction of the tax on auctioned goods instituted "after the civil wars" (*post bella civilia*) and appropriated to help pay for the military treasury (Tac. *Ann.* 1.78.2).[65] The consolidation of these provinces was assigned to two friends of Germanicus, Q. Veranius and Q. Servaeus (Tac. *Ann.* 2.56.4). All these factors suggest that Tiberius was using Germanicus' mission to boost his profile as the next successor to Augustus' *statio*.

The military interventions and diplomatic missions overseen by Augustus and Tiberius were inextricably intertwined with the Roman

---

Tiberius. According to Pliny (*HN* 30.4), Tiberius eradicated (*sustulit*) the Druids in Gaul, presumably in the aftermath of this uprising.

[62] For references to the standards lost by Crassus and Antony's generals, as well as the negotiations for their return to Augustus, see Cooley 2009: 242–4.

[63] Low (2016: 230–1) sees Germanicus as being personally involved in installing a king favorable to Rome on the throne of Armenia. She also suggests he may have gotten involved in the dispute between Rhescuporis and Cotys of Thrace.

[64] Low hypothesizes that Germanicus was sent east, among other things, to make "arrangements for the provincialization of Cappadocia" (2016: 230). Tiberius played a role in Cappadocia's being without a king (Tac. *Ann.* 2.42.2–3; Dio 57.17.3–7; Suet. *Tib.* 37.4). Tacitus indicates Cilicia was also without a king but never specifically states that Tiberius sent a governor there as he did with Cappadocia and Commagene. Goodyear (1981: 321) believes Cilicia was likely annexed at this time.

[65] Strobel 2002: 51. Schrömbges (1987: 14–15, with n. 69) sees the tax cut mentioned at Tac. *Ann.* 2.42 as not only connected to the annexation of Cappadocia but also as a promotion of the success of the imperial family, especially Germanicus, who was consul in that year and had recently celebrated a triumph.

notion of *pax*.[66] It is no accident that Tacitus places his apology for the lack of exciting battles towards the beginning of the second half of the Tiberian hexad (*Ann.* 4.32). The later years of Tiberius' reign were relatively peaceful. Despite the exaggerated assertion of Suetonius (*Tib.* 41), the retreat of the emperor to Capri had little effect on the provinces, and the threat of prosecution from the increasingly powerful delators, as well as Tiberius' notorious prorogation of governors, may actually have helped to prevent provincial maladministration.[67] Even Tiberius' harshest critics would have to agree that the provinces benefitted from the emperor's strictness. Unwilling to provoke insurrection, Tiberius was scrupulous in punishing governors who had overstepped their boundaries.[68] We have already mentioned in our discussion of the imperial cult that the temple in Smyrna dedicated to Tiberius, Livia, and the Senate was prompted by the punishment of abusive governors, most notably C. Silanus and Lucilius Capito (Tac. *Ann.* 4.15). Tiberius' famous maxim, that it was the quality of a good shepherd that his sheep be shorn, not flayed (*boni pastoris esse tondere pecus, non deglubere*, Suet. *Tib.* 32; cf. Dio 57.10.5), symbolizes his awareness that provinces would pay taxes more willingly if they were not overburdened. His motives were hardly altruistic, but they served their purpose of ensuring economic stability without imperial expansion. Tacitus (*Ann.* 4.6) concedes that Tiberius took care for the provinces so that they should not be disturbed by new burdens, and so that they would tolerate the old ones without the greed and cruelty of their governors.

In order to avoid the abuses of the provinces which had occurred in the late Republic, Tiberius notoriously employed the same men for long periods of time in the same position, sometimes without even allowing them to administer their provinces in person.[69] According to Josephus, Tiberius explained the reason for his policies with a fable. A wounded man was being hounded by flies. A passer-by, taking pity on him, moved to swat away these flies. The wounded man responded that the passer-by

---

[66] On the monopolization of *pax* by Augustus and his family, see Cornwell 2017: 155–86.

[67] Orth (1970: 122) concurs, noting that any marked difference in Tiberius' reign which appears in the historical writers is not supported by the archaeological evidence in the provinces.

[68] According to Brunt's statistics (1961, Table II), more men were condemned for provincial maladministration under Tiberius than under any emperor between Augustus and Trajan. Alföldy (1965: 832) asserts that the control and repression of abuse was probably never more organized than during the reign of Tiberius. See also Philo, *In Flaccum* 12,105–6; 13 108–18.151 and Millar 1977: 443.

[69] The cases can be found in Orth 1970, *Anhang* I. On governors being held in Rome, see Orth 1970: 82.

should not bother the flies, saying, "you would put me in a worse position if you drove them off. For since these flies have already had their fill of blood, they no longer feel such a pressing need to annoy me but are in some measure slack. But if others were to come with a fresh appetite, they would take over my now weakened body and that would indeed be the death of me" (*AJ* 18.173–6; Loeb trans. Feldman). As Hurlet explains (2006: 113), before his retreat to Capri, Tiberius extended the governorships of only two proconsuls, L. Afranius and Q. Blaesus, both of whom were dealing with the war with Tacfarinas in Africa. Augustus had already begun to keep governors in their *provinciae* during crises (Dio 53.13.6); Tiberius saw the wisdom in this and followed suit. After he withdrew to Capri, he became even more conservative in trusting men with provinces (and armies). While the aristocracy at Rome may have resented the lack of political (and financial) opportunities offered by governing provinces, the provinces benefitted from Tiberius' tendencies to keep men in office.[70]

Jews, Worshippers of Isis, and Astrologers

According to the ancient sources, Augustus had shown great tolerance towards the Jews.[71] Thus, an incident which is assigned by Tacitus (*Ann.* 2.85) to the year 19 has raised significant questions among scholars. Tacitus relates the action against the Jews in a larger section on the restoration of moral order and setting boundaries to female lust. The first part of this section concerns the case of Vistilia, a noblewoman who had registered as a prostitute to circumvent adultery laws. Then Tacitus briefly narrates (*Ann.* 2.85.4) an action of the Senate against both Jews and worshippers of Isis:

> Action was taken regarding the expulsion of Egyptian and Jewish rites, and a *senatus consultum* was passed that 4,000 freedmen infected by this superstition who were of suitable age would be transported to the island of Sardinia to control brigandage there; and if they died on account of the violence of the climate, it would be a cheap loss. The others were to leave Italy unless they disavowed their sacrilegious rites before a certain day.

---

[70] Tiberius was also following Augustan precedent in allowing provincial governors and legates to bring their wives with them, even on campaign. The motion by Caecina Severus that wives should not be allowed to accompany men sent to govern provinces was ultimately quashed by Tiberius' son Drusus, who alludes to the presence of his own wife Livilla during the times he was performing official duties (Tac. *Ann.* 3.32–5). As Barrett states, "if Augustus did not allow his legates to be accompanied by their wives, Drusus' final words would surely be tantamount to a serious insult to his father's predecessor" (2006: 137–8).

[71] See especially Josephus, *AJ* 16.162 and Philo, *Leg. ad Gaium* 154.

actum et de sacris Aegyptiis Iudaicisque pellendis, factumque patrum consultum, ut quattuor milia libertini generis ea superstitione infecta, quis
idonea aetas, in insulam Sardiniam veherentur, coercendis illic latrociniis
et, si ob gravitatem caeli interissent, vile damnum; ceteri cederent Italia nisi
certam ante diem profanos ritus exuissent.

Immediately following this particular action of the Senate, Tacitus records
a motion by Tiberius to replace Occia, who had served as a Vestal Virgin
for fifty-seven years with "the utmost chastity" (*summa sanctimonia*).

Tacitus does not specifically state why the Jews were exiled, or for that
matter the worshippers of Isis. Josephus' account of these events (*AJ*
18.3.4–5) only complicates matters further, as the stories he relates
regarding two separate women corrupted due to their religious beliefs bear
too many similarities for both to be true, especially since both women have
a husband with the same name (Saturninus) who was a close friend of
Tiberius.[72] Josephus begins with the story of a noblewoman named
Paulina, chaste and devoted to the worship of Isis, who was seduced by a
young man pretending to be the god Anubis. When her husband reported
the matter to Tiberius, the emperor ordered the Temple of Isis in Rome to
be destroyed and the statue of the goddess to be cast into the Tiber. In the
same year, Josephus says, another noblewoman named Fulvia was swindled
by Jewish priests into sending gifts to the Temple in Jerusalem, which they
then embezzled for themselves:

> Saturninus, the husband of Fulvia, at the instigation of his wife, duly
> reported this to Tiberius, whose friend he was, whereupon the latter
> ordered the whole Jewish community to leave Rome. The consuls drafted
> four thousand of these Jews for military service and sent them to the island
> of Sardinia; but they penalized a good many of them, who refused to serve
> for fear of breaking the Jewish law. And so, because of the wickedness of
> four men, the Jews were banished from the city. (*AJ* 18.3.5; Loeb trans.
> Feldman)

While certain details of the narrative overlap with those related by Tacitus,
Josephus, seconded by Suetonius (*Tib.* 36), is more likely correct here that
the Jews were merely banished from Rome, not the whole of Italy.[73]

Because of these narratives, Tiberius' treatment of the Jews has been
portrayed as a departure from the precedent of Augustus, whom Philo
praised (*Leg. ad Gaium* 154) as being respectful of the Jewish faith.

---

[72] The expulsion of the Jews is also related, although out of chronological context, by Suet. *Tib.* 36,
Dio [*EV* John of Antioch] 57.18.5a, Philo, *Leg. ad Gaium* 159–161, and Sen. *Ep.* 108.22.

[73] On the problems with Tacitus' narrative, see Goodyear 1981: 442–3.

Nevertheless, as Gruen observes, Augustus' tolerance was limited to just that; he took no measures to protect Jews (2003: 300).[74] Philo and Josephus, being Jewish, were sensitive to any possible persecution. More importantly, by exaggerating Augustus' benefactions to the Jews, they were attempting to influence the actions of the emperors under whom they were writing. Philo in particular was trying to persuade Caligula to intervene on behalf of the Jews in the provinces. He thus sets up Augustus as a benefactor of the Jews and criticizes the expulsion under Tiberius. While Philo blames this persecution of the Jews on Sejanus, a fitting scapegoat for someone pleading a case to Caligula, Tacitus asserts that Sejanus did not become supremely powerful with Tiberius until after the death of Drusus in 23. It is difficult to understand why Tiberius would go against Augustan precedent in order to punish a few bad actors or to please Sejanus.

Gruen offers a different explanation, pointing to the political problems which had plagued the early years of Tiberius' reign. While we cannot be entirely sure of the chronology as Tacitus often groups together measures of the Senate which were passed at different times, he relates the expulsion of the Jews and worshippers of Isis subsequent to his account of the death of Germanicus, who had spent his last days touring the East, most notably Egypt. There, Germanicus had visited the Apis bull. Pliny the Elder (*HN* 8.71) states that Apis refused to take food from the hand of Germanicus, signaling his impending death.[75] During his time in Egypt, according to Suetonius (*Aug.* 93), Octavian/Augustus conspicuously avoided the shrine of Apis; he later praised his adopted son Gaius for not offering prayers in Jerusalem when passing through Judaea. In the wake of the unrest caused by the death of Germanicus, Tiberius could have been forced to act.[76] As under Augustus, foreign religions could be tolerated only up to a certain point.

Two other factors must be mentioned in connection with the expulsion of the worshippers of Isis and the Jews in 19. One is the shortage of grain in that year, perhaps caused by Germanicus opening up the granaries

---

[74] One notable exception involved the distribution of grain. If it fell on the Sabbath, Augustus allowed the distributors to set aside a portion for the Jews to pick up the next day (Philo, *Leg. ad Gaium* 158). Jews, along with astrologers, had been expelled from Rome under the Republic in 139 BC (Val. Max. 1.3.3 [*Par.* and *Nepot.*]). Temples of Isis and Serapis were destroyed in 50 BC (Val. Max. 1.3.4 [*Par.*]).

[75] Mueller (2002: 100) points to an earthquake in that year mentioned by Pliny (*HN* 2.202) as engulfing some places and creating new ones, possibly creating the impression of a bad omen. Pliny dates the earthquake to June 8, well before the death of Germanicus, and does not connect the two events.

[76] On this possibility of political unrest as a factor in these expulsions, see Williams 1989.

during his visit to Egypt.[77] While Tacitus relates the grain shortage (*Ann.* 2.87) two chapters after his narrative of the expulsion of the worshippers of Isis and the Jews (2.85), it is likely the situation had been brewing for some time. When the crisis had reached the tipping point, Tiberius himself intervened and subsidized the price of grain. According to Suetonius (*Aug.* 42.3), during a severe grain shortage Augustus had ordered the expulsion from the city of slaves on the sales block, gladiators, and any foreigners who were not necessary for the public welfare. Tiberius was following Augustan precedent in expelling certain groups during a food shortage and at the same time curbing problematic sects promoting foreign rites.

Finally, some have questioned the assertion that 4,000 Jews were sent to Sardinia to combat brigandage, claiming that piracy was not endemic on the island at this time, even though Dio (55.28.1) mentions a special expedition sent to Sardinia by Augustus for just this purpose.[78] Woods (2008: 271) believes that when Augustus took over the province in 6 (it had been a senatorial province since 27 BC) and sent out troops to stamp out brigandage, he had been successful in doing so. Woods also argues against Tacitus' claim that it was hoped the climate of Sardinia would kill off the problematic conscripts, stating that the climate of Sardinia was no more pestilential than that of anywhere else in Italy (2008: 273).[79] Woods concludes that these troops were not being sent to Sardinia as a final destination but were instead on their way to Africa to help in the campaign against Tacfarinas.[80] He blames the original source for all three authors (Josephus, Suetonius, and Tacitus) for associating the conscription of new soldiers with the expulsion of the worshippers of Isis and the Jews from

---

[77] Rutland 1987: 158. Goodyear (1981: 377) reckons that Germanicus may not have opened granaries holding crops intended for Rome but perhaps reserves. "If he did, and if the harvest of 19 proved lean, he may indeed have caused the shortage in Rome, since reserves would not be left to ensure the quota for 19 was met." Rivière (2016: 320–31) asserts that the grain shipments would have already left Alexandria for Rome that year, thus denying Germanicus played any role in the famine which occurred in Rome in the succeeding year.

[78] Swan (2004: 189) lists other examples regarding piracy in Sardinia. See also Goodyear 1981: 442: "Sardinia was notorious for brigandage: cf. Varro, *R.R.* 1.16.2, Dio 55.28.1 (AD 6), who says that for this reason, it was taken from the Senate and placed under a military governor." One other possibility is that these conscripts were to be used in the mines on Sardinia. For lead mines on Sardinia under imperial control, see Hirt 2010: 81. On soldiers working in mines, see Hirt 2010: 196–8.

[79] For Sardinia's unhealthy climate, see Livy 23.34.11, Mela 2.123, Paus. 10.17.11, Plut. *C. Gracchus* 2.2, and, above all, Strabo 5.2.7, who relates the failure of authorities to fully control the brigands due to the pestilential conditions obtaining during the summer. On this passage of Strabo, see Roller 2018: 236.

[80] For a rather strong rebuttal to Woods' assertion that these conscripts were being sent to Africa, see Gnoli 2013: 87–8 n. 18.

Rome. Ultimately, those expelled from the city were those who refused to serve in the army. While all of this is highly speculative, it, like the explanation regarding the grain shortage, would ultimately show Tiberius to be upholding Augustan precedent, not undermining it. In 9, Augustus went to extreme measures in recruiting troops (Dio 56.23.2–3). Rocca believes, unlike Woods, that there were legitimate reasons for troops to be sent to Sardinia and that the conscription related by Tacitus and Josephus was not about punishing the Jews; rather, "Like Augustus, Tiberius was highly respectful of Jewish particularism and thought it best to create an all-Jewish unit" (2010: 25).[81]

Thus, despite the narratives of later historians, Jews fared no worse under Tiberius than they had under Augustus. Indeed, Philo praises Tiberius for intervening when a sycophantic Pontius Pilate installed shields in his honor at the palace in Jerusalem (*Leg. ad Gaium* 38.299–305). Philo claims to quote a letter of the Jewish king Agrippa, who had every reason to be hostile to Tiberius.[82] According to Agrippa, once Tiberius learned that Pilate had agitated the Jews, "without even postponing it to the morrow he wrote to Pilate with a host of reproaches and rebukes for his audacious violation of precedent and bade him at once take down the shields and have them transferred from the capital to Caesarea on the coast surnamed Augusta after your great-grandfather, to be set up in the temple of Augustus, and so they were" (*Leg. ad Gaium* 38.305; Loeb trans. Colson). Tiberius followed Augustus' policy of respecting the sensitivities of the Jews and turned a gesture meant to honor himself into one that would honor Augustus.

Like the expulsion of the Jews and the worshippers of Isis, the expulsion of astrologers from Rome is sometimes portrayed as a deviation from Augustan policy. But the situations are not entirely unconnected when one considers the exotic nature often attributed to practitioners of astrology.[83] Cicero (*Div.* 1.132) denounces anyone who makes money from predicting the future, including astrologers who hang around the circus (*de circo astrologos*) and followers of Isis who profess to be seers (*Isiacos coniectores*). Such practitioners were often consulted by the Roman elite, including Augustus and Tiberius. Tiberius was notorious for his friendship with the astrologer Thrasyllus. Augustus had also been friends with

---

[81] Rocca also points out that in both narratives the Senate originates the conscription of Jewish freedmen, not Tiberius (2010: 14–15).

[82] See especially Josephus, *AJ* 18.161–237.

[83] Ripat (2011: 129) points out the difficulty in identifying members of this fluid and ill-defined group.

Thrasyllus (Suet. *Aug.* 98.4); but both Augustus and Tiberius understood that normally harmless astrological knowledge could sometimes prove politically dangerous.[84] Augustus was known to express interest in his own horoscope. The fact that Augustus made his own horoscope public and Tiberius never did has led to a misconception that Tiberius was secretly guarding astrological knowledge. The expulsion of astrologers in 16 and/or 17 has been used by some to lend support to this depiction.[85] However, Octavian banned astrologers from Rome in 33 BC during a dangerous time (Dio.49.43.5).[86] Dio's use of the word *goētas* (see LSJ γόης 2) to describe those banned along with the astrologers indicates that men claiming expertise and knowledge were cheating and defrauding Roman citizens. Gradually, this ban was ignored, and the problem arose again in the early reign of Tiberius.

This was reflected in the trial of Libo, who was conned by men claiming he would achieve extreme wealth and power (Tac. *Ann.* 2.27.1): "Firmius Catus, a senator, due to his close friendship with Libo, was able to drive the naive young man, pliable to vanities, to the promises of the Chaldaeans, the rites of the magi, and the interpreters of dreams" (*Firmius Catus senator, ex intima Libonis amicitia, iuvenem inprovidum et facilem inanibus ad Chaldaeorum promissa, magorum sacra, somniorum etiam interpretes impulit*). Tacitus (*Ann.* 2.32.3) does not explicitly state that the senatorial decree banning astrologers from the city was the result of Libo's trial. However, the fact that he reports that decree immediately after his account of that trial would suggest that the two were connected.[87]

In addition to the expulsion of astrologers in 33 BC, Augustus limited such practices in 11. According to Dio, "the seers were forbidden to prophesy to any person alone or to prophesy regarding death even if others should be present" (56.25.5; Loeb trans. Cary).[88] Dio describes those singled out as "seers" (*tois mantesin*), which could describe just about anyone who predicts the future. In this case, Dio does not say that these practitioners were expelled, only that people were forbidden from

---

[84] On the ways in which Manilius and other writers may reflect this notion that astrology is only for the select few, see Green 2011: 134.

[85] For the date, see Mallan's commentary (2020: 217–19) on Dio 57.15.8–9.

[86] While Dio attributes the expulsion to Agrippa, there can be no doubt that it was done with Octavian's approval, if not at his suggestion.

[87] Goodyear (1981: 285) notes that even though Ulpian dates the ban to 17, Tacitus' placement of the edict in his narrative for 16 is not necessarily contradictory if the law was prompted by Libo's trial.

[88] Green (2014: 105) conjectures, "It is particularly tempting, therefore, to see the influence of Thrasyllus behind the Augustan edict of AD 11," without explaining why such an edict would be beneficial to Thrasyllus.

consulting them concerning death. Dio immediately mentions that Augustus published his own horoscope. These practitioners were likely being consulted, at least some of them, regarding the death of the princeps.[89] Thus, it was in the best interests of the *domus Augusta* to control access to astrological knowledge.

In 11, Augustus was trying to ensure a peaceful transition from himself to Tiberius. In 17, Tiberius was trying to secure his own position and the future transfer of power from himself to Germanicus. Both men had been threatened by the supposed conspiracy of Libo. If there was not an immediate cause and effect between the trial of Libo and the expulsion of the astrologers, there is at least a sense that perceived political threats had created an atmosphere of suspicion. In expelling astrologers from Rome, Tiberius and the Senate were using Augustan precedents, set in 33 BC in the midst of the insecurity of civil war and again in 11, when Augustus' death was impending. This was not a witch hunt. It was an attempt to stamp out the use of astrology to stir up discontent or encourage the ambitious (like Libo) to aspire beyond their destiny. According to Dio (57.15.8) and Suetonius (*Tib.* 36), pardon was offered to those who promised not to practice astrology again. This same pardon was offered two years later to Jews and worshippers of Isis who promised to renounce their faith. The ban on astrologers was repeated by subsequent emperors, mainly because once the crisis leading to the expulsion of astrologers was over, the ban failed to be enforced (see esp. Tac. *Hist.* 1.22.1).[90]

In a similar vein, Tiberius enforced Augustus' policy of strict personal control over the Sibylline Books. Dio ([Xiph.] 57.18.4–5) tells us that in 19 Tiberius, "disturbed not a little by an oracle reputed to be an utterance of the Sibyl," conducted his own investigation regarding spurious verses. Notably, this incident in the reconstruction of Dio's text is immediately followed by the expulsion of the Jews and woven into the narrative of the death of Germanicus. The destruction of the Temple of Isis, the crackdown on the Jews, the expulsion of astrologers, and the strict review of the Sibylline Books all occurred following Libo's trial and the death of Germanicus, times of dynastic crisis. Tacitus tells us (*Ann.* 6.12.2) that in 32 Tiberius rebuked the Senate for adopting as authentic a volume of reputed Sibylline prophecies.[91] He referred specifically to the precedent of

---

[89] Green (2014: 73 n. 38), noting that Dio's account does not specifically state when Augustus published his horoscope and drawing on the vagueness of the statement from Suet. *Aug.* 94.12, argues that Octavian actually published his full horoscope early on, at the same time that he began to advertise himself as having been born under the sign of Capricorn.

[90] Ripat 2011: 137.   [91] On the details of this episode, see Woodman 2017: 141–3.

Augustus. Augustus had already codified the verses by having them copied by the quindecimviri in their own hand, "so that no one else might read them" (Dio 54.17.2). According to Suetonius (*Aug.* 31.1), Augustus personally reviewed all Sibylline verses as Pontifex Maximus, having over 2,000 spurious verses burned. Tacitus' evidence regarding the spurious Sibylline verses indicates that even in his absence from Rome Tiberius took dangerous prophecies which could threaten the stability of the Augustan system very seriously, especially in the wake of another dynastic crisis, the alleged plots of Sejanus against the *domus Augusta*.

Conclusions

As discussed in the previous chapter, the imperial cult was central to propagating the charisma of Divus Augustus. But had Tiberius disowned his predecessor's political policies, Divus Augustus, like Divus Iulius, would have become just another name in the pantheon. By preserving Augustus' policies, Tiberius ensured that the charismatic image of Augustus as a wise ruler outlived the mortal princeps. More importantly, Tiberius made sure to repeatedly cite Augustan precedent so that the Senate and other orders of Roman society would understand his reverence for the divine mind of his predecessor. His treatment of the Senate echoed Augustus' desire to preserve the integrity of that body. His economic policies ensured security in Rome and the provinces. When a crisis did arise, he used Augustus' practice of making short-term loans to stabilize the real estate market. His reluctance to claim credit for *liberalitas* enhanced the memory of Augustus' many benefactions, visible on the inscription of the *Res Gestae* attached to his mausoleum. Finally, Tiberius was instrumental in creating and preserving the *pax Augusta*. When possible, he used foreign threats to enhance the charismatic image of the *domus Augusta*. Germanicus was awarded a triumph for his victories in Germania and then sent east on a diplomatic tour to advertise himself as future princeps. Both before and after Germanicus' death, threats to the *domus Augusta* from foreign sects were thwarted. Even after the *domus Augusta* had been emptied of potential heirs and the princeps himself had retreated to Capri, Tiberius continued to portray himself as being guided in his policies by Divus Augustus.

CHAPTER 4

The Power of Images of Augustus in the Age of Tiberius

The merging of Divus Augustus as cult figure with the charismatic *auctor* of precedents which must be preserved created continuity between the two reigns. We see this image projected in material remains such as coins, inscriptions, and sculpture. As in the case of divine honors, in public imagery Tiberius allowed himself to recede into the background in order to perpetuate the impression that Divus Augustus continued to watch over the *domus Augusta* and the state. This was particularly true in times of dynastic crisis, as after the death of Germanicus and the downfall of Sejanus. The messages found on coins and inscriptions focus on the peace brought by Divus Augustus and the continuation of that *status* under his family. Statue groups likewise focus on the unity of the *domus Augusta*. Those messages can be seen reflected in smaller objects such as the Boscoreale Cups and various cameos.

The Currency of Divus Augustus Pater

To those who used coinage, its value was guaranteed by the state. By the late Republic that guarantee was reinforced by images reflective of the men or, after Actium, man, who controlled the state. In recent years, scholars have tended to see the images on coins as a mutual exchange of messages from the princeps, members of the Senate, and officials of the imperial government outside of Rome.[1] The average low-wage worker on the outskirts of the empire might not have paid attention to coin types. But municipal and provincial aristocrats certainly did. The *tresviri monetales* were responsible for coins issued by imperial mints at Rome and Lugdunum (provincial coinage will be discussed later). While these officials likely consulted the princeps regarding coin types, even if they did

---

[1] On selection of coin types, see Levick 1982, Wallace-Hadrill 1986, Cheung 1998, and Noreña 2011. On coins as "monuments in miniature," see Meadows and Williams 2001 and Elkins 2015. For a review of recent works on imperial imagery in general, see Hekster 2020.

not, they were young politicians looking to advance on the *cursus honorum*.[2] They would have been very careful in choosing the images minted. Whether or not the princeps personally chose coin types, those types were meant to reflect the best aspects of his reign. Relatively few coin types were issued under Tiberius. These coins tended to focus on two things: the charismatic power of Divus Augustus and Tiberius' role as the continuator of the Augustan system. Besides a prevalence of coin types featuring Augustus during the reign of Tiberius, there is also a predominance of examples of such coins in the archaeological remains. In a statistical analysis of Tiberian coins found at various sites in Rome, Divus Augustus Pater coins outnumber those which feature only Tiberius.[3]

As the Tiberian regime attempted to reinforce the image of a smooth transition, we see continuity in the coins issued by the mint at Lugdunum (*RIC* 1^2 1–32), which was responsible for precious-metal coinage in the last years of Augustus' reign. Not only did production continue without interruption, but the images on coins in precious metals varied little in the early years of Tiberius' reign from those issued in the later years of Augustus.[4] The only *aes* issues attributed to the mint at Lugdunum (*RIC* 1^2 31–2) feature on the reverse the altar of Roma and Augustus, dedicated by Drusus the Elder in 12 BC (Livy, *Per.* 139; Suet. *Claud.* 2. 1). As we have already seen in Chapter 2, Tiberius restored the Temples to Concordia and the Dioscuri under Augustus in both his name and that of his deceased brother. Although this coin from Lugdunum may feature a local monument, it also subtly recalls the charismatic bond between Augustus as Jupiter and the Dioscuri represented by the dead Drusus and the living Tiberius. The publicizing of this monument would also, presumably, have enhanced the charismatic image of Drusus' son, Germanicus.

Even more telling are the issues of bronze coinage minted at Rome. Here, the predominant message advertised the continuity of Augustus as a divine father to Tiberius (and to all Romans). An analysis of the coin types identified in *Roman Imperial Coinage* (2nd ed.) demonstrates the prevalence of Roman *aes* not only advertising Divus Augustus Pater but also failing to advertise the reigning Tiberius.[5] As Seager (2005: 150)

---

[2] On mint officials consulting the emperor, see Sutherland and Carson 1984: 14 and Pollini 1990: 339.

[3] Molinari (2015: 29–30) analyzes 519 coins, of which 319 (61.5%) promote Divus Augustus Pater and 200 (38.5%) feature Tiberius.

[4] See especially Szaivert 1984: 27.

[5] However, many types with legends honoring Divus Augustus Pater on the obverse (*RIC* 1^2 49, 56, 57, 62, 63, 68, and 69) do feature the picture of Tiberius on the reverse. Some will be discussed below.

Figure 4.1   Divus Augustus Pater *aes*
RIC I^2 72. Image courtesy of the American Numismatic Society

observes, although Octavian did advertise himself as *divi filius*, Tiberius emphasized the *divus* over the *filius*. Of the undated *aes* coinage minted at Rome featuring Divus Augustus Pater on the obverse, only one type (*RIC* I^2 70) features Tiberius on the reverse (with no legend). The other types (71–83) all contain the letters SC with various images, including a draped female figure often identified as Livia (71–3); a round temple, most likely that of Vesta (74–6);[6] Victory holding an oval shield inscribed SPQR (77–8); SC inscribed in an oak wreath (79); the Ara Providentiae discussed in Chapter 2 (80–1); an eagle standing on a globe (82); and a winged thunderbolt (83). With the exception of the Ara Providentiae, none of these images had any strong ties to Tiberius; and the Ara Providentiae was constructed to advertise the *providentia* of Augustus in adopting Tiberius.

Not only was Divus Augustus Pater frequently advertised; the imagery used also reinforced his divinity. On several issues (*RIC* I^2 49, 70–83. Figure 4.1.) he is depicted wearing a radiate crown, a sign of his deification. Augustus was not depicted on coinage wearing a radiate crown in his own lifetime, and Tiberius was never depicted in that way. This is not unexpected since Tiberius, as discussed in Chapter 2, was never deified, nor did he seem interested in deification after his death. However, the radiate crown was not used on coins advertising Divus Iulius or Divus

---

[6] Sutherland argued (1941: 115–16 n. 25) that the Temple of Vesta was temporarily used for the worship of Augustus before the completion of his grand temple in the Forum. Elkins is more circumspect (2015: 70).

Claudius.[7] The other frequently used image of Augustus portrayed him standing in a quadriga drawn by elephants (*RIC* I² 56, 62, 68). Latham (2016: 107) has observed that the elephant-drawn chariot would remind viewers that Augustus was a great conqueror who brought peace to the *orbis terrarum*. Augustus is wearing a radiate crown and holding a laurel wreath, a reminder of his connection to Victory, reinforced also by the Divus Augustus Pater types featuring a seated Augustus wearing a radiate crown on the obverse and Victory with a shield on the reverse (*RIC* I² 77–8).

The final *aes* type which promoted Divus Augustus Pater does not have a portrait of Augustus (*RIC* I² 57, 63, 69). Instead, the legend DIVO AVGVSTO SPQR surrounds a shield with the inscription OB CIVES SER flanked by an oak wreath (*corona civica*) and two Capricorns. The *corona civica* and the legend OB CIVES SER(VATOS) provide a clear reference to the award made by the Senate to Augustus in 27 BC and advertised in the *Res Gestae* (34). In addition to highlighting the end of the civil wars under Augustus, these coins remind their audience that Tiberius' succession preserved that peace. The presence of Capricorn on Tiberian coins is noteworthy as it was the advertised birth sign of Augustus, not Tiberius (Scorpio).[8] Trillmich (1988: 486) observes that provincial issues used Capricorn as a mark of Augustus as a divine savior.[9] In fact, as Terio (2006: 213) remarks, although imperial mints outside Italy had produced coins featuring Capricorn during Augustus' lifetime, the first coins minted at Rome which featured Capricorn were actually struck late in the reign of Tiberius, when he was struggling to secure the succession for a *princeps* from the *domus Augusta*.[10]

The virtues advertised most commonly on Tiberian coins, especially *moderatio* and *clementia*, were meant to reassert his connection to Divus Augustus and reassure everyone that there would be stability during his reign. While both Julius Caesar and Augustus were known for their

---

[7] On the radiate crown in imperial imagery in general, see Bergmann 1998. For other images of Augustus which featured a radiate crown, see Pollini 2012: 149–51.

[8] On the debate over Augustus' horoscope, see especially Lewis 2008 and Volk 2009: 148–51.

[9] On provincial issues featuring Capricorn as a specific allusion to Augustus, see Calomino 2015: 63. See also Burnett et al. 1992: 46. A coin from Cyprus (*RPC* I 3916) dated "Under Augustus?" features Capricorn on one side and Scorpio on the other. *RPC* I 644 from Panormus in Sicily, issued under Tiberius, features the radiate head of Augustus with a thunderbolt and star on the obverse; on the reverse is the name of the local duovir with a Capricorn and triskeles.

[10] Coins from imperial mints featuring Capricorn during Augustus' lifetime: Emerita *RIC* I² 124–30 [denarius], *CBN* 1354, 1358, 1264, *BMCRE* I 344–7; Ephesus *RIC* I² 477 [cistophoros]; Pergamum *RIC* I² 488 [cistophoros], 521–2 [aureus], *BMCRE* I 679–80; uncertain mints after 27 BC *RIC* I² 541–2 [denarius], *BMCRE* I 664, *CBN* 1011; *RIC* I² 547a and b, 548, *BMCRE* I 305 and 307, *CBN* 1278; Lugdunum (12 BC) *RIC* I² 174, *BMCRE* I 465–6.

clementia, moderatio was a uniquely Tiberian virtue.[11] As Cowan (2009a: 482–3) has shown, *moderatio* was particularly exemplified by Tiberius' restraint in exercising power and accepting honors. Other virtues were also advertised besides *clementia* and *moderatio*, including *iustitia, salus,* and *pietas.*[12] Fears (1981b: 890) makes an important connection regarding the dates of these issues, seeing them as "'anniversary' types, marking the fiftieth anniversary of the awarding of the clupeus Virtutis," the shield of virtues presented to Augustus by the Senate (*RG* 34). The virtues specified in the *Res Gestae* as being celebrated on the shield are *clementia, iustitia,* and *pietas.*

One other virtue advertised during the reign of Tiberius evokes the end of the reign of Augustus – *concordia.* Coins dated to 34/35 feature the Temple of Concordia without any concurrent legend. This commemorated not only the twenty-fifth anniversary of Tiberius' dedication of the Temple of Concordia but also the twentieth anniversary of his acceptance of his father's *statio.* While Cox argues (1993: 261) that Tiberius was attempting to distinguish himself from Augustus at this point, she admits that other *aes* issues from this time period (*RIC* I² 56 and 57, dated to 34/35; 62 and 63, dated to 35/36; 68 and 69, dated to 36/37) all celebrate Augustus, especially in his aspects as victor and the savior who ended the civil wars. No symbol could be more apt to celebrate Tiberius as having preserved this stability than the Temple of Concordia, which Tiberius both vowed and completed while Augustus was still princeps, dedicated in his own name and in that of his brother Drusus, grandfather of the soon-to-be princeps Caligula.

While images on coins minted by the government in Rome may have been influenced by Tiberius and his advisers, provincial coins reflect the perception of the messages the princeps was sending. Burnett et al. give a solid analysis of the complicated process for choosing designs for coins by provincial mints in their catalog of *Roman Provincial Coinage* (1992: 1.1–54). The contributors (1992: 3) agree that "permission was a requirement" for provincial coinage, both for the issues themselves and for the images chosen for those issues. Local mint officials, like the *tresviri monetales* at Rome, would have been ambitious politicians attempting to win favor. They would be imitating Roman coin types or responding to messages distributed officially through state documents, all the while

---

[11] On *clementia* and *moderatio* on coins under Tiberius, see Levick 1975 and Sutherland 1979. On Tiberian *clementia* (and *severitas*) in literary sources, especially Velleius and Tacitus, see Cowan 2016. On *clementia* in general, see Dowling 2006.

[12] Iustitia *BMCRE* I 79–80, *RIC* I² 46; Salus Augusta *BMCRE* I 81–4, *RIC* I² 47; Pietas *BMCRE* I 98, *RIC* I² 43; Clementia *BMCRE* I 85–9, *RIC* I² 38; Moderatio *BMCRE* I 90, *RIC* I² 39–40.

attempting to promote themselves and/or their cities. Once again, as in the case of Roman issues, Augustus features prominently on provincial coins minted during Tiberius' reign. Hekster (2015: 172) notes that Divus Augustus was depicted on provincial coins from thirty-seven mints in the reign of Tiberius and only from twenty-two mints under all the other Julio-Claudians combined.

Not only legends and portraits but even specific images might be copied by provincial mints. For example, Mytilene issued coins imitating the previously mentioned *aes* issues from Rome which honored Divus Augustus Pater and showed him in a quadriga pulled by elephants (*RPC* 1 2343). Coins from Cyprus (*RPC* 1 3917–8) also copied Roman issues honoring Augustus. In the West, a similar trend can be seen, especially in coins issued by Spanish mints. Tarraco, site of the Temple of Divus Augustus discussed in Chapter 2, only struck provincial issues during the reigns of Augustus and Tiberius. Coins issued under Tiberius focused heavily on Tarraco as having been granted the right to build the first official Temple of Divus Augustus in the provinces. Of the Tiberian coins from Tarraco featured in *Roman Provincial Coinage*, catalog numbers 218–20 are inscribed DIVVS AVGVSTVS PATER and show Augustus wearing a radiate crown; 219 has on its reverse an octastyle temple with C V T T AETERNITATIS AVGVSTAE, advertising the right to build the provincial temple; 221–4 feature the legend DEO AVGVSTO and show Augustus seated holding Victory on a globe, with 222 and 224 having the same image as 219 on the reverse; 225–7 feature Tiberius on the obverse, with 226 having the same reverse as 219; 228–30 have Tiberius wearing a laurel crown on the obverse and Divus Augustus Pater with a radiate crown on the reverse. Thus, only two coins issued during the reign of Tiberius in Tarraco neglected to honor Divus Augustus directly. One of these (225) features on its reverse an altar with a palm, likely a reference to an altar to Augustus built while he was living.[13] That leaves only one issue (227) which seems to have no direct connection to Divus Augustus (other than the legend surrounding the portrait of Tiberius, TI CAESAR DIVI AVG F AVGVSTVS). Tarraco had a specific reason to advertise its support of the cult of Divus Augustus. Other Spanish cities followed suit, including Romula (*RPC* 1 73), Italica (*RPC* 1 66–7), and Emerita (*RPC* 1 20–37).

This trend of provincial mints following the patterns of coins issued from Rome was widespread both temporally and geographically. Indeed,

---

[13] Quint. 6.3.77. See Fishwick 2014.

while one might expect provinces to honor the living princeps as opposed to a dead one, we do not see this under Tiberius. According to the index of *Roman Provincial Coinage*: 101 cities issued coins with dedications to Divus Augustus under Tiberius, 8 under Caligula, 17 under Claudius, and 8 under Nero. One city issued coins honoring Germanicus under Augustus, 31 under Tiberius, 31 under Caligula, 2 under Claudius; 5 coins were issued honoring the twin sons of Drusus the Younger; 9 cities issued coins honoring Drusus and Nero, sons of Germanicus; 7 cities issued coins under Tiberius honoring Caligula. The evidence is clear. Provincial mints found it easier to look backwards than forwards during the reign of Tiberius. They were taking their lead from Rome itself, where Tiberius continually promoted the image of Divus Augustus Pater, sometimes at the expense of prospective heirs. Calomino observes, "On both imperial and provincial coinage Divus Augustus is essentially an 'obverse,' i.e., an emperor; he has maintained his authority even as a deified ruler" (2015: 75). Calomino gives the example of coins minted by Italica and Romula in Spain under Tiberius which include the formula PERM(ISSV) DIVI AVG (VSTI) (*RPC* 1 64–5, 73). Even after his death, Augustus served as an authority figure and guarantor of security.

While many provincial coins featured clear imitations of images from Rome, some were more ambiguous. In analyzing the messages on provincial coins, we run into the problem, particularly in eastern issues, of nomenclature. On coins from the Lugdunum and Roman mints, Tiberius is usually titled TI CAESAR DIVI AVG F AVGVSTVS. However, provincial mints in the East were unclear about how to deal with the hereditary titles "Caesar" and "Augustus." As Burnett (2011: 15) shows, the second most common designation used for Tiberius on eastern coins was simply SEBASTOS (ΣΕΒΑΣΤΟΣ), which appears 22 times, as opposed to 25 for TI KAISAR SEBASTOS. Surprisingly, this confusion regarding whether "Sebastos" was a title or a name did not carry over into the reigns of later emperors. A similar confusion arises over the portraits of the emperor which appear on provincial coins, especially when they occur without a legend. For example, *RPC* 1 2558 (Dioshieron) could be either Augustus or Tiberius. This phenomenon began under Tiberius and continued under Caligula and Claudius. Augustus' heirs were simply an extension of Divus Augustus.

Divus Augustus in Tiberian Documents

The most important documents from the reign of Tiberius concern his adoptive father Augustus and his adopted son Germanicus. The *Res Gestae* was a document written by Augustus and promoted by Tiberius.[14] Indeed, Scheid (2016: 50–1) proposes that we should not view Augustus as the sole author of the *Res Gestae*, likening it to speeches given by modern politicians. Given the role played by Tiberius late in the reign of Augustus, Tiberius may have helped Augustus edit the document in its final form. The publication of the *Res Gestae Divi Augusti* has been closely connected to the propagation of the cult of Divus Augustus, as the most complete (and famous) copy was found at the Temple of Augustus and Roma at Ankyra. Although a copy has not been found at Rome, we know that it was inscribed on bronze tablets placed outside the Mausoleum of Augustus. In this respect, it served many functions, including justifying the deification of Augustus, providing *exempla* for later generations, and giving prestige to the living members of the *domus Augusta*.[15]

Peachin (2013: 269) argues that Augustus was publicly leaving instructions to shape the post-Augustan principate. In this light, we must look at certain ways in which the *Res Gestae* fashioned Tiberius' own self-presentation. In a passage where he specifically refers to his son Tiberius as his colleague in the *lustrum* ending the census of 14, Augustus states, "By the passage of new laws I revived many *exempla* of our ancestors at the time passing out of our custom, and I myself handed down *exempla* of many things for posterity to imitate" (*Legibus novis latis complura exempla maiorum exolescentia iam ex nostro usu revocavi et ipse multarum rerum exempla imitanda posteris tradidi, RG* 8.5). The reference to Tiberius as his son and the notion of *exempla imitanda* signal the need for Augustus' successor to imitate his *exempla*. Moreover, these *exempla* demonstrate the charismatic nature of Augustus' position as princeps. He professes to have done things no one else had ever done, carefully framing his achievements within the comfort zone of those wanting to believe in the myths of the past. As Ferrary (2003: 421) observes, it was not the offices which he accumulated that made Augustus princeps but the extraordinary honors he was awarded. By inheriting the *statio* of his father, Tiberius had to walk a fine line between excessive honors and refusal of power. As we have seen in the difficulties he experienced negotiating his position with the Senate, as well as in the criticism described by Tacitus regarding his refusal of divine honors, he was not always successful. And yet, Tiberius' refusal of many of

---

[14] For the text and English translation, see Cooley 2009; cf. Scheid 2007, who also provides the text and a French translation. For Tiberius' responsibility in the dissemination of the *Res Gestae*, see Millar 1988: 11–12.

[15] On the possible functions of the *Res Gestae*, see Scheid 2016. On the exemplary nature of Augustus' *Res Gestae*, see Yavetz 1984.

the honors awarded to Augustus preserved and in some cases increased the reverence of all classes of Roman society for the founder of the principate.

This reverence can be seen in another document from the East in the early years of Tiberius' reign. An inscription in both Greek and Latin regarding the requisitioning of carts in Pisidia suggests the language which the governor of this region felt was appropriate. The inscription, transcribed and translated by Mitchell (1976), begins as follows:

> Sextus Sotidius Strabo Libuscidianus, *legatus pro praetore* of Tiberius Caesar Augustus, says: It is the most unjust thing of all for me to tighten up by my own edict that which the Augusti, one the greatest of gods, the other the greatest of emperors, have taken the utmost care to prevent, namely that no one should make use of carts without payment.[16]

Regardless of when the decree was published, the wording designates Augustus as the greatest of gods and Tiberius as the greatest of principes, maintaining the distinction between the two which Tiberius preserved throughout his reign.[17] However, both men are considered Augusti. As we have already seen in the case of coinage, Augustus/Sebastos was the most frequent designation for Tiberius besides his own name in the East. The legate adds to his own authority mandates handed down by a *princeps optimus* (ll. 6–7). While it may not seem clear initially whether the inscription refers to Augustus or Tiberius here, Mitchell (1976: 113) believes it must be Augustus. Either way, the ambiguity expresses the governor's respect for the power of Rome. The charismatic nature of Augustus' reign has been enshrined in the notion that his hand-picked successor will also be a *princeps optimus*.[18]

Unquestionably, the most famous documents dating to the reign of Tiberius surround the death of Germanicus: the *Tabula Siarensis*, the *Tabula Hebana*, and the *Senatus Consultum de Cn. Pisone patre*.[19] We will discuss Piso's supposed involvement in Germanicus' death and its portrayal in later sources in Chapter 6. Here we are concerned solely with the way in which the Senate and Tiberius presented these events publicly. The *Tabula Hebana* (*TH*) and the *Tabula Siarensis* (*TS*), along with fragments grouped under *CIL* VI 31199, are together referred to as

---

[16] ll. 3–4: *Est quidem omnium iniquissimum me edicto meo adstringere id quod Augusti alter deorum alter principum // maximus diligentissime caverunt, ne quis gratuitis vehiculis utatur.* The Greek version uses the phrase ὑπὸ τῶν Σεβαστῶν τοῦ μὲν θεῶν τοῦ δὲ αὐτοκρατόρων μεγείστου.

[17] Mitchell (1976: 113) dates the document to shortly after Augustus' death but acknowledges the language is consistent with Tiberius' attitude throughout his reign.

[18] On contemporary references to Tiberius as *optimus princeps*, see Cowan 2009a: 483–5.

[19] This section is revised from the previously published Edwards 2012.

the *lex* or *rogatio Valeria Aurelia* and detail the posthumous honors decreed to Germanicus.[20] The *Tabula Siarensis*, discovered in Spain in the 1980s, is a senatorial decree detailing resolutions passed in December of 19, roughly two months after the death of Germanicus (October 10). The decree ends with a resolution to bring the matter before the people. This then led to the *rogatio* inscribed on the *Tabula Hebana*, discovered in Italy in the 1950s. The list of honors on these inscriptions includes some which had already been enacted and others that would still follow.

Before looking at these honors, we should briefly discuss the authorship of these decrees and how they were created. The *Tabula Siarensis* explicitly states that Tiberius selected the honors in consultation with other members of the *domus Augusta*, specifically Drusus, Livia, and Antonia (*TS* 1, 4–8). At one point in the *Tabula Siarensis*, discussed further below, the Senate cites Tiberius as the source of a particular proposition. Tiberius and the Senate clearly worked together to select the honors granted to Germanicus.[21] And while many of the honors are reminiscent of those granted posthumously to Augustus' grandsons/adopted sons Gaius and Lucius, others have more specific connotations. In particular, we see honors granted to Germanicus which ensure that his memory will live on. We also see Germanicus incorporated into the annual rituals which celebrate the divinity of the *domus Augusta*.[22] But most importantly, we see the charismatic Germanicus associated with the future of the Augustan system even after his death.[23]

In these documents, the Senate ordered the construction of three arches: one in Rome, one in Germania, and one in Syria.[24] The arch of Germanicus in Rome was to be placed near statues of Divus Augustus and other members of the *domus Augusta* (*TS* 1, 10).[25] This mention of the statuary group advertises Augustus' role as founder of the *domus Augusta*.

---

[20] For a reconstruction with commentary, see Crawford 1996: 1.507–45. Sánchez-Ostiz Gutiérrez 1999 has an extensive commentary on the various emendations to the *Tabula Siarensis*, especially by Lebek (1986, 1987, and 1993), since its original publication by González (1984); cf. González and Fernández 1981. On the list of honors at Tac. *Ann.* 2.83 and their relationship to these decrees, see González 1999.

[21] On Tiberius' role in shaping this decree, see Lebek 1986: 32–5 and Rowe 2002: 60.

[22] Lebek 1993.

[23] "The honors granted for the memory of Germanicus were numerous and lasting, more lasting than the honors granted to any other imperial prince" (Weinstock 1966: 898). Cf. Weinstock 1957.

[24] On these arches, see Lebek 1987.

[25] This statuary group in the Circus Flaminius was dedicated by C. Norbanus Flaccus in 15 during his tenure as consul. The statues are now lost, along with any inscription(s) which may have used the phrase *domus Augusta*. For suggestions about the possible statues included in the group, see Flory 1996.

Moreover, certain associations are summoned by the phrase *domus Augusta*, here used for the first time in a senatorial decree.[26] Tiberius is completely absent from the arch itself, which was to feature statues of Germanicus, Drusus the Elder, Antonia, Livilla, Claudius, and Germanicus' children (*TS* 1, 18–21). Flory (1996: 302) believes that the absence of Tiberius and Livia from the statuary on Germanicus' arch minimizes Germanicus' role in the succession scheme and moves him back into the *gens Claudia*.[27] Then why build the arch so close to a statuary group celebrating the *domus Augusta*, which was founded on the *gens Iulia*? Agrippina, Antonia, and Germanicus' children, all blood relatives of Augustus, were to be featured on the arch. Surely, the intention was to secure Augustus' charisma for the next generation, the sons of Germanicus and Agrippina.

The associations between Augustus and Germanicus continue in the list of honors related to certain religious festivals. Germanicus' *sellae curules* were to be displayed at the Ludi Augustales. Statues of Germanicus were to be taken from the Temple of Concordia and displayed at the Ludi Victoriae (*TS* 111b, 2–12).[28] Eventually, they would be housed in the temple of his deified grandfather, which was currently under construction. In the meantime, they were to be exhibited in the Temple of Mars Ultor (*TH* 50–4), the temporary house of worship for Divus Augustus. Likewise, his name would be included in the Salian Hymn (*TH* 4–5; *TS* 11c, 18–9). While Tiberius never received this honor, it was granted to Augustus within his own lifetime (*RG* 10). Finally, every year the Sodales Augustales would perform a sacrifice before a *tumulum* (*TH* 59–62). Weinstock (1966: 896; cf. Crawford 1996: 1.521, 542) believes this to be the Mausoleum of Augustus, where Germanicus was buried (Tac. *Ann.* 3.4.1). Germanicus' memory would be preserved, as would his prominence as the grandson of Divus Augustus.

Germanicus' image was further commemorated through *imagines clipeatae* of both himself and his father Drusus, which were to be displayed in the porticus of the Temple of Apollo on the Palatine (*TH* 1), a temple

---

[26] For the repercussions of this designation on the imperial cult, see Chapter 2. On the history of the term and its significance, see Corbier 1994, Wardle 2000, and Corbier 2001. The specific phrase *domus Augusta* first appears in Ovid, *Ex Ponto* 2.2.74. For more on Ovid's use of the phrase, see Chapter 5.

[27] Tiberius could hardly advertise himself as Germanicus' father without awkwardly usurping his brother's position as Antonia's husband.

[28] For a reconstruction of these lines, see Lebek 1988; his suggestions are followed by Sánchez-Ostiz Gutiérrez 1999: 263–80.

built by Augustus adjacent to his own house.[29] These *imagines* of Germanicus and Drusus were to be located next to a statue of Apollo, a god with whom Augustus expressed a special affinity.[30] The *Tabula Siarensis* specifies that this *senatus consultum* would be inscribed in the porticus where the Senate regularly met (*TS* 11b, 20–21).[31] In addition to the *senatus consultum*, the deeds of Germanicus would be incised on bronze and publicly displayed with speeches by Tiberius and Drusus which praised Germanicus (*TS* 11b, 11–19).[32] The Senate does not clarify the location, but it would undoubtedly have been a place tied to the *domus Augusta* and Divus Augustus.

The agitation of the people over the death of Germanicus led them to enter into a voluntary state of mourning. The state declared an official *iustitium* on December 8. By the end of the month, the Senate had drawn up the documents recorded on the *Tabula Siarensis* and the *Tabula Hebana*. The arrival of Agrippina in Rome, bearing the ashes of Germanicus, brought a renewal of public outrage, directed in particular at Tiberius, his mother, and their friends Piso and Plancina. Tiberius decided to bring the matter before the Senate. An inscription found on bronze tablets in Spain, known as the *Senatus Consultum de Cn. Pisone patre* (*SCPP*), was deliberately written for publication in Rome, the provinces, and, perhaps most importantly, legionary camps (*SCPP* 169–72).[33] The *SCPP* was ratified on December 10, 20, roughly one year after the publication of the *Tabula Siarensis* and *Tabula Hebana*. The language of the *SCPP* was constructed to reassure all citizens of the Roman Empire, the plebs, and the army in particular that the *domus Augusta* and the *res publica* were healthy after the crisis produced by Piso's insubordination.[34] Tiberius was directly responsible for sending Piso to accompany Germanicus in the East; thus, he was the target of suspicion and public

---

[29] On the house of Augustus and the adjacent buildings, see Wiseman 2019.

[30] On Apollo in Augustan Rome, see Miller 2009.

[31] See especially Thompson 1981 and Corbier 1992.

[32] *[...]men, quod Ti(berius) Caesar Aug(ustus) in eo ordine a(nte) d(iem) XVII K(alendas) Ian(uarias) // [...] suo proposuisset, in aere incisum figeretur loco publico // [...] placeret...* (11–13). The lacuna at *TS* 11b, 11 has been variously interpreted as *carmen* or *volumen*. I prefer the reading of Lebek 1986: 38–41, who tentatively proposes *volumen* as preferable to González and Fernández 1981: 10, who suggest *carmen*; cf. Schillinger-Häfele 1988: 73–81 and Dumont 2000: 189–200.

[33] The definitive edition of the *SCPP* is that of Eck et al. 1996. For reviews with further analysis, see Griffin 1997, Potter 1998, and Yakobson 1998. New fragments have been discovered that contain parts of the inscription already published; see Stylow and Corzo 1999 and Bartels 2009.

[34] On the use of the *SCPP* to create *consensus* by exaggerating the danger presented by Piso, see Hurlet 2009: 135–40.

outrage.[35] As a result, the *SCPP* foregrounds the charisma of Divus Augustus and the family of Germanicus (through which, of course, the bloodline of Augustus would be continued), charisma which would guarantee the stability of the empire.

The *Tabula Siarensis* and *Tabula Hebana* state that the imperial family was consulted regarding the honors accorded to Germanicus, but the Senate ultimately takes responsibility. The *SCPP* (4–11), however, explicitly states that the decree was passed in response to *relationes* which Tiberius brought before the Senate. Throughout the document the Senate refers to Tiberius as *princeps noster*. Calboli concludes (1998: 129) that, while this is certainly in line with Augustan precedent, it also emphasizes Tiberius' role as *princeps senatus*. We can see further evidence of Tiberius aligning himself with the Senate in his *subscriptio*, written in the first person: *Ti. Caesar Aug(ustus) trib (unicia) potestate (vicesimo secundo) manu mea scripsi* (174). In his *subscriptio*, Tiberius uses only his *tribunicia potestas*.[36] Severy (2000: 334) believes that Tiberius was trying to distance himself from his family, especially his mother, who is clearly identified in the document as having protected Piso's wife, Plancina. Perhaps, but in doing so he removes his own currently unpopular persona from an otherwise charismatic family. This enhances the image of the *domus Augusta*.

As Tiberius aligns himself with the Senate, Augustus becomes the representative of the *domus*. The importance of Augustus in this decree is clear from the beginning. Augustus (not including the epithets *Iulia Augusta* and *domus Augusta*) is mentioned directly by name eight times in the *SCPP*.[37] When the Senate commences its declarations regarding the punishment of Piso, it offers thanks to the gods that Piso was not successful in his nefarious plans which threatened the *tranquillitatem praesentis status r(ei) p(ublicae)* (13–4). As the editors of the *SCPP* have noted, this phrase recalls Augustan parallels. The fact that the *res publica* was *tranquilliore statu* thanks to Augustus was celebrated on the coins of the *triumvir monetalis* L. Mescinius Rufus (*BMCRE* I 91–4).[38] The Senate condemns Piso's attempt to disturb the peace enjoyed "for a long time now through the *numen* of Divus Augustus and the virtues of Tiberius Caesar

---

[35] Drogula (2015) argues that Germanicus was actually sent to spy on Piso and not the other way around.

[36] The introduction to the *relationes* lists his other titles as well (4–5).

[37] Lines 4 (*Divi Augusti filius* in Tiberius' title), 46, 52, 69, 86, 92, 138, 142.

[38] For other parallels in Suetonius, Velleius, and Valerius Maximus, see Eck et al. 1996: 142. See also Potter 1998: 442.

Augustus" (47). The *SCPP* further states that Piso threatened the military discipline instituted by Divus Augustus and preserved by Tiberius (52–3).

Other references to Divus Augustus occur unexpectedly. The most prominent of these is the charge that Piso violated the *numen* of Augustus.[39] The text is damaged; the extant parts make it clear that Piso committed an offense against the memory and images of Divus Augustus before his deification (*ante quam in deorum numerum referretur*, 68–70).[40] Fishwick (2007: 297–300) proposes that the offenses committed by Piso would have occurred just after the death of Augustus. The accusation that Piso disrespected the *numen* of Divus Augustus immediately follows charges that Piso rejoiced at the death of Germanicus (62–8). If Fishwick is correct, Piso disrespected Augustus shortly after his death just as he did Germanicus. The *SCPP* specifies that Piso's name would be erased from the statue of Germanicus dedicated by the Sodales Augustales near the Ara Providentiae (82–4). As we have already discussed in Chapter 2, this altar commemorated Tiberius' adoption of Germanicus and Augustus' adoption of Tiberius. Piso's name on this inscription, his betrayal compounded by the fact that he was a member of the Sodales Augustales, was a painful reminder that he scorned the *domus Augusta* and tried to upset the arrangement laid out so carefully by Divus Augustus.

After detailing the proceedings against Piso and his family, the Senate turns to the imperial family, offering all the members of the *domus Augusta* praise for their conduct in this affair. This *gratiarum actio*, which also thanks the various *ordines* of Roman society for their devotion, occupies about a quarter of the text (roughly 40 lines of the extant 176). The Senate emphasizes the relationship certain members of the *domus* have to both Augustus and Germanicus. They also stress the importance of the *domus* to the safety of the empire and encourage all orders of society to maintain loyalty to the house of Augustus. The Senate addresses Tiberius first, proclaiming that Tiberius' *pietas* exceeded that of all other parents (123–4). Tiberius displayed the same *pietas* towards his adopted son which he had shown to his adoptive father. After the exhortation to Tiberius, the Senate briefly recognizes Livia and Drusus as having learned virtues from Tiberius, especially *moderatio* and *iustitia*, virtues celebrated, as we have already seen, on Tiberian coins.[41] They too are praised for their *pietas*

---

[39] As Cowan notes, this charge does not appear in the original *relatio*: "The senate may even have sought to stress that this charge was their own addition" (2009a: 473).

[40] For further discussion of this passage, see Marcone 2015.

[41] On the connection between virtues attributed to members of the *domus Augusta* and those inscribed on the Augustan *clipeus virtutis*, see Potter 1998: 450.

towards Germanicus (132–6). The Senate then moves on to the other members of the *domus Augusta*.

Eck et al. (1996: 243) have noted in their commentary that the unusual *gratiarum actio* conveyed on the behalf of the Senate to the women of the imperial household, especially to Agrippina, pointedly connects them to Augustus and not Tiberius. The Senate refers to Agrippina as having been *probatissima* to Divus Augustus and having lived in unique *concordia* with her husband, Germanicus (137–9). The Senate concludes by admiring Agrippina's fertility. Her children continue the bloodline of Augustus and ensure the future prosperity of the *domus Augusta*. The Senate also praises Antonia, the mother of Germanicus (140–2). Antonia's close relationship (*tam arta propinquitate*) to Divus Augustus is emphasized as well as the fact that she was worthy of this relationship due to the sanctity of her moral conduct. The Senate applauds her chastity and loyalty to her deceased husband Drusus, the father of Germanicus. Antonia, as the niece of Augustus, passed on his blood to her son Germanicus. Through the offspring of his marriage to Agrippina, the granddaughter of Augustus, Germanicus has ensured the continuity of the *domus Augusta*. Livilla, the sister of Germanicus (and wife of Drusus the Younger), also receives her share of accolades. Her presence here among the more prominent members of the family seems ironic in light of the accusations that she later betrayed that family to Sejanus.[42] In comparison with Agrippina, the other daughter-in-law of Tiberius, Livilla's place (and that of her children) is minimized. Livilla had given birth to twins in the midst of the turmoil surrounding the death of Germanicus (Tac. *Ann.* 2.84). Tacitus claims that the birth of these twins caused concern among the plebs that Germanicus' line would be supplanted. While the *SCPP* praises Agrippina's fertility, mentioning her eldest son Nero by name (147), it is silent on the subject of Livilla's offspring.[43]

After giving thanks to the members of the imperial family, the Senate turns its attention to the other orders of Roman society. The stratified classes all share one common trait, loyalty toward the house of Augustus. First, the Senate acknowledges the equestrian order (152–4). The Senate praises the *equites* for recognizing that the *salus* of the *domus* was the *salus omnium*. Next, the Senate commends the plebs for its *pietas* (155–8). The *pietas* of the plebs towards Tiberius is paired with their reverence for the

---

[42] As Eck et al. (1996: 242) comment, Livilla is omitted from the list of those thanked by the Senate in Tacitus' narrative (*Ann.* 3.18.3).

[43] The document thanks Germanicus' brother Claudius last (148), corroborating Tacitus (*Ann.* 3.18.3–4)

memory of Germanicus. The *SCPP* admits that the fervor demonstrated by the plebs against Piso was nearly out of control but gives this enthusiasm a positive spin by asserting that the restraint the plebs exhibited in not lynching Piso was modeled on the actions of their princeps. The *SCPP* exploits a negative episode to advertise the extreme loyalty the plebs felt towards the *domus Augusta*.

Last, but certainly not least, the Senate thanks the army (159–65). Again, their *pietas* towards the *domus Augusta* is praised as is their awareness that the *salus* of the empire depends on this one family. As the editors of the *SCPP* have commented (Eck. et al. 1996: 251), throughout the other parts of the *gratiarum actio* the Senate extols the past actions of members of the imperial house and Roman society. Here, however, the language stresses the need for future loyalty from the army. The Senate encourages the army to cultivate the *nomen Caesarum*. Only a few years earlier the legions of Germania and Pannonia had mutinied upon news of Augustus' death. The *Tabula Siarensis, Tabula Hebana*, and *SCPP* seem to have effectively reassured the soldiers that Germanicus' memory would not be forgotten. Moreover, the *Senatus Consultum de Cn. Pisone*, like the *Tabula Siarensis* and *Tabula Hebana*, foregrounds the images of Augustus and Germanicus, both dead, as opposed to those of Tiberius and Drusus, the living princeps and his heir. The charismatic members of the family provide legitimacy to those who lack charisma.

Divus Augustus in Tiberian Sculpture

As Vout has observed, the need for Tiberius to appear to be the son of Augustus alongside the numerous images of Augustus which were installed in his lifetime led to a dilemma. Tiberius had to portray himself as "'Augustus two,' authentic and indisputable, but in an environment in which the original Augustus is still omnipresent, in building and statuary" (2013: 61). Koortbojian (2013: 188) has also noted the perception from public imagery in the early reign of Tiberius that Augustus was actually still emperor and Tiberius was merely a cipher. The proliferation of images of Augustus from before his death, combined with a new emphasis on Augustus' divine charisma in numerous posthumous statues, helped to reinforce Tiberius' presentation of himself as continuing to rule under the auspices of Augustus.[44]

---

[44] Von den Hoff (2011: 31) cites more than 200 "rundplastische Bildnisse" of Augustus, of which only about 50 percent date to his own lifetime. Højte, in his analysis of statue bases, concludes, "The

By far the most famous extant image of Augustus is the full-length statue of him wearing a breastplate found at Livia's villa at Prima Porta.[45] For years, scholars have tied this statue to the return of Roman standards from the Parthians in 20 BC. However, especially given the find site, it may have been designed and sculpted significantly later. Few scholars have been willing to go so far as to assert that the image is posthumous, but there is no definitive proof.[46] Since the image was found at Livia's villa, the soldier featured on the breastplate and accepting submission from a barbarian (Parthian or otherwise) could very well be Augustus' most trusted general in the latter part of his reign, Tiberius. Although Tiberius did not personally receive the standards returned to the Romans by the Parthians, his march on Armenia was instrumental in forcing the Parthian king to make a diplomatic agreement with Augustus.[47] Even if the Roman soldier depicted is not Tiberius, the image itself is a reminder of the role Tiberius played in helping Augustus subjugate recalcitrant barbarians, echoed on other works, most notably the Boscoreale Cups and the Gemma Augustea.

The statue from Prima Porta was found in a private setting but may have been modeled on a public monument. Augustus' lengthy tenure as princeps had produced an unprecedented number of statues honoring him throughout the Roman world. There has been much debate in recent decades regarding the creation of portrait types based on models made in the capital.[48] Here I would like to focus on the consensus regarding images of Augustus, especially after his death, and images of Tiberius, both subsequent to his adoption by Augustus and after becoming princeps. Whether or not the assimilation of "Augustan" features in portraits of Tiberius was a result of pressure from above or perception from below (or most likely a combination of both), there is little doubt that images of Augustus after his death enhanced his divine aspects. At the same time, while portraits of Tiberius took on certain physical characteristics to make him look more as if he were the son of Augustus, the divine father and the mortal son were clearly differentiated.

---

bases indicate that nearly one-quarter of all portraits of Augustus were created posthumously"
(2005: 192; cf. 133).

[45] On the find spot, see Reeder 1997.

[46] Simpson speculates: "If we accept Kähler's [1959] suggestion that the statue was sculpted after Augustus's death, it may be observed that the iconography of the Prima Porta breastplate corresponds closely to Augustus's nearly contemporary final testament" (2005b: 89).

[47] Popkin 2018: 275.

[48] See especially the series *Das römische Herrscherbild*, with volumes on Augustus by Boschung (1993a) and on Tiberius by Hertel (2013). See also von den Hoff 2011 and Hekster 2020.

The portrayal of Augustus as the divine *paterfamilias* and *pater patriae* casts a long shadow over the reign of Tiberius. We have already mentioned above the statue group in Rome, dedicated by C. Norbanus in 15 and now lost, honoring Divus Augustus and the *domus Augusta*. There was also a statue of Augustus dedicated by Livia and Tiberius near the Theater of Marcellus.[49] Since neither of these images still exists nor do any detailed descriptions of them, we are forced to rely on extant pieces. In instances where bases have been found, Augustus' status as a *divus* is clear. But, given certain allowances made during his own lifetime for types of divine worship (as discussed in Chapter 2), it is often difficult to interpret statues found out of context. For example, many images of Augustus have been found, especially outside of Rome, in which he is nude or semi-nude. The state of undress has often been used to identify these images as representing Divus Augustus. However, images of Tiberius also exist which are semi-nude, and he was never deified. Hallett (2005: 224–30) has convincingly argued that while there are superhuman or heroic aspects of nude or semi-nude statues, more often than not Divus Augustus is depicted as togate, even with his head covered (*capite velato*).

In particular, Hallett (2005: 230) points to the addition of the radiate crown to images of Augustus as a definitive marker of deification, akin to the star used to designate Divus Iulius.[50] Unfortunately, our best evidence for images of Augustus wearing a radiate crown comes from coins (see above), cameos, and statues outside of Italy.[51] Márquez (2019: 266) believes that a statue from Baetica of Divus Augustus Pater bears holes which would have been used to hold a radiate crown and that this image was modeled on the statue dedicated by Livia and Tiberius near the Theater of Marcellus.[52] Bergmann (1998: 118) asserts that this radiate crown was superior to the star which appeared on the head of some images of Divus Iulius. First, the very idea of a crown was something which, in Republican tradition, had to be awarded by the state, either as an oak

---

[49] Tacitus (*Ann.* 3.64) mentions the dedication under the year 22 as having happened not long before Livia's illness. Flory (1996: 288) assumes this means the statue was dedicated in that year, but it may have been dedicated in a previous year. The *Fasti Praenestini* gives the date of the dedication as April 23 and corroborates Tacitus' assertion that Livia's name preceded that of Tiberius. See the *Acta Fratrum Arvalium* (Scheid 1998: 30) for a sacrifice *ante simulacrum divi Augusti*.

[50] On the use of various crowns in imperial iconography, see Bergmann 2010. On the radiate crown as a signifier of Augustus' deification, see Bergmann 1998: 107–26.

[51] Divus Augustus is wearing a radiate crown on the Grand Camée as well as on a cameo of Livia as priestess of Augustus now in the Kunsthistorisches Museum in Vienna. See below for further discussion.

[52] He believes this to be the statue depicted on *RIC* I^2 49.

crown (*corona civica*) or as a triumphal laurel crown (*corona laurea*). This reinforced the fact that Augustus was deified by the Senate immediately upon his death, a stark contrast to the tumultuous path Caesar took to become a god. Secondly, the radiate crown was associated with the sun god Sol, or in the case of Augustus, Apollo. Like the sun, Augustus looked down on his subjects from the heavens and ensured the continuation of his divine beneficence. The radiate crown also recalled the idea of a golden age initiated by Augustus. The radiate crown became the province solely of Augustus during the reign of Tiberius and was used to underscore the difference between the deified Augustus and the human Tiberius.

Clearly, Augustus was portrayed as Divus Augustus Pater during the reign of Tiberius. But how did portraits of Tiberius connect him to Augustus while maintaining reverence for the *divus*? The analysis and dating of different portrait types poses challenges. In recent years, scholars, especially in Germany, have identified portraits of male members of the imperial family based on their hairstyles.[53] Despite detailed descriptions and sketches of various "locks," the three main scholars who have produced studies on portraits of Tiberius in recent years have failed to come to an agreement. Dietrich Boschung (1990, 1993b, 2002) laid the ground-work in his studies of portraits of the imperial family, designating six different portrait types for Tiberius. John Pollini, in his publications on two newly discovered busts of Tiberius (2005 and 2008), offered his own numerical portrait types, which differed slightly from those created by Boschung. Finally, Dieter Hertel, in his catalog of Tiberian portraits for *Das römische Herrscherbild* series (2013), proposed yet another arrange-ment and dating scheme for portrait types of Tiberius, one which was criticized by Boschung in his review of this work (2014). As seen in Table 4.1, there is no definitive agreement as to which portrait type of Tiberius was created first and which was created last.[54]

Including posthumous, spurious, and relief portraits of Tiberius, Hertel (2013) has catalogued 225 sculptural images. Many of these were pro-duced before Tiberius' reign, even before his adoption by Augustus. Von

---

[53] Although, as Pollini (1999: 725) comments, adhering too scrupulously to this method can be problematic. Perhaps more promising, although in its early stages, is the use of facial recognition technology. See the study by Srirangachar Ramesh et al. 2022. For background and discussion of the study of imperial portraiture in modern scholarship, see Heijnen 2021, which includes an extensive catalog of statues termed "The Roman Imperial Portraits Dataset" and appendices examining findspots.

[54] For other studies of Tiberian portraiture, see Polacco 1955, Mlasowsky 1996: 308–27, and Megow 2000.

Table 4.1 *Portraits of Tiberius as identified by Boschung, Pollini, and Hertel*

Type	Boschung	Pollini	Hertel
I	Basel, created 27 BC	Basel, created ca. 19 BC	Ephesos-Munich, created between 16 & 11 BC
II	Copenhagen 623, created 11 BC	Copenhagen 623, created 11 BC	Basel, created between 13 & 8 BC
III	Ephesos-Munich, created before 4	Berlin-Naples-Sorrento, created ca. 4	Copenhagen 623, created between 11 & 7 BC
IV	Berlin-Naples-Sorrento, created ca. 4	Ephesos-Munich, created ca. 10	Berlin-Naples-Sorrento, created 4
V	Chiaramonti, late Augustan	Copenhagen 624, post 14	Chiaramonti, created between 10 & 13
VI	Copenhagen 624, post 14	Chiaramonti, post 31	Copenhagen 624, post 14

den Hoff (2011: 31) notes that very few posthumous portraits of Tiberius exist, most of them dating to the reigns of Caligula and Claudius. For the purposes of this study, we will concentrate on the similarities (and differences) between portraits of Tiberius and Augustus. Even before his adoption, Tiberius' portraits would have been associated with those of Augustus. The portraits in the first group as Hertel labels them include Type Ephesos-Munich, Type Basel, and Type Copenhagen 623 (Figure 4.2); all predate the adoption of Tiberius by Augustus. While Boschung orders them differently, he too dates all three of these portrait types before 4. Hertel (2013: 91) believes portraits in this group are modeled in particular on a portrait of Octavian dated by Boschung (1993a, 2002: 182) and Pollini (1999) as having been created around 29 BC, referred to as Type Louvre 1280 (Figure 4.3). Thus, Tiberius, the stepson of the man now known as Augustus, and also, after the death of Agrippa, Augustus' son-in-law and most important general, was identified with the youthful Octavian at the time of his great victories.

Pollini sees a similar trend. He proposes (2005: 64) that Tiberius' first portrait type, which he considers to be Type Basel, was designed in 19 BC in conjunction with Tiberius' victory in Armenia, a victory which was instrumental in influencing the Parthians to return the standards taken from Crassus and Antony's generals, as well as in celebration of Tiberius' marriage to Vipsania, daughter of Agrippa.[55] Even when Tiberius was no

---

[55] Pollini identifies a bust in Naples (Farnese Collection, Archaeological Museum, inv. 6052) as a strong representative of the Type Basel, thus renaming it the Naples-Basel type. He further

Figure 4.2   Tiberius, Copenhagen 623/IN 1445
© Ny Carlsberg Glyptotek, Copenhagen / Jo Selsing

more than Augustus' stepson, his portraits were modeled on those of the first princeps.[56] Massner (1982: 51, 61) sees a connection between portraits of Tiberius and those of Marcellus. This would make sense, considering that Tiberius and Marcellus were paired together several times in their youth, most notably in Augustus' Actian Triumph (Suet. *Tib.* 6.4).

As their relationship grew closer, portraits of Tiberius would bear even closer resemblance to those of Augustus. After the death of Agrippa, Tiberius was famously forced to divorce his beloved Vipsania and marry Augustus' daughter Julia. Pollini has dubbed this the "son-in-law type," for which he believes the best representation is Copenhagen 623. According to Pollini, "it drew inspiration also from Augustus' fourth and fifth portrait types ('Louvre MA 1280' type and 'Prima Porta' type respectively)" (2005: 65). Hertel (2013: 92) sees a greater differentiation in the later portraits of this group, especially Type Copenhagen 623, perhaps due to Tiberius' increasing isolation from the rest of the family as Gaius and Lucius made their debuts in public life, and Tiberius left Rome for Rhodes. Massner

observes, "The hairstyle of the Naples-Basel type also reflects to some extent Octavian's fringe of locks" (2005: 63).

[56] As were those of Drusus the Elder. See Boschung 2002: 185.

Figure 4.3   Augustus, Louvre MA 1280
© RMN-Grand Palais / Art Resource, NY

(1982: 50), on the other hand, sees a direct connection between this early portrait type of Tiberius and portraits of Octavian from the so-called Actium Type (from Zanker 1973), referred to by Pollini (2005) as Type III and by Boschung (1993a) as the Alcudia Type. Regardless of its name, this type was associated with Octavian/Augustus in the years when he was presenting himself as the victor of the civil wars and the bringer of peace. Thus, portraits of the young Octavian served as a model for Tiberius and other members of the imperial household who were playing an important role in military affairs.

All three scholars who have categorized the portraits have identified Berlin-Naples-Sorrento as the type created upon Augustus' adoption of Tiberius. While images of Tiberius before his adoption were modeled more closely on portrait types of Octavian, the Type Berlin-Naples-Sorrento, like images of Gaius and Lucius, takes on features of the Prima

Figure 4.4   Augustus of Prima Porta
© Governorate of the Vatican City State – Directorate of the Vatican Museums

Porta type (Figure 4.4).[57] Indeed, as Massner (1982: 61) observes, the Prima Porta Type which predominated until Augustus' death was the embodiment of everything that made Augustus a unique charismatic leader.[58] Tiberius' portrayal as the son of the man who ended the civil wars would reassure all orders of society that the transition from the first to the second princeps would be peaceful, and that Augustus would continue to watch over his family and the state.

Upon becoming princeps, Tiberius was represented by a new portrait type, Type Copenhagen 624 (Figure 4.5), which both Boschung (1990: 377) and Hertel (2013: 103) believe to be the last portrait type created of Tiberius.[59] Pollini (2005: 67), on the other hand, argues that the Type

---

[57] See Hertel 2013: 114–15. Contra Mlasowsky 1996: 319.   [58] Cf. Boschung 2002: 182.

[59] Højte (2005) catalogs 41 statue bases for images of Tiberius before his accession, 27 percent of the total of 153. He further points out (2005: 127) the incongruity that if Boschung (1993b) is correct, five of the six types of Tiberian portraiture were created before his accession.

Figure 4.5   Tiberius, Copenhagen 624/IN 1750
© Ny Carlsberg Glyptotek, Copenhagen / Jo Selsing

Chiaramonti (Figure 4.6) was created after Tiberius survived the supposed coup led by Sejanus. Both Boschung (2002: 187) and Hertel (2013: 101) date Type Chiaramonti to the years after Tiberius' victories in Pannonia and Germania but before his succession to Augustus' *statio*. All three of these scholars see a marked deviation in Tiberius' portraits once he became princeps. Pollini (2005: 67) sees the changes as the result of Tiberius trying to establish his independence. But as Vout argues, and as we have already mentioned above, the images created while Augustus was still alive would undoubtedly have played a role in the way Tiberius would have been portrayed as his successor. She asserts (2013: 66) that this is one of the reasons why Tiberius was so upset when Granius Marcellus was accused of replacing the head of a statue of Augustus with that of Tiberius (Tac. *Ann.* 1.74).[60] If Tacitus is to be believed, Tiberius was more concerned with his legacy than with the survival of physical monuments to himself (*Ann.* 4.37–8). In the same speech, Tiberius expressed concern that honor for Augustus would be diminished if excessive honors were granted to himself.

---

[60] Since the charges of treason were dropped, Tiberius was likely upset that the prosecutor was trying to use his loyalty to his father's image to draw Tiberius into setting a precedent regarding *maiestas* which he was, at that point, reluctant to set. For more on this case, see Chapter 6.

Figure 4.6   Tiberius, Chiaramonti
© Governorate of the Vatican City State – Directorate of the Vatican Museums

The differentiation of portraits would remind everyone that while Augustus was a god, the current princeps was worthy of only mortal honors.

The majority of scholars who have studied the portraits of Tiberius see a more "Republican" ideology in Type Copenhagen 624.[61] Perhaps this is true, as his *Frisur* is more linear, and we see less influence from the interwoven locks of Augustus' Prima Porta Type. However, the classicizing tendency to hide his age still predominates. Tiberius was 55 when he ascended to his father's *statio*. Compared to images of Julius Caesar, who died at that age, or Crassus, who died around age 60, images of Tiberius display no wrinkles or signs of a receding hairline.[62] Hertel (2013: 120) sees in the expression and bearing of Tiberius' post accession portrait type the Augustan ideal of *dignitas*. Thus, while the arrangement of Tiberius' hair may not be "Augustan" and this portrait may show more "Claudian" features, there are still aspects of Tiberius' accession portrait which mirror the image Augustus tried to present of himself as princeps. Just as Tiberius had tried, less than successfully, to recall aspects of Augustus' *recusatio*

---

[61] See especially Polacco 1955: 139, Massner 1982: 83–6, Hertel 2013: 116, and Boschung 2014: 364.
[62] Contra Boschung 2002: 189, who sees *"faltige Wangen"* in Tiberian portraits.

imperii, he also likely felt the need to create a new image indicating his own intention to continue Augustus' revival of the traditions of the past.[63]

Boschung and Hertel believe that Copenhagen 624 was the last portrait type created of Tiberius and that it was used with variations throughout his reign. Massner and Pollini argue that there were later portrait types created during the reign of Tiberius. Massner (1982: 103) proposes that a type was created in 22/23, based on images of Tiberius from *aes* coinage of that year. She sees this as being similar to the first portrait type issued upon Tiberius' accession but with an even greater resemblance to Augustus' Prima Porta type. She observes an increasing trend to return to Augustan traditions as Tiberius' reign progressed. Pollini (2005: 68) also believes that a new portrait type was created for Tiberius during his reign. He identifies that as Type Chiaramonti, which both Boschung and Hertel date to the period between Tiberius' adoption and his accession. Pollini argues such a type was necessary to drive home Tiberius' "divine" right to rule by virtue of his adoption by Divus Augustus and to show him as more vigorous in the wake of the coup supposedly planned by Sejanus. As does Massner, Pollini sees a return to Augustan tradition as a way to bolster the position of the young Caligula, Augustus' great-grandson.

Finally, we should briefly discuss the reverse trend, whereby images of Augustus produced under Tiberius began to look more "Claudian." Boschung (1993a: 73–4) dates certain portraits of Augustus (e.g., Louvre, MA 1246; Figure 4.7) to the reign of Tiberius based not upon the resemblance of Tiberius to Augustus but rather the resemblance of Augustus to Tiberius. He notes that certain portraits of Augustus show a more linear hairstyle, as seen in the portraits of the reigning Tiberius. Likewise, certain features of Tiberius which mark him distinctively as a Claudian – unusually large eyes with thick eyelids, receding mouth, and prominent chin – can be seen encroaching upon portraits of Augustus supposedly created in the reign of Tiberius.

Portraits of Augustus and Tiberius were often found in public groups honoring the *domus Augusta*. The catalogues of Rose, *Dynastic Commemoration and Imperial Portraiture in the Julio-Claudian Period* (1997), and Boschung, *Gens Augusta* (2002), provide invaluable context for these images. As was the case for coins and inscriptions, members of the elite both in Italy and the provinces would have taken the opportunity to advertise their loyalty to the *domus Augusta*, in this case by erecting images of members of that family. There was no specific authorization or

[63] Hertel 2013: 116 n. 131.

Figure 4.7   Augustus, Louvre MA 1246
© RMN-Grand Palais / Art Resource, NY

permission necessary for the erection of a statue group. The process developed alongside the principate itself.[64] Municipalities angling within this new system to proclaim their loyalty to the *domus* would have been careful not to risk offense. In Rose's study, "Of the eighteen portraits of Augustus that survive from dynastic groups, six are Augustan, five Tiberian, two Caligulan, and five Claudian" (1997: 60).[65] The number of portraits of Augustus which survive from statue groups erected during his four decades as princeps is thus roughly equivalent to the number erected during the twenty-three-year reign of Tiberius (or the thirteen-year reign of Claudius for that matter).

Perhaps the best example of this presentation of Augustus as the divine *paterfamilias* of the *domus Augusta* can be seen in a statue group from Leptis Magna, found at a site identified as the Temple of Augustus and Roma.[66] The temple was probably begun in the late Augustan era and

---

[64] On this process, see Pekáry 1985.

[65] Højte catalogs fifteen bases for posthumous statues of Augustus which belonged to statue groups. "In most of these the statue of Divus Augustus was included to lend an aura of divinity to his successors" (2005: 133).

[66] On this statue group and its significance, see Boschung 2002: 8–18.

finished early in the reign of Tiberius. The inner cella housed statues of Augustus and Roma; the pronaos, statues of Tiberius and Livia. The parallelism of the two statue pairs is obvious, but the size ratio makes it clear that Augustus is superior. Augustus' head measures .92m, whereas Tiberius' measures .74m. As Boschung has noted (2002: 15), the pairing of Augustus and Roma is similar to that on the Gemma Augustea, which we shall look at more closely below. Likewise, the pairing of Tiberius and Livia matches that on the Grand Camée of Paris. These pairings may have been somewhat commonplace in imperial iconography.

Statues are generally considered to be public objects, often set up in a temple or forum as a way for a local magistrate to demonstrate his loyalty. The relief sculpture found on decorative pieces such as the Boscoreale Cups, the "Sword of Tiberius," and various cameos is another story. The Boscoreale Cups, a pair of silver embossed drinking vessels found in the eponymous town in Campania, were most likely created late in the reign of Augustus and have been much studied, particularly by Ann Kuttner (1995). The two cups have come to be nicknamed the "Augustus cup" and the "Tiberius cup" as they feature scenes of each man. The Augustus cup depicts two separate scenes. On one side, Augustus sits on a camp stool with his lictors, receiving a party of conquered barbarians, including their infant children. They are accompanied by a Roman soldier, commonly identified as Drusus the Elder.[67] The scene presumably refers to the conquests made by Tiberius and his brother under the auspices of Augustus. The other side of the Augustus cup depicts Augustus seated on a *sella curulis*. He is facing figures commonly identified as Roma, Venus, and Cupid. Venus presents a Victoriola to Augustus. Along with these is a figure Kuttner identifies as the Genius of the Roman People. Behind Augustus, Mars leads personifications of conquered provinces. This mingling of human and divine has compelled some to reject the theory that these cups were originally based upon monumental art in Rome. But as Kuttner (1995: 35) notes, Augustus is wearing the toga of a Roman magistrate.

Like the Augustus cup, the Tiberius cup (Figure 4.8) celebrates military glory. One side depicts Tiberius making a sacrifice before he heads off to war; the other depicts him returning in triumph. These two scenes have faced much scrutiny by scholars attempting to identify the exact triumph being celebrated. The possible presence of Drusus the Elder on the Augustus cup has led many to date the events as taking place before his

---

[67] The cups were severely damaged after their discovery. The figure of the soldier is now missing, but photographs taken in the early part of the twentieth century suggest that he may be Drusus.

Figure 4.8   Tiberius Cup, Triumph Scene
© RMN-Grand Palais / Art Resource, NY

death. However, as discussed in Chapter 2, Tiberius made dedications in 6 (Castor and Pollux) and 10 (Concordia) in the name of himself and his brother even though the latter was long dead. Hildebrandt (2017: 375) has suggested a significantly later date between 12–14, or possibly even after the death of Augustus. He also suggests that the soldier on the Augustus cup is not Drusus but his son Germanicus.

Since there is no way to date these cups for certain, let us instead note that their depiction of Tiberius differs radically from that of Augustus. By examining the difference, we shall see a pattern that will continue until the very end of Tiberius' reign. Behind Tiberius stands a *servus publicus*, whose job it was to remind the triumphator of his mortality. As Kuttner observes, "this depiction of the *servus publicus* is extraordinary and unique. Nowhere else in Republican or imperial art do we see this shadowy figure" (1995: 149). Kuttner (1995: 151–2) uses this as evidence to date the cups to the reign of Augustus by arguing that, had they been produced under Tiberius, the artist would have tactfully omitted the *servus publicus*. Kuttner overlooks the iconography of Tiberius as the mere agent of Augustan *victoria* both before and during his own reign. Throughout his reign, Tiberius is consistently depicted in both private and public art as subordinate to Augustus. The *servus publicus* would be the perfect image to provide a contrast between the mortal Tiberius and the divine (if perhaps not yet deified) Augustus.

Figure 4.9   The Sword of Tiberius
© The Trustees of the British Museum

Another metal object, commonly called the "Sword of Tiberius," was probably created to commemorate Germanicus' recovery of the standards lost by Varus.[68] The bronze relief on this sword sheath found in Germany and now in the British Museum depicts a seated, semi-togate Tiberius receiving a Victoriola from a youthful soldier commonly identified as Germanicus (Figure 4.9). Next to Tiberius is a shield with the inscription FELICITAS TIBERII. Behind him stands a full-sized Victory, bearing a shield inscribed VIC(toria) AVG(usti). The hierarchy denoted by these inscriptions is summarized by Gagé (1930: 13–4), who demonstrates that the victories won under Tiberius were repeatedly attributed to Divus Augustus. The sheath portrays Tiberius as princeps, yet indicates that Augustus was still guiding the Roman army to victory. *Felicitas* is a passive

---

[68] On this and other decorative military pieces featuring the imperial family from this period, see Dahmen 2001: 105–17. Von Gonzenbach (1966: 183–208) sees the relief as a vehicle for propaganda among the soldiers of Tiberius.

virtue. As Wistrand (1987: 38) notes, in the words of Cicero (*Inv.* 1.94), it would be inconsistent if anyone, when he wanted to praise someone, spoke about his *felicitas*, not his *virtus*. The message depicted on the sheath is then clear, but who was the intended audience? The sword was found in Mainz and appears to have come from a soldier who fought with Germanicus, presumably in the campaign to recover the standards lost by Varus. Dahmen (2001:108) also sees a possible recollection of the return of the Parthian standards recovered under Augustus by Tiberius. The figure of Mars Ultor is positioned directly between Germanicus and Tiberius, a reminder of the temple built by Augustus, which housed the standards recovered from the Parthians and where the cult statue of Divus Augustus was being displayed until his own temple could be completed.

That Tiberius derived his *felicitas* from *victoria Augusti* is also celebrated on decorative gemstones. Two cameos, one in Vienna and one in Paris, depict the hierarchy of charismatic fortune both while Augustus was living and after his death. These showpieces were most likely created for a small audience of the ruling elite. Their imagery is often difficult to interpret. Most scholars agree that the Gemma Augustea (Figure 4.10) was produced late in the reign of Augustus, probably after Tiberius' campaigns in Pannonia but before his triumph was celebrated in Rome (9–12).[69] General consensus identifies the primary figures in the upper register as, from left to right: Tiberius (shadowed by Victory), Germanicus, Roma, Augustus, and three deities seated behind Augustus. The identification of Tiberius is fairly solid based upon his portraiture as well as the Scorpio on the shield below him, which probably represents his birth sign.[70] The identification of Augustus is even more certain. Above his head is a Capricorn, his chosen birth sign. The goddess Oikumene/Cybele behind him holds over his head the *corona civica* that he was granted by the Senate in 27 BC. An eagle stands below his chair, a reminder that Augustus was often portrayed as Jupiter's proxy on earth. The Gemma Augustea is a clear manifestation of the dynastic scheme which dominated the end of the reign of Augustus. The victories achieved by Tiberius and Germanicus were won under the auspices of Augustus. The semi-divine aspects of Augustus in this image also foreshadow his impending deification, a

---

[69] For a table showing various dates and identification of figures on the cameo, see Zwierlein-Diehl et al. 2008: 270–3.

[70] The Scorpio was also associated with the Praetorian Guard, presumably due to Tiberius' patronage of the unit. See Kelly 2020: 135.

Figure 4.10   The Gemma Augustea
© KHM-Museumsverband

reminder that even after his death he will continue to watch over the *domus Augusta* and the people of the empire.

The Gemma Augustea forms a template for another piece, the Grand Camée (Figure 4.11). Unlike the Gemma Augustea, the date and identification of the figures on this piece are highly controversial. It has been dated from early in the reign of Tiberius to as late as the reign of Claudius.[71] There seems little dispute that the central figures are Tiberius and Livia. While most scholars see the figure in the radiate crown at the top of the piece as Augustus, Giard (1998: 21) has proposed that it is Divus Iulius, identifying the figure riding the Pegasus as Augustus. Since the image of Divus Iulius all but disappeared in the reign of Tiberius, these identifications are highly unlikely. Augustus was frequently depicted with a radiate crown in images created under Tiberius; he is almost certainly the central

---

[71] For a discussion of the various theories about date and the identification of figures on the cameo, see Zwierlein-Diehl 2007: 160–6.

Figure 4.11   The Grand Camée
© Bibliothèque Nationale de France

figure in the upper register. The figure on horseback is likely Drusus the Elder, a reminder of his association with the Dioscuri. As was the case in the Gemma Augustea, Augustus is the divine protector watching over Tiberius as he continues to serve the empire. On the Grand Camée, Tiberius is wearing a laurel crown. This contrasts with the oak wreath over the head of Augustus in the Gemma Augustea and reminds the viewer that while Tiberius earned triumphs, Augustus saved citizens by ending civil war. The lap of the seated Tiberius is covered with the aegis. Tiberius has the protection of Jupiter but not the attributes of Jupiter found with respect to Augustus on the Gemma Augustea. Moreover, his companion is not the goddess Roma but his mother, his primary connection to Augustus. Livia has many attributes of the goddess Cybele/Rhea and seated below her is a figure resembling Attis. This connection of Livia to Cybele may be meant to reinforce an identification of Augustus with Saturn.[72] This would, of course, remind the viewer of the golden age associated with Augustus and its continuation during the reign of Tiberius under Augustus' divine auspices.

While the identification of Augustus, Tiberius, and Livia is fairly clear, that of the other figures on the cameo is much more problematic. The placement of Livia next to Tiberius suggests that the cameo was created before her death in 29. The question then arises whether the young men prominent in the middle register represent Germanicus and Drusus the Younger or Nero and Drusus, the sons of Germanicus. If we identify these figures as Germanicus and Drusus, we are left with the problem of identifying the young men in the upper register flanking Augustus. We are also left with the issue of the boy to the far left, usually identified as Caligula. It is much more likely that this cameo dates to the period 23–29, after the death of Drusus the Younger, when the fortunes of the house of Germanicus seemed secure.[73] We have already seen the support for the charismatic bloodline of Augustus in the inscriptions published after Germanicus' death. The Grand Camée would then be a piece akin to the Gemma Augustea, celebrating the apparent succession plan.[74]

As a coda to our discussion of the two most famous cameos featuring Tiberius and Augustus, we should mention two cameos featuring Livia, the link between the two men. The first, now in the Museum of Fine Arts in Boston (Figure 4.12), shows Livia and Tiberius facing in three-quarter profile towards each other and the viewer.[75] Gagetti (2016) has argued that the imagery on the cameo reflects that of Venus Genetrix with her son Cupid. If that is the case, then the stone emphasizes Tiberius' connection

---

[72] Both Bergmann (1998: 109) and Zwierlein-Diehl (2007: 161) emphasize this point.

[73] Boschung (1989: 64–5) and Zwierlein-Diehl (2007: 163–4) both propose this time frame.

[74] I find it hard to accept Jeppesen's identification (1974, 1993) of the young soldier standing before Tiberius as Sejanus. The figure clearly has the Claudian chin. Champlin (2012: 371) is convinced by Jeppesen's arguments.

[75] The Boston MFA website identifies the male figure as Augustus (?), based primarily on the hairstyle, but acknowledges that it could also be one of Livia's sons. The telltale Claudian chin makes the latter identification much more likely. Traditionally, the male figure has been identified as Tiberius.

Figure 4.12   Livia and Tiberius
© 2024 Museum of Fine Arts, Boston

to the Julian line through his adoption. Gagetti dates the stone to shortly after the death of Augustus. However, there is no way to know for certain whether Augustus was alive or dead when this particular image was created. Another cameo in the Kunsthistorisches Museum of Vienna (Figure 4.13) depicts Livia as the priestess of Divus Augustus, holding a bust of him *capite velato* and with a radiate crown, much as he appears on the Grand Camée, only here in profile.[76] Again, Livia has attributes which appear to link her to Cybele. She is wearing the mural crown and holding sheaves of wheat. Unlike the other cameo featuring Livia and Tiberius, this one can clearly be dated after the death of Augustus (and before that of Livia). And like the Grand Camée, it advertises the image of Augustus as Saturn, continuing to watch over Rome's golden age, perpetuated through Livia by her son.

---

[76] On this cameo, see Zwierlein-Diehl et al. 2008: 126–33.

Figure 4.13   Livia and Augustus
© KHM-Museumsverband

Conclusions

The emphasis on the connection of Augustus and Tiberius to Livia in both of these cameos as well as the parallels between the Gemma Augustea and the Grand Camée display a similar pattern to that found in coinage, inscriptions, and other images: Tiberius is mortal; Augustus is a god. The frequent presence of Augustus in Tiberian imagery, combined with the consistent portrayal of Augustus as superior to Tiberius, both before and after the latter's accession, created the illusion that Divus Augustus Pater continued to watch over his son and Rome. Indeed, Tiberius becomes merely a link in a chain from Augustus to the future successors from his charismatic bloodline, particularly Germanicus and then Caligula. While Tiberius does not fade completely into the background, Augustus remains very much in the foreground.

CHAPTER 5

Charismatic Images of Augustus in Tiberian Authors

The most respected author writing in the reign of Tiberius from a modern perspective, Ovid is usually considered to be Augustan. Millar (1993: 2), however, considers the other Augustan poets, namely Vergil, Horace, and Propertius, to have been writing in a different era than Ovid, labelling them "triumviral" poets. He sees a clear separation for the period 2 BC to AD 29, the year Livia died. The exiles of the two Julias, the turmoil after the death of Germanicus, and the downfall of Agrippina and her eldest sons all created confusion about which members of the *domus Augusta* one should praise. Ovid, especially after his exile in 8, reflects this era of uncertainty. Authors of this era also perceived the importance of *exempla* as seen in the *Res Gestae* and the documents produced after the death of Germanicus. Valerius Maximus' work is entirely focused on historical *exempla* meant to provide instruction to the ruling class as well as the ruled.[1] Velleius Paterculus wrote an extremely condensed history highlighting the moments which shaped Rome until his own day, culminating in the peace and prosperity brought about by Augustus and Tiberius.

While Goodyear (1984) portrays the literary world under Tiberius as plagued by oppression and censorship, Gowing comments that, "in terms of sheer volume, more accounts of Rome's civil wars appear to have been produced during the Tiberian period than at any other" (2010: 250). Naturally, the portrayal of the civil wars and their horrors enhanced the image of peace and prosperity brought about by the principate. In this chapter, we will examine in somewhat chronological order the way in which authors writing in the reign of Tiberius represented Augustus and other members of the *domus Augusta*. As we shall see, many of these authors reflect the policies discussed in Chapter 3 and the imagery discussed in Chapter 4. All of them express a reverence for the charismatic

---

[1] On the evolution and "situation ethics" of *exempla* in Roman literature from the late Republic and early principate, see Langlands 2018, especially Chapter 11.

protection of Divus Augustus and a desire that his family continue to preserve the *status* he created.

Ovid: *L'Enfant Terrible*

Ovid by most accounts died around three years after Augustus. Yet in many ways he is a quintessential example of how writers had to adapt to the new situation under Tiberius.[2] Regardless of the circumstances surrounding his exile, Ovid did not return to Rome after Augustus' death.[3] Nevertheless, both Ovid's *carmen* and *error* gave him a sort of literary immortality which inextricably linked him to the last years of the first princeps and the first years of the second. In Ovid's poetry from exile and his revisions to the *Fasti*, we see a poet who had spent his career pushing the boundaries of what was considered acceptable, and then, after his appeals for clemency fell upon deaf ears, openly transgressing those boundaries.[4] Fantham (1985: 244) has shown that the revisions to the *Fasti* made after Augustus' death are closely linked to the last letters Ovid wrote from exile, Book 4 of the *Epistulae ex Ponto*. Thus, I would like to begin with some of the bolder statements Ovid makes in the *Tristia*, written before the death of Augustus as the succession of Tiberius became inevitable, following them to their natural conclusion in the *Epistulae ex Ponto* and the revised *Fasti*, where Ovid engages in blatant flattery of the *domus Augusta* which could also be seen as undermining the charismatic power of Divus Augustus.

Many scholars in recent years have read Ovid's praise of Augustus as ironic.[5] Even if we move beyond a somewhat subjective notion that Ovid was being tongue-in-cheek when he praised Augustus, in certain passages

---

[2] "Ovid is the first poet to write about one of the greatest novelties in Roman life, a novelty in some ways even greater than the principate itself: the succession to the principate" (Feeney 2006: 471 n. 12).

[3] Knox (2004) has gone as far as to claim that Tiberius, not Augustus, was responsible for the poet's exile. Herbert-Brown (1994: 168 n. 76) had already suggested as much but did not pursue the matter. I have no intention here of engaging in speculation as to Ovid's *error*. For an overview of hypotheses, see Claassen 2008: 229–33. The *Ars Amatoria* may have been the greater impetus for Ovid's exile if Augustus viewed it as having encouraged the behavior that led to the exile of his daughter, granddaughter, and, possibly, grandson/adopted son. One wonders what would have happened if Ovid had done as D. Silanus did and returned to Rome after Augustus' death without asking permission (Tac. *Ann.* 3.24).

[4] See Dowling 2006: 121.

[5] For readings of Ovid as subversive or ironic, see Boyle 1997 and 2003, Barchiesi 1997, Johnson 1997, Claassen 2008, and Herbert-Brown 2011. Cf. also Luisi and Berrino 2010, who push their arguments regarding irony in Ovid's treatment of Livia and Tiberius to the extreme. For those who see him as sincere, see Fantham 1985, Millar 1993, Flory 1996, and Green 2004.

of the exile poetry Ovid openly attacks the princeps, especially in *Tristia* 2, a book which consists of only one poem, addressed to Augustus and perhaps modeled on Horace, *Ep.* 2.1. In the letter, which White considers "one of the most outspoken manifestos addressed by any subject to any emperor during the principate" (2002: 16), Ovid pleads his case as a poet. He begins with a general defense of elegiac poetry and then moves on to a specific defense of the *Ars Amatoria*, the *carmen* responsible in part for his exile. The manner in which Ovid defends his work confronts Augustus with a dilemma. Either the princeps has not read his work, in which case he is judging in ignorance, or the princeps has read the work but has not read it correctly.[6] And if Augustus has misjudged Ovid's work, then he has just as likely misjudged Ovid himself.

Nugent points out the contradictory nature of Ovid's address to the *clementia* of Augustus. "Specifically, he alludes to the emperor's edict of relegation as *immite minaxque* (135). Clearly, this clashes with the poet's first address to Augustus as *mitissime Caesar* (27)" (1990: 252–3). In this address to Augustus, Ovid calls as character witnesses two of his later poems, the *Metamorphoses* and the *Fasti*. In the former, he predicted the deification of Augustus. The latter was apparently originally dedicated to Augustus. However, the *Fasti* as we know it begins with an invocation to Germanicus almost certainly inserted after Augustus' death. We shall discuss the revisions to the *Fasti* in greater detail below; regardless, neither of these poems shows the gods on their best behavior. And if Augustus were to be equated with Jupiter, as he frequently is in Ovid's exilic poetry, the injustices committed by Jupiter in the *Metamorphoses* would have seemed less than flattering.[7]

Ovid had every reason to portray Augustus as a tyrant. He was exiled without a public hearing and never allowed to return. Throughout the exile poetry, he treads a fine line between expressing his bitterness and begging for clemency. When Ovid does beg for clemency, his appeal is directed towards the appeasement of the *ira Caesaris*.[8] Ovid also repeatedly hints that he is not the only one who should fear the wrath of Augustus. At *Tristia* 1.1.69–70, Ovid describes his book as tentatively arriving in

---

[6] Nugent (1990: 254) sees this poem as the opposite of a true apology or defense. Cf. Boyle 2003: 12.
[7] See Nugent 1990: 256 and Boyle 2003: 5.
[8] As McGowan notes: "the term *ira* is most often joined with *Caesar, princeps, deus, numen,* or *Iuppiter* and nearly always refers to Augustus. In fact, by my own account, only five of the seventy-eight uses of *ira* in the *Tristia* and *Epistulae ex Ponto* do *not* refer directly or indirectly to the anger of the *princeps*" (2009: 193; her italics).

Rome and cautiously approaching the house of Augustus. While on the surface Ovid is telling his book that these instructions are necessary to make the best impression on Augustus, the description creates an atmosphere of fear and oppression. He tells the book that he considers his life to be the "gift of a god" (*munus dei*, *Tr.* 1.1.20), implying Augustus would have him killed if he followed his book to Rome. This portrayal continues throughout the exile poems. Ovid draws attention to the fact that he does not name any of the recipients of his letters in the *Tristia*; and in the *Epistulae ex Ponto*, he qualifies mentioning friends by name. Ovid asserts that the recipient of *Ex Ponto* 3.6 desired to remain anonymous. As Williams observes, "The more Ovid insists that Augustus poses no threat, the clearer it becomes that his friends suspect otherwise" (2002: 367).

Moreover, throughout the exilic poetry, Ovid pointedly uses the name Augustus in a negative manner. In *Tristia* 2, Ovid calls on the princeps as Augustus to question the latter's presentation of himself as a moral reformer. As mentioned, Ovid rebukes Augustus for his inability to correctly read the *Ars Amatoria*. One particular theme in that work is the use of public spaces for meeting members of the opposite sex. Ovid points out that not only is Augustus responsible for creating these public spaces, but also that the games which the princeps sponsors may be encouraging immoral behavior:

> Inspect the expenses of your games, Augustus;
> you will find many such things purchased by you at a great price.
> You yourself have watched these games and have often given games to be watched –
> your majesty is so obliging everywhere –
> and you, with your own eyes, by which the whole world benefits,
> have indifferently watched adulteries played out on stage.

> inspice ludorum sumptus, Auguste, tuorum;
> empta tibi magno talia multa leges.
> haec tu spectasti spectandaque saepe dedisti –
> maiestas adeo comis ubique tua est –
> luminibusque tuis, totus quibus utitur orbis
> scaenica vidisti lentus adulteria. (*Tr.* 2.509–14)

In a clear attempt to expose the princeps' hypocrisy, Ovid contrasts the associations of the name Augustus as well as his *maiestas*, a word with certain connotations regarding persecutions of free speech towards the end of Augustus' reign, with *scaenica adulteria*.

At *Ex Ponto* 2.5.17–8, Ovid states regarding his place of exile that you could scarcely find anywhere which enjoyed the *pax Augusta* less: *vix hac invenies totum, mihi crede, per orbem, | quae minus Augusta pace fruatur humus.*[9] By adding the epithet *Augusta* to *pax*, Ovid specifically under-mines the myth of Augustus as a charismatic bringer of peace, a myth that was the foundation for the entire principate.[10] Ovid regularly complains about the barbarians, which could in and of itself be embarrassing to the regime, and adds that the barbarian inhabitants of Tomis are frequently attacked by even more barbaric barbarians. Ovid's pleas for a recall to Rome, or at least a better place of exile, would be a constant reminder to Augustus and his heirs that the *pax Augusta* was, for some, a farce.

After his exile in 8 by Augustus, Ovid had a vested interest in appealing to other members of the *domus Augusta* who could succeed the first princeps. As for why Ovid was never allowed to return to Rome, the answer lies not in his addressing his plea for recall to Germanicus instead of Tiberius. Indeed, we have no evidence that Germanicus made any attempt to intervene on Ovid's behalf. Some have even argued that Tiberius might have been an admirer of Ovid's poetry, as Ovid is included in Velleius' list of literary luminaries (2.36.3), while Horace, whose mentions of Tiberius and Drusus are fairly laudatory (*Carm.* 4.4, 4.14), is not. Helzle (1989: 28) speculates Tiberius might have shared common interests with Ovid, including their love of Hellenistic poetry.[11] He also notes that Tiberius was said to have emulated Ovid's patron Messalla as an orator (Suet. *Tib.* 70) and that Tiberius was friends with Messalla's son Cotta Maximus Messalinus (Tac. *Ann.* 6.5), the addressee of multiple letters from Ovid (*Ex Ponto* 1.5, 1.9, 2.3, 2.8, 3.2, and 3.5).

Thakur (2014) argues that several passages in *Tristia* 2 were meant to mark the shift in Ovid's appeals from Augustus to Tiberius. He dates *Tristia* 2 in the wake of the Varian disaster, when Augustus was vulnerable and Tiberius was the bulwark of the empire. Thakur (2014: 79) believes Ovid's references to Tiberius' campaigns were meant to invite comparison with parts of his earlier work, which featured a *propempticon* (*AA* 1.177–228) for Augustus' other adopted heir, Gaius, as he was about to set out for the East. More importantly, *Tristia* 2.225–30 celebrates the securing of various parts of the empire by someone addressed with the second-person pronoun *tu*. While traditionally *tu* has been understood as referring to Augustus, Thakur convincingly demonstrates that the places mentioned by Ovid – Pannonia, Illyricum, Raetia, Thrace, Armenia,

[9] Cf. *Tr.* 5.10 and *Ex Ponto* 2.7.57–68.
[10] Claassen 2008: 33. Cf. Dowling 2006: 117–18. Millar (1993: 10) observes that Tomis was a Greek city and not as remote as Ovid suggests.
[11] Cf. Herbert-Brown 1994: 178.

Parthia, and Germania – were all associated with victories won by Tiberius. Thus, it seems more likely that the *tu* here is not Augustus but Tiberius, who is mentioned earlier in the poem (*Tristia* 2.165).

If Tiberius was an admirer of Ovid, why does he appear so infrequently in Ovid's post-exilic poetry? One all-too-easy answer would be metrical (in)convenience. In Tiberius' praenomen, the first three syllables are all short; so, in general, his name will not scan in a line of hexameter or pentameter.[12] Accordingly, Tiberius is never cited by his praenomen. Germanicus is cited four times in the *Fasti* (three times in Book 1), always in the vocative, and five times in the *Epistulae ex Ponto*, three times in the vocative and twice in the nominative. Augustus is cited by name seventeen times in various cases. At *Fasti* 1.531, the plural of Augustus occurs, referring to the fact that the guardianship of Rome will remain with Augustus and his designated heirs (*penes Augustos patriae tutela manebit*), presumably Tiberius and Germanicus. By far the most frequent designation, Caesar is used fifty-one times dating back to the *Amores*. The fact that Julius Caesar, Augustus, Tiberius, and Germanicus were all subsumed under the name Caesar adds to the general confusion. But in a way, that confusion is precisely the point. Ovid's poetry after exile is often quite vague with regard to whom he is addressing as Caesar. He is casting a wide net, appealing to Tiberius through his reverence for Augustus, as well as to friends of Livia and Germanicus.

After the death of Augustus, Ovid revised the first book of the *Fasti*, dedicating the work not to the reigning Tiberius but to his heir apparent Germanicus.[13] Yet while Germanicus is addressed more frequently, the larger focus is the continuation of the dynasty founded by Caesar, consolidated by Augustus, and confirmed by the peaceful succession of Tiberius. Even before the phrase *domus Augusta* first appeared in Tiberian documents like the *Tabula Siarensis*, Ovid used the phrase in his panegyric to members of that family, praising Augustus, Livia, Tiberius, Germanicus, Drusus the Younger, *ceteraque Augustae membra... domus* (*Ex Ponto* 2.2.74). This letter was written to Cotta Messalinus, a friend of Tiberius. Moreover, the poem celebrates Tiberius' triumph over Dalmatia, a triumph which Ovid had enacted in the previous poem, dedicated to Germanicus. In both these poems, it is unclear which Caesar is actually the focus of the triumph. While ostensibly the victory was won by Tiberius, he was helped by Germanicus, and they were both

---

[12] Knox 2004: 16 n. 102.

[13] On the rededication to Germanicus, see Myers 2014. Although, as White points out (2002: 24), Tiberius is also prominent in Book 1 (*Fasti* 1.9–12; 1.533–4; 1.613–16; 1.645–8; 1.707–8).

fighting under the auspices of Augustus, mirroring the imagery we find in the "Sword of Tiberius" and other contemporary artwork discussed in the previous chapter. At *Ex Ponto* 2.8.1–4, Ovid thanks Messalinus for sending him silver images of Augustus and Tiberius (along with Livia), *Caesar cum Caesare.*[14] Ovid also praises Drusus and Germanicus, worthy of both their grandfather and father (*vel avo dignos, vel patre nepotes*), who aid in securing the empire (except, of course, for Tomis).

In his revision of Book 1 of the *Fasti* after the death of Augustus, Ovid not only looks toward Germanicus, he also looks back upon the filial relationship between Augustus and Tiberius. As Green comments: "In 527-8, Aeneas' duty is to carry his father. In 533-4, the duty of Augustus/Tiberius in taking control of the Empire is explained in a manner which cleverly alludes to this image: they both have the duty of carrying the 'weight of their father' (*pondera... paterna feret* (534))" (2004: 242). The notion of the empire as a burden is also seen in Ovid's portrayal of Tiberius taking up the *imperii frena* (*Fasti* 1.529–34; cf. *Ex Ponto* 4.13.27–8). This echoes Tiberius' words as reported by Tacitus that only the mind of Divus Augustus could manage such a great burden as the empire (*solam divi Augusti mentem tantae molis capacem, Ann.* 1.11.1). While in *Tristia* 2 and *Ex Ponto* 2.5, poems written before Augustus' death, Ovid was willing to mock Augustus' cognomen, in the revised *Fasti*, he shows due reverence. Ovid fuses together the two meetings of the Senate in January 27 BC, commemorating both on January 13 (*Fasti* 1.587–90) and indicating that this was the day on which Augustus assumed the cognomen "Augustus" (which actually occurred on January 16). In comparison with other traditional Roman honorific names, only Augustus' name is divine. Ovid invokes Augustus, conflating him with Jupiter (*hic socium summo cum Iove nomen habet,* 1.608) as a protective deity for the empire and for Germanicus, who will one day inherit the name: "may he increase the empire of our leader, may he increase his years, | and may the oak wreath protect your doors, | heir of such a great cognomen, so that with the auspicious gods | and omen by which his father did, he may take up the burden of the world" (*augeat imperium nostri ducis, augeat annos,* | *protegat et vestras querna corona fores,* | *auspicibusque deis tanti cognominis heres* | *omine suscipiat, quo pater, orbis onus,* 1.613–6). The vagueness of the language makes it unclear who is the *heres* and who is the *pater*. Regardless, only the family of Augustus is capable of taking up the burden of the empire.

---

[14] On the subversive nature of this poem, see Pandey 2020.

As in the other poems from exile, in his revision of the *Fasti* Ovid shifts his focus away from Augustus and towards the other members of the family, attempting to portray a unified *domus Augusta* in the wake of the scandals which involved Agrippa Postumus and Julia the Younger, scandals which may have played some part in Ovid's exile, even if indirectly. But his previous works, especially the *Ars Amatoria*, had already shown too much disrespect to Augustus and the Rome he envisioned. Even writing a calendar which would rival the official one set forth by Augustus could be seen as problematic.[15] Moreover, as in the *Metamorphoses*, in the *Fasti* Ovid portrays gods behaving badly. A hasty revision of Book 1 and a new dedication to Germanicus did little to defuse the tension in certain parts of the work. If anything, changing the dedicatee only called attention to Ovid's lack of respect for its original dedicatee, Augustus.

For Ovid, not only the stability of the Roman Empire but also his own chances for recall depended upon the *clementia* of a sympathetic ruler. Knowing that Tiberius' claim to the principate was founded upon his adoption by Augustus, Ovid drives home the idea that the entire family was committed to peaceful transitions of power.[16] As we shall see below, these same themes would be echoed in the works of authors considered to be loyalists to the regime, such as Valerius Maximus and Velleius Paterculus. So why was Ovid never recalled? Probably because, despite his attempts to extol the *domus Augusta*, he had made too many subtle and not-so-subtle attacks on its founder. *Tristia* 2 alone would be enough to convince Tiberius (and likely Germanicus) that Ovid was much safer from a distance. Any attack on the charismatic founder and his principles would undermine the stability of a principate experiencing its first transition.

Germanicus and Manilius: Written in the Stars

After the death of Augustus, Ovid rededicated the first book of his *Fasti* to Germanicus. Perhaps he was relying on the young man's reputation as *comis*. Or he was appealing to a fellow poet who had also composed a sort of calendar. The translation of Aratus' *Phaenomena* attributed to Germanicus has its difficulties. Even if the traditional ascription of the text to Germanicus is correct, no one has been able to pinpoint exactly

---

[15] Boyle 1997: 8.

[16] "Ovid emphasizes a number of ideas about the dynastic house: the descendants of Augustus have a divine right to rule (*Fast.* 1.532); the family and household of Augustus are sacred and sacrosanct (*Fast.* 6.810); only Augustus' family has the right to celebrate triumphs (*Tr.* 3.1.41); and finally, the *domus Augusta* will rule in perpetuity (*Tr.* 4.2.10; *Fast.* 1.721)" (Flory 1996: 301).

when it may have been written.[17] Possanza (2004: 233–5) believes it was originally written between 4 and 7, with revisions after the death of Augustus.[18] Lewis (2008: 332) follows this dating but connects Germanicus' identification of Virgo as Iustitia (*Phaen.* 104) with the institution of a cult to Iustitia in 13. In the introduction to his Belles Lettres translation, Le Boeuffle (2003: x) prefers a date of composition for the entire work around 16–17. This seems unlikely given Germanicus' official duties during that time. Germanicus probably began the poem after his adoption and revised it later to reflect changes in the *domus Augusta*.

Thus, to a certain degree, we run into some of the same problems faced in reading the revised *Fasti*; namely, to whom are the most panegyrical passages of the poem being addressed? One of the more confusing passages in this respect is the *proemium*:

> Aratus began his poem with mighty Jove,
> but you are the greatest authority for us, parent;
> I honor you and bring you a sacred offering of this learned labor,
> the first fruits. The ruler and begetter of the gods himself approves.

> Ab Iove principium magno deduxit Aratus.
> carminis at nobis, genitor, tu maximus auctor,
> te veneror tibi sacra fero doctique laboris
> primitias. probat ipse deum rectorque satorque. (1–4)

The passage ends with the lines, "While I attempt to proclaim these things with Latin Muses, | may your peace and you yourself be present and may you as a divine power show favor to your offspring" (*haec ego dum Latiis conor praedicere Musis,* | *pax tua tuque adsis nato numenque secundes,* 15–16). The confusion arises from a literal reading of the terms *genitor* and *natus*. If the addressee of the poem is the deified Augustus, then these words could indicate Tiberius as the author. If the addressee of the poem is the ruling princeps Tiberius, that would indicate Germanicus as the author. On the other hand, *genitor* often refers to the founder of one's line. The parallelism between the *genitor* of his own line and the *sator* of the gods indicates that Germanicus is invoking his grandfather, Divus Augustus.[19]

In beginning his poem with an invocation to the *genitor* of the *domus Augusta*, Germanicus invites a comparison with Jupiter/Zeus. As Possanza (2004: 108–9) comments, Germanicus rewrites Aratus' proem so that

---

[17] For a solid treatment of the difficulties with dating and authorship, see Possanza 2004: 219–43.
[18] Cf. Terio 2006: 81–2 and Stiles 2017: 881.
[19] For other arguments that Germanicus is addressing his grandfather, see Steinmetz 1966: 450–6 and Stiles 2017.

Augustus becomes the bringer of order, not Zeus. Tiberius will ensure that order continues. Unlike Ovid, who glorifies the *domus Augusta* from a distance, Germanicus was an integral part of that dynasty. His focus on Augustus reflects the general trend towards portraying Augustus, even during his own lifetime, as having supernatural abilities and as having created a system that preserves peace through divine sanction. The poem most likely celebrates the recent deification of Augustus, but the *proemium* is deliberately ambiguous to indicate that the *numen* of Augustus continues to rule through the inspiration which it provides for both the poet (and future princeps) and the reigning princeps.[20]

Germanicus again glorifies his divine grandfather in his treatment of Capricorn (558–60). As we have seen in the Gemma Augustea, Capricorn was connected to Augustus as a superhuman being who preserved Rome, flanked by deities and sporting a *corona civica*.[21] Germanicus pronounces: "this one (Capricorn), Augustus, has brought your *numen* from its natal body, | through dumbstruck races and a frightened fatherland, | to heaven and restored it to its ancestral stars" (*hic, Auguste, tuum genitali corpore numen | attonitas inter gentis patriamque paventem | in caelum tulit et maternis reddidit astris*). While this may bear some similarities to Mars carrying off Romulus or Venus bringing Caesar to the heavens as a star in Ovid's *Metamorphoses* (14.805–28; 15.745–870), in Germanicus' poem Capricorn merely transports Augustus as he returns to the heavens. This is not, strictly speaking, a catasterism. Augustus does not become a heavenly body. He already was one before he became a *praesens divus* on earth.[22] The fact that Augustus has returned to the heavens (and that he came from there in the first place) has implications for Tiberius and Germanicus. They themselves are from divine lineage and will presumably one day ascend to the stars. More importantly, as he had done while he was alive, Augustus will continue to preserve Rome.

Germanicus was not the only poet of this age who imitated the astronomical works of Hellenistic Alexandria. Manilius too seems to have been writing in the late Augustan and/or early Tiberian era.[23] Again, the disagreement in dating Manilius' *Astronomica* revolves around references to a Caesar who cannot be readily identified. In particular, passages concerning Libra and Virgo may glorify the natal signs of Julius Caesar,

---

[20] Lausdei 1987: 181.
[21] On Augustus' horoscope, see especially Lewis 2008 and Volk 2009: 148–51.
[22] Possanza 2004: 183–4.   [23] For a discussion of the various dates, see Volk 2011.

Augustus, or Tiberius.[24] Nevertheless, we can see clear references throughout the poem to the *domus Augusta*. The most obvious (1.898–900)
concerns the Varian disaster, which took place in 9. Thus, we have a
terminus post quem for at least this version of the poem. Volk (2009:
143–6) argues that the work must be entirely Augustan because passages
which glorify a Caesar all seem to refer to Augustus. However, as we have
seen in the poems of Ovid and Germanicus, although Tiberius was
princeps, he was not the focus of attention, particularly in the early years
of his reign. Even after painstakingly going through all the ambiguous
passages and arguing that they do refer to Augustus, Volk concedes, "many
of Manilius' references to the emperor are vague and admit of differing
interpretations" (2009: 160). Ultimately, as was the case with Ovid, that is
the point. The charismatic *numen* of Augustus casts its shadow over the
reign of Tiberius so that all the Caesars blend into one "Caesar."

Strabo: The World According to Augustus

Just as Ovid and Manilius had appealed to the interest of the imperial
family in the calendar and astrology, Strabo's *Geography* demonstrates an
awareness of the ways in which one should discuss the terrestrial world in
the reigns of Augustus and Tiberius. He may have had specific reasons for
choosing his subject and his tone. At 2.5.33, Strabo states: "And Libya is –
as the others show, and indeed as Cn. Piso, who was once the prefect of
that country, told me – like a leopard's skin; for it is spotted with inhabited
places that are surrounded by waterless and desert land" (Loeb trans.
Jones). The Piso mentioned above is none other than the one-time friend
of Augustus and Tiberius who was later driven to commit suicide over
accusations that he had, among other things, murdered Germanicus.
Strabo's connections to the inner circle of the imperial court may go even
further. Dueck (2000: 7) suggests that Strabo was connected to Sejanus
through his relationship with Aelius Gallus, who, she believes, may have
made Strabo a Roman citizen and was Sejanus' adoptive father. While such
a close connection to Sejanus is rather speculative, Strabo certainly knew
Piso and relatives of Sejanus.

Strabo reinforces the notion that by the death of Augustus the Romans
had conquered (or forced into obeisance) every part of the world worth
conquering. In Book 6, Strabo remarks on Rome's success in expanding its

---

[24] For some serious maneuvering to identify the figures associated with these passages, see Lewis 2008.

territory. He sees the rule of the Augustus and his heirs from the *domus Augusta* as the culmination of Roman imperialism:

> As for Italy itself, though it has often been torn by factions, at least since it has been under the Romans, and as for Rome itself, they have been prevented by the excellence of their form of government and of their rulers from proceeding too far in the ways of error and corruption. But it were a difficult thing to administer so great a dominion (χαλεπὸν δὲ ἄλλως διοικεῖν τὴν τηλικαύτην ἡγεμονίαν) otherwise than by turning it over to one man, as to a father; at all events, never have the Romans and their allies thrived in such peace and plenty as that which was afforded them by Augustus Caesar, from the time he assumed the absolute authority, and is now being afforded them by his son and successor, Tiberius, who is making Augustus the model of his administration and decrees, as are his children, Germanicus and Drusus, who are assisting their father. (6.4.2; Loeb trans. Jones)

Lasserre (1982: 885) has gone so far as to assert that the ideas expressed here are taken from a speech given by Tiberius in the Senate after the death of Augustus.[25] Certainly, there are echoes of Tiberian sentiments, including the famous phrase from Tacitus that Tiberius observed all of Augustus' words and actions as though they were law (*Ann.* 4.37.3). We also see here the idea of the empire as a burden which must be borne by one man, reminiscent of the language supposedly used in Augustus' *recusatio* in 27 BC and its reprisal by Tiberius in 14. Although Tiberius was clearly the reigning emperor at the time this was written, Augustus is mentioned more frequently, and the passage ends with an emphasis on Tiberius' sons.

In Strabo's work, we run into some of the same issues mentioned in our discussion of Ovid, Germanicus, and Manilius. Tiberius' desire to stress continuity with his predecessor creates confusion about dating. Since Tiberius was clearly ruling at the time Strabo wrote the passage above, the question then arises as to how late into the reign of Tiberius the text stretches. Some, for example, have pointed to an absence of passages about Germanicus' trip to the East as a sign that the work was written before then.[26] However, Pothecary (2002: 402) believes the work was written after the death of Germanicus, when Tiberius would have wished attention to be focused on Drusus. That said, neither of Tiberius' sons plays a huge role in the work. Nor does Tiberius himself. Dueck dates the *Geography* to 18–24, yet considers the *Geography*, "A Tiberian work chronologically, but an Augustan thematically" (2000: 151). Dueck (2000: 97) contends that

---

[25] For a rather different opinion, see Cowan 2009a: 469–70.
[26] For references, see Pothecary 2002: 389–90.

Strabo used Augustus' *Res Gestae*, a document written by Augustus but published by Tiberius, as a source throughout his *Geography*.[27] This would explain the inclusion of certain peoples outside Rome's *imperium*. Strabo expresses the ideology which Augustus had promoted regarding the state of the empire upon his death – that Rome controlled the entire *oikumene* and had received submission from exotic places which were not worthy of total conquest.

Not only does Strabo stress continuity with the Augustan regime; he thrusts Augustus into the forefront and lets Tiberius, who, as mentioned in Chapter 3, did most of the fighting to consolidate the *pax Augusta*, recede into the background. When praising Tiberius, Strabo takes the opportunity to praise his predecessor. At 12.8.18, Strabo compares Tiberius' generosity towards the cities of Asia after an earthquake in 17 with the aid from Augustus to Tralles and Laodicea after earthquakes in 26 and 25 BC. Strabo ignores the reallocation of provinces from the control of the Senate and the people to the princeps by Tiberius, "exaggerating continuity both within Augustus's reign, and between Augustus and Tiberius" (Pothecary 2002: 414; cf. Clarke 1997: 105 n. 72). Strabo states: "But the Provinces have been divided in different ways at different times, though at the present time they are as Augustus Caesar arranged them" (17.3.25; Loeb trans. Jones). Strabo explains that the division of provinces was necessary; only Augustus could command the army and ensure peace. This passage occurs at the end of the work and may have been written as late as 24. Strabo was aware of the need to stress the stability, even ten years later, of the *pax Augusta* under Tiberius.

Velleius Paterculus: Witness to History

Historically, Velleius Paterculus has often been unfairly labeled as an apologist for the Tiberian regime.[28] Beginning with Woodman's commentaries (1977 and 1983), scholars have generally veered away from painting Velleius with such a broad brush. Nevertheless, Velleius admittedly benefitted from associations with the imperial family. He boasts of his service with Tiberius and of his (and his brother's) election to the praetorship for 15 as *candidati Caesaris* (2.124.3–4).[29] His history ends with the

---

[27] Cf. Lasserre (1982: 884), who posits that the memoirs of Augustus may have been used.
[28] See especially Syme 1978b.
[29] On Velleius' career, see Sumner 1970. See also Levick 2011, who composed a fictional manuscript in the Bodleian written by the sons of Velleius.

consulship of M. Vinicius, to whom the work as a whole was dedicated. Vinicius was consul in 30, serving from January 1 until the end of June. Vinicius was also married to Livilla, daughter of Germanicus. The celebration of Vinicius' consulship plus the fairly laudatory tone toward Sejanus at the end of the work indicates that Velleius' history can be firmly dated no later than the early part of 31.[30] The period 23–31 was certainly a difficult time for anyone attempting to write a history which would include praise of members of the *domus Augusta*. As we shall discuss in the next chapter, after the death of Drusus, the sons of Germanicus were designated as the heirs apparent. But their mother's inability to cooperate with Tiberius ultimately led to the exile of Agrippina and her eldest son, Nero, as well as the imprisonment in Rome of her second son, Drusus. Whereas Strabo praises Germanicus and Drusus as helping their father Tiberius to preserve the *pax Augusta*, by 24 the main *socius laborum* to Tiberius was Sejanus. Thus, more so than Ovid, Manilius, Strabo, and perhaps even Germanicus, Velleius appears to reflect the desired image being sent forth from the Tiberian court. When Tiberius agreed to accept the principate, he claimed to have done so with the idea that one day he could retire. Augustus had professed similar ideas throughout his reign as well. One can certainly doubt their sincerity, but one cannot doubt the message being transmitted that the empire was a burden which required superhuman strength to sustain. Velleius seems to have understood this.[31]

Like Strabo, Velleius may also have used Augustus' *Res Gestae* as a source.[32] Galimberti (2015: 298) points to two particular passages, 2.61.1–3 and 2.89.3–4, as having been influenced by the *Res Gestae*.[33] The first deals with the introduction of Octavian onto the political scene during the *dominatio* of Mark Antony. The second celebrates Octavian's triumphal return to Italy after Actium and the restoration of order after the civil wars (more on this passage below). Velleius is careful to distance the young heir to Julius Caesar from the actions of Antony and Lepidus. Antony is the clear scapegoat for all of the evil wrought by the proscriptions and other unsavory acts.[34]

---

[30] Rich (2011: 84–87) lays out the arguments for a swift composition of a year or less. Balmaceda (2017: 138) observes that Velleius' praise of Sejanus shows signs of concern, esp. at 2.131.2.

[31] Hillard 2011: 234.

[32] Perhaps not coincidentally, Velleius' history and the *Res Gestae* can both be found in the same Loeb volume.

[33] Hellegouarc'h and Jodry (1980) also argue that Velleius used the *Res Gestae* as a source.

[34] Connal 2013: 54.

Velleius, as one might expect of someone writing in the reign of Tiberius, focuses on the career of Divus Augustus, not Octavian the heir of Julius Caesar. When relating the birth of Augustus in 63 BC, Velleius states that the event added more than a little honor to Cicero's consulship (*Consulatui Ciceronis non mediocre adiecit decus natus eo anno divus Augustus*, 2.36.1). Although he had just been born, Octavius is referred to here as Divus Augustus, the title he received after his death. And his birth gave honor to the consulship of Cicero, connecting the baby to the salvation of the *res publica* by the same man whom Antony wickedly killed. Velleius predicts the preeminence of the newborn who will cast a shadow with his greatness over all men of all races. Likewise, at 2.60.1–2, the young Octavius is faced with the difficult decision of whether to accept the inheritance left to him by the recently assassinated Caesar. As his mother and stepfather try to dissuade him, fate steps in. The fates are beneficial (*salutaria*), and they are the fates of not just the *res publica* but the entire world (*orbis terrarum*). These salutary fates lay claim to Octavius, overriding the hesitation of his family because he is destined to become a new founder (*conditorem*) and the savior (*conservatorem*) of the Roman name. As he makes his decision, Octavius' divine soul (*caelestis animus*) spurns human counsels, affirming his divine origin as the son of Caesar (*divi filius*) and prefiguring his own deification. In pursuing the highest good, Octavius will be risking his own safety. Both at Octavius' birth and at his rebirth as Caesar, Velleius asserts that he had divine qualities, qualities which would help him save Rome. As mentioned in Chapter 1, this is one of the foremost characteristics of a charismatic leader.

Velleius further gives Augustus his due, setting the stage for praise of the current princeps. Velleius' description of Augustus' "restoration of the Republic" prefigures that of Tiberius' succession to the principate. At 2.89, Velleius describes Octavian's return to Rome after Actium:

> Men are able to ask, then, nothing from the gods, and the gods are able to offer nothing to men, nothing is able to be conceived by a vow, nothing to be consummated by good fortune, which Augustus did not bestow upon the Republic, the Roman people, and the entire world after his return to Rome. Civil wars had been ended after twenty years, foreign wars were suppressed, peace restored, madness of arms everywhere quieted, force restored to the laws, authority to the courts, majesty to the Senate, the imperium of the magistrates was restored to its ancient form, aside from the fact that two praetors were added to the existing number of eight. That former and ancient form of the Republic was restored.

> Nihil deinde optare a dis homines, nihil dii hominibus praestare possunt, nihil voto concipi, nihil felicitate consummari, quod non Augustus post

reditum in urbem rei publicae populoque Romano terrarumque orbi repraesentaverit. Finita vicesimo anno bella civilia, sepulta externa, revocata pax, sopitus ubique armorum furor, restituta vis legibus, iudiciis auctoritas, senatui maiestas, imperium magistratuum ad pristinum redactum modum, tantummodo octo praetoribus adlecti duo. Prisca illa et antiqua rei publicae forma revocata.

While Augustus is not called Divus here, he is given divine attributes. Velleius states that Augustus gave to the Republic, the Roman people, and the entire world everything which men could wish from the gods and everything which the gods could give to men. At the end of the passage, Velleius states, "that former and ancient form of the Republic was revived." Those who see Velleius, and Tiberius, as having "Republican" tendencies are not mistaken. However, so did Augustus. The great deception in Tiberian authors was not just establishing continuity between Augustus and Tiberius but also from the Republic to Tiberius through the facade created by Augustus. Velleius' examples from the Republican past display a deliberate attempt to show his readers that the principate was connected to the Republic, and that the princeps was capable of living up to the *mos maiorum*.[35]

One reason for this seamless transition (or is it? see below) is the relationship between Augustus and Tiberius, which Velleius portrays as sincerely familial.[36] At 2.103.3, Velleius states that Augustus wanted to adopt Tiberius after the death of Lucius while Gaius was still alive, but Tiberius refused. One wonders what the dynamic of power would have been, given how, according to Velleius (2.99.2), Tiberius withdrew to Rhodes so that Gaius and Lucius could come into their own.[37] Velleius does include (2.104.2) the proclamation made by Augustus that when he adopted Tiberius, he did so for the sake of the state (*rei publicae causa*).[38] Velleius uses this statement as a springboard to launch into the accomplishments of Tiberius, especially in Illyricum and Germania. Velleius then describes the tender scene when Augustus recalled Tiberius to Nola after he had set out for Illyricum, "since he knew, if he wanted to leave everything secure after him, whom he must summon" (*cum sciret, quis*

---

[35] Lobur 2008: 184. Bloomer argues (2011: 114–17) that Velleius aims to convince his audience that *admiratio* for the Caesars must replace the *invidia* of the late Republic. See also Gowing 2005: 35–36; cf. Gowing 2007.
[36] Balmaceda 2014: 352; cf. Balmaceda 2017: 147.
[37] On Velleius' handling of dynastic tensions, see Schmitzer 2000: 229–31.
[38] Suetonius includes the same statement (*Tib.* 21.3) but does so in excusing Augustus' adoption of Tiberius despite awareness of his faults.

volenti omnia post se salva remanere accersendus foret, 2.123.1). Augustus, upon seeing Tiberius, embraced him and said that he was now without care (*securum se Augustus praedicans*). Augustus revived a little upon seeing the face of the one dearest to him (*carissimi sibi*, 2.123.2). This affection is rather different from the relationship described in Suetonius and Tacitus. At the same time, the foremost theme running through Velleius' portrayal of the bond between Augustus and Tiberius is their shared concern for the state. The dying Augustus commends to Tiberius their mutual labor (*sua atque ipsius opera*). Throughout, Velleius depicts Tiberius as doing his duty to both his *pater* and the *pater patriae*.[39]

As one might expect from what has been said above, Velleius' narrative of Tiberius' succession portrays Tiberius in a positive light. However, it is also quite complicated. If Augustus had brought about peace after civil wars, and if his relationship with Tiberius was as cordial as Velleius portrays it to have been, why was the transition a time of great anxiety? Velleius states at 2.124 that after Augustus "returned his divine spirit to heaven" (*animam caelestem caelo reddidit*, 2.123.2), the whole world was in a state of panic. From an outsider's perspective, this seems understandable. The principate was a position uniquely created by and for Augustus. The succession to a charismatic leader like Augustus was fraught with all sorts of questions, as discussed in Chapter 1. But Velleius has, for the most part, portrayed Augustus and Tiberius as being of the same mindset and has endeavored to demonstrate that Tiberius was the only man who could have succeeded Augustus. By drawing attention to the anxiety created by the death of Augustus, Velleius drives home the fact that, thanks to the relationship forged by Augustus and Tiberius, civil war will not be renewed.[40] The charisma of Augustus will ensure a peaceful succession.

The way in which Velleius describes the relief of the Roman world when Tiberius stops refusing the principate closely resembles the description of Augustus' restoration of the Republic after Actium discussed above (2.124). In a similar vein, Velleius summarizes the first sixteen years of Tiberius' reign:

> Trust has been restored to the forum, sedition removed from the forum, canvassing from the Campus Martius, discord from the Senate, and justice,

---

[39] Pieper (2021) demonstrates that for Velleius an important aspect of Tiberian *moderatio* was Tiberius' willingness to stay in the background even after equaling Augustus in political power.

[40] Regarding Velleius' account of Livia's escape with baby Tiberius (2.75.2–3), Gowing observes: "Velleius regularly draws attention to an important aspect of Tiberius' talent: his ability to hold in check those forces that would renew civil war at Rome" (2010: 255).

equity, industry, once buried and obscured, have been returned to the state; authority has been added to the magistracies, majesty to the Senate, gravity to the courts.

> Revocata in forum fides, summota e foro seditio, ambitio campo, discordia curia, sepultaeque ac situ obsitae iustitia, aequitas, industria civitati redditae; accessit magistratibus auctoritas, senatui maiestas, iudiciis gravitas. (2.126.2)

Both passages refer to the restoration of *maiestas* to the Senate; both passages use the participle *revocata* to describe the restoration, in the passage featuring Augustus, of the former and ancient form of government (*prisca illa et antiqua rei publicae forma*), and, in the passage celebrating Tiberius, of trust in public affairs (*in forum fides*). While under Augustus the *imperium* of various magistracies was restored (*imperium magistratuum ad pristinum redactum modum*), under Tiberius authority was added to the magistracies (*accessit magistratibus auctoritas*).[41] By highlighting the unique circumstances of the transition of power, Velleius enhances the glory of both the first successor to the newly created principate and the man who ensured a peaceful succession. He also emphasizes that, despite a brief period of public anxiety, Tiberius was able to restore order and build upon the stable foundation Augustus had left behind.[42] Velleius, like Tacitus, understood that the most important test for the stability of the unique system created by Augustus was Tiberius' acceptance (and consolidation) of *paterna statio*.

Valerius Maximus and the Exemplary Emperors

For many years, scholars have believed that Valerius Maximus must have written at least part of the *Facta Dictaque Memorabilia* after the fall of Sejanus. At 9.11 ext. 4, under the heading of *Dicta Improba aut Facta Scelerata*, Valerius rebukes an unnamed *parricidium*. While most of his outrage could be used to describe any number of threats to the imperial family, Valerius specifies that the offense involved a breach of the loyalty of friendship (*amicitiae fide*) and that the offender had tried to seize the reins

---

[41] In pointing out the similarities between the passages, Schmitzer concludes, "the logic implicit in the text suggests that Augustus had not succeeded in retaining this ideal state of the *res publica* permanently after it had been recovered. Rather, Tiberius again had to address chaotic circumstances, as before the initial restoration of the *res publica*" (2011: 190). For a different interpretation, see Cowan 2009a: 477–8.

[42] Cf. Galimberti 2015: 306 and Balmaceda 2017: 144. Contra Cowan (2009a: 479), who argues that Velleius "saw Tiberius as much more than Augustus' 'continuator.'"

of the Roman Empire (*habenas Romani imperii*). Given that an altar was built celebrating Tiberius' friendship with Sejanus in 28 (Tac. *Ann.* 4.74.2) and that Tacitus uses similar language to describe Sejanus and Tiberius as having been freed from the reins which restrained them by the death of Livia (*velut frenis exsoluti proruperunt*, *Ann.* 5.3.1), Sejanus seems the most likely candidate for Valerius' rancor.[43] Nevertheless, Bellemore (1989) has argued that the conspirator was actually Libo or some *ignotus*.[44] Her primary reasoning for such an early dating is the lack of *exempla* which showcase the *domus Augusta*. While Valerius acknowledges Tiberius is princeps and Augustus is now Divus, the only *exemplum* which directly includes Tiberius is his race to the deathbed of his brother Drusus. However, Valerius mentions at 2.6.8 an incident he personally witnessed while travelling with Sextus Pompeius to Asia. Sextus Pompeius was consul in 14 and served as governor of Asia in 25. The incident in this passage likely occurred in 25, giving a reasonable *terminus post quem*.[45]

If Valerius Maximus' work was published after the death of Sejanus, why does he include so few *exempla* which glorify Augustus and Tiberius? In many ways, Valerius' work is similar to that of Velleius. Velleius spends a significant amount of time on the history of Rome before his own era, all the while claiming to race towards the culmination of the Republic, the reign of Tiberius; but the historian only allots eight chapters to the sixteen years of Tiberius' reign which precede the consulship of his dedicatee, Vinicius. Like Velleius, Valerius' focus on the Republican past is not a slight aimed at Augustus or Tiberius. Rather, it is an attempt to stress the continuity between the system which existed before the civil wars and the one which followed their end. We can see this especially in Valerius' prefatory address to Tiberius, which uses language reminiscent of that found in the authors discussed earlier. Augustus has brought peace and stability to the Roman world, and Tiberius is responsible for preserving that state: "Therefore, I invoke you, Caesar, surest salvation of our father-land, for this undertaking, for whom the *consensus* of gods and men has wished there to be rule over sea and land, and by whose celestial

---

[43] As mentioned earlier, the phrase *frena imperii* predates Tacitus. It is used twice by Ovid in describing Tiberius as reluctantly accepting power (*Fasti* 1.532; *Ex Ponto* 4.13.27–8).

[44] Bellemore was expanding on a suggestion already made by Carter (1975).

[45] Briscoe (1993: 398–404) argues for a *terminus post quem* of 24–26 for Book 2 and a *terminus ante quem* of 29 for Book 6. He refutes Bellemore's major arguments in favor of a date shortly after the trial of Libo and firmly establishes Book 9 as being written in the aftermath of the fall of Sejanus. Briscoe repeats these arguments in the introduction to his commentary on Book 8 of Valerius (2019: 2–4).

providence the virtues of which I am about speak are most kindly fostered and vices most severely punished" (*Te igitur huic coepto, penes quem hominum deorumque consensus maris ac terrae regimen esse voluit, certissima salus patriae, Caesar, invoco, cuius caelesti providentia virtutes, de quibus dicturus sum, benignissime foventur, vitia severissime vindicantur*). Valerius refers to the *consensus* of men and gods as having granted to Tiberius rule over sea and land, echoing the phrase in the *Res Gestae* that Augustus had brought peace through victory over land and sea (*terra marique parta victoriis pax*, RG 13).

As discussed in Chapter 1, *consensus* was a key concept in the charismatic ideology of Augustus, especially in the notion that *tota Italia* swore an oath supporting him against Antony (*RG* 25.2). We also see *consensus* in his acclamation as *pater patriae* by the *populus Romanus universus*, the Senate, and the equestrian order (*RG* 35.1). Likewise, just as Augustus was considered to have saved Rome from endless civil war, Tiberius is hailed as the surest salvation (*certissima salus*) for the fatherland. As we saw in Chapter 2, an altar was built celebrating the *providentia* of Augustus in adopting Tiberius and of Tiberius in adopting Germanicus; thus, Tiberius is celebrated for his heavenly providence (*caelesti providentia*). Finally, while every great man was celebrated for his virtues, Augustus was famously presented with a *clipeus virtutis* by the Senate (*RG* 34), a symbol of his fostering the virtues which brought stability to the state (*virtus, iustitia, clementia*, and *pietas*). Tiberius, according to Valerius, now stands as the arbiter of such virtues, for, by Tiberius' divine providence, "virtues are most kindly fostered and vices most severely punished."[46]

Notably, Tiberius is referred to here as Caesar. In Valerius, we run into some of the same ambiguities in the use of the name we have already seen in other authors. After invoking Tiberius in the *praefatio*, Valerius foreshadows Tiberius' deification in much the same way Augustan authors had that of his predecessor: "your divinity seems equal, by the present trust, to your father's and grandfather's star, by whose distinguished radiance much glorious splendor has been added to our own rites: for we have accepted other gods; we have produced the Caesars" (*tua [divinitas] praesenti fide paterno avitoque sideri par videtur, quorum eximio fulgore multum caerimoniis nostris inclutae claritatis accessit: reliquos enim deos accepimus, Caesares dedimus*). Valerius equates the divine virtue of Tiberius with his father's and grandfather's star. He ends by stating that while the Romans had

---

[46] On the rewarding of virtues and the punishment of vices in Valerius using the lens of *severitas*, see Langlands 2008.

accepted the other gods as gods, they had given (to the world) the Caesars (as gods). This rather blatant statement of the deification of emperors may seem somewhat cynical if taken out of context.[47] But it is clearly tied to Valerius' entire mission – to show the Caesars as embodying all of the virtues which were exemplified individually by previous Romans.

Nevertheless, the charismatic princeps Augustus evolved from the young man Octavian, who did some rather unsavory things. Like Velleius, Valerius treads very carefully when discussing Octavian's rise to power.[48] Briscoe notes that although the proscriptions are mentioned eleven times, "in none of them is Octavian himself named – *proscriptus a triumviris* is a common phrase" (1993: 403). Valerius does include an episode before Philippi, also found in Plutarch, which could have painted the young heir of Caesar in a less-than-favorable light. According to Plutarch (*Brut.* 41.7; cf. *Ant.* 22.2), on the eve of battle Octavian was warned to leave his camp by a friend who had seen a vision in his sleep. Octavian did indeed leave; his camp was sacked and his men slaughtered.[49] Pliny the Elder (*HN* 7.148) says that Octavian spent three days hiding in the marshes while Antony continued the (ultimately victorious) campaign. Valerius, on the other hand, spins this story in a positive manner. Octavian was saved by divine intervention. Valerius opens his account under the heading of "Dreams" (*De Somniis*) by stating that he could begin at no better place than from the most sacred memory of Divus Augustus (1.7.1). Valerius narrates that before Philippi the goddess Minerva appeared to Octavian's doctor in a dream and instructed him not to let his patient's sickness keep him from battle. Thus, Octavian was in battle (having been carried on a litter), not in hiding, when his camp was sacked. Valerius concludes the narrative with the exclamation: "What, therefore, should we think other than that action was taken by a divine *numen* lest a head already destined for immortality should suffer violence from fortune unworthy of that celestial spirit?" (*Quid ergo aliud putamus quam divino numine effectum ne destinatum iam immortalitati caput indignam calesti spiritu Fortunae violentiam sentiret?*)

Perhaps not coincidentally, this passage is immediately followed by a narrative of Calpurnia's dream on the eve of Caesar's assassination. Caesar,

---

[47] Mueller (2002: 13) compares this with importation of Juno of Veii and Aesculapius, who were immediately accepted in Rome.

[48] Bloomer 1992: 223. Cf. Gowing 2010: 254.

[49] Appian much more succinctly states, "Octavian himself was not there, having been warned in a dream to beware of that day, as he has himself written in his *Memoirs*" (*BC* 4.110; Loeb trans. White)

of course, did not listen to his wife. Valerius states that the gods willed that Octavian/Augustus be saved because he had not yet accomplished the deeds that would prove his divinity while Caesar had (1.7.2). At the same time, Valerius portrays Augustus as showing more respect to the signs of the gods. Likewise, Valerius juxtaposes Caesar and Augustus at 7.6.5–6. Caesar, running low on timber at Munda, built a rampart out of enemy corpses. By contrast, during a grain shortage in the Bosporus caused by the threat of an impending Parthian attack, the *cura* of Augustus solved the crisis.

Elsewhere, Valerius shows Augustus in his role as *pater patriae*, protecting both the state and the family. At 7.7.3, C. Tettius had been disinherited by his father. Valerius, without giving any further details about the case, says that Divus Augustus, having used his judgment as *pater patriae*, ordered the young man to take possession of his father's property. Divus Augustus also annulled the dispositions of Septicia, who had attempted to disown her sons (7.7.4). Valerius rebukes Septicia, asserting that Aequitas herself could not have given a more just or considered decision (*si ipsa Aequitas hac de re cognosceret, potuitne iustius aut gravius pronuntiare*). He concludes by stating that even in the underworld Septicia had been blasted by a celestial thunderbolt (*caelesti fulmine*), a reminder of Augustus' association with Jupiter. Valerius later (7.8.6) presents another case where Augustus seemingly exhibits divine judgement in the case of wrongdoing, this time against himself. Under the heading, "Wills Which Remained Valid Although There Were Reasons They Could Have Been Annulled" (*[Testamenta] quae rata mansuerunt cum causas haberent cur rescindi possent*), Valerius calls out T. Marius, who had been shown favor by Divus Augustus and repeatedly promised to include his *imperator* in his will. Apparently, he lied. Nevertheless, the will was still considered valid.[50]

The protection of the Roman family was a key part of Augustus' program. But the protection of his own family, the *domus Augusta*, was even more important. While in the cases mentioned above Augustus showed *iustitia* in preserving the rights of heirs, he could punish severely when his own family was threatened. At 9.15.2, Valerius recounts an accusation against the chastity of Augustus' sister Octavia. He begins, "Not even the most excellent *numen* of Divus Augustus, still then ruling earth, was untried by this kind of injury." A young man declared himself to be the abandoned child of Octavia. This not only insulted Octavia's

---

[50] Anyone who has read Tacitus knows that later it would become standard practice for men to leave property to bad emperors in the hopes that their wills would remain valid: *a bono patre non scribi heredem nisi malum principem, Agr.* 43.

famous chastity; it also would presumably have entitled him to the position for which at one time Octavia's son Marcellus had been marked. According to Valerius, this would stain the most sacred household (*sanctissimi penates*). Augustus had the pretender sentenced to the galleys. This awkward story, not found elsewhere, seems a counterpoint to the supposititious false Agrippa and false Drusus, who both caused problems in the reign of Tiberius. It reasserts the charismatic privilege of true members of the *domus Augusta*.

At 8.15 *praef.*, Valerius provides his own explanation as to why there are so few mentions of the imperial family in his catalog of *exempla*. Valerius expresses that the divinity of Augustus has been transferred to his *domus*: "But even if my mind in this place were being borne away by every impetus straightaway towards the *domus Augusta*, a most beneficent and honored temple (*benificentissimum et honoratissimum templum*), it will be better restrained, since for one to whom the path to heaven lies open, earthly tributes, however great they are, are still less than what is owed." The *domus Augusta*, both as a family and as a physical space, is considered a *templum*.[51] But because Augustus (and presumably Tiberius) is destined for the heavens, Valerius claims he will focus his tributes on those outside of the *domus Augusta*.

Even after his death, Augustus is celebrated as *pater patriae* and *paterfamilias* of the *domus Augusta*. Indeed, while Tiberius is praised in the *praefatio* as the Caesar who preserves order, and who, along with Augustus, thwarted the conspiracy of the *parricidium*, in the only *exemplum* which directly features Tiberius he is a *frater*, not *pater*.[52] Under the heading "Pietas," one of the cardinal virtues from the *clipeus virtutis* of Augustus, Valerius describes Tiberius' speedy trip to his brother's deathbed. In introducing the brothers, he asserts that they once belonged to the Claudian *gens* but now are part of the Julian (5.5.3), despite the fact that Drusus was never adopted by Augustus. Having learned of Drusus' injury and subsequent illness, Tiberius raced day and night. While he had only one human companion, he was escorted by the most sacred *numen* of Pietas herself, the gods who foster exceptional virtues, and the most faithful guardian of the Roman Empire, Jupiter (*sanctissimum pietatis*

---

[51] In his overview of triumphs, Valerius omits Actium but mentions the oak wreath granted to Augustus *qua postes Augustae domus sempiterna gloria triumphant* (2.8.7). As Briscoe points out (2019: 222), in both references, "V. means the actual house, not the imperial family (surprisingly no other author uses the phrase)."

[52] Despite the focus on his role as brother and son, Tiberius is referred to here as *princeps parensque noster*.

numen et di fautores eximiarum virtutum et fidissimus Romani imperi custos Iuppiter comitatus est). As mentioned previously, Augustus had been frequently associated with Jupiter throughout his lifetime. This affirms the identification of the two brothers with the Dioscuri. Valerius further compares the *pietas* of Tiberius to that of Pollux. Drusus was still alive when Tiberius arrived. He met his brother and saluted him as *imperator*. He yielded honor to his brother in allocating general's quarters *(fraternae maiestati cessit)*.[53] Then he died. Drusus' recognition of his brother's *maiestas* foreshadows Tiberius' future role as princeps. Valerius does make another indirect allusion to Tiberius in his mention of Tiberius' ancestors, the consuls of 207 BC, Livius Salinator and C. Claudius Nero. These two men also held the censorship together in 204 BC. They did not get along. Valerius reflects on their ignorance. If they had only known the mingling of their *imagines* would lead to the birth of "our beneficial princeps" *(salutaris principis nostri)*, they would have made a pact of *amicitia* (2.9.6a). Just as in the *praefatio*, Tiberius is the *salus patriae*.

Which brings us back to the attempted *parricidium* that threatened to destroy the Roman state (9.11 ext. 4). In Valerius' narrative, the gods who save Rome are not just the traditional tutelary deities but also the Caesars themselves:

> But the eyes of the gods were keeping watch, the stars preserved their own strength, the altars, divine couches, and temples were protected by the present *numen*; nothing which was obligated to protect the head of Augustus and the fatherland handed itself over to sloth; and in particular the author and safeguard of our welfare took care with divine counsel lest his own most excellent benefactions should collapse with the ruin of the whole world.

> sed vigilarunt oculi deorum, sidera suum vigorem obtinuerunt, arae pulvinaria templa praesenti numine vallata sunt, nihilque quod pro capite Augusti ac patria excubare debuit torporem sibi permisit, et in primis auctor et tutela nostrae incolumitatis ne excellentissima merita sua totius orbis ruina conlaberentur divino consilio providit.[54]

At 4.3.3, Valerius had referred to Augustus and Tiberius as the divine eyes of the state *(duobus rei publicae divinis oculis)*. In the *praefatio*, Tiberius' *divinitas* is equal to the stars of his father and grandfather. Thus, while

---

[53] As Wardle (2002: 439) notes, Tiberius is the only one of his contemporaries to whom Valerius attributes *maiestas*. We will discuss the concept of *maiestas* under Tiberius in the next chapter.

[54] Following the text of Briscoe's Teubner edition (1998). Shackleton-Bailey's Loeb (2000) has *pro capite augusto*.

Valerius does not explicitly state as much, Divus Augustus seems to be included among the protective deities who thwart the *parricidium*. Likewise, the altars, sacred couches, and temples were protected by a *praesens numen*. This phrase was often used of Augustus during his lifetime. If Valerius is referring to Tiberius here as Augustus, it would be the only time he does so. Regardless, Tiberius is blessed by divine will to bring prosperity to the world. And thus, he is the "guardian of our safety" (*tutela nostrae incolumitatis*), who uses his divine counsel (*divino consilio*) to thwart the plots against the state. In saving Rome, Tiberius is both protected by and has become assimilated with Augustus. In Valerius' text we see an awareness of the routinization of Augustus' charismatic position.

Phaedrus: Telling Tales about the Principate

Traditionally, Phaedrus has been considered a Tiberian author. He narrates stories involving Augustus (3.10) and Tiberius (2.5) as if they were recent events. He does not mention Caligula or Claudius. And, most tellingly, he claims to have been persecuted by Sejanus (3 Pr.). While some scholars have challenged the traditional narrative that Phaedrus was a freedman of Augustus, Champlin argues not only that Phaedrus was an elite lawyer, but also that he was writing in the reign of Claudius and Nero: "In brief: the fables of Phaedrus were not yet available around AD 43, and they (or at least their first book) were in circulation by about AD 70" (2005: 102). Champlin relies heavily on Seneca's statement in the *Consolatio ad Polybium* (8.3) that fables were a genre as yet untried by Roman talents. He dismisses any possible argument for this omission, citing only a (typically) cryptic remark by John Henderson (2001: 206 n. 10; cited at Champlin 2005: 101 n. 8). While Champlin's arguments against the traditional biography of Phaedrus are enticing, his dismissal of evidence for a Tiberian date seems unwarranted.[55]

Although we can never know for certain when the *Fables* first became available to a wider audience, the persona of Phaedrus tells us certain things about perceptions of the princeps in the reign of Tiberius. We know that Tiberius himself often spoke allusively, even resorting to fables. Phaedrus' rationale for using fables was a limitation on *libertas*, a limitation felt by the second princeps, who was often misunderstood by the Senate as

---

[55] See Edwards 2015. Pieper (2010) and Renda (2012) also question Champlin's dating. In Champlin's discussion of authors imitated by Phaedrus (2005: 109), none date later than Ovid.

he tried to continue the system founded by his charismatic predecessor while acknowledging his own inferiority. Moreover, the claim to be persecuted by Sejanus could be seen as a badge of honor after his downfall.[56] Given that at least Books 3–5 were written after the fall of Sejanus, like Velleius and Valerius, Phaedrus provides us with a view of a time when the *domus Augusta* was in crisis. Germanicus and Drusus were dead, the children of Germanicus were still young, their mother Agrippina was jostling with her sister-in-law Livilla, and Sejanus was lurking in the background. Even after the fall of Sejanus and the designation of Caligula as heir presumptive, Tiberius' absence from Rome demonstrated the weaknesses in a government which depended upon one man. Thus, in a collection of Aesop's fables, Phaedrus includes two narratives featuring the first and second principes.

In *Fabula* 3.10, a poem likely written after the fall of Sejanus, Phaedrus paints Augustus as a wise judge, able to see past the manipulation of a greedy freedman and resolve a sad legal case involving a Roman *matrona*, purportedly protecting her adolescent son.[57] The freedman had tricked the *paterfamilias* into believing his wife was having an affair. The husband pretended to leave town. The wife, wanting to protect her own and her son's chastity, compelled her son to sleep in her bed. The husband returned and mistakenly killed his own son.[58] Realizing what he had done, he then killed himself, leaving the wife without any corroborating witnesses to her innocence. When Divus Augustus is called upon to settle the case, he "dispels the shadows of calumny, and finds the certain source of the truth" (3.42–3).[59]

Phaedrus' portrayal of Augustus can be compared with that of Tiberius in Book 2. In *Fabula* 3.10, Divus Augustus is a wise ruler publicly intervening to ensure justice for a wronged family. In 2.5, Tiberius is a solitary emperor sardonically mocking a courtier. An *ardalio* attempts to earn a great reward for a small price. The word *ardalio* appears only here and in two poems by Martial (2.7.8, 4.78.10). It is translated variously as "busybody" (*OLD*), "harlequin" (Loeb trans. Perry), and "mucker" (Henderson 2001: 9).[60] In Martial 2.7, the addressee is a jack-of-all-trades

---

[56] Jennings 2009: 242. Cf. Henderson 2001: 66–70.
[57] As Henderson points out, 3.10 is "the longest extant *fabula* in Phaedrus" (2001: 37).
[58] Neither Phaedrus nor Augustus seems to consider the possibility of incest.
[59] See Henderson (2001: 38) and Wiegand (2013: 217) for this poem's positive image of Augustus. Libby (2010: 555) observes that Phaedrus blends the narrative in such a way that it is difficult to tell where the wisdom of Augustus stops and that of the poet begins.
[60] For more discussion on the etymology of this word, see Henderson 2001: 20 and 196 n. 15.

and master of none. Martial 4.78 lambasts an older man who seems overly enthusiastic about *salutationes* and other flatteries which would better befit a younger man starting his career. Regardless of the various subtleties of translation, an *ardalio* is a prime target for satire.

Thus, the entire tone of *Fabula* 2.5 is rather different from that of 3.10. Divus Augustus scatters clouds of deception. He is the wise judge, the protector of the family, and perhaps most importantly, is in Rome. Tiberius, on the other hand, is at Misenum. Given the location, it seems fairly clear that this poem was written after Tiberius' permanent withdrawal from Rome.[61] It may even have been written after the fall of Sejanus. Phaedrus' Tiberius is a man living in solitude, surrounded by *ardaliones*. When one tries to earn the favor of his master by sprinkling water on the dusty ground, Tiberius mocks him. He utters a Tiberian witticism which is subject to interpretation but which basically tells the *ardalio* that his effort has been wasted.[62] In stark contrast to the charismatic Divus Augustus, Tiberius could be any great man dealing with overzealous servants at his Campanian villa.

Phaedrus examines the very nature of the principate in a curious anecdote from Book 5, which may have been written after the death of Tiberius and the accession of Caligula (or even Claudius). In *Fabula* 5.7, Phaedrus narrates an odd anecdote about a flute-player named Princeps. The story is set in the reign of Augustus, as Phaedrus states that Princeps accompanied Maecenas' favorite, Bathyllus. Phaedrus also indicates that the incident happened in his own time.[63] Princeps breaks his leg. He is absent from the stage while his leg heals. When a boisterous ovation breaks out upon his return to the scene with the chant that "Rome, secure, rejoices because its princeps is safe" (*laetare incolumis Roma salvo principe*), the flute-player assumes the chant is for him. He soon realizes when the crowd begins to mock him that they are not applauding him but the *domus divina*. The "pretender" is tossed off stage. Given that this incident supposedly takes place before we have any record of the phrase *domus divina* becoming common, there are clearly some anachronistic elements. Indeed, the incident has more in common with the reign of Tiberius, when the princeps had to deal with multiple impersonators challenging his right to rule. Phaedrus underscores the theater of the *domus divina* itself;

---

[61] Wiegand (2013: 191) sees this poem as a means to dating at least Book 2 to the mid-20s.
[62] The interpretation hinges on the word *alapa*, which could be symbolic of manumission. See Henderson 2001: 30.
[63] On the "historicity" of the incident, see Henderson 2001: 97–100.

the only thing necessary for one to be beloved by the crowd is to be included in the divine house of Augustus. Anyone who does not fit that bill but tries to usurp those privileges, no matter how much he was previously beloved, will suffer, just as Princeps does in the fable, and, historically, in a much more brutal way, Sejanus and his family.

Seneca the Elder: The Rhetoric of Augustan Charisma

Seneca the Elder gives us insight into the ways in which rhetoric changed under the principate, a transformation cynically recognized by Tacitus' *Dialogus*, from meaningful oratory on behalf of the state to declamation practiced among a small group of elites. Seneca likely began writing the *Controversiae* before the death of Tiberius. At 7.1.27, Seneca refers to Julius Montanus, *qui comes fuit <Tiberii>*.[64] Although the past tense might seem confirmation that at this point Tiberius was dead, we know from Seneca's son (*Ep.* 122.11) that Julius Montanus fell from favor with Tiberius (*tolerabilis poeta et amicitia Tiberi notus et frigore*). The only other mention of Tiberius in the work of Seneca the Elder is much less ambiguous. At *Suasoriae* 3.7.7, Tiberius, himself a student of Theodorus of Gadara (cf. Suet. *Tib.* 57.1), was offended *Nicetis ingenio* and was thus delighted by a quip from Junius Gallio which referred to an old joke at the expense of Nicetes. The use of the imperfect tense (*offendebatur*) would again suggest that Tiberius was no longer living but is not decisive.[65] The most important evidence for dating the bulk of Seneca's work until after the death of Tiberius is the frequent mention of authors whose works were supposedly banned under Tiberius, most notably Cremutius Cordus. Seneca, whose son wrote a *consolatio* to Cordus' daughter, may have had a contraband copy of Cordus' history; nevertheless, he could not safely cite it until after the work had been pardoned by Caligula (Suet. *Cal.* 16).

While Seneca seems indifferent to Tiberius, he reveres Augustus. Augustus is mentioned by name seven times. In five of those instances (*Contr.* 2.4.13.9, 2.4.13.18, 2.5.20.6, 4 pref. 5.3, 4 pref. 7.5), he is dubbed Divus Augustus even though he was still alive at the time of the narrative. He is also referred to as Caesar Augustus in the same narrative contained in

---

[64] The insertion of *Tiberii* was first proposed by Kiessling. See the note on this passage in Håkanson 1989: 181.

[65] Sussman (1987: 93) summarizes, "Written after the *Controversiae* (2.4.8), the *Suasoriae* contain many more contemporary references. This suggests that Seneca compiled the *Controversiae*, which only contain a few, shortly before the death of Tiberius, and that the *Suasoriae* were written afterwards."

those first two citations, as well as at *Contr.* 2.4.12.12 and 10 pref. 14.1. Seneca seems to make no distinction between the two nomenclatures. All of the mentions of Augustus occur within the *Controversiae*. In the first narrative where Augustus appears (*Contr.* 2.4.12-13), he is listening to Porcius Latro declaim on a case which criticizes a man for adopting grandchildren of lower birth. This was clearly a sensitive subject; at the time Augustus was about to adopt the sons of Agrippa. Seneca reports that in the face of insults to his closest friend and confidant, Augustus allowed free speech: "So great was the *libertas* under Divus Augustus... Divus Augustus seems to me worthy of admiration since under his reign so much was permitted." Likewise, regarding the trial of Titus Labienus narrated at *Contr.* 10 pref. 3, Griffin observes, "[Seneca] is careful to lay the blame on Labienus' personal enemies in the Senate rather than on Augustus, where it probably belongs" (1972: 14). At *Contr.* 4 pref. 5.3, Seneca praises Augustus for not growing excessively angry with his friend Pollio, who threw a dinner party shortly after news of the death of Gaius arrived in Rome. Pollio explains to Augustus that he had done the same when his own son had died, one of many instances in Roman literature of a father bearing the death of a son with stoic calmness.[66] Seneca states that Divus Augustus, as was the custom for that most merciful man (*illi clementissimo viro*), dealt with the situation not only with civility but even with friendliness (*non civiliter tantum sed etiam familiariter*). We will discuss in the next chapter the role played by Augustus in setting the stage for the treason trials which ran rampant in the reign of Tiberius. Here, Seneca portrays him as the model of tolerance.

Augustus appears in other narratives as a literary critic. Whereas Seneca takes a rather neutral attitude towards Tiberius' literary tastes, in the *Controversiae* Augustus responds to witticisms and makes his own quips *eleganter* (*Contr.* 2.5.20.6) and *optime* (*Contr.* 4 pref. 7.5). He seems to foster talent rather than stifle it. Seneca reports (*Contr.* 10 pref. 14.1) that Augustus praised the declamations of Gavius Silo, whom he frequently had heard pleading cases in Tarraco. This incident must have taken place in the earlier part of Augustus' reign. Augustus' promotion of oratorical talent in Spain would have resonated with Seneca. If the *Controversiae* were indeed written late in the reign of Tiberius, then these passages praising Augustus would reflect Tiberius' desire to highlight the charismatic image of his predecessor to ensure a peaceful succession by one of his descendants.

---

[66] E.g., Horatius (Livy 2.8); Cato the Elder (Plut. *Cat. Mai.* 24.6); and Tiberius (Tac. *Ann.* 4.8; cf. Suet. *Tib.* 52.1)

Finally, we must mention the historical work of Seneca the Elder, which survives only in fragments and a reference from his son. A fragment from Seneca the Younger's *Vita Patris* (*FRH* Seneca the Elder T1) reads: "whoever had read his history from the beginning of the civil wars, from whence first the truth retreated, up until practically the day of his own death, would have greatly valued knowing. . ." (*Quisquis legisset eius historias ab initio bellorum civilium, unde primum veritas retro abiit, paene usque ad mortis suae diem, magno aestimasset scire. . .*). Seneca the Younger's testimony indicates that his father's work was published posthumously. Some have even argued that the work was never published.[67] However, recent work on the papyri at Herculaneum challenges that view. Valeria Piano (2019) and Maria Chiara Scappaticcio (2018) have re-evaluated Papyrus 1067. They both argue that the fragments belong to the *Histories* of Seneca the Elder. This would justify the assertion that the Seneca cited as a source by Suetonius (*Tib.* 73; cf. *Cal.* 12, without the attribution to Seneca) in his narrative of the death of Tiberius was the Elder, not the Younger. Particularly noteworthy among Piano's and Scappaticcio's readings of the fragments are the occurrences of the names Augustus and Tiberius. Augustus appears in the vocative case, which suggests that the fragment in question belongs to a speech or letter addressed to Augustus. The phrase *vir prudens* also occurs. *Prudentia* is closely related to *providentia*, a virtue widely advertised, as we have seen, in Augustus' plans for Tiberius to succeed to his *statio*. While these readings are not definitive, the passage in the fragmentary papyrus may have dealt with the transition from Augustus to Tiberius. This supports Seneca the Younger's claim that his father wrote a history from the beginning of the civil wars until almost his own death. Seneca the Elder was presumably working on the *Suasoriae* at this time, so the positive image of Augustus and the neutral image of Tiberius seen in Seneca's works on declamation were likely also reflected in the historical work. But until more fragments are analyzed or uncovered, we cannot know for sure.

Conclusions

As in the material remains examined in the previous chapter, in literary works from the age of Tiberius Divus Augustus is front and center. His charismatic image as a divine protector overshadows the portrayal of Tiberius as a mortal man. While Ovid, Velleius, and Valerius depict

---

[67] See Griffin 1972: 10 and Levick in *FRH* (2013b: 1.506–8).

Tiberius as somewhat superhuman, his powers derive from his adoptive charismatic father. This leads to frequent confusion in nomenclature, particularly in the use of the title Caesar. As Tiberian authors struggled to explain the succession from one princeps to another, they found themselves needing to assimilate the chief male members of the *domus Augusta*, including Germanicus, who, had he not died prematurely, would have succeeded to the *statio* Tiberius inherited from Augustus. This transfer of Augustan charisma to the entire house created serious legal difficulties in the reign of Tiberius. If the *salus* of Rome depended upon the *salus* of one man or one family, then any threat to the *maiestas* of that man or family could be seen as a threat to the state. Thus, the door was open for accusations of treason against the disloyal. While initially Tiberius curbed these accusations, the crisis in the *domus Augusta* after the death of Drusus, Tiberius' own absence from Rome, and the eagerness of senators to prove their devotion to the house of Augustus ultimately led to an embarrassing "reign of terror."

CHAPTER 6

Maiestas *and the Protection of Augustan Charisma*

As we have already seen in Chapter 2, the cult of Divus Augustus and reverence for the *domus divina/Augusta* were integral to the succession of Tiberius. Nevertheless, Tiberius was scrupulous in refusing divine honors for himself, mostly due to his own *moderatio*, but also lest the divine honors voted to Augustus should lose their distinction. The foundations for prosecutions of *maiestas laesa* had been laid in the late Republic. Towards the end of the reign of Augustus, prosecutors began to use *maiestas* laws to attack those libeling members of the nobility. Soon, verbal attacks on the princeps were considered *maiestas laesa*. Even members of the *domus Augusta* were exiled, unofficially condemned for undermining the *maiestas* of their *paterfamilias*. Once Augustus had been deified, a strong message was sent that his charismatic image and that of his family must be protected to ensure the preservation of the *status* he created.

When delators tried to bring forth *maiestas* charges in the early years of his reign, Tiberius treated such cases in much the same way Augustus had during his later years. Anything which threatened the state, such as the supposed conspiracy of Libo or the military insubordination of Piso, had to be punished. Lesser offences were dismissed. However, even if we take Tacitus' comments at the beginning of Book 4 of the *Annals* with a grain of salt, there was a fundamental shift in the emperor's attitude towards the prosecution of *maiestas* and related crimes in the latter part of his reign.[1] Tiberius' absence from Rome allowed senators free rein to attack their personal enemies. More importantly, the crisis within the *domus Augusta*

---

[1] I am using the term *maiestas* here very broadly to encompass anything which was called *maiestas* or implied to be treasonous by ancient authors in their narratives of Tiberius' reign. On the difficulties in defining *maiestas* in the reign of Tiberius, see Yakobson 2003: 76. For technical, if somewhat problematic, analyses of *maiestas* laws in the Republic and early principate, see Bauman 1967 and 1974. For a list of the *maiestas* and other legal cases narrated by Tacitus as well as their outcomes, see Appendix II of Walker 1960. On the discrepancy between "fact" and "impression" in Tacitus' narration of Tiberian treason trials, see Walker 1960: 82–137.

triggered by the attacks on Agrippina the Elder and her son Nero created an atmosphere of distrust, exacerbated by the downfall of Sejanus. The only way for senators to prove their loyalty to the state was through charges against each other for showing disloyalty to the *domus Augusta*.

Republican and Augustan Precedents

Laws protecting the *maiestas* of the Roman people existed during the Republic, beginning with the law introduced by Saturninus around 100 BC, the *lex Appuleia de maiestate*.[2] However, the details are unclear. Cicero (*Pis.* 50) gives us some sense of a *lex Cornelia de maiestate*, most likely introduced by Sulla in 81 BC, which covered provincial misgovernment.[3] Cicero also mentions a law concerning *maiestas* introduced by Julius Caesar, the *lex Iulia de maiestate*. Cicero cites this law specifically to attack Antony for his failure to uphold the acts of Caesar: "And what of this, that those laws of Caesar's are in part altered which declare that he who is convicted of riot, and also he who is convicted of treason (*maiestas*), shall be refused water and fire (*aqua et igni interdici*)?" (Phil. 1.9.23; Loeb trans. Ker).[4] The Julian law seems to be a modification of the Sullan law, both of which defined punishment for those found guilty as loss of citizenship and exile from Italy.[5]

While the ancient sources generally restrict their accounts of trials regarding *maiestas* to the later years of Augustus' reign, epigraphic evidence suggests that precedents for attacks on the princeps being encompassed by *maiestas* laws go back much earlier. The Second Cyrene Edict (E.-J.[2] 311), dated by Augustus' titles to 7/6 BC, recounts a dispute between Roman citizens and native aristocrats. After investigating the initial matter, Augustus detained a Roman citizen living in Cyrene over the accusation that this man had removed a statue of Augustus, or possibly just a statue inscribed with Augustus' name, from a public place. Peachin (2015: 551–2) conjectures that Augustus was personally offended and may have

---

[2] See *Rhet. Her.* 1.21 and Cic. *De Or.* 2.25.107, 2.39.164 for Saturninus' law of *maiestas minuta*.

[3] Bleicken (1962: 28) argues that the *lex Cornelia* would also have encompassed acts that could otherwise be considered *perduellio*.

[4] For citations on the *lex Iulia de maiestate*, see Schilling 2010: 85–8, who notes (87 n. 111) that there is no evidence in the sources for an Augustan law. On the lack of evidence for an Augustan law, see also Allison and Cloud 1962.

[5] Schilling (2010: 88) speculates that Caesar's law added a clause including confiscation of half the convicted person's property.

punished the accused for *maiestas laesa*. The people of Cyrene commemorated the incident on a public monument to demonstrate their loyalty.

Augustus' treatment of the two Julias and their lovers also indicates that he believed their actions violated his *maiestas*.[6] Although Augustus declared his daughter and granddaughter to be exiled before the Senate, they were not tried in any public court. Presumably, their exiles could be subsumed under the punishment for the *lex Iulia de adulteriis coercendis*.[7] Their lovers were also punished; most notably, Iullus Antonius was sentenced to death. Bauman contends that the charge was "some form of *maiestas*" (1967: 205). The question then arises as to whether or not the *lex Iulia de maiestate* entailed the death penalty. As mentioned above, under Julius Caesar the law seems to have prescribed a penalty of exile with loss of citizenship. Schilling posits that Augustus felt a need to institute the death penalty due to a very real threat against his life (2010: 91).[8] If this was the case, Augustus, not Tiberius, first enabled *maiestas* to be punished by death, specifically in a case where there was a perceived threat to Augustus and his family.

Tiberius was also not responsible for associating provincial mismanagement with *maiestas*. As mentioned above, this was already part of the Sullan law. Moreover, when C. Silanus was on trial before the Senate on charges of *maiestas* and extortion, Tiberius cited papers of Augustus concerning the provincial misconduct of Volesus Messalla (Tac. *Ann.* 3.68). Schilling (2010: 106–8) believes these cases were both tried under the *lex Iulia repetundarum* but with additional accusations of *saevitia* inflicted on the provinces. This would then explain why Tiberius cited Augustus' documents on the trial of Messalla as a precedent in the trial of Silanus. However, Messalla may also have been indicted on charges of diminishing the *maiestas* of the Roman people by abusing provincial subjects. Both Messalla and Silanus would have been liable for *maiestas* under the Sullan law.

Most of the discussion regarding the application of *maiestas* laws under Augustus centers around censorship cases generally dated to the end of his reign. Tacitus (*Ann.* 1.72.3–4) states that Augustus first allowed the application of the *lex Cornelia de famosis libellis* under the heading of

---

[6] Fantham 1985: 266. For varying interpretations of Tacitus' statement that in punishing his daughter and granddaughter, Augustus exceeded his own laws (*suasque ipse leges egrediebatur*, *Ann.* 3.24.2), see Woodman and Martin 1996: 225–9.

[7] For the history of this law and known punishments, see Schilling 2010: 80–5.

[8] See also Allison and Cloud (1962: 720–2), who analyze the problems in our sources for the punishment of the two Julias.

maiestas. The two cases of which we know both occurred late in his reign and are perhaps indicative of a movement to suppress free speech.[9] In the preface to Book 10 of the *Controversiae*, Seneca the Elder writes of Labienus, whose books were burned as a "new punishment":[10]

> His freedom of speech was so great that it exceeded the definition of freedom, and since he indiscriminately attacked all orders and men, he was called Rabienus. Among his faults were a powerful mind, one violent in line with his talent and which had not yet put aside its Pompeian sympathies despite such great peace. Against this first a new penalty was thought up; it was accomplished through his enemies that all his books be burned: a new and extraordinary affair – that punishment should be exacted from literary works.

> Libertas tanta ut libertatis nomen excederet, et quia passim ordines hominesque laniabat Rabienus vocaretur. Animus inter vitia ingens et ad similitudinem ingeni sui violentus et qui Pompeianos spiritus nondum in tanta pace posuisset. In hoc primum excogitata est nova poena; effectum est enim per inimicos ut omnes eius libri comburerentur: res nova et invisitata supplicium de studiis sumi. (Seneca, *Contr.* 10 pref. 5).

Seneca then wishes the same fate upon Labienus' accuser and recounts the final fate of Labienus (whom he elsewhere (*Contr.* 4 pref. 2) styles as a man with a mind even more bitter than his tongue (*homo mentis quam linguae amarioris*)).[11] Not wishing to outlive his work, Labienus shut himself up in his familial tomb, afraid that the flame which had been applied to his work would be denied to his body (*Contr.* 10 pref. 7). Although Seneca does not specify the charges, the previous statements regarding the *libertas* of Labienus are compounded by the anecdote that Labienus considered parts of his history too outspoken to be read until after his death (*Contr.* 10 pref. 8). Moreover, Labienus apparently provoked Maecenas by insulting his beloved freedman Bathyllus.[12] Hennig (1973: 253) argues that Labienus was the first person to be tried under Augustus' new conception

---

[9] Suetonius (*Aug.* 36) adds that Augustus suppressed the publication of the *acta senatus*.

[10] On book burning in the later Republic and early principate, see Cramer 1945, Rohmann 2013, and Howley 2017. Howley (2017: 224) adds to the examples more commonly cited a story from Seneca (*Contr.* 10.5.22), where Timagenes burned his own *historias rerum ab illo gestarum* in protest at being excluded from Augustus' house.

[11] Labienus' accuser is often thought to be Cassius Severus, whom Seneca (*Contr.* 10 pref. 8) refers to as most hostile to Labienus (*hominis Labieno invisissimi*); however, Seneca follows this assessment by stating that Cassius Severus claimed that if Labienus' books were to be burned, he himself should be burned alive as he knew them all by heart. See Cornell in *FRH* (2013: 1.472) and Howley 2017: 217 n. 25.

[12] Labienus seems to have given his enemies plenty of ammunition. Seneca summarizes (*Contr.* 10 pref. 4): *summa egestas erat, summa infamia, summum odium.*

of the *lex Iulia de maiestate* to include *iniuriae* punishable under the *lex Cornelia de famosis libellis*.

Suetonius (*Cal.* 16.1) states that early in his reign Caligula allowed the books of Labienus and Cassius Severus to be read again. Their writings had been banished by the Senate (*scripta senatus consultis abolita*). Cassius Severus, was, according to Tacitus (who does not mention Labienus), the victim of the first case of *maiestas* prosecuted for libelous writing or speech.[13] Tacitus specifically accuses Augustus of being the first to apply the laws of *maiestas* to defamatory writings. Augustus was provoked by the licentiousness (*libidine*) with which Severus defamed illustrious men and women (*Ann.* 1.72.3). Severus' writings were burned and he was relegated to Crete. Not having learned his lesson, he continued his attacks against prominent members of the Senate (*Ann.* 4.21). While Tacitus concedes that the application of the laws of *maiestas* was expanded in the later years of Augustus, he does not hold him to the same level of accountability as he does Tiberius. Nevertheless, the consular historian seems to acknowledge here, as he does elsewhere, that Tiberius was bound by Augustan precedent and the servility of the Senate to allow such trials to proceed.[14]

One more name should be mentioned in the context of *maiestas* and censorship in the later years of Augustus' rule. Ovid says that the reason for his exile was *carmen et error* (*Tristia* 4.10.89–90). The *carmen* was the scandalous *Ars Amatoria*; but this had been published years before. The *error* was something Ovid claimed to have seen but kept secret, about what we will never truly know. Nevertheless, the fact that Ovid viewed the *carmen* as *a* reason, if not necessarily *the* reason, for his exile indicates that the last years under Augustus were characterized by an increasing control over the content and tone of literature. Williams (1978: 55) connects the case of Ovid with those of Labienus and Cassius Severus as part of a general movement in the years 6–12. Whatever freedom of speech Augustus had hesitated to censure previously was now curbed by the *senatus consulta* authorizing the destruction of the works of Labienus and Severus. Ovid's works, while not burned by a *senatus consultum*, were, like their author, exiled from Rome. According to the *Tristia* (3.1.59–82;

---

[13] For a somewhat laudatory description of Cassius Severus and his oratorical style, as well as an explanation as to why he was so bad at declamation, see Seneca, *Contr.* 3 pref. Quintilian (10.1.116–17) admires him but admits he could display *acerbitas* and sometimes *plus stomacho quam consilio dedit*. In the *Dialogus* (26.4–5), Tacitus has Messalla say of Severus, *in magna parte librorum suorum plus bilis habeat quam sanguinis* and *non pugnat, sed rixatur*.

[14] On the role played by the Senate in these incidents, see Rohmann 2013: 146.

3.14.5–18), the erotic works of Ovid were banned from public libraries.[15] As mentioned in the previous chapter, Ovid specifically states that he was exiled by Augustus, not the Senate (*Tristia* 2.131–8).

The cases of Labienus, Severus, and Ovid date to the period after the exiles of Agrippa Postumus and Julia the Younger. In addition to the convulsions within the *domus Augusta*, fires, famine, and foreign disasters were plaguing the *pax Romana*. While overtly the cases of Labienus and Severus were concerned with libel against any member of the elite, the seeds had been sown for prosecution of verbal/written attacks against the princeps and his family.[16] Thus, by the end of the reign of Augustus we can sense a distinct shift in the definition of *crimen maiestatis*. During the Republic, *maiestas* laws were used to prosecute magistrates who tarnished the image of the Roman people, either through military ineptness or provincial mismanagement, and to protect magistrates from abuse. If *maiestas* laws protected magistrates, and the princeps always held some form of magisterial power (through *imperium* and *tribunicia potestas*), then the princeps was always covered by the laws involving *maiestas*.

Moreover, any attempts by members of the *domus Augusta* to undermine the authority of the *pater familias/pater patriae* could be seen as treasonous. Suetonius (*Aug.* 25) specifically refers to Augustus' refusal to allow anyone, even members of his family, to be overly familiar with the army:

> After the civil wars, neither in assemblies nor in documents did he address any of the soldiers as comrades, but just soldiers, and he did not allow them to be called otherwise, even by his sons or stepsons who held military command, thinking it more ambitious than military strategy or the peace of the times or the *maiestas* of himself and his house required.

> neque post bella civilia aut in contione aut per edictum ullos militum commilitones appellabat, sed milites, ac ne a filiis quidem aut privignis suis imperio praeditis aliter appellari passus est, ambitiosius id existimans, quam aut ratio militaris aut temporum quies aut sua domusque suae maiestas postularet.[17]

---

[15] Naturally, by playing up the fact that his books were publicly banned, Ovid likely increased private demand for them.

[16] Hennig (1973: 254) sees the cases as connected to a general movement to censor libel mentioned by Dio (56.27.1). Woodman (2018: 193–4) acknowledges the problems in Tacitus' narrative and concludes: "A more likely interpretation of [*Ann.*] 1.72.3 is that, in the troubled last decade of his principate, Augustus, alerted by Cassius Severus' extreme behavior to the potential damage which defamation could do, extended the *lex maiestatis* to cover speech and writings aimed at the imperial family but ensured that Severus himself was punished under some other law." See also Bauman 1967: 263.

[17] As Fantham (1985: 266) remarks, the phrase *sua domusque suae maiestas*, "may cite the princeps' own words."

Two things stand out in this context. The first is that after the civil wars Augustus did not refer to his soldiers as *commilitones*. This implies that he did allow himself to be overly familiar with his soldiers during the civil wars, as the circumstances demanded. As we have already seen, the image of Octavian/Augustus as a charismatic military leader who brought peace through victory was central to consolidating his power and that of his family. The other striking thing in this passage is the comparative adverb *ambitiosius*, implying that once peace and stability had been established, neither Augustus himself nor his family needed to solicit the favor of the army since their *maiestas* already secured such loyalty. But should anyone else do so, he could be seen as challenging the *maiestas* of Augustus.

Despite all attempts to reconstruct laws surrounding treason under Augustus, what constituted *maiestas* was probably never clearly defined. Augustus was secure enough in his own charisma and *auctoritas* to ensure laws of treason were applied only when there was a genuine threat. Tiberius, however, relied heavily, especially in his early years, on the charismatic image of Divus Augustus. His desire to protect the memory of his predecessor, combined with his own insecurity, allowed various "bad actors" to take advantage. Pliny remarks in his *Panegyricus* (11.1), contrasting Trajan's deification of Nerva with that of Augustus, "Tiberius dedicated Augustus to heaven, but in order that he could introduce the charge of *maiestas*" (*Dicavit caelo Tiberius Augustum, sed ut maiestatis crimen induceret*). Despite Pliny's cynicism, the passage points to the most vulnerable aspect of Tiberius' regime. Tiberius promoted the charismatic image of his predecessor to such an extent that others, especially in the Senate, felt compelled to prove their loyalty by protecting it.

Protecting the *Maiestas* of Divus Augustus

Suetonius, after extolling Augustus' clemency regarding insults to himself, records a letter Augustus had written to Tiberius: "My Tiberius, do not indulge your youth in this matter and become too indignant if someone speaks evil about me; for it is enough that we know that no one is able to do evil to us" (*Aetati tuae, mi Tiberi, noli in hac re indulgere et nimium indignari quemquem esse, qui de me male loquatur; satis est enim, si hoc habemus ne quis nobis male facere possit, Aug.* 51). Even at a young age and before he was Augustus' *filius*, Tiberius was aware of the importance of protecting Augustus' *maiestas*. Certainly, Tiberius has borne the brunt of the blame for allowing prosecutions encompassed under the heading of *maiestas*. But our evidence for such trials under Augustus is sketchy, while that for Tiberius' reign was assembled by a skilled orator.[18] Many of the early prosecutions which Tiberius allowed to proceed, following Republican and Augustan precedent, involved the preservation of the *pax Augusta*. As we shall see, several of those accused of *maiestas* under Tiberius were also charged with extortion or other crimes allegedly committed during their governance of a province.[19] Nevertheless, prosecutions for *maiestas* escalated under Tiberius, and we see a marked shift in policy after he withdrew from Rome.

The Senate clearly sensed Tiberius' reverence for his predecessor. Delators first tested the waters for prosecutions of *maiestas* and related crimes with charges brought against Faianius, a Roman knight.[20] He was accused of two insults to Divus Augustus: including a notorious *mimus* among his Augustales and having sold a statue of Augustus along with his estate. Despite Tacitus' assertion that these trials were manipulated *Tiberii arte*, in this instance Tiberius wrote to the Senate, saying, "his father had not been decreed a god so that this honor could be used to harm citizens... nor was it against religious scruples that his statue was added to the sale of the house and gardens, as was the case for statues of other gods" (*non ideo decretum patri suo caelum ut in perniciem civium is honor verteretur... nec contra religiones fieri quod effigies eius, ut alia numinum simulacra, venditionibus hortorum et domuum accedant, Ann.* 1.73.3). All the charges were dismissed. Rubrius, another *eques*, was accused of committing perjury after swearing an oath by the newly deified Augustus. Tiberius refused to hear the case, saying famously, "injuries to the gods are the concern of the gods" (*deorum iniurias dis curae, Ann.* 1.73.4).

Tacitus (*Ann.* 1.74) follows these cases with that of Granius Marcellus, who, in addition to *sinistros sermones* against Tiberius, was accused of placing his own statue higher than those of the Caesars and of replacing the head of a statue of Augustus with one of Tiberius. At this point in the accusation, Tiberius expressed an outburst of anger. Tacitus would have us believe that the outburst was due to disgust with the sinister statements against himself, but the sequence of the narrative tells otherwise. Tiberius erupted immediately after he learned that a statue of Augustus had been decapitated. Given the reverence Tiberius had shown for Augustus as well as his own refusal of excessive honors, Tiberius was more likely upset over

---

[18] Rutledge 2001: 89–90. On the overemphasis on treason trials in Tacitus, see Tuori 2016: 147–8.
[19] While it is difficult to know the exact circumstances for each case, sources indicate that Cn. Piso, Caesius Cordus, Antistius Vetus, C. Silanus, and C. Silius were all prosecuted for crimes in their provinces. We will discuss these cases in further detail below.
[20] On the arguments in favor of Faianius instead of Falanius, see Coarelli 2005.

the informal *damnatio memoriae* of the newly deified Divus Augustus.[21] Granius Marcellus was absolved of the charges of *maiestas*, but the princeps' displeasure at defacement of statues of Augustus, especially in an attempt to flatter himself, was made perfectly clear.[22]

Although these cases were dismissed, Tiberius did not make any blanket statement that *maiestas* could *not* be used to prosecute insults to Divus Augustus. Indeed, soon after Tacitus records the trials mentioned above, he has Tiberius state in a debate regarding riots in the theater that he would follow the precedent of Augustus, as it would not be right (*fas*) for him to infringe on his predecessor's *dicta* (*Ann.* 1.77.3). In this same debate, Tacitus states that Tiberius was offering the Senate the image of freedom (*simulacra libertatis*). While inevitably much of our view of this matter is colored by Tacitus' narrative, these two elements – Tiberius' long leash for the Senate and his public reverence for Augustus – created the perfect environment for the growth of prosecutions for *maiestas*. Tiberius did not create the laws of *maiestas*, nor was he the first to apply the laws to insults against the princeps. Moreover, he was not the one who brought the first charges for *maiestas* forward. He was asked by a praetor whether or not the law should be enforced and replied (what else could he reply given the Augustan precedent?) that the laws must be enforced (*exercendas leges esse*, Suet. *Tib.* 58 and Tac. *Ann.* 1.72.3; both cite the same phrase).

Tiberius had inaugurated his reign as Augustus' successor by deifying his predecessor. He now either needed to defend the fact that Augustus was a god to be treated like all the other gods or allow Augustus' image to be mocked and his own legitimacy undermined. The primary issue at hand was a lack of legislative precedent for prosecutions of impiety. Tiberius and the Senate had to find their own way to protect the image of Augustus as well as that of the *domus Augusta*.[23] The vagueness of what constituted a charge of *maiestas* as well as Tiberius' professed reverence for his adoptive father led the Senate to use the *crimen maiestatis* for multiple purposes, especially to show flattery to the imperial household and to eliminate their

---

[21] On this view see Shotter 1966 and Bauman 1974: 76.

[22] Tacitus does admit that Granius Marcellus, like many others accused of *maiestas*, was guilty of other crimes.

[23] Cf. Dio's statement as he praises the early part of Tiberius' reign that "he would not by any means have it appear that he had been insulted or impiously treated by anybody (they were already calling such conduct *maiestas* (ἀσέβειάν) and were bringing many suits on that ground), and he would not hear of any such indictment being brought on his own account, though he paid tribute to the majesty of Augustus in this matter also (καίπερ τὸν Αὔγουστον καὶ ἐν τούτῳ σεμνύνων)" (57.9.2; Loeb trans. Cary).

enemies.[24] In the later years of Augustus' reign, an opening had been made for insults against members of the imperial household to be considered *maiestas*. Now, at the beginning of Tiberius' reign, certain senators were trying to expand that opening.[25]

Faianius and Rubrius were Roman knights; neither was a major political player. But the next case involving *maiestas* in the early reign of Tiberius featured a substantially bigger threat. M. Scribonius Libo Drusus (or Drusus Libo), as the name suggests, was related to Scribonia, the first wife of Augustus and the mother of his only child, Julia.[26] Drawing on Suetonius' assertion (*Tib.* 25) that Tiberius was reluctant to accept the principate due to the threats from Libo and Clemens, Pettinger (2012) has gone so far as to detail an elaborate plot stemming back to the death of Augustus. If Tiberius suspected Libo, he played his cards close to the vest. L. Scribonius Libo, most likely the brother of the would-be conspirator, was consul in 16, the year of the trial. Likewise, while Tacitus (*Ann* 2.28.2) states that Tiberius was suspicious of Libo thanks to accusations from informers, he also tells us that Tiberius named Libo praetor.[27] Fulcinius Trio brought the charges to the Senate.[28] Unlike the cases of Faianius and Rubrius, which seemed harmless, both the nature of the charges and the connections of the defendant prompted a much more serious inquiry. While Tacitus (*Ann.* 2.30) blames Tiberius for the insidious innovation of ordering Libo's slaves to be sold to the *actor publicus* in order to testify against their master, Tiberius was following a precedent set by Augustus. According to Dio (55.5.4), people were displeased with Augustus because he ordered that slaves should be sold to the *actor publicus* whenever the need arose. Dio explicitly connects this policy change with conspiracies in 8 aimed against Augustus and other magistrates.[29] As Thomas points out

---

[24] On the use of *maiestas* to destroy one's enemies, see Levick 1977.

[25] According to Suetonius, Tiberius tried to warn the Senate that if they opened the window to such attacks, they would be flooded with such cases: "*si hanc fenestram aperueritis, nihil aliud agi sinetis; omnium inimicitiae hoc praetexto ad vos deferentur*" (*Tib.* 28).

[26] Tacitus (*Ann.* 2.27.1) calls him Libo Drusus. Suetonius (*Tib.* 25.1) and Dio (57.15.4) mistakenly refer to him as L. Scribonius Libo. On the mistake, see Mallan 2020: 211. Pettinger (2012: 219–20) argues for Drusus Libo. On Libo's family connections, see Pettinger 2012, Appendix 1.

[27] Goodyear (1972: 271) believes that Tacitus' statement that Tiberius *ornat* Libo with the praetorship refers to the designation of Libo as a praetor for 17. Bauman (1967: 178) sees parallels between the trial of Libo and that of Q. Salvidienus Rufus under Octavian. Velleius Paterculus (2.129.2) praises Tiberius for his swift action against a man *ingratum et nova molientem*; Seneca (*Epist.* 70.10) calls Libo *stolidus*.

[28] For Fulcinius Trio's subsequent promotion of the cult of Divus Augustus in Spain, see Chapter 2.

[29] Birch (1981: 454; with reference to Levick 1999 [1976]: 335) expressly connects the torture of slaves by the state with the investigation into the events leading up to the exile of the younger Julia

(1998: 480), such a policy was unprecedented. In fact, although there were exceptions in extreme cases, under the Republic a master had the right to refuse to allow his slaves to testify.[30]

Tacitus never uses the term *maiestas* in his account of Libo's trial. However, he does begin his narrative, "then first the means were found which eroded the state through so many years" (*tum primum reperta sunt, quae per tot annos rem publicam exedere, Ann.* 2.27.1). Dio states that Libo was suspected of "revolutionary designs" (*ti neōterizein*, 57.15.4). Among the specifics, Libo was accused of consulting necromancers and making sinister, secretive marks (*atroces vel occultas notas*) in his own handwriting (confirmed by witnesses and slaves) next to the names of members of the *domus Augusta* and the Senate (*Ann.* 2.29.2).[31] Tiberius supposedly remained neutral in the case. Despairing of his situation, Libo committed suicide. This should have ended the proceedings, but the prosecutors persisted. The posthumous punishments determined for Libo were similar to those handed down later after the suicide of Cn. Piso, which we will discuss below. Libo's *imago* was banned from funerals; the cognomen "Drusus" was no longer to be used by any of the Scribonii; a *supplicatio* was declared; dedications were made to Jove, Mars, and Concordia; and the Ides of September, the day on which Libo killed himself, was to be declared *dies festus* (Tac. *Ann.* 2.32). Tiberius asserted that he would have pardoned Libo had he been given the chance (*Ann.* 2.31.3). Ultimately, we are left wondering about the nature of Libo's attempted revolution. Pettinger believes it was a serious plot and part of a larger movement. Perhaps he is right. The *Fasti Amiternini* for the Ides of September refers to nefarious plots (*nefaria consilia*) against the welfare of Tiberius, his sons, and other leading men of the state.[32] But none of our sources specifies the exact crime of which he was accused.

In the same year, Tacitus reports that Clemens, one of Agrippa Postumus' former slaves, unable to save his master from death, began to imitate him and cause trouble for Tiberius. Tacitus even asserts that had Clemens not been stopped, "he would have shaken the state with discord

---

and Ovid. Dettenhofer (2000: 159) believes this was a sign that Augustus was becoming more totalitarian.

[30] According to Cicero (*Pro Mil.* 59), slaves could testify against their masters in matters involving religious violations. They could also do so in cases of incest or treason (*de incestu et de coniuratione, Part. Or.* 34). Cf. *Pro Sex. Rosc.* 120 and *Pro Deiot.* 1.3. See Schilling 2010: 120–1 n. 293 for further discussion.

[31] On the charges involving magic, see Rives 2006: 62. Potter (1994: 174) associates this case with the ban on consulting fortune tellers in 11 (see Chapter 3).

[32] Levick (2013a: 45) agrees that there was a serious plot. See also Rogers 1935: 12–20.

and civil war" (*discordiis armisque civilibus rem publicam perculisset, Ann.* 2.39.1).[33] While Tacitus reports the movements of Clemens after the trial of Libo, his efforts would likely have begun shortly after his master's death in 14. Pettinger speculates (2012: 207–17) that the conspiracy of Libo and the activities of Clemens were intimately connected. He is not the first to do so. Levick (1999 [1976]: 150–2; following Rogers 1935: 22) proposed as much in her study on Tiberius. However, Pettinger goes too far when he speculates that Libo, along with supporters of Agrippa Postumus, wanted to restore the Republic. While Libo may have been the great-grandson of Pompey, he was also related to Agrippina and Germanicus through his great-aunt Scribonia. Nothing indicates that Clemens was advocating for a restoration of the Republic, whatever that would entail. He supposedly had many supporters from the house of the princeps, as well as knights and senators (Tac. *Ann.* 2.40.3), more in line with a movement to agitate greater support for Germanicus and Agrippina, Agrippa's sister. When Clemens was apprehended and brought before Tiberius, the dialogue did not revolve around restoring the Republic but rather about what it took to be a Caesar. Thus, when Tiberius pointedly asked Clemens how he became Agrippa, Clemens responded, "*quo modo tu Caesar*" (Tac. *Ann.* 2.40.3; cf. Dio 57.16.4). In contrast to the very public trial of Libo, the matter of Clemens was handled secretly by Sallustius Crispus, who was involved in the death of Agrippa Postumus.[34]

Throughout these narratives, no mention is made of Germanicus or Agrippina. The dedication to Concordia included in the Senate's decree against Libo reveals a concerted effort to emphasize family harmony. In the same year, an arch was dedicated near the Temple of Saturn to celebrate Germanicus' recovery of the standards (at least some of them) lost by Varus as well as a temple to Fors Fortuna along the Tiber near the gardens left to the Roman people by Julius Caesar (Tac. *Ann.* 2.41). Both advertised the military success of Germanicus. In addition to these dedications, Tacitus mentions the shrine (*sacrarium*) to the Julian *gens* and the statue of Divus Augustus dedicated at Bovillae (see Chapter 2). Whatever the nature of the conspiracies involving Libo and Clemens, in their aftermath, strong messages were sent advertising the charisma (and *concordia*) of the *domus Augusta*.

The purported conspiracies of Libo and Clemens indicate the general instability of the government during the early part of Tiberius' reign. The

---

[33] Dio (57.16.3) says that Clemens went to Gaul first and then "marched on Rome."
[34] Tac. *Ann.* 1.6. Suetonius (*Tib.* 22) is noncommittal as to who gave the order to kill Agrippa. Dio (57.3) places the blame squarely on Tiberius. See Allen 1947, Detweiler 1970, and Sordi 1979.

case of Appuleia Varilla is tangential to these cases as she was distantly related to the *domus Augusta*. Appuleia was accused of adultery, exacerbated by the fact that she was the granddaughter of the elder Octavia, Augustus' half-sister. Tiberius seemed to regard her case as that of any other noblewoman who had committed adultery and entrusted her punishment to her relatives. Her adulterer was banned from Africa and Italy (Tac. *Ann.* 2.50.3). However, Appuleia was also accused of *maiestas* because she had mocked Divus Augustus, Tiberius, and Livia with slanderous speeches (*probrosis sermonibus*). Tiberius insisted that these charges be treated separately. Concerning statements about himself, Tiberius responded that he did not want them to be considered in the trial. When asked about the slanders against his mother, Tiberius, as in the letter to Gytheion (see Chapter 2), said that he would consult her; her response, not surprisingly, mirrored his. Suetonius (*Tib.* 28), Tacitus (*Ann.* 2.50), and Dio (57.9) all assert that in the early years of Tiberius' reign he refused to allow slanderous speech against himself to be a cause for capital charges. Nevertheless, Tiberius asked that the charge of *maiestas* be distinguished and that she should be condemned if she had spoken impiously about Augustus (*si qua de Augusto inreligiose dixisset*, Tac. *Ann.* 2.50.2). Although Tiberius ultimately freed (*liberavit*) Appuleia from the charge of *maiestas*, this case set a dangerous precedent which encouraged delators to prosecute slanders against Divus Augustus.[35]

A few years after the trial of Appuleia, another public trial featured a prominent woman accused of disrespecting the imperial family. Like Appuleia, Aemilia Lepida was connected to noble families.[36] In addition to being a member of the ancient and powerful Aemilii, Lepida was the great-granddaughter of both Sulla and Pompey. Lepida was accused of faking a pregnancy by the wealthy and childless Quirinius, who was disliked by the people. She was also accused of adultery and attempting to poison Quirinius, a charge which Tacitus (*Ann.* 3.23.2) admits was proven to be true. More importantly, she was accused of consulting Chaldaeans regarding the imperial family (*Ann.* 3.22.1), which is reminiscent of the charges against Libo.[37] Although Tiberius initially had asked the Senate not to consider the charges of *maiestas*, he then suborned the

---

[35] Bauman (1974: 78–9) goes as far as to say, "The *senatus consultum* accepting the charge of *inreligiose dicta* against Appuleia Varilla is the most important single ruling in the entire history of *impietas in principem*." Cf. Yakobson 2003: 94–5.

[36] Although the trial of Cn. Calpurnius Piso may predate that of Aemilia Lepida, I have transposed the two for thematic reasons. Both trials took place in 20.

[37] On the similarities in Tacitus' narrative of the two trials, see Woodman and Martin 1996: 211–12.

former consul M. Servilius, among others, to bring these charges forward (*Ann.* 3.22.2). Unlike Appuleia, who seems to have put up little resistance, Lepida had her brother M.' Lepidus defend her. When it became clear the evidence was against her, she made a public display of herself in the theater of her great-grandfather Pompey.[38] The people were particularly moved by remembering that she was once destined to be the wife of Lucius Caesar and the daughter-in-law of Divus Augustus (*Ann.* 3.23.1). Notably, Tiberius not only remained neutral himself, despite having proof that Lepida was guilty of trying to poison Quirinius, but also prevented Drusus from speaking first on the case as consul designate. The Senate, having received mixed signals, condemned Lepida, presumably of *venenum*, and sentenced her to exile.

All of these cases demonstrate a general lack of support for Tiberius among certain factions in the aristocracy. But nothing threatened to destabilize the principate of Tiberius more than the death of Germanicus and the accusation that Tiberius had facilitated his murder through Cn. Calpurnius Piso. The sensational charge of poisoning, dropped due to lack of evidence, overshadows the actual charges in the narratives of Tacitus (*Ann.* 3.7–19) and Suetonius (*Tib.* 52; *Cal.* 1–2).[39] In the document detailing the outcome of the trial, the *Senatus Consultum de Cn. Pisone patre* (see Chapter 4), published at the request of Tiberius himself, the charges are more clearly laid out. The most significant involve Piso's return to Syria upon the death of Germanicus and his attempt to stir up civil war (*bellum etiam civile excitare conatus sit*, *SCPP* 45–6). The *SCPP* (55–6) refers to factions of Pisonians and Caesarians. Piso was complicit in the failed escape attempt of Vonones, the exiled former king of Parthia, who, after being chased out by the Parthians, had seized Armenia. Given that part of Germanicus' mission in the East was to settle a new king on the throne of Armenia and renew the detente with the Parthians, this was a serious offence. Ultimately, Vonones was killed trying to escape custody in Cilicia (Tac. *Ann.* 2.68).[40]

---

[38] "Her appeal to the statue of Pompey (at whose feet Caesar had been murdered) in particular suggests something of her rebellious spirit, confirming her fundamentally 'treasonous' behavior" (Gowing 2009: 99).

[39] Dio's account of this trial, now lost, is summarized by Xiphilinus and Zonaras, who only mention the murder charge (57.18.10). On how their summaries may reflect Dio's actual narrative, see Mallan 2020: 238. For the problems with dating the trial in Tacitus' narrative, see Woodman and Martin 1996: 67–75.

[40] Vonones had been confined under surveillance in Syria in 16 by Creticus Silanus (Tac. *Ann.* 2.4). In accordance with a request from the new Parthian king, Germanicus had Vonones removed to Pompeiopolis in Cilicia (*Ann.* 2.58).

In addition to the troops in Syria which he had corrupted during his time as governor, Piso also drew support from Cilician chieftains in his attempt to retake his former province (Tac. *Ann.* 2.78). After the recent death of King Philopator (*Ann.* 2.42), the Romans had not yet had time to stabilize this region. Piso, taking advantage of this, seized a fortress in Cilicia, from which he was expelled by Sentius, whom Germanicus had put in charge of Syria upon Piso's abrupt departure (*Ann.* 2.80–1). Piso struck an agreement with Sentius which allowed him to go to Rome to face trial, where he believed Tiberius would somehow protect him. In the event, he was proven gravely mistaken. More than anything, as the *SCPP* shows, Tiberius was disgusted at the revival of the specter of civil war, a concept which was supposedly eradicated after Augustus' victory at Actium. As discussed in Chapter 4, Piso was also found guilty of undermining the *maiestas* of the *domus Augusta* (*neclecta maiestate domus Aug (ustae)*, *SCPP* 32–3) and insulting the *numen* of Divus Augustus (*numen quoq(ue) Divi Aug(usti) violatum esse*, *SCPP* 68).[41] Piso's case seems to be the first in which someone was found guilty of *maiestas* in the traditional sense *and* condemned for irreligious actions against Divus Augustus. Piso, despite committing suicide before the conclusion of the trial, was censured in a document constructed by his fellow senators and displayed throughout the empire, particularly the winter camps of all the legions.

Notably, while allowing the son of Piso to inherit most of his property, Tiberius separated some property in Illyricum which had been given to Piso by Augustus from his *bona*, claiming that the neighbors had complained of abuses at the hands of Piso and his staff (*SCPP* 84–90). This falls in line with Tiberius' use of *renuntiatio amicitiae*, by which he had tried to distance himself from certain aspects of the prosecution of Piso (Tac. *Ann.* 3.12).[42] This concept is revisited when Tacitus narrates (*Ann.* 3.24) the return of D. Silanus, who had been accused of adultery with the younger Julia. As was the case for Ovid, D. Silanus' exile was not carried out through an order of the Senate. Thus, when his brother M. Silanus accomplished his return, Tiberius had to walk a fine line between pardoning someone who had sinned against the *domus Augusta* and ignoring the will of the Senate. While acknowledging that there was no legal reason D. Silanus should not have returned to Rome, he preserved Augustus' *renuntiatio amicitiae*, effectively ending any future political career D. Silanus might have had. Tiberius specifically maintained, at least

---

[41] On the nuances of these distinctions, see Corbier 2001: 192.
[42] On the idea of *renuntiatio amicitiae*, see Rogers 1959.

according to Tacitus, that he was preserving the wishes of Augustus in the matter (*sibi tamen adversus eum integras parentis sui offensiones, neque reditu Silani dissoluta, quae Augustus voluisset, Ann.* 3.24.4).

Although delators could use *maiestas* to add weight to other accusations, there were risks involved. In 21, the Senate punished two *equites* on Tiberius' authority for accusing a praetor of *maiestas* (Tac. *Ann.* 3.37.1). Tiberius was apparently trying to rein in specious prosecutions. But only a few sentences later, Tacitus (*Ann.* 3.38.1) confuses the issue by stating that Tiberius and the delators were untiring.[43] Caesius Cordus, on trial for extortion, was also charged with *maiestas*. Tacitus refers to such a charge as the complement of all other accusations. What Tacitus does not say (until *Ann.* 3.70.1) is that Cordus was found guilty of extortion. Tacitus does not explain what happened to the charge of *maiestas* or the foundation of that charge. In the same chapter in which he claims Tiberius was not wearying of treason trials, Tacitus recounts the case of Antistius Vetus, whose case actually was brought before the Senate at Tiberius' direction. Antistius was accused of *maiestas*, specifically for interfering in Thrace after the death of Cotys on behalf of Rhescuporis, who had wanted a war against Rome (*Ann.* 3.38.2). Antistius was punished with relegation to some island far from Macedonia or Thrace. The punishment indicates that he was indeed found guilty of *maiestas* under the Sullan law.

In these cases, no mention is made of *maiestas* involving attacks on Divus Augustus and the *domus Augusta*; the next case narrated by Tacitus (*Ann.* 3.49–51), that against Clutorius Priscus, hinges upon such a charge.[44] Tacitus does not specify the charges against Clutorius, only that they involved a poem eulogizing Drusus, who was not yet dead. In the debate in the Senate, for which Tiberius was not present, Haterius Agrippa proposed that Clutorius be put to death. M. Lepidus countered that Clutorius had not committed a crime. However, the use of the phrase *nefaria voce* in Lepidus' defense evokes the accusations against Libo for suspicious marks by the names of members of the imperial family and Appuleia's *inreligiose dicta* against Divus Augustus.[45] Given the recent trial of Piso, condemned for celebrating the death of Germanicus, the charges against Clutorius were not as innocuous as Tacitus makes them

---

[43] On Tacitus' attempt to mislead the reader, see Woodman and Martin 1996: 319.

[44] The case is also related by Dio ([Xiph.] 57.20.3–4), who refers to the defendant as C. Lutorius. On the name, which may be C. Clutorius Priscus, see Mallan 2020: 251.

[45] Bauman asserts, "The trouble was that the crime did not fall under any of the public criminal laws. It belonged under the *malum carmen*, the spell or curse for which the xii Tables had ordained the death penalty" (1996: 58). This may be true, but none of our sources make this connection.

seem.[46] Lepidus (at least in Tacitus' narrative) admits that even if Clutorius were guilty of *maiestas*, the punishment would not be death but exile, confiscation of one's property, and interdiction from fire and water (*Ann.* 3.50.3). The Senate sided with Haterius, and Clutorius was immediately executed. The hasty execution prompted Tiberius to rebuke the Senate. In response, the Senate passed a law that would delay executions (Tac. *Ann.* 3.49–51; Suet. *Tib.* 75.2; Dio [Xiph.] 57.20.4).[47] Both Tacitus and Dio indicate that Tiberius was more upset about not being consulted than with the actual punishment. Tacitus (*Ann.* 3.51.2) asserts that Tiberius never did take advantage of the ten-day moratorium to override a condemnation by the Senate. But he also states that Tiberius ambiguously praised the Senate for its loyalty while declaring he would have pardoned Clutorius. These mixed messages continued to sow confusion about to what degree attacks on the *domus Augusta* constituted *maiestas*.

As in the trial of Piso (*SCPP* 32–3, 68), charges of violating the divinity of Augustus and spurning the *maiestas* of the *domus Augusta* (*violatum Augusti numen, spretam Tiberii maiestatem*, Tac. *Ann.* 3.66.1) were appended to accusations of provincial mismanagement against C. Silanus. Silanus was guilty of using *saevitia* against and extorting money from the subjects in his province of Asia (*nec dubium habebatur saevitiae captarumque pecuniarum teneri reum*, *Ann.* 3.67.1). Bauman (1996: 59) observes, "In assessing the penalty for *repetundae* aggravated by *saevitia* the accusers went back to Republican precedents," while Tiberius made a specific reference to Augustan precedent. As mentioned earlier, in rebuking Silanus, Tiberius cited Augustus' punishment of Volesus Messalla, another corrupt governor of Asia.[48] Silanus was condemned; we do not know on what charges. He was relegated to Cythnus after Tiberius, supposedly at the request of Silanus' sister, a Vestal Virgin, interposed his clemency on the original sentence of relegation to Gyarus.

While the case of Silanus may have been a clear example of traditional *maiestas laesa*, the delators had not given up on their attempts to widen the

---

[46] Dio ([Xiph.] 57.22.5) records under the year 23 a trial involving Aelius Saturninus, accused of composing inappropriate poems (*epē ouk epitēdeia*) against Tiberius. He was condemned in the Senate and thrown from the Tarpeian Rock. The case is not mentioned by Tacitus or any other source.

[47] Cowan (2016) sees this case as the turning point in the dialogue on *clementia* vs. *severitas* between the Senate and Tiberius.

[48] According to the younger Seneca (*De Ira* 2.5.5), Volesus as governor of Asia had beheaded 300 people in one day and boasted that it was a "kingly act" (*o rem regiam*).

definition of that crime to include insults to images of the princeps and his family. As in the cases of Faianius and Granius Marcellus, L. Ennius, an *eques*, was accused of desecrating a statue.[49] Only this time it was one of Tiberius, not Divus Augustus. Ennius supposedly melted down a silver statue of Tiberius to use the metal for other purposes. One would think the delators would remember that Augustus had melted down silver statues of himself and made donations to the Temple of Apollo (*RG* 24). Not surprisingly, Tiberius stopped the prosecution. However, Ateius Capito interposed an ironic objection that in preventing the case from being tried, Tiberius was infringing on the rights of the Senate (Tac. *Ann.* 3.70). Capito equated attacks on the emperor with attacks on the state (*rei publicae iniurias*). Tiberius persisted in his refusal to allow the case to proceed. But the delators would find new ways to advance the line Tiberius was trying to draw with respect to prosecutions for *maiestas*.

Related to the case of Ennius was a motion in the Senate in the previous year to curb the abuse of seeking asylum at images of members of the *domus Augusta*. The breaking point was reached when the senator C. Cestius, having been harassed by a woman named Annia Rufilla, decided to take his case before the Senate. He argued that while the principes stood in the same position as gods, not even the gods listened to unjust prayers, nor was anyone able to seek refuge at the Capitol or any other temple as a shield for one's sins (Tac. *Ann.* 3.36.2). Having successfully prosecuted Annia Rufilla for *fraus*, he was being insulted by her in public as she clung to an *effigies* of the *imperator*. Cestius' fellow senators attested to similar experiences. Drusus, presiding over the Senate, ordered Rufilla to be imprisoned (*publica custodia*). The precedent was presumably then set which would last down to the time of the writers of the *Digest*:

> It was decreed by a *senatus consultum* that no one should carry an image of the emperor for the purpose of harming someone else: and one who did so should be arrested.[50]

> Senatus consulto cavetur, ne quis imaginem imperatoris in invidiam alterius portaret: et qui contra fecerit, in vincula publica mittetur. (Scaevola, *Lib. iv regularum Dig.* 47.10.38)

---

[49] Woodman and Martin (1996: 471) believe, "He was the son-in-law of Thrasyllus, Tib.'s astrologer." However, Tacitus does not make that connection, which seems like a missed opportunity.

[50] For the connection between this passage in the *Digest* and the case of Annia Rufilla, see Rogers 1935: 60. On the seemingly contradictory evidence of *Dig.* 48.19.28.7, see Bauman 1974: 87 and Gamauf 1999: 146.

Cestius and his fellow senators placed enough faith in Drusus, and by association Tiberius, that they felt they could complain about this phenomenon without fear of prosecution for *maiestas*.[51] But if Tacitus is to be believed, Tiberius and other members of the *domus Augusta* were becoming increasingly assimilated to *divi*, especially Divus Augustus. The prosecutions for *maiestas* involving irreligious speech and actions against Divus Augustus would be extended to encompass everyone in the *domus Augusta*.

In addition to the cases discussed above, Suetonius and Seneca highlight supposedly trivial accusations of *maiestas*. In his account of the "bad" Tiberius, Suetonius adds the following vague examples of abuses of the *maiestas* laws:

> When the defendant had been condemned, he gradually proceeded to this kind of false accusation, so that these things also were capital crimes: to have beaten a slave around an image of Augustus; to have changed one's clothes there; to have brought a coin or a signet ring with his image into a latrine or a brothel; or to have criticized any word or deed of his.

> Damnato reo paulatim genus calumniae eo processit, ut haec quoque capitalia essent; circa Augusti simulacrum servum cecidisse, vestimenta mutasse, nummo vel anulo effigiem impressam latrinae aut lupanari intulisse, dictum ullum factumve eius existimatione aliqua laesisse. (*Tib.* 58)

The condemned man whom Suetonius sees as the beginning of all these trivial charges seems to be none other than Granius Marcellus, who was not condemned for *maiestas*, at least according to Tacitus. The lack of evidence from other sources makes it likely that the other examples also involved cases where charges of *maiestas* were introduced but later dismissed. More importantly, the accusations involve desecration of the divinity of Augustus, not Tiberius.

In his essay *De Beneficiis*, Seneca relates the story of a senator saved from doom by his quick-thinking slave. The man was carrying a chamber pot while wearing a ring bearing the image of Tiberius. The passage bears closer examination:

> Under Tiberius Caesar there was such a common and almost universal frenzy for bringing charges of treason that it took a heavier toll of the lives of Roman citizens than any Civil War; it seized upon the talk of drunkards, the frank words of jesters; nothing was safe – anything served as an excuse to shed blood, and there was no need to wait to find out the fate of the accused since there was but one outcome. (3.26.1; Loeb trans. Basore)

---

[51] Contra Gamauf 1999: 141–2.

> Sub Tib. Caesare fuit accusandi frequens et paene publica rabies, quae omni civili bello gravius togatam civitatem confecit; excipiebatur ebriorum sermo, simplicitas iocantium; nihil erat tutum; omnis saeviendi placebat occasio, nec iam reorum expectabantur eventus, cum esset unus.

The language of Seneca relates two important factors. First, the accusations took place under Tiberius but not necessarily at the instigation or by the will of Tiberius. Secondly, the exaggerated language of the slaughter as greater than that of all the civil wars is countered by the fact that in this particular case the accuser dropped the charges when he realized there was no evidence.

Immediately following upon this story of the *beneficium* done by a slave for his master under Tiberius, Seneca writes that under Augustus words were not yet dangerous but could be troublesome (*Sub divo Augusto nondum hominibus verba sua periculosa erant, iam molesta,* 3.27.1). The anecdote recounts verbal slanders which landed a senator named Rufus in hot water. An inebriated Rufus jokingly wished that Augustus would not return safely from a journey he was planning, quipping that all the bulls and calves that would be sacrificed upon his return wished the same. When he had sobered up, a slave encouraged him to make haste and apologize to Augustus while he still could. The dangerous litigation which burst forth under Tiberius was looming in the reign of Augustus. The key difference was that Augustus could rely upon his personal charisma and *auctoritas*; Tiberius could not. His power was based on protecting the image of his divine father.

Sejanus, *Socius Laborum*

All of our sources for the reign of Tiberius denote a drastic change in the emperor's attitude towards prosecutions for *maiestas* at some particular point, leading to a "reign of terror." Lurking in the background of these accounts is the growing influence of the Praetorian Prefect Aelius Sejanus, especially after the deaths of Germanicus and Drusus. Tacitus introduces Sejanus in full at the beginning of Book 4 of the *Annals*, attributing his rise to the lack of a credible heir after Sejanus and Livilla had allegedly murdered Drusus. While Sejanus' appearance on stage in Book 4 is a literary tour-de-force, he had been waiting in the wings for some time. At *Ann.* 1.24.2, Tacitus mentioned that Sejanus, who was accompanying Drusus to deal with the mutiny in Pannonia, had been appointed Prefect of the Praetorian Guard alongside his father, Seius Strabo. Tacitus does not specify whether Augustus or Tiberius appointed Sejanus to that position. Sejanus' presence at the Pannonian mutiny makes sense since Drusus was accompanied by cavalry from the Praetorian Guard. But despite the fact that Sejanus had only recently been appointed Praetorian Prefect, Tacitus indicates he was already powerful as he was being sent as a mentor for Drusus as well as to threaten or persuade others (*ceteris periculorum praemiorumque ostentator*). Likewise, at *Ann.* 3.29.4 Tacitus contrasts the people's joy at Nero, son of Germanicus, making his entry into public life with their disdain for Claudius' son being betrothed to Sejanus' daughter.[52] Sejanus is also mentioned when one of his protégés, Junius Otho, joins the prosecution of C. Silanus (*Ann.* 3.66.3). Finally, Tacitus hints at the growing power of Sejanus at *Ann.* 3.72, where he is credited with helping to put out a fire in the Theater of Pompey, for which he was honored with a statue.

Given the characterization of Sejanus and his growing influence over Tiberius at the beginning of Book 4 of the *Annals*, it should come as no surprise that he plays an increasingly large role in treason trials after the death of Drusus. In particular, Tacitus portrays Sejanus as preying upon Tiberius' suspicions that Agrippina was trying to speed up the succession of her son Nero. The insertion of the names of Nero and his younger brother Drusus in the annual vows for the health of the princeps (Tac. *Ann.* 4.17) likely brought back memories for Tiberius of the situation he experienced during the advancement of Gaius and Lucius.[53] Only Tiberius had no Tiberius. That is to say, with the deaths of Germanicus and Drusus, that generation of the succession had been wiped out. If Tiberius intended to groom one of Germanicus' children for the position of princeps, he would have to rely on someone else in the meantime. Thus, in contemporary writers (Velleius 2.127) and in the letters which Tacitus claims Sejanus and Tiberius exchanged regarding Livilla's hand (*Ann.* 4.39–40), Sejanus is inevitably compared to Augustus' *adiutor*, Agrippa.[54]

According to Tacitus, after murdering Drusus, Sejanus was determined to destroy Agrippina and her children. Tacitus (*Ann.* 4.18.1) links the prosecutions of C. Silius and Titius Sabinus to this effort, even though they took place four years apart. While the trial of Sabinus is highly

---

[52] Cf. *Ann.* 4.15.3, where Nero makes a speech of thanks before the Senate after they grant permission to the cities of Asia to build a temple to Tiberius, Livia, and the Senate. According to Tacitus, the people's favor for him was increased by their awareness of Sejanus' hatred.

[53] Indeed, Augustus himself had rebuked Tiberius for placing Gaius at his side during a festival, leading to excessive enthusiasm from the crowd (Dio 54.27.1).

[54] As Woodman (2018: 216) comments, in Tacitus' version of these letters, Sejanus makes several appeals to Augustan precedent as a form of *captatio benevolentiae*. Champlin (2012: 374) discounts the notion that Sejanus was intended to serve as regent for the son of Drusus.

problematic, the prosecution of Silius seems to have been warranted. Velleius links Silius with Libo and Piso in the only sentence in his history which addresses treason attempts under Tiberius (2.130.3). According to Tacitus (*Ann.* 4.18.2), Silius was accused of boasting that he was responsible for handing Tiberius power by keeping his legions in check when others had rebelled. More importantly, he was accused of colluding with Sacrovir (*conscientia belli Sacrovir diu dissimulatus*) and then engaging in excessive greed after his victory over that enemy (*victoria per avaritiam foedata, Ann.* 4.19.4). When Silius objected that he was being prosecuted by the consul Varro, Tiberius supposedly used language reminiscent of the old Republican *senatus consultum ultimum* (*ne quod res publica detrimentum caperet, Ann.* 4.19.3). Tacitus admitted that the defendant was guilty of extorting money from his province. Silius committed suicide before he could be condemned. His wife Sosia Galla, accused of sharing in his mismanagement of the province, was exiled.

After Silius' suicide, Tacitus states that his property was confiscated (*saevitum tamen in bona, Ann.* 4.20.1). Tacitus specifies that property given to Silius by Augustus was returned to the *fiscus* (*liberalitas Augusti avulsa*). Tacitus, intending to paint a portrait of an increasingly tyrannical Tiberius, says that this was the first time Tiberius showed such attention to someone else's money.[55] But the *Senatus Consultum de Cn. Pisone patre* specifies that property was returned to Tiberius which had been presented to Piso by Divus Augustus (*SCPP* 85–6). In that document, the Senate states that Tiberius confiscated these lands because neighbors had complained of abuse by Piso's freedmen and slaves. Given the parallels between the arrogance of Silius and that of Piso, Tiberius may have confiscated Silius' property for a similar reason. In ensuring that gifts from Divus Augustus were not used improperly, Tiberius was protecting the legacy of his predecessor, even at his own expense. Moreover, according to Dio (53.23.7), in 26 BC the Senate voted to condemn Cornelius Gallus and to award his estate to Augustus.[56] Thus, "the practice of confiscating the

---

[55] On the debate over confiscation of goods of those who committed suicide before their condemnation, see Rivière 2002: 491–3. Cf. Millar (1977: 163–74), who traces the evolution of the confiscation of property by the princeps, citing Suet. *Vit. Verg.* p. 9 of the OCT, Suet. *Aug.* 41.1, and Ovid, *Trist.* 5.2.57. See also Lucinio 2004.

[56] The case of Cornelius Gallus remains enigmatic. Daly (1979) argues that if Gallus were tried under a law of *maiestas*, it would have been the *lex Cornelia*, not the *lex Iulia*. Gallus committed suicide before matters could come to a head, and later tradition focuses on Augustus' *renuntiatio amicitiae* rather than any formal charges. For more on the situation, see Kaster 1995: 184–6. Richardson (1997: 517) argues that the case of Gallus set the precedent for moving hearings involving *maiestas* from the traditional *quaestio* to the Senate.

properties of condemned men by the imperial *fiscus* had begun during the reign of Augustus" (Mallan 2020: 175).

Perhaps connected to the case of Silius is the prosecution of Vibius Serenus, accused by his son of stirring up war in Gaul (Tac. *Ann.* 4.28). The elder Vibius, having served as proconsul of Hispania Ulterior, had already been exiled to Amorgus for *vis publica* (*Ann.* 4.13.1). Ultimately, the prosecution came to nothing and Vibius was returned to Amorgus.[57] Tacitus dwells on this case because an accused co-conspirator of Vibius, Caecilius Cornutus, committed suicide before being condemned. The Senate then debated whether or not the accusers should receive their rewards. Supposedly, Tiberius intervened on behalf of the accusers, stating that such men were guardians (*custodes*) of the laws (*Ann.* 4.30).[58] Despite Tacitus' criticism of Tiberius' stance, the Roman legal system depended on men taking up prosecutions on behalf of the state.

In the same year, Tacitus records (*Ann.* 4.31) a case where C. Cominius was convicted of reciting a *probrosum carmen* against Tiberius. After a plea from Cominius' brother, Tiberius let Cominius go. Notably, Cominius' slanders were against Tiberius not Divus Augustus. Nor was it a poem predicting the death of a member of the *domus Augusta* as in the case of Clutorius Priscus. In the same chapter, Tacitus reports that Tiberius intervened in the trial of P. Suillius, who had once served as quaestor for Germanicus. Tiberius altered the Senate's punishment of exile from Italy to relegation to an island, swearing that he was doing so in the interests of the state (*e re publica*). Tacitus admits that, despite the resentment Tiberius earned for this, he was later proven right when Suillius exerted a sinister influence over Claudius. Tiberius also intervened in the case of Firmius Catus, who, instead of being exiled, was removed from the Senate after trying to prosecute his own sister for *maiestas*.

In Book 4 of the *Annals*, Tacitus uses various narrative techniques to depict a state in which cases of *maiestas* were becoming more frequent and more vicious. Vibius Serenus was brought to trial by his own son. Firmius Catus tried to prosecute his own sister. Never mind that neither of these prosecutions was successful. Indeed, even though the succession was in doubt and Tiberius was growing increasingly tired of handling his responsibilities, in the vast majority of these cases the defendants either were found guilty of some other crime or committed suicide before their trial was completed. But the delators would not give up so easily, and,

---

[57] On Vibius and the nature of this case, see Woodman 2018: 120–2.
[58] On this passage, see Rivière 2002: 67.

according to Tacitus, they were being encouraged by Sejanus, who was determined to destroy the children of Agrippina, a task made all too easy by Agrippina's efforts to thrust her sons into the spotlight without consulting Tiberius.

As seen in Chapter 5, Velleius (2.124.1) writes about the fear of civil war at the death of Augustus. It should come as no surprise, then, that authors who wrote favorably about those on the losing side in the civil wars would face scrutiny in the reign of Tiberius. The trial of Cremutius Cordus is one of the most studied passages of Tacitus. In the speech which Tacitus puts in the mouth of Cremutius, he protests that he was not provoking rebellion by praising Brutus and Cassius as if they were still on the field at Philippi (*Ann.* 4.35.2); however, as Martin and Woodman (1989: 183) remark, "It would not have been difficult to interpret Cordus' narrative as criticism of the principate and a call to arms."[59] In 22, just a few years before Cordus' trial, Tacitus (*Ann.* 3.76.2) highlights the fact that at the funeral of Junia, wife of Cassius and sister of Brutus, their *imagines* were conspicuously absent. Gowing (2010: 252) observes that Tiberius' own experiences during the civil wars would undoubtedly have caused him to be wary of any imagery which could be seen as inciting such conflict. Support for Brutus and Cassius would also undermine Augustus' charismatic image as the avenger of his divine father and the man who restored order to the *res publica.*

And yet Velleius showed respect towards Brutus and Cassius, while recognizing that their assassination of Caesar was wrong. In his comparison of the two, he states that one would rather have Brutus as a friend and would fear Cassius more as an enemy. Cassius had more *vis*; Brutus, more *virtus*. Velleius even speculates that, had they won at Philippi, Brutus would have been a better princeps than Cassius (2.72). Velleius did not go quite as far as Cordus was alleged to have done; but he did not condemn the tyrannicides as severely as some other authors of the time.[60] Velleius' praise of Brutus and Cassius is restrained; his praise of Sejanus (2.127–8) reads, even to those who are generous in their assessment of Velleius, as excessive. Thus, it seems more likely that it was Cordus'

---

[59] On the historicity of Cordus' speech in Tacitus, see Levick 2013b: 1.498. On the speech as part of Tacitus' historiographic agenda, see Moles 1998 and McHugh 2004. As Moles notes (1998: 145), Tacitus' own statements that history can be dangerously misinterpreted undermine some of the protests found in Cordus' speech.

[60] Bloomer concludes that in the work of Valerius Maximus, "With the exclusion of those passages where Brutus, Decimus Brutus, and Cassius are raised in passing to identify a partisan and so to orient the reader, these three are uniformly abused as the traitorous assassins" (1992: 222).

criticism of Sejanus, mentioned by Seneca (*Ad Marc.* 22.4–7), Tacitus (*Ann.* 4.34.1), and Dio (57.24.2), rather than his praise of Brutus and Cassius, which provoked prosecution. Although Tacitus may focus more heavily on Cordus as a historian being persecuted for his writings, he also admits that the trial was instigated by *Seiani clientes* (*Ann.* 4.34.1). We know from Seneca the Younger, who wrote a *consolatio* to the daughter of Cordus, that Cordus insulted Sejanus on multiple occasions, most famously with his quip regarding the statue voted to him by the Senate in gratitude for saving the Theater of Pompey from being destroyed by fire, that the theater was now truly ruined (*exclamavit Cordus tunc vere theatrum perire*, *Ad Marc.* 22.4). Seneca also says that Cordus' history could teach readers what a Roman man was, a man untamed by the yoke of Sejanus when everyone else had submitted, a man free in character, in spirit, and in action (*quid sit vir Romanus, quid subactis iam cervicibus omnium et ad Seianianum iugum adactis indomitus, quid sit homo ingenio, animo, manu liber, Ad Marc.* 1.3).

Sejanus may have taken advantage of passages in Cordus' work which were provocative. According to Suetonius (*Cal.* 16), one of the first acts of the newly installed Caligula was to allow the works of Cordus to circulate again.[61] But Quintilian states that even if the writings of Cordus had been allowed to see the light of day after being carefully protected by Cordus' daughter Marcia, they were published in an expurgated form: "Cremutius' frankness also has its admirers, and rightly so, though the passages which ruined him have been cut out of the text. There are still plenty of lofty spirit and bold *sententiae* to be found in what survives" (*Inst. Orat.* 10.1.104; Loeb trans. Russell).[62] If the writings of Cordus retained their bite even after they had been censored for dangerous material, one must wonder whether his history was really innocuous. According to Dio ([Xiph.] 57.24.3–4), Cordus was accused not only of praising Brutus and Cassius but also of having attacked *(kathēpsato)* the *populus Romanus* and the Senate.[63] The original definition of *maiestas* involved diminishing the *maiestas* of the Roman people. Under the *lex Cornelia*, the Senate came to be included under that definition. If Cordus had derided the people and

---

[61] Bellemore (1992) argues that Seneca's *Ad Marciam* was written late in the reign of Tiberius, after the fall of Sejanus. If that were the case, Cordus' history would have been widely available even before the restoration attributed to Caligula by Suetonius.

[62] Rohmann (2013: 129) argues that passages of Cordus' works may not have been expunged due to state censorship but rather due to prudence on the part of his daughter.

[63] On this passage, see Mallan 2020: 264–5.

the Senate, the Senate might have been motivated to prosecute Cordus on its own behalf.

Dio asserts that Cordus' work, which he had produced long before, recounting Augustus' deeds and which Augustus himself had acknowledged, was the cause of his trial. Suetonius (*Tib.* 61.3) states with respect to an unnamed historian who must be Cordus and a tragedian who is probably Mamercus Scaurus that their works were destroyed under Tiberius although they had been recited many years before with Augustus in the audience. Interestingly, Tacitus makes no mention of this in his account of the trial, although he does have Cordus claim that Augustus used to tease Livy for his admiration for Pompey (*Ann.* 4.34.3).[64] According to Dio ([Xiph.] 57.24.3), while Cordus had said nothing bad about Caesar or Augustus, he also did not show much reverence (*ou... huperesemnune*) for them either.[65] As Cordus' work no longer survives, we have no clear idea of what he actually said about Augustus. Aside from the fragment relating the death of Cicero and cited by Seneca the Elder (*Suas.* 6.19), our only other clearly historical fragment from the actual work of Cordus paints Augustus in a less than positive light.[66] Suetonius (*Aug.* 35) claims Cordus wrote that at one point Augustus was so afraid of the Senate he would not admit any senator into his presence unless he was alone and had been thoroughly searched. As discussed in the previous chapter, both Valerius Maximus and Velleius Paterculus were careful to avoid any hint of wrongdoing by the youthful Octavian in his rise to power. If Cordus did praise the liberators in his narrative of the Battle of Philippi, he also likely reported the proscriptions in a way which did not properly deflect the blame onto Antony. Indeed, Seneca (*Ad Marc.* 26.1) glorifies Cordus by saying that "he proscribed the proscribers for all time."

As we have already discussed, in the later years of his reign Augustus was increasingly willing to prosecute speech considered dangerous or

---

[64] As for Augustus' tolerance of Livy's purported Pompeian sympathies, Martin (2016: 161) argues that the later books of Livy were not published until after the death of Augustus.

[65] Corbier (2001: 165–6) contends that at Tacitus, *Ann.* 4.34, when Cremutius Cordus is defending himself since his offenses were aimed neither at the princeps nor the parent of the princeps (*sed neque haec in principem aut principis parentem, quos lex maiestatis amplectitur*), the princeps is Augustus and the *parens* Julius Caesar. This seems a bit of a stretch, as Tiberius was the current princeps. Either way, an insult to Augustus is implied. On interpretations of Tacitus' meaning, see Woodman 2018: 193.

[66] There are two additional fragments cited by Pliny the Elder which deal with birds called "Memnon's daughters" and a tree which never comes into full leaf as it was the tree from which Phyllis hanged herself (*HN* 10.74 and 16.108). See "Cremutius Cordus" in *FRH*.

defamatory. But the praise of Brutus and Cassius may have been dangerous even before then. Suetonius refers to an orator named C. Albucius Silus who narrowly escaped punishment for addressing a statue of Brutus as the author and defender of the laws and liberty (*legum ac libertatis auctorem et vindicem, Rhet.* 6). Suetonius ties this incident to a case Silus was pleading before the proconsul L. Piso at Mediolanum. Piso was consul in 15 BC; he was probably serving as proconsul shortly after that.[67] If so, this plants Silus' praise of Brutus firmly in the middle of the reign of Augustus, long before the supposed oppression which took place later. Moreover, Suetonius (*Aug.* 85.1) states that Augustus wrote a response to Brutus' eulogy of Cato. He adds that Augustus gave a recitation of this work, and when he grew tired, he had Tiberius continue the reading. Perhaps the work of Brutus was again circulating and Augustus felt the need to write a defense of his own actions. Cordus was quoting Brutus himself when he called Cassius "the last of the Romans."[68] Even if the history for which Cordus was put on trial was the same history which had been "pardoned" by Augustus and not a revised version, things had changed significantly since Augustus' death, and more importantly, since the beginning of Tiberius' reign. Attacks on Augustus as the charismatic bringer of peace were particularly dangerous at a time when the lack of a credible successor threatened the *status* he had created.

Cordus killed himself before the conclusion of his trial. Although he may not have been actually condemned, his works were banned, like those of Labienus and Cassius Severus at the end of Augustus' reign.[69] In the aftermath of Cordus' trial, treasonous speech increasingly provided grounds for prosecution. At *Ann.* 4.42, Tacitus recounts a treason case against Votienus Montanus which involved the testimony of a military man. But the case is far more complicated than he would have us believe.[70] Bauman reasons, "the presence of a military witness suggests that Montanus may have been guilty of inciting soldiers to sedition" (1974:

---

[67] Kaster (1995: 315) states, "All the evidence above tends to place A.'s career at Rome in the last quarter of the 1st cent. BCE and the first years of the 1st cent. CE." He believes the incident may actually be related to a different Piso and dated to the triumviral period but concedes, "If the incident belongs to the mid-10s, A. must have returned to plead the case in his native region when already active at Rome," citing the precedent of Porcius Latro in Spain found at Sen. *Contr.* 9 pref. 3. (1995: 323).

[68] For Brutus referring to Cassius as the "last of the Romans," see Plutarch, *Brut.* 44 and Appian, *BC* 4.114.

[69] For the similarities in Dio's accounts of these purges, see Bauman 1967: 271.

[70] Votienus Montanus had already been tried *apud Caesarem* on some charge brought by the colony of Narbo (Sen. *Contr.* 7.5.12). See Koestermann 1965: 144. That trial may have taken place under Augustus or Tiberius.

120). The witness, Aemilius, is identified by Shotter (1991: 21) as "the man who served with Germanicus in Germany (*Ann.* 2.11.2), and more importantly the Paulus Aemilius whose career was recorded at Capua (*CIL* x 3881 = *ILS* 2686). This would indicate that at the time of the trial of Montanus, Aemilius was a tribune in the Praetorian Guard, therefore presumably hand-picked by Sejanus (*Ann.* 4.2.3)." Combined with the case of Silius, the case of Montanus indicates a growing uneasiness between the military and Tiberius, likely spurred by the popularity of Agrippina and her sons.[71]

In the same chapter as the trial of Votienus, Tacitus mentions (*Ann.* 4.42.3) that Tiberius removed Apidius Merula from the Senate for refusing to swear by the *acta* of Divus Augustus. While this may seem fairly trivial, it is mirrored shortly afterwards by the argument which Tacitus relates (*Ann.* 4.52) between Agrippina and Tiberius regarding who best represented the image of Augustus. The argument started over the prosecution of Agrippina's cousin, Claudia Pulchra, eventually condemned of adultery but also accused of threatening poison and curses against Tiberius (*veneficia in principem et devotiones*, *Ann.* 4.52.1), charges reminiscent of those against Appuleia Varilla and Aemilia Lepida.[72] According to Tacitus, Agrippina rushed to confront Tiberius and found him sacrificing to Augustus (*sacrificantem patri*, 4.52.2). The source for this incident is none other than Agrippina's daughter, Agrippina the Younger (*Ann.* 4.53.2). Thus, a hostile source concedes that even in private Tiberius was showing reverence for Divus Augustus. After a verbal exchange in which Agrippina rebuked Tiberius, saying that it was hypocritical to sacrifice to Divus Augustus while attacking his descendants (*mactare divo Augusto victimas et posteros eius insectari*), Tiberius reminded Agrippina that she was not being wounded simply because she did not rule (*Ann.* 4.52.3; cf. Suet. *Tib.* 53). As the struggle for succession intensified, Tiberius and Agrippina were locked in a battle to determine who controlled the image of Augustus. By actively promoting the cult of Divus Augustus, Tiberius had fostered the cultivation of the *domus Augusta* as a *domus divina*, giving Agrippina the opportunity to capitalize on her claim to be a true descendant of

---

[71] Under the year 33, Dio (58.21.6) states that Tiberius precluded anyone who had served in the army from "giving evidence" (*exētasmenou*). Tacitus does not mention this, and Dio's account is too vague to allow for any legal conclusions.

[72] Claudia Pulchra's son was later attacked by the same prosecutor, Domitius Afer, but Tacitus does not tell us either the charges or the outcome (*Ann.* 4.66). On their relationship to Agrippina, see Woodman 2018: 257.

Augustus (as opposed to the interloper Tiberius).[73] Never mind that her vision of her sons ruling at such a young age undermined the system Augustus had created and Tiberius was struggling to preserve.

Tacitus had already foreshadowed the prosecution of Titius Sabinus as a supporter of Agrippina in his narrative of the trial of Silius (*Ann.* 4.18.1). The alleged reason for Sabinus' downfall was his allegiance to the cause of Agrippina, along with treasonous statements concerning Tiberius and Sejanus, statements Sabinus made in the misguided belief that he was speaking in confidence (*Ann.* 4.68–70).[74] The chief accuser, L. Latiaris, induced three fellow senators to hide in the rafters of Sabinus' house while he proceeded to lead Sabinus to make inflammatory comments about the princeps and his *adiutor*.[75] Since by this point Tiberius had left Rome for good, Tacitus (*Ann.* 4.70.1) records a letter from the princeps, read in the Senate on New Year's Day of 28, accusing Sabinus of tampering with imperial freedmen and attacking the princeps. Given his connection with the increasingly *atrox* Agrippina, it seems highly probable that Sabinus was guilty of some sort of treason.[76] In the passage immediately preceding the trial of Sabinus, Tacitus recounts (*Ann.* 4.67.4) the insinuations that Agrippina and Nero were being watched by Sejanus, with agents urging them to flee to the Rhine legions or to clasp the effigy of Divus Augustus in the Forum and incite the people and the Senate. The elder Pliny prefaces a story about a loyal dog by saying that Sabinus and his slaves were punished for intrigue with Nero, the son of Germanicus (*ex causa Neronis Germanici filii*, *HN* 8.145). This correlates with the letter Tacitus records from Tiberius to the Senate after Sabinus was executed:

> a letter followed thanking them because they had punished a man hostile to the republic, with an addendum that the emperor feared for his own life due to suspected plots by his enemies, although no one was named specifically; nevertheless, there was no doubt that he meant Nero and Agrippina.

> secutae insuper litterae grates agentis, quod hominem infensum rei publicae punivissent, adiecto trepidam sibi vitam, suspectas inimicorum insidias,

---

[73] As mentioned in Chapter 2, Tacitus (*Ann.* 4.52.2) has Agrippina claim that Claudia Pulchra was being attacked because she had chosen Agrippina *ad cultum*.

[74] Cf. Dio [Xiph.] 58.1b.

[75] Tacitus calls him Latinius Latiaris at *Ann.* 4.68.2 and Lucanius Latiaris at *Ann.* 6.4.1. On the name, see Koestermann 1965: 201, Syme 1970: 70, and Woodman 2017: 104–5. For the other accusers, see Woodman 2018: 314–15.

[76] Rutledge 2001: 145.

nullo nominatim conpellato; neque tamen dubitabatur in Neronem et Agrippinam intendi. (*Ann.* 4.70.4)

While certainly Tacitus paints a dark portrait of the persecutions of the so-called "party of Agrippina," those persecuted may actually have been plotting against Tiberius, or at least undermining his authority. Agrippina, like her mother Julia, believed her sons were worthy of the hereditary rule established by Augustus. But just as Augustus had deferred the advancement of Gaius and Lucius, Tiberius wanted the young men to earn their position.[77]

Tiberius' treatment of his daughter-in-law Agrippina as well as his grandsons Nero and Drusus must inevitably be compared with Augustus' exile of his daughter, granddaughter, and grandson/adopted son.[78] According to Suetonius (*Aug.* 65), Augustus sent a *libellus* to the Senate regarding his daughter Julia. Augustus himself was not present at this meeting, and the *libellus* was read by one of the quaestors. Suetonius does not tell us whether the Senate had been consulted about Julia's crimes or punishment, but does state that Augustus subsequently isolated himself and contemplated having Julia executed. Tiberius likewise communicated his grievances against members of his family to the Senate. The narratives of these events in Tacitus and Dio are fragmentary. The extant texts disagree on the details concerning the persecution of Agrippina and her two eldest sons.[79] Tiberius had probably already made up his mind when he sent the letter to the Senate which began the proceedings against Agrippina and Nero (Tac. *Ann.* 5.3). But the ambiguity of his letter to the Senate led to confusion as to what, exactly, Tiberius wanted them to do. Tiberius then wrote again, saying, according to Tacitus (*Ann.* 5.5), that by the intercession of one senator (Junius Rusticus) the *maiestas* of the *imperator* had been publicly mocked.

Deline (2015: 770) argues that Tacitus has reversed two stages of the prosecution of Agrippina in his accounts for the years 27 and 29.[80] Deline believes that Tiberius first communicated his concerns to the Senate in 27, accusing Agrippina of insubordination and Nero of *inpudicitia*.[81] She was

---

[77] Barrett 1990: 19.   [78] Fertik 2019: 49.

[79] Caligula supposedly burned the *commentarii* concerning the trials of his mother and brothers (Suet. *Cal.* 15.4; cf. Dio 59.4.3).

[80] She builds upon points already made by Meise (1969: 240) and Levick (1999 [1976]: 167–70). Dio ([Xiph.] 58.2) records the death of Livia immediately after the trial of Sabinus and makes no mention of any action against Agrippina (or her two older sons) in 29.

[81] Schilling notes that Nero, having been accused of sodomy, should have been put to death under the *lex Scantinia* (2010: 170).

then exiled from Rome or kept under house arrest. In 29, Tiberius was able to escalate his punishment of Agrippina because she was no longer under the protection of Livia, who had recently died. Deline (2015: 768) points out that Suetonius (*Cal.* 10.1) states that Livia took care of Caligula after his mother had been exiled. Velleius (2.130.4–5) and Pliny the Elder (*HN* 8.145) also indicate that the condemnation of Agrippina preceded the death of Livia. At some point, the situation escalated, with charges being added that Agrippina and Nero planned to break out of house arrest in order to claim sanctuary at an image of Augustus and/or flee to the Rhine legions. These accusations of outright treason led to their relegation to Pandateria (Agrippina) and Pontia (Nero). By including the letter under his account of the final condemnation of Agrippina instead of under his account of the initial complaint, Tacitus has misled his readers. Tiberius seems to be overreacting to Agrippina's insubordination. If the allegations that Agrippina intended to stir up the Rhine legions were even partially true, Tiberius faced a very real threat. As the granddaughter of Augustus and the widow of Germanicus, Agrippina could have used their charismatic images to convince the army to advance the claims of her sons, potentially triggering a civil war and overthrowing the peaceful *status* established by her grandfather.

The Fall of Sejanus and the Aftermath

Sejanus had grown increasingly powerful after saving Tiberius' life at Sperlonga (Tac. *Ann.* 4.59; cf. Suet. *Tib.* 39), being honored with an altar of friendship (*Ann.* 4.74.2) and cultivated for access to Tiberius, who was now mostly residing at Capri (*Ann.* 4.74; Dio [Xiph.] 58.5).[82] Tacitus sees the ultimate turning point in Sejanus' ambitions as the death of Livia (*Ann.* 5.3). Notably, at the same time that Livia's death "unleashed" Sejanus and Tiberius (*velut frenis exsoluti*, Tac. *Ann.* 5.3.1) on Agrippina and Nero, Caligula was chosen to give the eulogy for his great-grandmother from the rostra (*Ann.* 5.2.1). So why did Tiberius betray his "Agrippa" and throw his support behind Caligula?[83] Schilling (2010:

---

[82] While Tacitus (*Ann.* 4.67) and Suetonius (*Tib.* 40) may portray Capri as a fortress of solitude, the archeological evidence shows that the Villa Jovis and other parts of the island were not significantly different from other villas on the Bay of Naples in their capacity to serve as "working vacation" homes. See especially Krause 2003. Augustus had acquired the island and spent time there before his death (Strabo 5.4.9, Suet. *Aug.* 92.2 and 98.4, and Dio 52.43.2).

[83] On the overemphasis of the role played by Antonia in protecting Caligula in later sources, see Nicols 1975.

173) asserts that the discovery of Drusus' murder was the key, arguing that Sejanus was not only convicted of *maiestas* but also of murder under the *lex Cornelia de sicariis et veneficiis*. This would explain why Sejanus was condemned to death. However, that does not explain the precautions taken by Tiberius in secretly replacing Sejanus with Macro as head of the Praetorian Guard or the persecution of Sejanus' supporters after his death. Our sources (such as they are) point to attacks on Caligula and schemes with Livilla rather than retribution for the murder of Drusus. Indeed, Birley (2007: 141) suggests that the marriage of Sejanus and Livilla may have been part of the reason Tiberius acted when he did.[84]

Cogitore (2002: 227) claims that Tiberius used Sejanus as a weapon to reinforce the claims of the Claudian side of the dynasty against those of the Julian. Severy (2003: 199) disputes the idea of Julians and Claudians. By the second generation, the Julians had mixed blood with the Claudians. The children of Agrippina, a Julian, were also the children of Germanicus, a Claudian (by birth). Agrippina's exchange with Tiberius (Tac. *Ann.* 4.52) established that the most important factor in the contest for power was being related to Divus Augustus. Instead of Julians and Claudians, we should focus on connections to Divus Augustus within the *domus Augusta*. Ultimately, Tiberius did concede priority to Caligula, who had closer blood ties to Divus Augustus, over his biological grandson Gemellus. Despite her argument that Tiberius was trying to eliminate Julians, Cogitore (2002: 226) notes that the celebration of Sejanus' downfall by games presided over by the various priestly colleges, including the Sodales Augustales (Dio 58.12.4–5), signaled that the *aegis* of Divus Augustus had protected the city. Tiberius began his covert attack on Sejanus at a meeting of the Senate held at the Temple of Apollo on the Palatine, built by Augustus and closely tied to his *domus*. As seen in Chapter 4, Germanicus was commemorated through *imagines clipeatae* of both himself and his father Drusus in the *porticus* of that temple (*TH* 1). Moreover, the meeting of the Senate at which Sejanus was condemned took place in the Temple of Concordia (Dio 58.11.4), whose connections to the *domus Augusta* we have discussed in Chapter 2. The public celebration upon the

---

[84] For arguments that it was Livilla and not her daughter who was married or betrothed to Sejanus at the time of his death, see Bellemore 1995, who also believes that the marriage of Livilla and Sejanus may have prompted their downfall. She proposes that this may have been the information which Antonia brought to Tiberius' attention as opposed to some vague attack on Caligula or himself. Dio [Zon.] 58.3.9 states that Tiberius betrothed Sejanus to Julia, Livilla's daughter. On Dio's account, see Mallan 2020: 290 and 300.

death of the Praetorian Prefect once again reinforced the notion that the *domus* was being protected by its progenitor.

In the aftermath of the death of Sejanus, ancient sources paint the portrait of Tiberius as a paranoid tyrant ordering executions from his stronghold at Capri. But upon closer examination, attacks on those who were friends of Sejanus were more often initiated by senators seeking revenge for previous wrongs.[85] As Cogitore (2002: 227) observes, the mysterious letter which Tiberius sent from Capri did not directly indict Sejanus of any crime and allowed the Senate to make its own decision. The same is true in virtually all the cases involving Sejanus' alleged supporters. Schilling (2010: 187) concludes that more often than not Tiberius was responsible for mitigating penalties handed down by the Senate. If anything, Tiberius can be blamed for a lack of leadership in curbing members of the Senate from attacking each other. Undoubtedly, his absence from Rome created an environment of mistrust. When Tacitus' narrative resumes after the fall of Sejanus (*Ann.* 5.8), the first named victim of the purge of Sejanus' supporters is P. Vitellius, who committed suicide after he was alleged to have offered the military treasury for "revolutionary purposes" (*militarem pecuniam rebus novis obtulisse, Ann.* 5.8.1).[86] According to Tacitus, at the same time Pomponius Secundus was accused of protecting Aelius Gallus, presumably a kinsman of Sejanus.[87] Tacitus vaguely states that Pomponius survived Tiberius, indicating that the charges were dropped (or at least deferred). As for the horrific execution of the children of Sejanus (*Ann.* 5.9), Tacitus does not say who was responsible. Given the general hatred for Sejanus expressed in Juvenal's satire (10.56–77; cf. Sen. *Tranq.* 11.11), the Senate may have been acquiescing to the will of the mob.

Sejanus' fall created an environment of paranoia and suspicion. More importantly, Tiberius' absence from the city left the Senate adrift as to the princeps' mindset. Tacitus (*Ann.* 6.2–3; cf. Dio 58.17) narrates failed attempts at flattery by Togonius Gallus, who suggested a bodyguard for Tiberius whenever he entered the Senate (which he would never do again), and Junius Gallio, who suggested that veterans of the Praetorian Guard should be shown the same respect as *equites* in the theater. Tiberius rejected the latter's proposal, citing the precedent of Augustus (Tac.

---

[85] See Schilling 2010: 178–9. Tacitus' account of the reign of Tiberius was undoubtedly colored by his own experiences under Domitian. One cannot help but think of Nerva's wise decision to outlaw prosecutions of former delators lest the Senate implode upon itself (Dio 68.1.1; cf. Pliny, *Ep.* 4.22).

[86] Vitellius had served as one of the prosecutors of Piso (Tac. *Ann.* 3.13.2).

[87] On Aelius Gallus, see Woodman 2017: 72.

Ann. 6.3.2; cf. Dio 58.18). Tacitus (*Ann.* 6.3.4) adds that in the same letter Tiberius initiated an indictment against Sextius Paconianus, accused of having assisted Sejanus in his plot against Caligula.[88] Tacitus does not specify the charge. Apparently, Paconianus had made enough enemies that, given the opportunity, the senators pounced. But he turned informer against Latiaris, who had helped Sejanus take down Titius Sabinus.

The protection of the *domus Augusta* served as an excuse for an attack on Ovid's and Tiberius' mutual friend (see Chapter 5) Cotta Messalinus. He had allegedly insulted the manhood of the heir presumptive, Caligula (Tac. *Ann.* 6.5).[89] After Cotta appealed to "his" Tiberius (*Tiberiolus meus*), the princeps sent the famous letter which Tacitus construes as the tyrant revealing his soul (*Ann.* 6.6; cf. Suet. *Tib.* 67).[90] Regardless of how one interprets Tiberius' letter, he was clearly exasperated at the Senate. Cotta was exonerated. Indeed, Cotta's accuser, Caesilianus, was punished instead – although Tacitus (*Ann.* 6.7) does not tell us how.[91] Dio narrates (58.19.1) an incident involving a man named Caesianus in the following year who was spared by Tiberius for being an associate of Sejanus.[92] If the two are the same man, the accusation against Cotta may have been a way of proving allegiance to Caligula and the *domus Augusta*. Dio connects the pardon of Caesianus with that of Terentius, the same man Tacitus provides as a mouthpiece for all nobles defending themselves against friendship with Sejanus (Dio 58.19; *Ann.* 6.8). In that case as well the accusers were punished for bringing a false charge (*Ann.* 6.9.1). Shortly afterward, a letter from Tiberius rebuked Sex. Vistilius, who had once been a friend of his brother Drusus. Tacitus implies (*Ann.* 6.9.2) that the charge was insulting Caligula. Only this time, the accusation was brought by the princeps himself. And yet, Tacitus' narrative suggests that Tiberius had only intended a *renuntiatio amicitiae*, not a formal prosecution. Vistilius' suicide may have been, like that of the future emperor Galba's brother (Tac. *Ann.* 6.40), a result of shame after disgrace.

---

[88] Woodman (2017: 103) argues for Sextilius as opposed to Sextius.

[89] Cotta had already been an advocate for prosecutions of Agrippina and Nero after Tiberius' mysterious letter to the Senate in 29 (Tac. *Ann.* 5.3.3). He had also proposed the ban on *imagines* of Libo (*Ann.* 2.32.1).

[90] For various interpretations, see Rogers, 1935: 134–5, Levick 1978b, and Morello 2006: 351–3. In general, see Woodman's commentary on this passage (2017: 109–14). Woodman (2017: 111) notes that Tiberius' language (*di me deaeque peius perdant*, *Ann.* 6.6.1), which is also cited by Suetonius (*Tib.* 67.1), echoes language used by Augustus in a letter to Tiberius (*di me perdant*, Suet. *Tib.* 21.7).

[91] On the name, see Syme 1970: 66.

[92] He was also accused of making fun of Tiberius' baldness. According to Dio, Tiberius took the joke in stride.

As the cases discussed above indicate, the Senate was at a loss as to how to properly honor the *domus Augusta* in the wake of Sejanus' downfall and the presumed ascendancy of Caligula. According to Dio (58.8.4), just before Tiberius brought about the demise of Sejanus, he banned sacrifices to living humans. This was connected to Tiberius' refusal of divine honors for himself. Tacitus (*Ann.* 6.18.2) makes no mention of this ban when introducing the case of the descendants of Theophanes. Tacitus is maddeningly vague, stating only that Tiberius drove Pompeia Macrina into exile and attacked her husband and father-in-law, who were Greek nobility. Pompeia's father and brother committed suicide, supposedly anticipating condemnation.[93] The charge was presented that divine honors were being given to the deceased Theophanes (*defuncto Theophani calestes honores*), who had been friends with Pompey. Tacitus does not state when these honors were decreed nor what they entailed.[94] Although it was not uncommon in the Republic for such honors to be awarded to provincial governors and local nobility, once Divus Augustus had been made a god by senatorial decree, it would be dangerous to put anyone else on his level.

Tacitus is our most reliable source for the reign of Tiberius; however, there is a distinct gap at times between "fact" and "impression" in his narrative. Thus, when he refers to a massive slaughter (*immensa strages*, *Ann.* 6.19) in 33 of supporters of Sejanus, we must read his narrative cautiously. Walker (1960: 83) believes Tacitus' *immensa strages* refers to an event narrated by Suetonius (*Tib.* 61) where twenty people were executed on one day. Bauman (1996: 179 n. 61), on the other hand, argues that Suetonius reckons the victims of only one day in a string of days of executions. But Suetonius also lists the execution on this day of virgins deflowered by the executioner, a clear reference to the incident already narrated by Tacitus (*Ann.* 5.9) regarding Sejanus' daughter. Dio seems to refer to the same event, but his explanation is quite different. While Tacitus says that those executed were accused of associating with Sejanus, Dio states that they were the most notorious of the delators (τούς τε ἐπιβοητοτάτους τῶν τὰς κατηγορίας ποιουμένων, 58.21.5; cf. 58.16.7). The two are not unrelated, as Tacitus had narrated multiple cases prosecuted by agents of Sejanus; yet Dio's account suggests that

---

[93] Pompeia's brother, Pompeius Macer, had served as praetor in 15. Ironically, he was the one who asked if cases involving treason ought to be heard (Tac. *Ann.* 1.72.3). For the complexities of this family tree, see White 1992.

[94] Rogers (1935: 145–6) believes there may be a political angle as well, possibly connected to the movements of the false Drusus in Achaea two years earlier. Seager (2005: 195) points out that, according to Strabo (13.2.3), the son of Theophanes was once a good friend of Tiberius.

Tiberius may have been trying to slow the carnage by eliminating the worst offenders and threatening others who would take their places.[95]

The deaths of Agrippina and her son Drusus followed not long after (*Ann.* 6.23–5). Her eldest son, Nero, had died in 31. According to Suetonius (*Tib.* 54), he was forced to commit suicide. Dio (58.8.4) does not report Nero's actual death; he does state that Tiberius sent a letter to the Senate to report it in which he seemed to slight Sejanus. Tiberius also made a point to send letters to the Senate reporting the deaths of Agrippina and Drusus. As Barrett (1990: 32) observes, these public reports were likely prompted by the appearance of the "false Drusus" in 31 (Tac. *Ann.* 5.10), as well as Clemens' earlier attempt to impersonate Agrippa Postumus.[96] A public declaration of their deaths would presumably quash any attempts to stir up rebellion on their behalf. Drusus' and Agrippina's deaths are prefaced in Tacitus' narrative by the death of Asinius Gallus (*Ann.* 6.23.1), accused of having an affair with Agrippina.[97] Tacitus asserts that the claim was unlikely given Agrippina's notoriety for chastity, yet he concedes that she was intolerant of an equal, greedy for power, and had substituted the concerns of men for the vices of women (*aequi impatiens, dominandi avida, virilibus curis feminarum vitia exuerat, Ann.* 6.25.2). Barrett's (1990: 20) supposition that Asinius Gallus was the prospective husband Agrippina had in mind when she confronted Tiberius during the prosecution of Claudia Pulchra is not unreasonable. This would certainly have lent some air of credibility to the accusations of an affair between the two, or at least an alliance which could be seen as a threat by Tiberius.

Soon after these deaths, accusers attacked Mamercus Scaurus.[98] While his authorship of a tragedy critical of tyrants earned him the mantle of a literary martyr alongside Cremutius Cordus (Suet. *Tib.* 61.3), Tacitus (*Ann.* 6.9) had already mentioned an attack on Scaurus two years earlier, noting that Tiberius deferred the prosecution to investigate the matter

---

[95] Bauman (1996: 179 n. 61; 1974: 192–4) contends that Dio has retrojected the punishment of delators from later reigns. As the delators and supporters of Sejanus are closely linked, I do not see any strong argument against taking Dio at his word. On the curious placement of this statement in Dio's narrative of the financial crisis of 33, see Mallan 2020: 330–1.

[96] Dio (58.25) reports the false Drusus as having appeared in 34. For arguments in favor of Tacitus' dating, see Tuplin 1987.

[97] Dio (58.23.6) reports Gallus' death after those of Agrippina and Drusus. For the prosecution of Gallus, see Dio [Xiph.] 58.3 and Rogers 1935: 104–5. The account found in Dio [*EV* 191] 58.3.1–3 indicates that Gallus was courting Sejanus, which made Tiberius jealous. On the problems with this suggestion, see Mallan 2020: 279.

[98] On the trial of Mamercus Scaurus in the *Annals*, see Woodman 2017: 213–16.

himself.[99] Dio (58.24.4) explicitly blames Scaurus' tragedy *Atreus* for his downfall, saying that Tiberius quipped he would make the author an Ajax. Tacitus (*Ann.* 6.29.3) asserts that Scaurus was attacked because he had run afoul of Macro and adds that the charges brought forward by the accusers were adultery with Livilla and magic rituals (*magorum sacra*). This resembles the charges against Libo and Aemilia Lepida, who were accused of intending to use magic against members of the *domus Augusta*. Tacitus does not tell us if the case was prosecuted further, only that Scaurus' wife joined him in committing suicide. Immediately afterwards, Tacitus admits that the prosecutors of Scaurus were themselves punished. No mention is made in Tacitus' narrative of any interference by Tiberius.[100] Whether or not Scaurus had been put on trial for treasonous speech, Tiberius was clearly aware of the negative publicity caused by such prosecutions. Tacitus (*Ann.* 6.38) states that Fulcinius Trio, unable to endure the increasing attacks of the accusers, had written slanders against Macro and Tiberius in his will. Fulcinius had been involved in the prosecutions of both Libo and Piso. Tacitus relates that after rewarding the other prosecutors of Piso, Tiberius advised Fulcinius not to undermine his eloquence with violence (*Ann.* 3.19.1).[101] Dio (58.25.2) introduces Trio as a friend of Sejanus and a prominent accuser who committed suicide after having been charged, presumably with *maiestas*. Tacitus does not state how he died. Tiberius had the will of Fulcinius read publicly.[102]

The suicide of Trio is followed in Tacitus' narrative (*Ann.* 6.38–9) by the deaths of Granius Marcianus, who committed suicide after being charged with *maiestas*; Tarius Gratianus, condemned to death for *maiestas*; Trebellienus Rufus, who committed suicide (Tacitus does not explicitly state he was facing prosecution); and Sextius Paconianus, executed for

---

[99] In addition to Scaurus, Annius Pollio, his son Annius Vinicianus, Appius Silanus, and Calvisius Sabinus were indicted for *maiestas* in 32. Silanus and Sabinus were released; Tiberius promised to launch an investigation regarding the other three. Rogers (1935: 140) remarks, "... of the five indicted in 32 three were themselves later involved in suspicion of treason, the family of the fourth supplied conspirators for two generations in the next three reigns, and only Silanus seems innocent of subsequent treasonable activity."

[100] Seneca the Elder (*Contr.* 10 pref. 3) states that seven speeches of Scaurus were burned by order of the Senate. "This seems to be unrelated to the offense against Tiberius. These speeches probably slandered senators because Seneca the Elder explicitly welcomes their destruction" (Rohmann 2013: 132).

[101] Apparently, Fulcinius did not take these words to heart. He ended up in a battle with his fellow consul Regulus, whom he accused of being slow in bringing down the remaining supporters of Sejanus (*Ann.* 5.11; cf. *Ann.* 6.4).

[102] Woodman (2017: 248–9) notes that Tiberius was following Augustus' precedent of allowing freedom of speech in wills (Suet. *Aug.* 56.1).

repeatedly reciting poems against the emperor while already in prison for conspiring with Sejanus against Caligula.[103] Tacitus claims that Tiberius was so close to the city that he could almost see the blood gushing forth. More specifically, Dio (58.25.2) states that around this time Tiberius was at Antium for the wedding of Caligula. While Dio may not be correct about the occasion, Tiberius likely stayed at Antium at least a few times.[104] If Caligula was with his grandfather, he may have instigated, either directly or indirectly, the downfall of these men.

The Succession of Caligula

According to Dio (58.23.4), when considering the inevitable succession of Caligula, Tiberius frequently quoted a line from Greek tragedy: "When I am dead, let the earth be overrun with fire." This recalls the suggestion that Augustus had chosen Tiberius as his successor so that he might appear better by comparison (Tac. *Ann.* 1.10.7; Suet. *Tib.* 21.2; Dio 56.45.3). But just as Augustus had backed himself into a corner by relying upon members of his close family, Tiberius was bound by his predecessor's precedent. The death of Drusus the Younger created a power vacuum in the *domus Augusta*. As the two elder sons of Germanicus came of age, their mother's ambition alienated them from the princeps. The rise of Caligula and the overthrow of Sejanus seem inextricably linked, even beyond the machinations of Sejanus' successor, Macro. Dio (58.7–8) connects Caligula's popularity with the masses to Sejanus' decline. In 29, Caligula delivered the funeral oration for Livia, just as Julius Caesar had done for his aunt, Augustus had done for his grandmother, and Tiberius had done for his father.[105] Soon afterwards, Caligula was made a priest alongside Sejanus and his sons.[106] Caligula was made quaestor in 33 at the same age at which his father had been advanced to the office, four years before he had reached the minimum age. He was also given the right to hold other offices five years earlier than the minimum age.

---

[103] On these men, see Woodman 2017: 249–50.
[104] Tacitus (*Ann.* 6.20.2) mentions the wedding two years earlier. Suetonius (*Cal.* 12.1) is no help. As Woodman (2017: 168; cf. 251) states: "There is no way of reconciling these three quite different dates for the marriage." Antium is roughly thirty-five miles from Rome. Tiberius also spent time in his later years at Tusculum (Dio 58.24.1), which is roughly thirteen miles from Rome.
[105] For references and other precedents, see Woodman 2017: 56.
[106] Portraits of Caligula are documented by at least 19 but became more abundant in 29. See Boschung 1989: 62.

While certainly his status as the last remaining son of the charismatic Germanicus and the great-grandson of Divus Augustus would have made him popular with the masses, Caligula had very few opportunities to interact with the Senate. Despite his political advancement, Caligula spent much of his time with his grandfather on Capri.[107] Although Tiberius had his reservations about the character of Caligula, he feared that if a successor were sought outside the *domus Augusta*, the memory of Augustus and the name of the Caesars would become fodder for jokes and insults (Tac. *Ann.* 6.46.2). At the same time, however, Dio (58.23.1) states that Tiberius warned the Senate against puffing up the young man with excessive honors. Tiberius did not adopt Caligula as his son. He did not give him extraordinary powers. In the end, Caligula's succession was the result of a process which had been going on during the entire reign of Tiberius, a process which had transformed the image of Augustus (and, to a lesser degree, Germanicus) into a charismatic power which ensured that the next three principes would claim the right to rule based solely on their membership in the *domus Augusta*.

Tiberius had resigned himself to the succession of Caligula. But there was another potential heir – Tiberius Gemellus, the son of Drusus the Younger. The historical sources present conflicting reports about Tiberius' attitude towards his biological grandson. Human nature would incline one to believe that he favored his own bloodline; the facts do not bear that out. Regardless of whether he believed Gemellus to be the product of adultery (Dio 58.23.2), Tiberius did not advance his career in the same way in which he had advanced those of Germanicus' sons, including Caligula.[108] Although Tiberius named Gemellus joint heir with Caligula in his will, Gemellus had held no public offices. Despite being seventeen, Gemellus had still not taken up the *toga virilis*. Tiberius was well aware that even if he named both his grandsons as heirs in his will (which was annulled), Caligula had the better claim. Indeed, both Tacitus (*Ann.* 6.46.4) and Dio (58.23.3) cite Tiberius' famous quip to Caligula that one day he would kill his cousin, and another would kill him.

---

[107] Tacitus (*Ann.* 6.20.1) describes him as *avo comes*.

[108] Bauman (1967: 204) suggests the intriguing possibility that Agrippa Postumus may have been thought to be the son of one of Julia's lovers, possibly Ti. Sempronius Gracchus. In that case, Tiberius would again be following Augustan precedent by dismissing a grandson born from adultery. According to Josephus (*AJ* 18.6.9), Tiberius tried to manipulate auguries in Gemellus' favor but was outwitted.

Caligula may have been designated Tiberius' successor, but there had only been one precedent for a peaceful transition of the *statio* of princeps. Caligula held none of the key powers Tiberius possessed upon the death of Augustus. His claim was based solely upon his position in the charismatic *domus Augusta*. Interested parties took measures to ensure Caligula's rule. While the timeline is uncertain, Caligula reputedly had an affair with the wife of Macro. Dio (58.28.4) tells us that her name was Ennia Thrasylla, perhaps the granddaughter of Thrasyllus, Tiberius' trusted adviser on astrology and other matters.[109] We can never truly know what role Macro played in Caligula's succession, which seemed to have been decided when Tiberius made his move against Sejanus.[110] Macro may have murdered Tiberius by smothering him with bedclothes (Tac. *Ann.* 6.50.5; Suet. *Tib.* 73.2, *Cal.* 12; Dio 58.28.3). But Tiberius was already seventy-eight. He was not going to live much longer.

Nevertheless, one last dynastic intrigue is reported before the inevitable succession of Caligula. In 37, as Tiberius' health was declining and Macro was increasingly secure in his control, Albucilla, a woman "notorious for her many lovers," was accused of *impietas in principem* on the evidence of her husband (Tac. *Ann.* 6.47; cf. Dio 58.27).[111] Macro presided over the case. Her lovers included Vibius Marsus, L. Arruntius, and most importantly, Cn. Domitius, husband of the younger Agrippina. The Senate procrastinated until Tiberius, who seemed oblivious to the proceedings, died. As Bauman (1974: 103) argues, what this alleged conspiracy hoped to achieve can likely be divined from the accuser. Macro, like Sejanus, was ridding himself of political enemies, or in the case of Domitius, threats within the *domus Augusta* to the power of the soon-to-be princeps Caligula.

Conclusions

The *maiestas* trials which plagued the latter part of Tiberius' reign were inevitable. While precedents had been set in the late Republic and under Augustus which allowed delators to bring such charges, the real impetus was the overwhelming reliance of Tiberius on the charismatic image of Divus Augustus. As that charismatic power was transferred to the position of the princeps and the *domus Augusta*, the scope of prosecutions expanded

---

[109] See Woodman 2017: 270.
[110] Of course, Macro himself suffered a fate similar to that of Sejanus in 38 (Dio 58.10.6).
[111] On the defendants and their various connections, see Forsyth 1969: 206.

exponentially. This was all compounded by multiple crises within the *domus*, many of them brought about by conflicts among those competing for power. Tiberius' retreat to Capri, effectively cutting off communication with the Senate except through the Praetorian Prefect, created an atmosphere of fear and mistrust. The inevitable result was confusion among the Senate, leading to a "reign of terror," and overwhelming support for the succession of the great-grandson of Divus Augustus.

Conclusions

When news of Tiberius' death reached Rome, the people supposedly shouted, "Into the Tiber with Tiberius" (Suet. *Tib.* 75.1). The eulogy delivered by Caligula focused mostly on Divus Augustus and Germanicus (Dio 59.3.8). Caligula recognized that his power stemmed not from any offices he may have held but his descent from two powerful charismatic figures. Suetonius (*Cal.* 13–14) states that Caligula was universally hailed as princeps by the army, the Senate, and the urban plebs. Eventually, despite everyone's hope that he would fulfill the charismatic potential of his great-grandfather and father, Caligula alienated the Praetorian Guard as well as the Senate and was assassinated. Claudius, the great-nephew of Augustus, was installed by the Praetorian Guard (Suet. *Claud.* 10). Claudius had held the consulship but had no extraordinary powers before his acclamation as princeps. His qualification for the position was his membership in the *domus Augusta* (Dio 60.1.3). While there may have been negotiations before the senators accepted Claudius as their princeps, they were really left with little choice.[1] Nero, Augustus' great-great-grandson was also installed by the Praetorians. Imitating Tiberius, he swore upon his ascension that he would rule according to the precepts of Augustus (*ex Augusti praescripto*, Suet. *Nero* 10.1).

Nero deified his adoptive father, making Claudius the first *divus* added to the pantheon after Augustus. As discussed in Chapter 2, the imperial cult was instrumental in legitimizing Tiberius' succession to his father's charismatic *statio*. Nero's failure to show the proper respect for either Divus Claudius or Divus Augustus, coupled with years of internecine slaughter within the *domus Augusta*, led to the first civil conflict since Actium.[2] The legions in Spain and Gaul proclaimed Galba emperor, only to be challenged

---

[1] On the negotiations between the Senate and Claudius after the death of Caligula, see Buongiorno 2017: 51–63, drawing especially on the accounts of Dio (60.1–4) and Josephus (*AJ* 19.157–272; *BJ* 2.205–14).

[2] On Nero's attitude towards Divus Claudius, see Griffin 1984: 96–9. Griffin (1984: 185–234) also analyzes the reasons for Nero's fall.

a few months later by the legions in Germania, who supported Vitellius. In the meantime, Otho had corrupted the Praetorian Guard, leading to the assassination of Galba and civil war with Vitellius. The ultimate victor of the "Year of the Four Emperors," Vespasian had plenty of experience in imperial government as well as military support. But he was not a member of the *domus Augusta*. Dio records an incident in Alexandria in which the crowd turned on Titus because of Vespasian's exaction of tribute. When Titus tried to appease the mob, they shouted, "We forgive him; for he knows not how to play the Caesar (*kaisareuein*)" (65.8.6; Loeb trans. Cary). This evokes Tiberius' exchange with the false Agrippa, Clemens. Vespasian did have his own charismatic aura (Suet. *Vesp.* 5–7; Tac. *Hist.* 81–2; Dio 65.8.1–2) but could never have become sole ruler if Tiberius had not routinized the charisma of Divus Augustus and thus the *statio* of princeps.

Even if, as Brunt (1977) has argued, every subsequent ruler after Tiberius formalized his power through some sort of negotiation with the Senate, all the so-called Julio-Claudians were able to hold that negotiation because of their relationship to the charismatic Divus Augustus.[3] Vespasian had won the title of princeps through civil war. He had to tread carefully in order to secure through legal/rational means the position that had once been held primarily by virtue of inherited charisma. Vespasian's overtures to the Senate reflected his desire to stabilize the principate as it had been under Augustus and Tiberius, both of whom had negotiated their powers with the Senate, as discussed in Chapter 1. At least part of this process is preserved in the *lex de imperio Vespasiani*.[4] The *lex de imperio Vespasiani* lays out the powers granted to the princeps by the Senate. While Tiberius and Claudius are mentioned as precedents, the *lex* focuses on Augustus.[5] Peachin (2007) emphasizes particularly the way Augustan *exempla* are used in the document to guide Vespasian's behavior according to the Senate's expectations. This recalls Augustus' own desire, inscribed in the *Res Gestae*, that he would serve as an *exemplum* for later Romans.

As seen in Chapter 3, Augustus did serve as an *exemplum* for Tiberius, who often cited Augustus as a model before the Senate. In the rare cases in which Tiberius deviated from Augustan precedent, he always gave his reasons for doing so. The most notorious of these deviations was his

---

[3] Levick (2009b: 14) rejects Brunt's conjecture that under the Julio-Claudians the process for accepting powers had already been streamlined.

[4] For various analyses of this document see Capogrossi Colognesi and Tassi Scandone 2009. For the *lex* as one element in a series of "Konsensakten," see Flaig 2019 [1992]: 525–30.

[5] Levick (2009b: 19) notes that only Augustus is referred to as Divus, emphasizing his role as the founder of the principate.

scrupulous denial of divine honors for himself, discussed in Chapter 2. Consistently, Tiberius reiterated his own mortality in contrast to the divine nature of his adoptive father. Tiberius propagated the idea that he was merely the reigning princeps; Divus Augustus was still guiding the empire. Material remains from the Tiberian period, analyzed in Chapter 4, show a strong emphasis on the continuation of Augustan charisma protecting the *res publica*. This is reflected in the works of authors from this era, examined in Chapter 5, who consistently praise Augustus and his divine qualities. Tiberius' heavy reliance on the charisma of Augustus to secure the principate opened the door for *maiestas* trials involving defamation of Augustus and, eventually, other members of the *domus Augusta*, as demonstrated in Chapter 6. Diminishing the *maiestas* of the princeps and his family was now equated with diminishing the *maiestas* of the state.

As Max Weber and others have shown, charismatic figures effect revolutionary change. Yet that change is ephemeral if it is not "routinized" into an institution. Tiberius inherited the *statio* of his father. No one quite understood what that entailed. Augustus had assembled an unprecedented amount of power cloaked in pre-existing titles and positions. He had magisterial control over Rome for over fifty years. The Senate had been led by its princeps to such a degree that it lacked the ability to function without one. Likewise, the armies could only show allegiance to one *imperator* (and his family). Julius Caesar had supposedly toyed with the idea of making himself something akin to a Hellenistic king. Had Germanicus succeeded Augustus, he might have followed in the footsteps of his grandfather Mark Antony and indulged himself in the cult of personality favored in the East. Tiberius, on the other hand, lacked the charisma to establish himself as princeps without claiming that he was ruling on the authority of Divus Augustus. Through his promotion of the imperial cult, his professed adherence to Augustan precedent, his propagation of Augustan imagery, and his tacit encouragement of prosecutions for those violating the *maiestas* of Augustus, Tiberius was responsible for enshrining the *statio* of Augustus into the system known as the principate.

Bibliography

Abdy, Richard and Nicholas Harling. 2005. "Two Important New Roman Coins." *NC* 165: 175–8.

Adair-Toteff, Christopher. 2005. "Max Weber's Charisma." *Journal of Classical Sociology* 5: 189–204.

2020. "Max Weber and the Sociology of Charisma." In *The Routledge International Encyclopedia of Charisma*, edited by J. P. Zúquete, 7–17. London: Routledge.

Alföldi, Andreas. 1971. *Der Vater des Vaterlandes im römischen Denken.* Darmstadt: Wissenschaftliche Buchgesellschaft.

Alföldy, G. 1965. "La politique provinciale de Tibère." *Latomus* 24: 824–44.

1992. *Studi sull'epigrafia augustea e tiberiana di Roma.* Rome: Casa editrice Quasar.

Allen, Walter. 1947. "The Death of Agrippa Postumus." *TAPA* 78: 131–9.

Allison, J. E. and J. D. Cloud. 1962. "The *Lex Julia Maiestatis.*" *Latomus* 21: 711–31.

Alpers, Michael. 1995. *Das nachrepublikanische Finanzsystem: Fiscus und Fisci in der frühen Kaiserzeit.* Berlin: de Gruyter.

Ando, Clifford. 2000. *Imperial Ideology and Provincial Loyalty in the Roman Empire.* Berkeley: University of California Press.

Arnaldi, A. 2008. "Testimonianze del culto imperiale nell'Etruria centro-settentrionale costiera." In *Nuove ricerche sul culto imperiale in Italia: atti dell'incontro di studio, Ancona, 31 gennaio 2004*, edited by L. Gasperini and G. Paci, 33–74. Tivoli: Tored.

Arthurs, Joshua. 2012. *Excavating Modernity: The Roman Past in Fascist Italy.* Ithaca: Cornell University Press.

Badian, Ernst. 2009. "From the Iulii to Caesar." In *A Companion to Julius Caesar*, edited by Miriam Griffin, 11–22. Chichester: Wiley-Blackwell.

Balmaceda, Catalina. 2014. "The Virtues of Tiberius in Velleius' *Histories.*" *Historia* 63: 340–63.

2017. *Virtus Romana: Politics and Morality in the Roman Histories.* Chapel Hill: University of North Carolina Press.

Balty, J.-C. 2007. "Culte impérial et image du pouvoir: les statues d'empereurs en 'Hüftmantel' et en 'Jupiter-Kostüm'." In *Culto imperial: política y poder. Actas del congreso internacional, Mérida, Museo Nacional de Arte Romano,*

18–20 de mayo, 2006, edited by T. Nogales Basarrate and J. González Fernández, 51–73. Rome: L'Erma di Bretschneider.

2012. "L'image de César dans les groupes statuaires julio-claudiens et le monnayage augustéen." In *César sous Auguste*, edited by Olivier Devillers and Karin Sion-Jenkis, 73–82. Pessac: Ausonius.

Barchiesi, Alessandro. 1997. *The Poet and the Prince: Ovid and Augustan Discourse*. Berkeley: University of California Press.

Barnes, T. D. 1974. "The Victories of Augustus." *JRS* 64: 21–6.

Barrandon, J.-N., A. Suspène, and A. Gaffiero. 2010. "Les émissions d'*as* au type Divvs Avgvstvs Pater frappées sous Tibère: l'apport des analyses à leur datation et à leur interprétation." *RN* 166: 149–73.

Barrett, Anthony. 1990. *Caligula: The Corruption of Power*. New Haven: Yale University Press.

2006. "Augustus and the Governor's Wives." *RhM* 149: 129–47.

Bartels, J. 2009. "Der Tod des Germanicus und seine epigraphische Dokumentation." *Chiron* 39: 1–9.

Bauman, Richard. 1967. *The Crimen Maiestatis in the Roman Republic and Augustan Principate*. Johannesburg: Witwatersrand University Press.

1974. *Impietas in Principem: A Study of Treason Against the Roman Emperor with Special Reference to the First Century AD*. Munich: Beck.

1996. *Crime and Punishment in Ancient Rome*. London: Routledge.

Bellemore, Jane. 1989. "When did Valerius Maximus Write the *Dicta et Facta Memorabilia?*" *Antichthon* 23: 67–80.

1992. "The Dating of Seneca's *Ad Marciam de Consolatione*." *CQ* 42: 219–34.

1995. "The Wife of Sejanus." *ZPE* 109: 255–66.

2003. "Cassius Dio and the Chronology of AD 21." *CQ* 53: 268–85.

2007. "Tiberius and Rhodes." *Klio* 89: 417–53.

2013. "The Identity of Drusus: The Making of a Princeps." In *The Julio-Claudian Succession: Reality and Perception of the "Augustan Model,"* edited by A. G. G. Gibson, 79–94. Leiden: Brill.

Bellen, Heinz. 1976. "Die Krise der italischen Landwirtschaft unter Kaiser Tiberius (33 n. Chr.)." *Historia* 25: 217–34.

Bergmann, Birgit. 2010. *Der Kranz des Kaisers: Genese und Bedeutung einer römischen Insignie*. Berlin: De Gruyter.

Bergmann, Marianne. 1998. *Die Strahlen der Herrscher: theomorphes Herrscherbild und politische Symbolik im Hellenismus und in der römischen Kaiserzeit*. Mainz: von Zabern.

Bernecker, Annemarie. 1976. "Zur Tiberius-Inschrift von Saepinum." *Chiron* 6: 185–92.

Beyer, J. M. and L. D. Browning. 1999. "Transforming an Industry in Crisis: Charisma, Routinization, and the Supportive Cultural Leadership." *Leadership Quarterly* 101 483–520.

Birch, R. A. 1981. "The Settlement of 26 June AD 4 and Its Aftermath." *CQ* 31: 443–56.

Birley, Anthony. 2007. "Sejanus: His Fall." In *Corolla Cosmo Rodewald*, edited by Nick Sekunda, 121–50. Gdansk: Foundation for the Development of Gdansk University.

    2020. "Introduction." In *Selected Correspondence of Ronald Syme, 1927–1939*, edited by A. Birley, 1–22. Newcastle: History of Classical Scholarship.

Bleicken, Jochen. 1962. *Senatsgericht und Kaisergericht: eine Studie zur Entwicklung des Prozessrechtes im frühen Prinzipat.* Göttingen: Vandenhoeck und Ruprecht.

Bloomer, W. Martin. 1992. *Valerius Maximus and the Rhetoric of the New Nobility.* Chapel Hill: University of North Carolina Press.

    2011. "*Transit Admiratio*: *Memoria, Invidia*, and the Historian." In *Velleius Paterculus: Making History*, edited by Eleanor Cowan, 93–119. Swansea: The Classical Press of Wales.

Bollinger, Traugott. 1969. *Theatralis Licentia. Die Publikumsdemonstrationen an den öffentlichen Spielen im Rom der früheren Kaiserzeit und ihre Bedeutung im politischen Leben.* Winterthur: Verlag Hans Schellenberg.

Bonnefond-Coudry, Marianne. 1989. *Le Sénat de la République Romaine. De la guerre d'Hannibal à Auguste.* Rome: École Française de Rome.

Börm, H. and W. Havener. 2012. "Octavians Rechtsstellung im Januar 27. v. Chr. und das Problem der 'Übertragung' der *res publica*." *Historia* 61: 202–20.

Borzsák, Stephan (István). 1970. "Zum Verständnis der Darstellungskunst des Tacitus. Die Veränderungen des Germanicus-Bildes." *Acta Antiqua Academiae Scientiarum Hungaricae* 18: 279–92.

    1992. *Cornelius Tacitus. Annales I–VI.* Stuttgart: Teubner.

Boschung, Dietrich. 1989. *Die Bildnisse des Caligula.* Berlin: Mann.

    1990. "Prinzenporträt des Tiberius." In *Antike Kunstwerke aus der Sammlung Ludwig III: Skulpturen*, edited by Ernst Berger, John Boardman, and Reinhard Lullies, 369–77. Mainz: P. von Zabern.

    1993a. *Die Bildnisse des Augustus.* Berlin: Mann.

    1993b. "Die Bildnistypen der iulisch-claudischen Kaiserfamilie: ein kritischer Forschungsbericht." *JRA* 6: 39–79.

    2002. *Gens Augusta: Untersuchungen zu Aufstellung, Wirkung und Bedeutung der Statuengruppen des julisch-claudischen Kaiserhauses.* Mainz: P. von Zabern.

    2014. "Review of D. Hertel, *Die Bildnisse des Tiberius.*" *Bonner Jahrbücher* 214: 362–4.

    2015. "Divus Augustus. Das Charisma des Herrschers und seine postume Beglaubigung." In *Das Charisma des Herrschers*, edited by Dietrich Boschung and Jürgen Hammerstaedt, 173–86. Paderborn: Wilhelm Fink.

Boyle, A. J. 1997. "Postscripts from the Edge: Exilic *Fasti* and Imperialised Rome." *Ramus* 26: 7–28.

    2003. *Ovid and the Monuments.* Bendigo, Vic.: Aureal Publications.

Bravi, A. 1998. "Tiberio e la collezione di opere d'arte dell'aedes Concordiae Augustae." *Xenia antiqua* 7: 41–82.

Brice, Lee. 2015. "Second Chance for Valor: Restoration of Order after Mutinies and Indiscipline." In *Aspects of Ancient Institutions and Geography: Studies in*

Honor of Richard J. A. Talbert, edited by Lee Brice and Daniëlle Slootjes, 103–21. Leiden: Brill.

Briscoe, John. 1993. "Some Notes on Maximus." *Sileno* 19: 395–408.

1998. *Facta et Dicta Memorabilia.* 2 vols. Stuttgart: Teubner.

2019. *Valerius Maximus, Book 8: Text, Introduction, and Commentary.* Boston: de Gruyter.

Brokopp, Jonathan. 2020. "Constructing Muslim Charisma." In *The Routledge International Encyclopedia of Charisma,* edited by J. P. Zúquete, 163–74. London: Routledge.

Brunt, P. A. 1961. "Charges of Provincial Maladministration under the Early Principate." *Historia* 10: 189–227.

1963. "Review of H. D. Meyer, *Die Aussenpolitik des Augustus und die augusteische Dichtung.*" *JRS* 53: 170–6.

1966. "The Fiscus and Its Development." *JRS* 56: 75–91.

1977. "Lex de Imperio Vespasiani." *Journal of Roman Studies* 67: 95–116.

1984. "The Role of the Senate in the Augustan Regime." *CQ* 34: 423–44.

Buongiorno, Pierangelo. 2017. *Claudio. Il Principe Inatteso.* Palermo: 21 Editore.

Burnett, Andrew. 2011. "The Augustan Revolution Seen from the Mints of the Provinces." *JRS* 101: 1–30.

Burnett, Andrew, Michel Amandry, and P. P. Ripollès. 1992. *Roman Provincial Coinage. Vol. 1: From the Death of Caesar to the Death of Vitellius (44 BC–AD 69).* London: British Museum Press.

Burrell, Barbara. 2004. *Neokoroi: Greek Cities and Roman Emperors.* Leiden: Brill.

Caballos Rufino, A. 2021. "Un senadoconsulto del año 14 d.C. en un epígrafe bético." *ZPE* 219: 305–26.

Calboli, G. 1998. "Le *Senatus Consultum de Cn. Pisone patre,* quelques considérations linguistiques." In *Moussyllanea: mélanges de linguistique et de littérature anciennes offerts à Claude Moussy,* edited by B. Bureau and N. Christian, 117–30. Louvain: Peeters.

Calomino, Dario. 2015. "Emperor or God? The Posthumous Commemoration of Augustus in Rome and the Provinces." *NC* 175: 57–82, plates 4–8.

Capogrossi Colognesi, L. and E. Tasso Scandone, eds. *La Lex de Imperio Vespasiani e la Roma dei Flavi: atti del convegno, 20–22 novembre 2008.* Rome: L'Erma di Bretschneider.

Carter, C. J. 1975. "Valerius Maximus." In *Empire and Aftermath. Silver Latin ii,* edited by T. A. Dorey, 26–56. London: Routledge.

Castritius, Helmut. 2015. "Die staatsrechtliche Situation beim Tod des Augustus." *ZRG* 132: 449–98.

Chamberland, G. 2007. "A Gladiatorial Show Produced *in Sordidam Mercedem* (Tacitus, *Ann.* 4.62)." *Phoenix* 61: 136–49.

Champlin, Edward. 1989. "The Testament of Augustus." *RhM* 132: 154–65.

2005. "Phaedrus the Fabulous." *JRS* 95: 97–123.

2011. "Tiberius and the Heavenly Twins." *JRS* 101: 73–99.

2012. "Seianus Augustus." *Chiron* 42: 361–88.

2015. "The Richest Man in Spain." *ZPE* 196: 277–95.

Charlesworth, M. P. 1936. "Providentia and Aeternitas." *Harvard Theological Review* 29: 107–32.

1939. "The Refusal of Divine Honors." *PBSR* 15 n.s. 2: 1–10.

Cheung, Ada. 1998. "The Political Significance of Roman Imperial Coin Types." *Schweizer Münzblätter* 191: 53–61.

Claassen, Jo-Marie. 2008. *Ovid Revisited: The Poet in Exile*. London: Duckworth.

Clarke, Katherine. 1997. "In Search of the Author of Strabo's *Geography*." *JRS* 87: 92–110.

Coarelli, Filippo. 2005. "P. Faianius Plebeius, Forum Novum and Tacitus." *PBSR* 73: 85–98.

Cogitore, Isabelle. 2002. *La légitimité dynastique d'Auguste à Néron à l'épreuve des conspirations*. Rome: École française de Rome.

Conger, J. and R. Kanungo. 1998. *Charismatic Leadership in Organizations*. Thousand Oaks, CA: SAGE Publications.

Connal, R. 2013. "Velleius Paterculus: The Soldier and the Senator." *CW* 107: 49–62.

Cooley, Alison. 2009. *Res Gestae Divi Augusti: Text, Translation, and Commentary*. Cambridge: Cambridge University Press.

2019. "From the Augustan Principate to the Invention of the Age of Augustus." *JRS* 109: 71–87.

Corbier, Mireille. 1992. "De la maison d'Hortensius à la *curia* sur la Palatin." *MEFRA* 104: 871–916.

1994. "À propos de la Tabula Siarensis: le sénat, Germanicus et la Domus Augusta." In *Roma y las provincias: modelo y difusión*, edited by T. Nogales Bassarate and Isabel Rodà, 39–85. Rome: L'Erma di Bretschneider.

2001. "*Maiestas Domus Augustae*." In *Varia epigraphica: atti del colloquio internazionale di epigrafia, Bertinoro, 8–10 giugno 2000*, edited by Maria Gabriella Bertinelli Angeli and Angela Donati, 155–99. Faenza: Fratelli Lega.

Cornell, T. J., ed. 2013. *The Fragments of the Roman Historians*. 3 vols: Oxford: Oxford University Press.

Cornwell, Hannah. 2017. *Pax and the Politics of Peace: Republic to Principate*. Oxford: Oxford University Press.

Cowan, Eleanor. 2009a. "Tiberius and Augustus in Tiberian Sources." *Historia* 58: 468–85.

2009b. "Tacitus, Tiberius and Augustus," *CA* 28: 179–210.

2016. "Contesting *Clementia*: The Rhetoric of *Severitas* in Tiberian Rome before and after the Trial of Clutorius Priscus." *JRS* 106: 77–101.

2018. "Velleius Paterculus and the Senate." In *Rappresentazione e uso dei senatus consulta nelle fonti letterarie della repubblica e del primo principato = Darstellung und Gebrauch der senatus consulta in den literarischen Quellen der Republik und der frühen Kaiserzeit*, edited by Andrea Balbo, Pierangelo Buongiorno, and Ermanno Malaspina, 407–28. Stuttgart: Franz Steiner Verlag.

2019. "Hopes and Aspirations. Res Publica, *Leges et Iura*, and Alternatives at Rome." In *The Alternative Augustan Age*, edited by K. Morrell, J. Osgood, and K. Welch, 27–45. Oxford: Oxford University Press.

Cox, Sarah. 1993. "The Temple of Concord on Tiberian *sestertii*." In *Actes du XIe Congrès international de numismatique: organisé à l'occasion du 150e anniversaire de la Société Royale de Numismatique de Belgique, Bruxelles, 8–13 septembre 1991 = Proceedings of the XIth International Numismatic Congress. v. II: Monnaies celtiques et romaines*, edited by Tony Hackens, Ghislaine Moucharte, Catherine Courtois, and H. Dewit, 259–64. Louvain-la-Neuve: Association Professeur Marcel Hoc.

2005. "The Mark of the Successor: Tribunician Power and the Ara Providentia under Tiberius and Vespasian." *Numismatica e antichità classiche* 34: 251–70.

Cramer, F. 1945. "Bookburning and Censorship in Ancient Rome. A Chapter from the History of Freedom of Speech." *Journal of the History of Ideas* 6: 157–96.

Crawford, Michael. 1996. *Roman Statutes*. 2 vols. London: Institute of Classical Studies.

Dahmen, Karsten. 2001. *Untersuchungen zu Form und Funktion kleinformatiger Porträts der römischen Kaiserzeit*. Münster: Scriptorium.

Dalla Rosa, Alberto. 2018. "Gli anni 4–9 d.C.: riforme e crisi alla fine dell'epoca augustea." In *Augusto dopo il bimillenario. Un bilancio*, edited by S. Segenni, 84–100. Milan: Le Monnier Università.

Daly, L. J. 1979. "The Gallus Affair and Augustus' *Lex Iulia Maiestatis*: A Study in Historical Chronology and Causality." *Studies in Latin Literature and Roman History* 1: 289–311.

David, Jean-Michel. 2002. "Review of C. Hatscher, *Charisma und Res Publica. Max Webers Herrschaftssoziologie und die römischen Republik*." *L'Antiquité Classique* 71: 440–2.

Deline, Tracy. 2015. "The Criminal Charges against Agrippina the Elder in AD 27 and 29." *CQ* 65: 766–72.

Dettenhofer, Maria. 2000. *Herrschaft und Widerstand im augusteischen Principat: die Konkurrenz zwischen res publica und domus Augusta*. Stuttgart: F. Steiner.

2002. "Die Wahlreform des Tiberius und ihre Auswirkungen." *Historia* 51: 349–58.

Detweiler, R. 1970. "Historical Perspectives on the Death of Agrippa Postumus." *CJ* 65: 289–95.

Dobiáš, J. 1960. "King Maroboduus As a Politician." *Klio* 38: 155–66.

Doboşi, A. 1935. "Bovillae. Storia e topografia." *Ephemeris Dacoromana* 6: 240–367.

Dowling, Melissa. 2006. *Clemency and Cruelty in the Roman World*. Ann Arbor: University of Michigan Press.

Drogula, Fred. 2015. "Who Was Watching Whom? A Reassessment of the Conflict between Germanicus and Piso." *AJP* 136: 121–53.

Dueck, Daniela. 2000. *Strabo of Amasia: A Greek Man of Letters in Augustan Rome*. London: Routledge.

Dumont, J. C. 2000. "*Carmen* et *libellvs* dans la *tabvla siarensis*." In *La commemorazione di Germanico nella documentazione epigrafica: convegno internazionale di studi, Cassino, 21–24 ottobre 1991*, edited by Augusto Fraschetti, 189–200. Rome: L'Erma di Bretschneider.

Eatwell, Roger. 2006. "The Concept and Theory of Charismatic Leadership." *Totalitarian Movements and Political Religions* 7: 141–56.

Eck, Werner. 2009. "Eine römische Provinz. Das augusteische Germanien links und rechts des Rheins." In *2000 Jahre Varusschlacht. Imperium*, edited by Haltern Westfälisches Römermuseum, 188–95. Stuttgart: Theiss.

———. 2011. "Augusto – la Germania – Varo – Tiberio. Il fallimento di una storia romana di successi." *Rivista storica italiana* 123: 5–25.

———. 2018. "*Consilium coercendi intra terminos imperii*: Motivationswandel in der augusteischen Expansionspolitik?" In *Augusto dopo il bimillenario*, edited by S. Segenni, 129–37. Milan: Le Monnier Università.

Eck, Werner, Antonio Caballos, and Fernando Fernández. 1996. *Das Senatus consultum de Cn. Pisone patre*. Munich: Beck.

Edwards, Rebecca. 2003. "Divus Augustus Pater. Tiberius and the Charisma of Augustus." Ph.D. dissertation, Indiana University.

———. 2012. "His Father's Son and His Son's Father: Augustus and Germanicus in Tiberian Documents," *Studies in Latin Literature and Roman History* 16: 398–414.

———. 2015. "Caesar Telling Tales: Phaedrus and Tiberius." *RhM* 158: 167–84.

Eich, Armin. 2009. "Der Wechsel zu einer neuen *grand strategy* unter Augustus und seine langfristigen Folgen." *Historische Zeitschrift* 288: 561–611.

Elkins, Nathan. 2015. *Monuments in Miniature: Architecture on Roman Coinage*. New York: American Numismatic Society.

Elliott, Colin. 2015. "The Crisis of AD 33: Past and Present." *JAH* 3: 267–81.

Fantham, Elaine. 1985. "Ovid, Germanicus and the Composition of the *Fasti*." *Papers of the Liverpool Latin Seminar* 5: 243–81.

Farrell, J. 2013. "Camillus in Ovid's *Fasti*." In *Augustan Poetry and the Roman Republic*, edited by J. Farrell and D. Nelis, 57–88. Oxford: Oxford University Press.

Fears, J. R. 1977. *Princeps a Diis Electus: The Divine Election of the Emperor as a Political Concept at Rome*. Rome: American Academy in Rome.

———. 1981a. "The Cult of Jupiter and Roman Imperial Ideology." *ANRW* II.17.1: 7–139.

———. 1981b. "The Cult of Virtues and Roman Imperial Ideology." *ANRW* II.17.2: 828–948.

Feeney, Dennis. 2006. "*Si Licet et Fas Est*: Ovid's *Fasti* and the Problem of Free Speech under the Principate." In *Oxford Readings in Ovid*, edited by P. Knox, 464–88. Oxford: Oxford University Press.

Ferrary, Jean-Louis. 2003. "*Res publica restituta* et les pouvoirs d'Auguste." In *Fondements et crises du pouvoir*, edited by Sylvie Franchet d'Espèrey, V. Fromentin, S. Gotteland, and Jean-Michel Roddaz, 419–28. Pessac: Ausonius.

Ferriès, M.-C. 2012. "L'ombre de César dans la politique du consul Marc Antoine." In *César sous Auguste*, edited by Olivier Devillers and Karin Sion-Jenkis, 55–72. Pessac: Ausonius.

Fertik, Harriet. 2019. *The Ruler's House: Contesting Power and Privacy in Julio-Claudian Rome.* Baltimore: Johns Hopkins University Press.

Fishwick, Duncan. 1987. *The Imperial Cult in the Latin West: Studies in the Ruler Cult of the Western Provinces of the Roman Empire. Part 1.* 2 vols. Leiden: Brill.

1990a. *The Imperial Cult in the Latin West: Studies in the Ruler Cult of the Western Provinces of the Roman Empire. Part 2, vol. 1.* Leiden: Brill.

1990b. "Prudentius and the Cult of Divus Augustus." *Historia* 39: 475–86.

1992. "On the Temple of Divus Augustus." *Phoenix* 46: 232–55.

1994. "Numinibus Aug(ustorum)." *Britannia* 25: 127–41.

2005. *The Imperial Cult in the Latin West: Studies in the Ruler Cult of the Western Provinces of the Roman Empire. Part 3, vol. 4. The Provincial Cult: Bibliography, Indices, Addenda.* Leiden: Brill.

2007. "Cn. Piso Pater and the Numen Divi Augusti." *ZPE* 159: 297–300.

2010. "Agrippa and the Ara Providentiae at Rome." *ZPE* 174: 251–58.

2014. "The Status and Location of the Altar of Augustus at Tarraco." *Phoenix* 68: 350–8.

2017. *Precinct, Temple and Altar in Roman Spain: Studies on the Imperial Monuments at Mérida and Tarragona.* Surrey: Ashgate.

Flach, Dieter. 1973. "Der Regierungsanfang des Tiberius." *Historia* 22: 552–69.

Flaig, Egon. 2004. "Review of C. Hatscher, *Charisma und Res Publica. Max Webers Herrschaftssoziologie und die Römische Republik.*" *Gnomon* 76: 523–30.

2007. "Falsche Bescheidenheit. Die *Cunctatio* des Tiberius – ein misslungener Rite de passage." In *Krumme Touren. Anthropologie kommunikativer Umwege,* edited by W. Reinhard, 77–105. Böhlau: de Gruyter.

2011. "The Transition from Republic to Principate: Loss of Legitimacy, Revolution, and Acceptance." In *The Roman Empire in Context: Historical and Comparative Perspectives,* edited by Johann Arnason and Kurt A. Raaflaub, 67–84. Chichester: Wiley-Blackwell.

2019. [1st ed. 1992]. *Den Kaiser herausfordern: die Usurpation im römischen Reich.* 2nd rev. ed. Frankfurt: Campus.

Flory, Marleen. 1984. "*Sic Exempla Parantur*: Livia's Shrine to Concordia and the Porticus Liviae." *Historia* 33: 309–30.

1996. "Dynastic Ideology, the Domus Augusta, and Imperial Women: A Lost Statuary Group in the Circus Flaminius." *TAPA* 126: 287–306.

Forsyth, Phyllis Young. 1969. "A Treason Case of AD 37." *Phoenix*: 204–7.

Frank, T. 1935. "The Financial Crisis of 33 AD." *AJP* 56: 336–41.

Franklin, James. 2001. *Pompeis Difficile Est: Studies in the Political Life of Imperial Pompeii.* Ann Arbor: University of Michigan Press.

Frederiksen, M. W. 1966. "Caesar, Cicero and the Problem of Debt." *JRS* 56: 128–41.

Friedländer, Saul. 1978. *History and Psychoanalysis: An Inquiry into the Possibilities and Limits of Psychohistory.* New York: Holmes and Meier.

Furedi, Frank. 2013. *Authority: A Sociological History.* Cambridge: Cambridge University Press.

Gagetti, Elisabetta. 2016. "La Turchese Marlborough: una gemma problematica." In *Intorno a Tiberio. 1. Archeologia, cultura e letteratura del Principe e della sua epoca*, edited by Fabrizio Slavazzi and Chiara Torre, 29–45. Firenze: All'Insegno del Giglio.

Gagé, J. 1930. "La Victoria Augusti et les auspices de Tibère." *RA* ser. 5 v. 32: 1–35.

Galimberti, Alessandro. 2015. "Velleio Patercolo, Augusto e l'ombra lunga di Tiberio." *Acta Antiqua Academiae Scientiarum Hungaricae* 55: 297–308.

Galinsky, Karl. 1996. *Augustan Culture: An Interpretive Introduction*. Princeton: Princeton University Press.

2015. "Augustus' *Auctoritas* and *Res Gestae* 34.3." *Hermes* 143: 244–9.

Gamauf, Richard. 1999. *Ad statuam licet confugere: Untersuchungen zum Asylrecht im römischen Prinzipat*. Frankfurt: P. Lang.

Garriguet, José Antonio. 2002. *El culto imperial en la Córdoba romana: una aproximación arqueológica*. Córdoba: Diputación Provincial de Córdoba.

Gartrell, Amber. 2021. *The Cult of Castor and Pollux in Ancient Rome: Myth, Ritual, and Society*. Cambridge: Cambridge University Press.

Gasperini, L. 2008. "L'Augusteo di Forum Clodii." In *Nuove ricerche sul culto imperiale in Italia: atti dell'incontro di studio, Ancona, 31 gennaio 2004*, edited by L. Gasperini and Gianfranco Paci, 91–134. Tivoli: Tored.

Geiger, Joseph. 2018. "The First Emperor? Augustus and Julius Caesar as Rival Founders of the Principate." In *Afterlives of Augustus, AD 14–2014*, edited by Penelope Goodman, 74–86. Cambridge: Cambridge University Press.

Gesche, Helga. 1968. *Die Vergottung Caesars*. Kallmünz: Verlag Michael Lassleben.

1978. "Die Divinisierung der römischen Kaiser in ihrer Funktion als Herrschaftslegitimation." *Chiron* 8: 377–90.

Giard, Jean-Baptiste. 1998. *Le Grand Camée de France*. Paris: Bibliothèque nationale de France.

Gibson, A. G. G. 2013. "Introduction." In *The Julio-Claudian Succession: Reality and Perception of the "Augustan model,"* edited by A. G. G. Gibson, 1–17. Leiden: Brill.

Gnoli, Tommaso. 2013. "Narona e Ravenna. Espressioni del culto imperiale tra Tiberio e Claudio." In *L'Augusteum di Narona*, edited by Giuseppe Zecchini, 83–116. Rome: L'Erma di Bretschneider.

Gonzenbach, Victorine von. 1966. "Tiberische Gürtel- und Schwertscheidenbeschläge mit figürlichen Reliefs." In *Helvetia Antiqua. Festschrift für Emil Vogt*, edited by R. Degen, 183–208. Zürich: Conzett und Huber.

González, J. 1984. "Tabula Siarensis, Fortunales Siarensis et Municipia Civium Romanorum." *ZPE* 55: 55–100.

1988. "The First Oath Pro Salvte Avgvsti Found in Baetica." *ZPE* 72: 113–27.

1999. "Tacitus, Germanicus, Piso, and the Tabula Siarensis." *AJP* 120: 123–42.

González, J. and F. Fernández. 1981. "Tabula Siarensis." *Iura* 32: 1–36.

Goodman, Penelope. 2018. "Twelve Augusti." *JRS* 108: 156–70.

Goodyear, F. R. D. 1972. *The Annals of Tacitus. Vol. 1: Annals 1–1.54.* Cambridge: Cambridge University Press.

1981. *The Annals of Tacitus. Vol. 11: Annals 1.55–81 and Annals 2.* Cambridge: Cambridge University Press.

1984. "Tiberius and Gaius: Their Influence and Views on Literature." *ANRW* 11.32.1: 603–10.

Gotter, Ulrich. 2008. "Die Nemesis des Allgemein-Gültingen. Max Webers Charisma-Konzept und die antiken Monarchien." In *Das Charisma – Funktionen und symbolische Repräsentationen. Historische, philosophische, islamwissenschaftliche, soziologische und theologische Perspektiven*, edited by Pavlína Rychterová, Stefan Seit, and Raphaela Veit, 173–86. Berlin: Akademie Verlag.

Gowing, Alain. 2005. *Empire and Memory: The Representation of the Roman Republic in Imperial Culture.* Cambridge: Cambridge University Press.

2007. "The Imperial Republic of Velleius Paterculus." In *A Companion to Greek and Roman Historiography*," edited by John Marincola, 411–18. Chichester: Wiley-Blackwell.

2009. "Urbs Roma: Tacitus on Tiberius and the City." In *Maxima Debetur Magistro Reverentia: Essays on Rome and Roman Tradition in Honor of R. T. Scott*, edited by P. Harvey and C. Coneybeare, 93–106. Como: New Press.

2010. "'Caesar Grabs My Pen': Writing Civil War under Tiberius." In *Citizens of Discord: Rome and Its Civil Wars*, edited by Brian W. Breed, Cynthia Damon, and Andreola Rossi, 249–60. Oxford: Oxford University Press.

Gradel, Ittai. 2002. *Emperor Worship and Roman Religion.* Oxford: Clarendon Press.

Grant, Michael. 1950. *Roman Anniversary Issues: An Exploratory Study of the Numismatic and Medallic Commemoration of Anniversary Years 49 BC–AD 375.* Cambridge: Cambridge University Press.

Green, Steven. 2004. *Ovid, Fasti 1: A Commentary.* Leiden: Brill.

2011. "Arduum ad Astra. The Poetics and Politics of Horoscopic Failure in Manilius' *Astronomica.*" In *Forgotten Stars: Rediscovering Manilius' Astronomica*, edited by Steven Green and Katharina Volk, 120–38. Oxford: Oxford University Press.

2014. *Disclosure and Discretion in Roman Astrology: Manilius and his Augustan Contemporaries.* Oxford: Oxford University Press.

Grenade, Pierre. 1961. *Essai sur les origines du principat, investiture et renouvellement des pouvoirs impériaux.* Paris: de Boccard.

Gresham, J. 2003. "The Collective Charisma of the Catholic Church: Werner Stark's Critique of Max Weber's Routinization Theory." *Catholic Social Science Review* 8: 123–39.

Griffin, Miriam. 1972. "The Elder Seneca and Spain." *JRS* 62: 1–19.

1984. *Nero. The End of a Dynasty.* New Haven: Yale University Press.

1997. "The Senate's Story." *JRS* 87: 249–63.

Gruen, E. 1990. "The Imperial Policy of Augustus." In *Between Republic and Empire: Interpretations of Augustus and his Principate*, edited by Kurt

Raaflaub and Mark Toher, 395–416. Berkeley: University of California Press.

2003. "The Emperor Tiberius and the Jews." In *Laurea internationalis: Festschrift für Jochen Bleicken zum 75. Geburtstag*, edited by Theodora Hantos, 298–312. Stuttgart: Steiner.

2005. "Augustus and the Making of the Principate." In *The Cambridge Companion to the Age of Augustus*, edited by Karl Galinsky, 33–51. Cambridge: Cambridge University Press.

Håkanson, L. 1989. *L. Annaeus Seneca Maior. Oratorum et Rhetorum Sententiae, Divisiones, Colores*. Leipzig: Teubner.

Hallett, Christopher. 2005. *The Roman Nude: Heroic Portrait Statuary 200 BC–AD 300*. Oxford: Oxford University Press.

Hänlein-Schäfer, Heidi. 1985. *Veneratio Augusti: eine Studie zu den Tempeln des ersten römischen Kaisers*. Rome: G. Bretschneider.

Harrison, J. R. 2012. "Diplomacy over Tiberius' Accession." In *New Documents Illustrating Early Christianity, v. 10. Greek and Other Inscriptions and Papyri Published 1988–1992*, edited by J. R. Harrison and S. R. Llewelyn, 64–75. Grand Rapids, MI: Eerdmans.

Haselberger, Lothar. 2007. *Urbem adornare: die Stadt Rom und ihre Gestaltumwandlung unter Augustus = Rome's urban metamorphosis under Augustus*. Portsmouth, R.I.: Journal of Roman Archaeology.

Hatscher, Christoph. 2000. *Charisma und res publica: Max Webers Herrschaftssoziologie und die Römische Republik*. Stuttgart: F. Steiner.

Heijnen, Sam. 2021. "Portraying Change: The Representation of Roman Emperors in Freestanding Sculpture (ca. 50 BC–ca. 400 AD)." Ph.D. dissertation, Radboud University.

Hekster, Olivier. 2015. *Emperors and Ancestors: Roman Rulers and the Constraints of Tradition*. Oxford: Oxford University Press.

2020. "When Was an Imperial Image? Some Reflections on Roman Art and Imagery." In *The Social Dynamics of Roman Imperial Imagery*, edited by A. Russell and M. Hellström, 275–88. Cambridge: Cambridge University Press.

Hellegouarc'h, Joseph and C. Jodry. 1980. "Les *Res Gestae* e l'*Historia Romana* de Velleius Paterculus." *Latomus* 39: 803–16.

Helzle, Martin. 1989. *Publii Ovidii Nasonis Epistolarum ex Ponto liber iv: A Commentary on Poems 1 to 7 and 16*. Hildesheim: Olms.

Henderson, John. 2001. *Telling Tales on Caesar: Roman Stories from Phaedrus*. Oxford: Oxford University Press.

Hennig, Dieter. 1972. "Zur Ägyptenreise des Germanicus." *Chiron* 2: 349–65.

1973. "T. Labienus und der erste Majestätsprozess *de famosis libellis*." *Chiron* 3: 245–54.

Herbert-Brown, Geraldine. 1994. *Ovid and the Fasti: An Historical Study*. Oxford: Oxford University Press.

2011. "Caesar or Augustus? The Game of the Name in Ovid's *Fasti*." *Acta Classica* 54: 43–77.

Hertel, Dieter. 2013. *Die Bildnisse des Tiberius.* Wiesbaden: Reichert Verlag.

Hickson, Frances. 1991. "Augustus *Triumphator*: Manipulation of the Triumphal Theme in the Political Program of Augustus." *Latomus* 50: 124–38.

Hildebrandt, Frank. 2017. "Silberne Prunkbecherpaare augusteischer Zeit und ihre Nachfolger." In *Augustus ist tot – Lang lebe der Kaiser! Internationales Kolloquium anlässlich des 2000. Todesjahres des römischen Kaisers vom 20.–22. November 2014 in Tübingen*, edited by Manuel Flecker, 367–80. Rahden: Verlag Marie Leidorf.

Hillard, Tom. 2011. "Velleius 2.124.2 and the Reluctant *Princeps*: The Evolution of Roman Perceptions of Leadership." In *Velleius Paterculus: Making History*, edited by Eleanor Cowan, 219–51. Swansea: The Classical Press of Wales.

Hirt, Alfred Michael. 2010. *Imperial Mines and Quarries in the Roman World: Organizational Aspects, 27 BC–AD 235.* Oxford: Oxford University Press.

Hoff, Ralf von den. 2011. "Kaiserbildnesse als Kaisergeschichte(n). Prolegomena zu einem medialen Konzept römischer Herrscherporträts." In *Zwischen Strukturgeschichte und Biographie: Probleme und Perspektiven einer neuen Römischen Kaisergeschichte 31 v. Chr.–192 n. Chr*, edited by Aloys Winterling, 15–43. Munich: R. Oldenbourg Verlag.

Hoffmann, Bert. 2009. "Charismatic Authority and Leadership Change: Lessons from Cuba's Post-Fidel Succession." *International Political Science Review* 30: 229–48.

Hoffman Lewis, Martha. 1955. *The Official Priests of Rome under the Julio-Claudians. A Study of the Nobility from 44 BC to 68 AD.* Rome: American Academy in Rome.

Højte, Jakob Munk. 2005. *Roman Imperial Statue Bases: From Augustus to Commodus.* Aarhus: Aarhus University Press.

Hollard, Virginie. 2010. *Le rituel du vote: les assemblées romaines du peuple.* Paris: CNRS Éditions.

Howley, Joseph. 2017. "Book-Burning and the Uses of Writing in Ancient Rome: Destructive Practice between Literature and Document." *JRS* 107: 213–36.

Hurlet, F. 1997. *Les collègues du prince sous Auguste et Tibère: de la légalité républicaine à la légitimité dynastique.* Rome: École française de Rome.

2006. *Le proconsul et le prince d'Auguste à Dioclétien.* Pessac: Ausonius.

2009. "Le consensus impérial à l'épreuve. La conspiration et ses enjeux sous les Julio-Claudiens." In *Ordine e sovversione nel mondo greco e romano: atti del convegno internazionale, Cividale del Friuli, 25–27 settembre 2008*, edited by Gianpaolo Urso, 125–43. Pisa: ETS.

2015. *Auguste: les ambiguïtés du pouvoir.* Paris: Colin.

Huttner, U. 2004. *Recusatio imperii: ein politisches Ritual zwischen Ethik und Taktik.* Hildesheim: Olms.

Instinsky, Hans. 1940. "Consensus Universorum." *Hermes* 75: 265–78.

Jakobson, A. and H. Cotton. 1985. "Caligula's *Recusatio Imperii*." *Historia* 34: 497–503.

Jennings, V. 2009. "Borrowed Plumes: Phaedrus' Fables, Phaedrus' Failures." In *Writing Politics in Imperial Rome*, edited by William J. Dominik, J. Garthwaite, and P. A. Roche, 225–48. Leiden: Brill.

Jeppesen, Kristian. 1974. *Neues zum Rätsel des Grand Camée de France*. Aarhus: Universitetsforlaget.

1993. "The Grand Camée of France." *MdI* 100: 141–75.

Johnson, Patricia. 1997. "Ovid's Livia in Exile." *CW* 90: 403–20.

Judge, E. A. 2019. *The Failure of Augustus. Essays on the Interpretation of a Paradox*. Newcastle: Cambridge Scholars.

Kähler, Heinz. 1959. *Die Augustusstatue von Prima Porta*. Cologne: M. Dumont Schauberg.

Kahlos, Maijastina. 2020. "Charismatic Leadership in Ancient Rome." In *The Routledge International Encyclopedia of Charisma*, edited by J. P. Zúquete, 65–76. London: Routledge.

Kaster, Robert. 1995. *Suetonius. De Grammaticis et Rhetoribus*. Oxford: Clarendon Press.

Kehne, Peter. 2002. "Limitierte Offensiven: Drusus, Tiberius und die Germanienpolitik im Dienste des augusteischen Prinzipats." In *Res publica reperta: zur Verfassung und Gesellschaft der römischen Republik und des frühen Prinzipats. Festschrift für Jochen Bleicken zum 75. Geburtstag*, edited by Jörg Spielvogel, 297–321. Stuttgart: Franz Steiner.

Kellum, B. A. 2000. "The City Adorned: Programmatic Display at the Aedes Concordiae Augustae." In *Between Republic and Empire*, edited by Kurt Raaflaub and Mark Toher, 276–97. Berkeley: University of California Press.

Kelly, Benjamin. 2020. "Court Politics and Imperial Imagery in the Roman Principate." In *The Social Dynamics of Roman Imperial Imagery*, edited by A. Russell and M. Hellström, 128–58. Cambridge: Cambridge University Press.

Kirbihler, François and Lilli Zabrana. 2014. "Archäologische, epigraphische und numismatische Zeugnisse für den Kaiserkult im Artemesion von Ephesus: der Kult der Dea Roma und des Divus Iulius unter dem Triumvirat." *JÖAI* 83: 101–31.

Knox, Peter. 2004. "The Poet and the Second Prince: Ovid in the Age of Tiberius." *MAAR* 49: 1–20.

Koestermann, Erich. 1963. *Cornelius Tacitus: Annalen, Band 1: Buch 1–3*. Heidelberg: Winter.

1965. *Cornelius Tacitus: Annalen, Band 2: Buch 4–6*. Heidelberg: Winter.

Koortbojian, Michael. 2013. *The Divinization of Caesar and Augustus: Precedents, Consequences, Implications*. Cambridge: Cambridge University Press.

Krause, Clemens. 2003. *Villa Jovis: die Residenz des Tiberius auf Capri*. Mainz: von Zabern.

Kuttner, Ann. 1995. *Dynasty and Empire in the Age of Augustus: The Case of the Boscoreale Cups*. Berkeley: University of California Press.

Lacey, W. K. 1963. "*Nominatio* and the Elections under Tiberius." *Historia* 12: 167–76.

1979. "*Summi fastigii vocabulum*: The Story of a Title." *JRS* 69: 28–34.

Laird, Margaret. 2015. *Civic Monuments and the Augustales in Roman Italy*. Cambridge: Cambridge University Press.

Langlands, Rebecca. 2008. "'Reading for the Moral' in Valerius Maximus: The Case of *Severitas*." *CCJ* 54: 160–87.

2018. *Exemplary Ethics in Ancient Rome*. Cambridge: Cambridge University Press.

Lasserre, F. 1982. "Strabon devant l'Empire romain." *ANRW* 11.30.1: 867–96.

Latham, Jacob. 2016. *Performance, Memory, and Processions in Ancient Rome: The Pompa Circensis from the Republic to Late Antiquity*. Cambridge: Cambridge University Press.

Lausdei, Claudio. 1987. "Sulla cronologia e sul proemio dei *Phaenomena* Arati." In *Germanico: la persona, la personalità, il personaggio: nel bimillenario dalla nascita*, edited by Giorgio Bonamente and Maria Paola Segoloni, 173–88. Rome: G. Bretschneider.

Le Bœuffle, André. 2003. *Germanicus. Les phénomènes d'Aratos*. 2nd ed. Paris: Belles Lettres.

Lebek, W. D. 1986. "Schwierige Stellen der Tabula Siarensis." *ZPE* 66: 31–48.

1987. "Die drei Ehrenbögen für Germanicus. Tab. Siar. frg. I 9–34; *CIL* VI 31199 a 2–17." *ZPE* 67: 129–48.

1988. "Die circensischen Ehrungen für Germanicus und das Referat des Tacitus im Lichte von Tab. Siar. Frg. II Col. C 2–11." *ZPE* 73: 249–74.

1990. "Standeswürde und Berufsverbot unter Tiberius: Das SC der Tabula Larinas." *ZPE* 81: 37–96.

1991. "Das SC der Tabula Larinas: Rittermusterung und andere Probleme." *ZPE* 85: 41–70.

1993. "Intenzione e composizione della Rogatio Valeria Aurelia." *ZPE* 98: 77–95.

Lendon, J. E. 2006. "The Legitimacy of the Roman Emperor: Against Weberian Legitimacy and Imperial 'Strategies of Legitimation.'" In *Herrschaftsstrukturen und Herrschaftspraxis: Konzepte, Prinzipien und Strategien der Administration im römischen Kaiserreich. Akten der Tagung an der Universität Zürich, 18.–20.10.2004*, edited by Anne Kolb. Berlin: Akademie Verlag.

Levene, D. S. 2012. "Defining the Divine in Rome." *TAPA* 142: 41–81.

Levick, Barbara. 1975. "Mercy and Moderation on the Coinage of Tiberius." In *The Ancient Historian and His Materials*, edited by C. E. Stevens, 123–37. Farnborough, Hants.: Gregg.

1977. "Review of R. Bauman, *Impietas in Principem*." *Gnomon* 49: 51–5.

1978a. "Concordia at Rome." In *Scripta Nummaria Romana: Essays Presented to Humphrey Sutherland*, edited by R. A. G. Carson and Colin Kraay, 217–33. London: Spink and Son.

1978b. "A Cry from the Heart from Tiberius Caesar." *Historia* 27: 95–101.

1982. "Propaganda and the Imperial Coinage." *Antichthon* 16: 104–16.

1983. "The Senatus Consultum from Larinum." *JRS* 73: 97–115.

1999 [1st ed. 1976]. *Tiberius the Politician*. 2nd ed. London: Routledge.

2009a. "Caesar's Political and Military Legacy to the Roman Emperors." In *A Companion to Julius Caesar*, edited by Miriam Griffin, 209–23. Chichester: Wiley-Blackwell.

2009b. "The Lex de Imperio Vespasiani: The Parts and the Whole." In *La Lex de imperio Vespasiani e la Roma dei Flavi: atti del convegno, 20–22 novembre*

2008, edited by Luigi Capogrossi Colognesi and Elena Tassi Scandone, 11–22. Rome: L'Erma di Bretschneider.

2011. "Velleius Paterculus as Senator: A Dream with Footnotes." In *Velleius Paterculus: Making History*, edited by Eleanor Cowan, 1–16. Swansea: Classical Press of Wales.

2013a. "The Conspiracy of Libo Drusus – and What Follows from It." *Politica Antica* 3: 43–50.

2013b. "A. Cremutius Cordus." In *The Fragments of the Roman Historians*, edited by T. J. Cornell, 1.497–501; 2.592–3; 3.592–3. Oxford: Oxford University Press.

Lewis, A.-M. 2008. "Augustus and His Horoscope Reconsidered." *Phoenix* 62: 308–37.

Libby, B. 2010. "The Intersection of Poetic and Imperial Authority in Phaedrus' Fables." *CQ* 60: 545–58.

Linderski, J. 2007. *Roman Questions II*. Stuttgart: Franz Steiner.

Lindholmer, M. O. 2020 "Augustus' Failure. Review of E. A. Judge, *The Failure of Augustus.*" *CR* 70: 183–5.

Lipps, Johannes. 2020. "Review of T. P. Wiseman, *The House of Augustus: A Historical Detective Story.*" *BMCR* 2020.09.23.

Littlewood, R. Joy. 2006. *A Commentary on Ovid: Fasti Book VI*. Oxford: Oxford University Press.

Lobur, John. 2008. *Consensus, Concordia, and the Formation of Roman Imperial Ideology*. London: Routledge.

Low, Katie. 2016. "Germanicus on Tour: History, Diplomacy and the Promotion of a Dynasty." *CQ* 66: 222–38.

Lucinio, A. 2004. "I processi contro Sosia Galla e Gaio Silio. La confisca dei beni degli incriminati suicidi." In *Epigrafia e territorio, politica e società: temi di antichità romane*, edited by Mario Pani, 241–56. Bari: Edipuglia.

Luisi, Aldo and Nicoletta F. Berrino. 2010. *L'ironia di Ovidio verso Livia e Tiberio*. Bari: Edipuglia.

Luttwak, Edward. 2016. *The Grand Strategy of the Roman Empire: From the First Century CE to the Third*. Rev. ed. Baltimore: Johns Hopkins University Press.

Lyasse, Emmanuel. 2008. *Le Principat et son fondateur: l'utilisation de la référence à Auguste de Tibère à Trajan*. Brussels: Latomus.

Madsen, Douglas and Peter Snow. 1991. *The Charismatic Bond*. Cambridge, MA: Harvard University Press.

Mallan, C. T. 2020. *Cassius Dio, Roman History: Books 57 and 58 (the Reign of Tiberius)*. Oxford: Oxford University Press.

Malloch, S. J. V. 2004. "The End of the Rhine Mutiny in Tacitus, Suetonius, and Dio." *CQ* 54: 198–210.

Marcone, Arnaldo. 2015. "Il Numen Augusti nel senatus consultum de Cn. Pisone patre." In *The Frontiers of Ancient Science: Essays in Honor of Heinrich von Staden*, edited by Brooke Holmes, Klaus-Dietrich Fischer, and Emilio Capettini, 397–406. Berlin: de Gruyter.

Marengo, S. M. 2008. "Aspetti del culto imperiale in area medioadriatica attraverso le fonti epigrafiche." In *Nuove ricerche sul culto imperiale in Italia: atti dell'incontro di studio, Ancona, 31 gennaio 2004*, edited by L. Gasperini and G. Paci, 147–72. Tivoli: Tored.

Márquez, Carlos. 2019. "The Seated Statue of Divus Augustus Pater Found in the Province of Baetica." In *Akten des 15. Internationalen Kolloquiums zum Provinzialrömischen Kunstschaffen. Der Stifter und sein Monument*, edited by Barbara Porod and Peter Sherrer, 262–72. Graz: Universalmuseum Joanneum.

Martin, P. M. 2016. "L'écriture de l'histoire sous Auguste: une liberté surveillée." In *Entre mots et marbre. Les métamorphoses d'Auguste*, edited by S. Luciani and P. Zuntow, 149–63. Bordeaux: Ausonius.

Martin, R. H. and A. J. Woodman. 1989. *Tacitus. Annals. Book IV*. Cambridge: Cambridge University Press.

Massner, Anne-Kathrein. 1982. *Bildnisangleichung: Untersuchungen zur Entstehungs- und Wirkungsgeschichte der Augustusporträts (43 v. Chr.–68 n. Chr.)*. Berlin: Mann.

Matthews, John. 2010. *Roman Perspectives: Studies in the Social, Political and Cultural History of the First to Fifth Centuries*. Swansea: Classical Press of Wales.

McGinn, T. A. J. 1992. "The SC from Larinum and the Repression of Adultery at Rome." *ZPE* 93: 273–95.

McGowan, Matthew. 2009. *Ovid in Exile: Power and Poetic Redress in the Tristia and Epistulae ex Ponto*. Leiden: Brill.

McHugh, Mary. 2004. "Historiography and Freedom of Speech: The Case of Cremutius Cordus." In *Free Speech in Classical Antiquity*, edited by I. Sluiter and R. M. Rosen, 391–408. Leiden: Brill.

McIntyre, Gwynaeth. 2016. *A Family of Gods: The Worship of the Imperial Family in the Latin West*. Ann Arbor: University of Michigan Press.

McWilliam, Janette. 2010. "Family as Strategy: Image-making and the Children of Germanicus." *Acta Patristica et Byzantina* 21: 121–40.

Meadows, Andrew and Jonathan Williams. 2001. "Moneta and the Monuments: Coinage and Politics in Republican Rome." *JRS* 91: 27–49.

Megow, W.-R. 2000. "Tiberius in Ephesos: Überlegungen zum frühaugusteischen Prinzenporträt." *JÖAI* 69: 249–95.

Meise, Eckhard. 1969. *Untersuchungen zur Geschichte der Julisch-Claudischen Dynastie*. Munich: Beck.

Mellor, Ronald. 1981. "The Goddess Roma." *ANRW* II.17.2: 950–1030.

Millar, Fergus. 1977. *The Emperor in the Roman World: 31 BC–AD 337*. Ithaca: Cornell University Press.

1988. "Imperial Ideology in the Tabula Siarensis." In *Estudios sobre la Tabula Siarensis*, 11–19. Madrid: C.S.I.C.

1989. "'Senatorial' Provinces: An Institutionalized Ghost." *AncW* 20: 93–7.

1993. "Ovid and the *Domus Augusta*: Rome Seen from Tomoi." *JRS* 83: 1–17.

Miller, J. 2009. *Apollo, Augustus and the Poets*. Cambridge: Cambridge University Press.

Miller, N. P. 1968. "Tiberius Speaks. An Examination of the Utterances Ascribed to Him in the *Annals* of Tacitus." *AJP* 89: 1–19.

Mitchell, Stephen. 1976. "Requisitioned Transport in the Roman Empire: A New Inscription from Pisidia." *JRS* 66: 106–31.

Mitford, T. B. 1960. "A Cypriot Oath of Allegiance to Tiberius." *JRS* 50: 75–9.

Mlasowsky, Alexander. 1996. "*Nomini ac fortunae Caesarum proximi*. Die Sukzessionspropaganda der römischen Kaiser von Augustus bis Nero im Spiegel der Reichsprägung und der archäologischen Quellen." *JDAI* 111: 249–388.

Moles, J. 1998. "Cry Freedom: Tacitus *Annals* 4.32–35." *Histos* 2: 95–184.

Molinari, Maria Cristina. 2015. *The Julio-Claudian and Flavian Coins from Rome's Municipal Urban Excavations: Observations on Coin Circulation in the Cities of Latium Vetus and Campania in the 1st Century AD.* Trieste: EUT.

Momigliano, Arnaldo. 1982. *New Paths of Classicism in the Nineteenth Century.* Middletown, CT: Wesleyan University Press.

Moreau, P. 2009. "Domus Augusta: l'autre maison d'Auguste." In *L'expression du pouvoir au début de l'empire. Autour de la Maison Carrée à Nîmes: actes du colloque organisé à l'initiative de la ville de Nîmes et du Musée archéologique, Nîmes, Carré d'art, 20–22 octobre 2005*, edited by Michel Christol and Dominique Darde, 33–43. Paris: France.

Morello, R. 2006. "A Correspondence Course in Tyranny: The *Cruentae Litterae* of Tiberius." *Arethusa* 39: 331–54.

Mueller, Hans-Friedrich. 2002. *Roman Religion in Valerius Maximus.* London: Routledge.

Myers, K. S. 2014. "Ovid, *Epistulae ex Ponto* 4.8, Germanicus, and the *Fasti.*" *CQ* 64: 725–34.

Nicols, John. 1975. "Antonia and Sejanus." *Historia* 24: 48–58.

Nippel, W. 2007. "New Paths of Antiquarianism in the Nineteenth and Early Twentieth Centuries: Theodor Mommsen and Max Weber." In *Momigliano and Antiquarianism: Foundations of the Modern Cultural Sciences*, edited by Peter Miller, 207–28. Toronto: University of Toronto Press.

Nilson, K. A, C. Persson, S. Sande, and J. Zahle. 2009. *The Temple of Castor and Pollux iii: The Augustan Temple.* Rome: L'Erma di Bretschneider.

Nogales Basarrate, T. 2007. "Culto imperial en Augusta Emerita: imágenes y programas urbanos." In *Culto imperial: política y poder: actas del congreso internacional, Mérida, Museo Nacional de Arte Romano, 18–20 de mayo, 2006*, edited by T. Nogales Basarrate and J. González Fernández, 449–539. Rome: L'Erma di Bretschneider.

Noreña, Carlos. 2011. "Coins and Communication." In *The Oxford Handbook of Social Relations in the Roman World*, edited by M. Peachin, 248–68. Oxford: Oxford University Press.

Nugent, S. G. 1990. "*Tristia* 2: Ovid and Augustus." In *Between Republic and Empire*, edited by Kurt Raaflaub and Mark Toher, 239–57. Berkeley: University of California Press.

Ober, J. 1982. "Tiberius and the Political Testament of Augustus." *Historia* 31: 306–28.

Orth, Wolfgang. 1970. *Die Provinzialpolitik des Tiberius*. Bonn: Rudolf Habelt Verlag.

Osgood, Josiah. 2013. "Suetonius and the Succession to Augustus." In *The Julio-Claudian Succession: Reality and Perception of the "Augustan model,"* edited by A. G. G. Gibson, 19–40. Leiden: Brill.

Paci, Gianfranco. 2008. "Tiberio e il culto imperiale." In *Nuove ricerche sul culto imperiale in Italia: atti dell'incontro di studio, Ancona, 31 gennaio 2004*, edited by L. Gasperini and G. Paci, 193–218. Tivoli: Tored.

Packer, James. 2010. "Pompey's Theater and Tiberius' Temple of Concord. A Later Republican Primer for an Early Imperial Patron." In *The Emperor and Rome. Space, Representation, and Ritual*, edited by B. Ewald and C. Noreña, 135–67. Cambridge: Cambridge University Press.

Palombi, D. 1993. "Curia in Palatio." In *Lexicon Topographicum Urbis Romae*, edited by E. M. Steinby, 1.334. Rome: Edizioni Quasar.

Pandey, Nandini. 2020. "*Publica numina*. Conspicuously Consuming the Imperial Image at Tomis." In *The Social Dynamics of Roman Imperial Imagery*, edited by Amy Russell and Monica Hellström, 76–99. Cambridge: Cambridge University Press.

Pani, Mario. 1987. "La missione di Germanico in Oriente: politica estera e politica interna." In *Germanico: la persona, la personalità, il personaggio: nel bimillenario dalla nascita*, edited by Giorgio Bonamente and Maria Paola Segoloni, 1–23. Rome: G. Bretschneider.

——— 2001. "L'imperium di Tiberio principe." *Epigrafia e territorio. Politica e società. Temi di antichità romane* 6: 253–62.

Parsi, B. 1963. *Désignation et investiture de l'Empereur romain: Ier et IIe siècles après J.-C.* Paris: Sirey.

Parsi-Magdelain, B. 1978. "L'avènement de Tibère." *Revue historique de droit français et étranger* 56: 391–425.

Pasco-Pranger, Molly. 2006. *Founding the Year: Ovid's Fasti and the Poetics of the Roman Calendar*. Leiden: Brill.

Peachin, Michael. 2007. "Exemplary Government in the Early Roman Empire." In *Crises and the Roman Empire: Proceedings of the Seventh Workshop of the International Network Impact of Empire, Nijmegen, June 20–24, 2006*, edited by Olivier Hekster, Gerda de Kleijn, and Daniëlle Slootjes, 75–93. Leiden: Brill.

——— 2013. "Augustus' *Res Gestae* and the Emerging Principate." In *Studia Epigraphica in Memoriam Géza Alföldy*, edited by Werner Eck, B. Fehér, and P. Kovács, 255–74. Bonn: Rudolf Habelt Verlag.

——— 2015. "Augustus' Emergent Judicial Powers, the 'Crimen Maiestatis,' and the Second Cyrene Edict." In *Il princeps romano: autocrate o magistrato? Fattori giuridici e fattori sociali del potere imperiale da Augusto a Commodo*, edited by Jean-Louis Ferrary and John Scheid, 497–554. Pavia: IUSS Press.

Pekáry, Thomas. 1966/67. "Tiberius und der Tempel der Concordia in Rom." *MDAI(R)* 73–74: 105–33.

——— 1985. *Das römische Kaiserbildnis in Staat, Kult und Gesellschaft*. Berlin: Mann.

Pelling, Christopher. 1993. "Tacitus and Germanicus." In *Tacitus and the Tacitean Tradition*, edited by A. J. Woodman and T. J. Luce, 59–85. Princeton: Princeton University Press.

2010. "The Spur of Fame: *Annals* 4.37–8." In *Ancient Historiography and Its Contexts: Studies in Honour of A. J. Woodman*, edited by Christina Shuttleworth Kraus, John Marincola, and C. B. R. Pelling, 366–84. Oxford: Oxford University Press.

Pettinger, Andrew. 2012. *The Republic in Danger: Drusus Libo and the Succession of Tiberius*. Oxford: Oxford University Press.

Phillips, Darryl. 2011. "The Temple of Divus Iulius and the Restoration of Legislative Assemblies under Augustus." *Phoenix* 65: 371–88.

Piano, Valeria. 2019. "P. Hercul. 1067 Reconsidered: Latest Results and Prospective Researches." In *Proceedings of the 28th International Congress of Papyrology, Barcelona 2016*, 231–40. Barcelona: Publicacions de l'Abadia de Montserrat, Universitat Pompeu Fabra.

Pieper, C. 2010. "Phaedrus' Ironie. Anmerkungen zum Prolog des dritten Fabelbuches." *Gymnasium* 117: 33–48.

2021. "*Tiberius Aequatus Augusto*. Augustan Intertexts for Tiberius' *Moderatio* in Velleius Paterculus 2.94.1 and 2.122.1." *Philologus* 165: 241–259.

Polacco, Luigi. 1955. *Il volto di Tiberio: saggio di critica iconografica*. Rome: L'Erma di Bretschneider.

Pollini, John. 1986. "Ahenobarbi, Appuleii and Some Others on the Ara Pacis." *AJA* 90: 453–60.

1990. "Man or God: Divine Assimilation and Imitation in the Late Republic and Early Principate." In *Between Republic and Empire*, edited by Kurt Raaflaub and Mark Toher, 334–63. Berkeley: University of California Press.

1999. "Review of D. Boschung, *Die Bildnisse des Augustus*." *The Art Bulletin* 81: 723–35.

2005. "A New Marble Head of Tiberius: Portrait Typology and Ideology." *Antike Kunst* 48: 55–72.

2008. "A New Portrait Bust of Tiberius in the Collection of Michael Bianco." *BABesch* 83: 149–54.

2012. *From Republic to Empire: Rhetoric, Religion, and Power in the Visual Culture of Ancient Rome*. Norman: University of Oklahoma Press.

Popkin, Maggie. 2018. "The Parthian Arch of Augustus and Its Legacy." In *Afterlives of Augustus, AD 14–2014*, edited by Penelope Goodman, 271–93. Cambridge: Cambridge University Press.

Possanza, D. Mark. 2004. *Translating the Heavens: Aratus, Germanicus, and the Poetics of Latin Translation*. New York: Peter Lang.

Pothecary, S. 2002. "Strabo, the Tiberian Author: Past, Present and Silence in Strabo's *Geography*." *Mnemosyne* 55: 387–438.

Potter, D. 1994. *Prophets and Emperors: Human and Divine Authority from Augustus to Theodosius*. Cambridge, MA: Harvard University Press.

1998. "Senatus Consultum de Cn. Pisone." *JRA* 11: 437–57.

Price, S. R. F. 1984. *Rituals and Power: The Roman Imperial Cult in Asia Minor.* Cambridge: Cambridge University Press.

1987. "From Noble Funerals to Divine Cult: The Consecration of Roman Emperors." In *Rituals of Royalty: Power and Ceremonial in Traditional Societies,* edited by David Cannadine and S. R. F. Price, 56–105. Cambridge: Cambridge University Press.

Ramage, E. S. 1985. "Augustus' Treatment of Julius Caesar." *Historia* 34: 223–45.

1998. "Augustus' Propaganda in Spain." *Klio* 80: 434–90.

Ramsey, J. 1994. "The Senate, Mark Antony, and Caesar's Legislative Legacy." *CQ* 44: 130–45.

Ramsey, J. and A. Lewis Licht. 1997. *The Comet of 44 BC and Caesar's Funeral Games.* Atlanta: Scholars Press.

Reeder, J. C. 1997. "The Statue of Augustus from Prima Porta and the Underground Complex." *Studies in Latin Literature and Roman History* 8: 287–308.

Renda, Chiara. 2012. *Illitteratum plausum nec desiderio: Fedro, la favola e la poesia.* Naples: Loffredo.

Ricci, Carla. 2006. *Gladiatori e attori nella Roma giulio-claudia: studi sul senato-consulto di Larino.* Milan: LED.

Rich, John. 2003. "Augustus, War and Peace." In *The Representation and Perception of Roman Imperial Power: Proceedings of the Third Workshop of the International Network Impact of Empire (Roman Empire, c. 200 BC–AD 476), Netherlands Institute in Rome, March 20–23, 2002,* edited by Lukas de Blois, 329–57. Amsterdam: J. C. Gieben.

2009. "Cantabrian Closure: Augustus' Spanish War and the Ending of His Memoirs." In *The Lost Memoirs of Augustus,* edited by Christopher Smith and Anton Powell, 145–72. Swansea: Classical Press of Wales.

2011. "Velleius' History: Genre and Purpose." In *Velleius Paterculus: Making History,* edited by Eleanor Cowan, 73–92. Swansea: Classical Press of W

2012. "Making the Emergency Permanent: Auctoritas, Potestas and the Evolution of the Principate of Augustus." In *Des réformes augustéennes,* edited by Y. Rivière, 37–121. Rome: École Française de Rome.

Rich, John and J. H. C. Williams. 1999. "Leges et Ivra P. R. Restitvit: A New Aureus of Octavian and the Settlement of 28–27 BC." *NC* 159: 169–213.

Richardson, J. S. 1997. "The Senate, the Courts, and the *SC de Cn. Pisone patre.*" *CQ* 47: 510–18.

Richardson, Lawrence. 1978. "Concordia and Concordia Augusta: Rome and Pompeii." *PP* 33: 260–72.

1988. *Pompeii: An Architectural History.* Baltimore: Johns Hopkins University Press.

Ripat, Pauline. 2011. "Expelling Misconceptions: Astrologers at Rome." *CP* 106: 115–54.

Rives, J. B. 1999. *Tacitus. Germania.* Oxford: Clarendon Press.

2006. "Magic, Religion, and Law: The Case of the *Lex Cornelia de Sicariis et Veneficiis.*" In *Religion and Law in Classical and Christian Rome,* edited by Clifford Ando and Jörg Rüpke, 47–67. Stuttgart: Steiner.

Rivière, Yann. 2002. *Les délateurs sous l'empire romain*. Rome: École française de Rome.

2016. *Germanicus, prince romain: 15 av. J.-C.–19 apr. J.-C.* Paris: Perrin.

Rocca, Samuel. 2010. "Josephus, Suetonius, and Tacitus on Military Service of the Jews of Rome: Discrimination or Norm?" *Italia* 20: 7–30.

Roddaz, Jean-Michel. 2003. "La Métamorphose: d'Octavien à Auguste." In *Fondements et crises du pouvoir*, edited by Sylvie Franchet d'Espèrey, V. Fromentin, S. Gotteland, and Jean-Michel Roddaz, 397–418. Pessac: Ausonius.

Rodewald, Cosmo. 1976. *Money in the Age of Tiberius*. Manchester: Manchester University Press.

Rogers, Robert Samuel. 1935. *Criminal Trials and Criminal Legislation under Tiberius*. Middletown, CT: American Philological Association.

1943. *Studies in the Reign of Tiberius: Some Imperial Virtues of Tiberius and Drusus Julius Caesar*. Baltimore: The Johns Hopkins Press.

1959. "The Emperor's Displeasure – *Amicitiam Renuntiare*." *TAPA* 90: 224–37.

Rohmann, D. 2013. "Book Burning as Conflict Management in the Roman Empire (213 BCE–200 CE)." *AncSoc* 43: 115–49.

Roller, Duane. 2018. *A Historical and Topographical Guide to the Geography of Strabo*. Cambridge: Cambridge University Press.

Rose, C. B. 1997. *Dynastic Commemoration and Imperial Portraiture in the Julio-Claudian Period*. Cambridge: Cambridge University Press.

Rowe, Greg. 2002. *Princes and Political Cultures: The New Tiberian Senatorial Decrees*. Ann Arbor: University of Michigan Press.

2013. "Reconsidering the Auctoritas of Augustus." *JRS* 103: 1–15.

2021. "*Luctatio Civitatis*. Augustus' *Res Gestae*, Tiberius' Accession, and the Struggle over Augustus' Legacy." In *Le Costume de Prince. Vivre et se conduire en souverain dans la Rome antique d'Auguste à Constantin*, edited by P. Le Doze, 139–63. Rome: École française de Rome.

Rutland, L. 1987. "The Tacitean Germanicus. Suggestions for a Re-evaluation." *RhM* 130: 153–64.

Rutledge, Steven. 2001. *Imperial Inquisitions: Prosecutors and Informants from Tiberius to Domitian*. London: Routledge.

Ryberg, Inez Scott. 1955. *Rites of the State Religion in Roman Art*. Rome: American Academy in Rome.

Sage, M. M. 1982/3. "Tacitus and the Accession of Tiberius." *AncSoc* 13/14: 293–321.

Sánchez-Ostiz Gutiérrez, Álvaro. 1999. *Tabula Siarensis: Edición, traducción y comentario*. Pamplona: Ediciones Universidad de Navarra.

Sande, Siri and Jan Zahle. 1988. "Der Tempel der Dioskuren auf dem Forum Romanum." In *Kaiser Augustus und die verlorene Republik: eine Ausstellung im Martin-Gropius-Bau, Berlin, 7. Juni–14. August 1988*, edited by M. Hofter, 213–224. Mainz: von Zabern.

Saquete, J. C. 2005. "L. Fulcinius Trio, Tiberio y el gran templo de culto imperial de Augusta Emerita." *Epigraphica* 67: 279–308.

Saquete, J. C. and J. M. Álvarez Martínez. 2007. "Culto imperial en Augusta Emerita: complejos monumentales y documentos epigráficos." In *Culto imperial: política y poder. Actas del congreso internacional, Mérida, Museo Nacional de Arte Romano, 18–20 de mayo, 2006*, edited by T. Nogales Basarrate and J. González Fernández, 397–414. Rome: L'Erma di Bretschneider.

Sawiński, P. 2018. *The Succession of Imperial Power under the Julio-Claudian Dynasty (30 BC–AD 68)*. Berlin: Peter Lang.

Scappaticcio, Maria Chiara. 2018. "Lucio Anneo Seneca e la storiografia sommersa: per l'esegesi di un nuovo testimone di antica tradizione diretta." *Latomus* 77: 1053–89.

Scheid, John. 1992. "L'investiture impériale d'après les commentaires des arvales." *Cahiers du Centre Gustave Glotz* 3: 221–37.

  1998. *Commentarii Fratrum Arvalium qui supersunt: les copies épigraphiques des protocoles annuels de la confrérie arvale: 21 av.–304 ap. J.-C.* Rome: École française de Rome.

  2007. *Res gestae divi Augusti = Hauts faits du divin Auguste*. Paris: Belles Lettres.

  2016. "Les 'Hauts faits du Divin Auguste.' Texte littéraire ou bilan politique?" In *Entre mots et marbre: les métamorphoses d'Auguste*, edited by Sabine Luciani, 39–52. Bordeaux: Ausonius.

Schilling, Andreas. 2010. *Poena extraordinaria: zur Strafzumessung in der frühen Kaiserzeit*. Berlin: Duncker und Humblot.

Schillinger-Häfele, U. 1988. "Die *laudatio funebris* des Tiberius für Germanicus (zu *Tabula Siarensis* Fr. ii, Col. B, 13–19)." *ZPE* 75: 73–81.

Schmid, Alfred. 2005. *Augustus und die Macht der Sterne: antike Astrologie und die Etablierung der Monarchie in Rom*. Cologne: Böhlau.

Schmitzer, Ulrich. 2000. *Velleius Paterculus und das Interesse an der Geschichte im Zeitalter des Tiberius*. Heidelberg: C. Winter.

  2011. "Roman Values in Velleius." In *Velleius Paterculus: Making History*, edited by Eleanor Cowan, 177–202. Swansea: Classical Press of Wales.

Schnurbein, S. von. 2003. "Augustus in Germania and His New 'Town' at Waldgirmes East of the Rhine." *JRA* 16: 93–107.

Schoonhoven, H. 1992. *The Pseudo-Ovidian Ad Liviam de Morte Drusi (Consolatio ad Liviam, Epicedium Drusi): A Critical Text with Introduction and Commentary*. Groningen: E. Forsten.

Schrömbges, Paul. 1986. *Tiberius und die Res publica Romana: Untersuchungen zur Institutionalisierung des frühen römischen Principats*. Bonn: Habelt.

  1987. "Zum römischen Staatshaushalt in tiberischer Zeit." *Gymnasium* 94: 1–49.

Scott, K. 1930. "Drusus, Nicknamed Castor." *CP* 25: 155–61.

  1932. "Tiberius' Refusal of the Title 'Augustus.'" *CP* 27: 43–50.

Seager, Robin. 2005. *Tiberius*. 2nd ed. Malden, MA: Blackwell.

Severy, Beth. 2000. "Family and State in the Early Imperial Monarchy: The Senatus Consultum de Pisone Patre, Tabula Siarensis, and Tabula Hebana." *CP* 95: 318–37.

2003. *Augustus and the Family at the Birth of the Roman Empire.* London: Routledge.

Shils, Edward. 1975. *Center and Periphery: Essays in Macrosociology.* Chicago: University of Chicago Press.

Shotter, D. C. A. 1966. "Tiberius and the Spirit of Augustus." *G&R* 2nd ser. 13: 207–12.

1991. "A Crucial Witness – a Note on Tacitus *Annales* 4.42." *LCM* 16: 21.

Simpson, C. J. 1991. "Livia and the Constitution of the Aedes Concordiae. The Evidence of Ovid, *Fasti* 1.637ff." *Historia* 40: 449–55.

2005a. "Rome's 'Official Imperial Seal'? The Rings of Augustus and His First Century Successors." *Historia* 54: 180–8.

2005b. "Where is the Parthian? The Prima Porta Statue of Augustus Revisited." *Latomus* 64: 82–90.

Sohm, Rudolf. 1892–1923. *Kirchenrecht.* 2 vols. Leipzig: Duncker und Humblot.

Sommer, Michael. 2011. "Empire of Glory. Weberian Paradigms and the Complexities of Authority in Imperial Rome." *Max Weber Studies* 11: 155–91.

Sordi, Marta. 1979. "La morte di Agrippa Postumo e la rivolta di Germania del 14 d.C." In *Studi su Varrone, sulla retorica, storiografia e poesia latina. Scritti in onore di Benedetto Riposati*, 481–95. Milan: Università cattolica S. Cuore.

Southern, Pat. 2014. *Augustus.* 2nd ed. London: Routledge.

Srirangachar, Ramesh, D., S. Heijnen, O. Hekster, L. Spreeuwers, and F. de Wit. 2022. "Facial Recognition as a Tool to Identify Roman Emperors: Towards a New Methodology." *Humanities and Social Sciences Communications* 9.78: 1–10.

Stahl, Michael. 2008. "Auctoritas und Charisma: Die Bedeutung des Persönlichen in der Herrschaft des Augustus." *Potestas* 1: 23–34.

Steinmetz, P. 1966. "Germanicus, der römische Arat." *Hermes* 94: 450–82.

Stelluti, Napoleone. 1997. *Epigrafi di Larino e della bassa Frentania. Vol. II. Studi sul Senatus Consultum di Larino.* Campobasso: Editrice Lampo.

Stevenson, Tom. 2007. "Roman Coins and Refusals of the Title *Pater Patriae*." *NC* 167: 119–41.

Stiles, Andrew. 2017. "*Non Potes Officium Vatis Contemnere Vates.* Germanicus, Ovid's *Fasti*, and the *Aratea*." *Mnemosyne* 70: 878–88.

Strobel, Karl. 2002. "Die Legionen des Augustus. Probleme der römischen Heeresgeschichte nach dem Ende des Bürgerkrieges: Die Truppengeschichte Galatiens und Moesiens bis in Tiberische Zeit und das Problem der *Legiones Quintae.*" In *Limes xviii. Proceedings of the xviiith International Congress of Roman Frontier Studies held in Amman, Jordan (September 2000)*, edited by Philip Freeman, Julian Bennett, Zbigniew Fiema, and Birgitta Hoffmann, 51–66. Oxford: Archeopress.

Strunk, T. 2012. "Review of A. Pettinger, *The Republic in Danger: Drusus Libo and the Succession of Tiberius*." *BMCR* 2012.12.67.

Stylow, A. 1977. "Noch einmal zu der Tiberius-Inschrift von Saepinum." *Chiron* 7: 487–91.

Stylow, A. and S. Corzo. 1999. "Eine neue Kopie des Senatus Consultum de Cn. Pisone patre." *Chiron* 29: 23–8.

Sumi, Geoffrey. 2009. "Monuments and Memory: The Aedes Castoris in the Formation of Augustan Ideology." *CQ* 59: 167–86.

2011. "Topography and Ideology: Caesar's Monument and the Aedes Divi Ivlii in Augustan Rome." *CQ* 61: 205–29.

Sumner, G. 1970. "The Truth about Velleius Paterculus: Prolegomena." *HSCP* 74: 263–97.

Suspène, A. 2001. "Tiberius Claudianus contre Agrippa Postumus: autour de la dédicace du Temple des Dioscures." *RPh* 75: 99–124.

Sussman, Lewis. 1978. *The Elder Seneca.* Leiden: Brill.

Sutherland, C. H. V. 1941. "Divus Augustus Pater. A Study in the Aes Coinage of Tiberius." *NC* 1: 97–116.

1979. "The *Clementiae* and *Moderationi* Dupondii of Tiberius: More Thoughts on the Chronology." *NC* 139: 21–5.

Sutherland, C. H. V. and R. A. G. Carson. 1984. *The Roman Imperial Coinage. Vol. i: from 31 BC to AD 69.* Rev. ed. London: Spink.

Swan, Peter. 2004. *The Augustan Succession: An Historical Commentary on Cassius Dio's Roman History, Books 55–56 (9 BC–AD 14).* Oxford: Oxford University Press.

Syme, Ronald. 1939. *The Roman Revolution.* Oxford: Clarendon Press.

1959. "Livy and Augustus," *HSCPh* 64: 27–87.

1970. *Ten studies in Tacitus.* Oxford: Clarendon Press.

1978a. *History in Ovid.* Oxford: Clarendon Press.

1978b. "Mendacity in Velleius." *AJP* 99: 45–63.

Szaivert, Wolfgang. 1984. *Die Münzprägung der Kaiser Tiberius und Caius (Caligula) 14/41.* Vienna: Verlag der Österreichischen Akademie der Wissenschaften.

Taeger, Fritz. 1957. *Charisma. Studien zur Geschichte des antiken Herrscherkultes.* 2 vols. Stuttgart: W. Kohlhammer.

Talbert, Richard. 1984. *The Senate of Imperial Rome.* Princeton: Princeton University Press.

Taylor, Lily Ross. 1929. "Tiberius' Refusals of Divine Honors." *TAPA* 60: 87–101.

1931. *The Divinity of the Roman Emperor.* Middletown, CT: American Philological Association.

Tchernia, André. 2016. *The Romans and Trade.* Oxford: Oxford University Press.

Telschow, Kurt. 1975. "Die Abberufung des Germanicus (16 n. Chr.). Ein Beispiel für die Kontinuität römischer Germanienpolitik von Augustus zu Tiberius." In *Monumentum Chiloniense: Studien zur augusteischen Zeit. Kieler Festschrift für Erich Burck zum 70. Geburtstag,* edited by Erich Burck and Eckard Lefèvre, 148–82. Amsterdam: Adolf M. Hakkert.

Terio, Simonetta. 2006. *Der Steinbock als Herrschaftszeichen des Augustus.* Münster: Aschendorff.

Thakur, Sanjaya. 2014. "Tiberius, the Varian Disaster, and the Dating of *Tristia* 2." *MD* 73: 69–97.

Thomas, Yan. 1998. "Les Procédures de la Majesté. La torture et l'enquête depuis les Julio-Claudiens." In *Mélanges de droit romain et d'histoire ancienne: hommage à la mémoire de André Magdelain*, edited by Michel Humbert and Yan Thomas, 477–99. Paris: Editions Panthéon-Assas.

Thompson, David. 1981. "The Meetings of the Roman Senate on the Palatine." *AJA* 85: 335–9.

Thornton, M. K. and R. L. Thornton. 1989. *Julio-Claudian Building Programs: A Quantitative Study in Political Management*. Wauconda, IL: Bolchazy-Carducci.

1990. "The Financial Crisis of AD 33: A Keynesian Depression?" *Journal of Economic History* 50: 655–62.

Timpe, Dieter. 2008. "Römische Geostrategie im Germanien der Okkupationszeit." In *Rom auf dem Weg nach Germanien: Geostrategie, Vormarschtrassen und Logistik: internationales Kolloquium in Delbrück-Anreppen vom 4. bis 6. November 2004*, edited by Johann-Sebastian Kühlborn and Cornelia Halm, 199–236. Mainz: P. von Zabern.

Toher, Mark. 2009. "Augustan and Tiberian Literature." In *A Companion to Julius Caesar*, edited by Miriam Griffin, 224–38. Chichester: Wiley-Blackwell.

2017. *Nicolaus of Damascus: The Life of Augustus and the Autobiography*. Cambridge: Cambridge University Press.

Trice, H. M. and J. M. Beyer. 1986. "Charisma and Its Routinization in Two Social Movement Organizations." *Research in Organizational Behavior* 8: 113–64.

Trillmich, W. 1988. "Münzpropaganda." In *Kaiser Augustus und die verlorene Republik: eine Ausstellung im Martin-Gropius-Bau, Berlin, 7. Juni–14. August 1988*, edited by M. Hofter and Martin-Gropius-Bau, 474–530. Mainz: von Zabern.

Tuori, Kaius. 2016. *The Emperor of Law: The Emergence of Roman Imperial Adjudication*. Oxford: Oxford University Press.

Tuplin, Christopher. 1987. "The False Drusus of AD 31 and the Fall of Sejanus." *Latomus* 46: 781–805.

Turpin, W. 1994. "*Res Gestae 34.1* and the Settlement of 27 BC." *CQ* 44: 427–37

Vanacker, Wouter. 2015. "*Adhuc Tacfarinas*. Causes of the Tiberian War in North Africa (AD ca. 15–4) and the Impact of the Conflict on Roman Imperial Policy." *Historia* 64: 336–56.

Vervaet, F. 2009. "In What Capacity Did Caesar Octavianus Restitute the Republic?" In *Le principat d'Auguste: réalités et représentations du pouvoir autour de la Res publica restituta. Actes du colloque de l'Université de Nantes, 1er–2 juin 2007*, edited by Frédéric Hurlet and Bernard Mineo, 49–71. Rennes: Presses universitaires de Rennes.

Veyne, Paul. 1990. *Bread and Circuses: Historical Sociology and Political Pluralism*. London: Penguin Press.

Vivas García, G. A. 2017. "El *Ottaviano Capoparte* de Mario Attilio Levi y su influencia en *The Roman Revolution* de Ronald Syme." *Gerión* 35: 279–97.

Volk, Katharina. 2009. *Manilius and His Intellectual Background*. Oxford: Oxford University Press.

2011. "Introduction: A Century of Manilian Scholarship." In *Forgotten Stars: Rediscovering Manilius' Astronomica*, edited by Steven Green and Katharina Volk, 1–10. Oxford: Oxford University Press.

Vout, Caroline. 2013. "Tiberius and the Invention of Succession." In *The Julio-Claudian Succession: Reality and Perception of the "Augustan Model,"* edited by A. G. G. Gibson, 59–77. Leiden: Brill.

Walker, B. 1960. *The Annals of Tacitus*. 2nd ed. Manchester: Manchester University Press.

Wallace-Hadrill, A. 1982. "Civilis Princeps: Between Citizen and King." *JRS* 72: 32–48.

1986. "Image and Authority in the Coinage of Augustus." *JRS* 76: 66–87.

Wardle, D. 2000. "Valerius Maximus on the Domus Augusta, Augustus, and Tiberius." *CQ* 50: 479–93.

2002. "The Heroism and Heroisation of Tiberius: Valerius Maximus and His Emperor." In *Hommages à Carl Deroux. II – Prose et linguistique, Médecine*, edited by Pol Defosse, 433–40. Brussels: Éditions Latomus.

Weber, Max. 1968. *Economy and Society: An Outline of Interpretive Sociology*. New York: Bedminster Press.

1992. *Max Weber Gesamtausgabe. Abt. I, Schriften und Reden. Wissenschaft als Beruf, 1917/1919; Politik als Beruf, 1919*. Tübingen: Mohr.

2005. *Max Weber Gesamtausgabe. Wirtschaft und Gesellschaft. Die Wirtschaft und die gesellschaftlichen Ordnungen und Mächte. Nachlass*. Tübingen: Mohr.

2013. *Wirtschaft und Gesellschaft: Soziologie: Unvollendet, 1919–1920*. Tübingen: Mohr.

Weingärtner, D. 1969. *Die Ägyptenreise des Germanicus*. Bonn: Habelt.

Weinstock, Stefan. 1957. "The Image and the Chair of Germanicus." *JRS* 47: 144–54.

1962. "Treueid und Kaiserkult." *MDAI(A)* 77: 306–27.

1966. "The Posthumous Honours of Germanicus." In *Mélanges d'archéologie et d'histoire offerts à André Piganiol*, edited by Raymond Chevallier, 891–8. Paris: S.E.V.P.E.N.

1971. *Divus Julius*. Oxford: Clarendon Press.

Weisser, B. 2016. "Roman Imperial Imagery of Time and Cosmos." In *Time and Cosmos in Greco-Roman Antiquity*, edited by Alexander Jones, 171–82. Princeton: Princeton University Press.

Wellesley, Kenneth. 1967. "The Dies Imperii of Tiberius." *JRS* 57: 23–30.

Wells, C. M. 1972. *The German Policy of Augustus: An Examination of the Archaeological Evidence*. Oxford: Clarendon Press.

Wharton, David. 1997. "Tacitus' Tiberius: The State of the Evidence for the Emperor's *Ipsissima Verba* in the *Annals*." *AJP* 118: 119–25.

White, Peter. 1988. "Julius Caesar in Augustan Rome." *Phoenix* 42: 334–56.

1992. "'Pompeius Macer' and Ovid." *CQ* 42: 210–18.

2002. "Ovid and the Augustan Milieu." In *Brill's Companion to Ovid*, edited by Barbara Weiden Boyd, 1–25. Leiden: Brill.

Whittaker, Hélène. 1996. "Two Notes on Octavian and the Cult of Divus Iulius." *SO* 71: 87–99.

Wiegand, Isabella. 2013. *Neque libere neque vere: die Literatur unter Tiberius und der Diskurs der res publica continua.* Tübingen: Narr.

Williams, Gareth. 2002. "Ovid's Exilic Poetry: Worlds Apart." In *Brill's Companion to Ovid*, edited by Barbara Weiden Boyd, 337–81. Leiden: Brill.

Williams, Gordon. 1978. *Change and Decline: Roman Literature in the Early Empire.* Berkeley: University of California Press.

Williams, M. H. 1989. "The Expulsion of the Jews from Rome in AD 19." *Latomus* 48: 765–84.

Willner, Ann. 1984. *The Spellbinders. Charismatic Political Leadership.* New Haven: Yale University Press.

Wiseman, T. P. 2019. *The House of Augustus: A Historical Detective Story.* Princeton: Princeton University Press.

Wistrand, Erik. 1987. *Felicitas Imperatoria.* Göteborg: Acta Universitatis Gothoburgensis.

Wohlmayr, W. 2013. "Der Herrschaftsantritt des Tiberius sowie einige offene Fragen zu den Anfängen des Kaiserkultes in Rom." In *Welt – Seele – Gottheit. Festschrift für Wolfgang Speyer zum 80. Geburtstag*, edited by W. Sonntagbauer and J. Klopf, 206–14. Salzburg: Verlag F. Berger und Söhne.

Wolters, Reinhard. 1999. *Nummi Signati: Untersuchungen zur römischen Münzprägung und Geldwirtschaft.* Munich: Beck.

2003. "The Emperor and the Financial Deficits of the *Aerarium* in the Early Roman Empire." In *Credito e moneta nel mondo romano. Atti degli Incontri capresi di storia dell'economia antica: Capri, 12–14 ottobre 2000*, edited by Elio Lo Cascio, 147–60. Bari: Edipuglia.

Woodman, A. J. 1977. *Velleius Paterculus. The Tiberian narrative, 2.94–131.* Cambridge: Cambridge University Press.

1983. *Velleius Paterculus. The Caesarian and Augustan Narrative, 2.41–93.* Cambridge: Cambridge University Press.

1998. *Tacitus Reviewed.* Oxford: Oxford University Press.

2006. "Mutiny and Madness: Tacitus, *Annals* 1.16–49." *Arethusa* 39: 303–29.

2017. *The Annals of Tacitus. Books 5 and 6.* Cambridge: Cambridge University Press.

2018. *The Annals of Tacitus. Book 4.* Cambridge: Cambridge University Press.

Woodman, A. J. and R. H. Martin. 1996. *The Annals of Tacitus. Book 3.* Cambridge: Cambridge University Press.

Woods, David. 2008. "Tiberius, Tacfarinas, and the Jews." *Arctos* 42: 267–84.

Yakobson, A. 1998. "The Princess of Inscriptions: *Senatus Consultum de Cn. Pisone patre* and the Early Years of Tiberius' Reign." *SCI* 17: 206–24.

2003. "*Maiestas*, the Imperial Ideology and the Imperial Family: The Evidence of the *Senatus Consultum de Cn. Pisone Patre.*" *Eutopia* n.s. 3: 75–107.

Yavetz, Zvi. 1984. "The *Res Gestae* and Augustus' Public Image." In *Caesar Augustus: Seven Aspects*, edited by Fergus Millar and Erich Segal, 1–36. Oxford: Clarendon Press.

Zanker, Paul. 1988. *The Power of Images in the Age of Augustus*. Ann Arbor: University of Michigan Press.

———. 2004. *Die Apotheose der römischen Kaiser: Ritual und städtische Bühne*. Munich: Carl Friedrich von Siemens Stiftung.

———. 2009. "The Irritating Statues and Contradictory Portraits of Julius Caesar." In *A Companion to Julius Caesar*, edited by Miriam Griffin, 288–314. Chichester: Wiley-Blackwell.

Zwierlein-Diehl, Erika. 2007. *Antike Gemmen und ihr Nachleben*. Berlin: de Gruyter.

Zwierlein-Diehl, Erika, Alfred Bernhard-Walcher, Paulus Rainer, and Wilfried Seipel. 2008. *Magie der Steine: die antiken Prunkkameen im Kunsthistorischen Museum*. Vienna: Brandstätter.

Index

Actium, 13, 15, 22, 37, 63, 86, 98, 119, 148–49, 151, 157, 180, 207
Aelius Gallus, 145, 198
Aelius Saturninus, 182
Aemilia Lepida, 178, 193, 202
Aemilia Musa, 79
Aemilius Lepidus, M., 79, 181–82
Aemilius Lepidus, M.', 179
Aeneas, 48, 141
Afranius, L., 90
Africa, 39, 87, 90, 93, 178
Agrippa Postumus, 2, 29, 61, 142, 157, 171, 176–77, 195, 201, 204, 208
Agrippa, M. Vipsanius, 22–23, 25, 44, 61, 72, 81, 83, 95, 117, 163, 186, 196
Agrippina the Elder, 22, 28, 51, 61, 73, 75, 87, 108–9, 112, 135, 148, 160, 167, 177, 186, 189, 193–201
Agrippina the Younger, 1, 193, 205
Albucilla, 205
Albucius Silus, C., 192
Annia Rufilla, 183
Annius Pollio, C., 202
Annius Vinicianus, 202
Antistius Vetus, 173, 181
Antium, 48, 203
Antonia Maior, 83
Antonia Minor, 107–8, 112, 196–97
Antonius, Iullus, 168
Antony, Marc, 11, 13–15, 21–22, 36–40, 51, 63, 67, 88, 117, 148–49, 154–55, 167, 191, 209
Apidius Merula, 24, 50, 193
Apis, 92
Apollo, 45, 47–48, 68, 108, 116, 183, 197
Appuleia Varilla, 177–79, 181, 193
Ara Fortunae Reducis, 81
Ara Pacis, 14, 16, 43–44
Ara Providentiae, 43–44, 100, 111
Armenia, 81, 88, 114, 117, 139, 179
Arminius, 85, 87

Arruntius, L., 205
Asia, 37, 41, 53–55, 75, 88, 147, 153, 182, 186
Asinius Gallus, C., 33, 201
Asinius Pollio, C., 163
astrologers, 92, 94–96, 178
Ateius Capito, C., 183
auctoritas, 10, 17–18, 22, 30, 35, 150, 152, 172, 185
Aurelius Pius, 78
Aventine mons, 74

Baetica, 23, 54, 115
Blaesus, Q. Junius, 27, 90
Boscoreale Cups, 98, 114, 125
Bovillae, 47–48, 177
Brutus, D. Junius, 189
Brutus, M. Junius, 11, 15, 189–92

Caecilius Cornutus, M., 188
Caecina Severus, A., 90
Caelian mons, 74
Caesius Cordus, 173, 181
Caligula, emperor, 1, 4, 6, 28, 30, 44, 47, 54, 64, 69, 92, 102–4, 117, 123, 131, 134, 159–62, 170, 190, 195–200, 202–6
Calvisius Sabinus, 202
Capitoline mons, 11, 183
Cappadocia, 75, 81, 88
Capri, 68, 89–90, 97, 196–98, 204, 206
Capricorn, 96, 101, 128, 144
Cassius Longinus, C., 15, 189–92
Cassius Severus, 169–71, 192
Castor, Temple of Pollux and, 38, 47, 58–63, 126
Cestius, C., 183
charisma, 2, 4–6, 24, 28–29, 35–36, 41, 43, 52, 57–58, 61, 65, 68, 97, 108, 110, 113, 151, 162, 165, 172, 177, 185, 208–9
Cicero, 11–12, 14–15, 37, 63, 67, 94, 128, 149, 167, 176, 191
Cilicia, 88, 179
Claudia Pulchra, 51, 193–94, 201

Claudius, emperor, 1, 4, 6, 28, 51, 101, 104, 108, 112, 117, 124, 129, 159, 161, 186, 188, 207–8
Clemens, 2, 29, 175–77, 201, 208
clementia, 101, 137, 142, 154, 182
Cleopatra, 13, 22
clipeus virtutis, 102, 111, 154, 157
Clutorius Priscus, 181, 188
comet of 44 BC, 38
Cominius, C., 188
Commagene, 88
Concordia, Temple of, 45, 47, 49, 58–64, 102, 108, 126, 176–77, 197
consensus, 9, 13, 15, 17, 30, 33, 109, 154
Consolatio ad Liviam, 62
Cornelius Gallus, C., 187
Cotta Maximus Messalinus, M. Aurelius, 139–40, 199
Cotys, 88, 181
Cremutius Cordus, 162, 189–92, 201
Creticus Silanus, Q. Caecilus Metellus, 179
Cybele, 128, 131–32
Cyprus, 24, 101, 103
Cyrene, 167
Cyzicus, 50

Divus Augustus, Temple of (Emerita), 49
Divus Augustus, Temple of (Rome), 47–48
Divus Augustus, Temple of (Tarraco), 48–49, 103
Divus Iulius, Temple of, 38, 47
Domitius Afer, Cn., 193
Domitius Ahenobarbus, Cn., 205
Domitius Ahenobarbus, L., 83
domus Augusta, 4, 6, 10, 17, 20, 23–24, 29, 38, 44–45, 47, 51, 54–59, 61, 63–65, 73, 75, 81, 85–86, 96–98, 101, 105, 107–15, 123–24, 129, 135–36, 139–40, 142–46, 148, 153, 156–57, 160, 165, 171, 174, 176–77, 180–84, 188, 193, 197, 199–200, 202, 204–6
domus divina, 4, 6, 20, 24, 52, 57, 161, 166, 193
Drusus the Elder, 3, 29, 58–65, 82–83, 99, 102, 104, 108–9, 112, 118, 125–26, 130, 139, 153, 157, 197, 199
Drusus the Younger, 25, 27, 32–33, 51, 55, 60, 69–70, 73, 86–87, 90, 92, 107, 109, 111, 113, 131, 140, 146–48, 160, 165, 179, 181, 183, 185–86, 189, 197, 203–4
Drusus, son of Germanicus, 73, 104, 131, 148, 157, 186, 200–1

economic crisis of 33, 67, 75–77, 79
Egypt, 4, 81, 86, 92–93
Elbe, 82–87
elections, reform of, 69–70

Emerita, 44, 49, 101, 103
Ennia Thrasylla, 205
Ephesus, 37, 101

Faianius, 173, 175, 183
Fidenae, 74
Firmius Catus, 95, 188
flamen Dialis, 50
flamen Divi Augusti, 50
flamen Divi Iulii, 39, 47, 50–51
Florus, Julius, 81, 86–87
Fors Fortuna, Temple of, 177
Forum Clodii, 42
Frisii, 87
Fulcinius Trio, L., 44, 49, 175, 202

Gaius Caesar, adopted son of Augustus, 22–23, 41, 45, 60, 69, 73, 81, 83, 88, 92, 107, 118, 139, 150, 163, 186, 195
Galba, emperor, 14, 199, 207
Gaul, 12, 81–87, 177, 188, 207
Gemellus, Ti., 60, 197, 204
Gemma Augustea, 114, 125, 128–29, 131, 134, 144
Germania, 26–29, 62, 81–88, 97, 113, 140, 150, 208
Germanicus, 1, 3–4, 17, 21–23, 26–29, 32–33, 43–44, 50, 55, 58–62, 65, 68–69, 72–73, 75, 81, 84–88, 92, 96–97, 104, 106–13, 126–28, 131, 134–35, 137, 139–48, 154, 160, 165, 177, 179, 181, 185–86, 188, 193, 197, 204, 207, 209
Grand Camée, 115, 125, 128–31
Granius Marcellus, 121, 174, 183–84
Granius Marcianus, 202
Gyarus, 182
Gytheion, 17, 53, 55, 178

Hadrian, emperor, 1
Haterius Agrippa, D., 181–82
Hercules, 46
Herod Agrippa, 94
Horace, 13, 135, 137, 139
Hortalus, M. Hortensius, 77–78

Illyricum, 81–84, 139, 150, 180
imperium, 1, 4, 20, 25–26, 28, 31, 86, 141, 147, 149, 152, 171
Isis, 90–96
iustitia, 102, 111, 143, 152, 154, 156

Jews, 90–96
Josephus, 89–94, 204, 207
Julia, daughter of Augustus, 1, 25, 63, 118, 168, 175, 195, 204

Julia, daughter of Drusus the Younger, 197
Julia, granddaughter of Augustus, 142, 168, 171, 175, 180, 195
Julius Caesar, 3, 5, 7, 14, 16–17, 30, 36–41, 45, 63, 67–68, 101, 116, 122, 140, 144, 148–49, 155–56, 167–68, 177, 189, 191, 203, 209
Junia, 189
Junius Gallio, 162, 198
Junius Otho, 186
Jupiter, 11, 45, 47–48, 52, 60, 62–63, 85, 99, 128, 131, 137, 141, 143, 156–57, 176

Labienus, 163, 168–71, 192
Latiaris, L., 194, 199
Leptis Magna, 42, 124
lex Appuleia de maiestate, 167
lex Cornelia de famosis libellis, 168, 170
lex Cornelia de maiestate, 167–68, 181, 187, 190
lex Cornelia de sicariis et veneficiis, 197
lex de imperio Vespasiani, 4, 208
lex Iulia de adulteriis coercendis, 71, 168
lex Iulia de maiestate, 167–68, 170, 187
lex Iulia repetundarum, 168
lex Valeria Cornelia, 69
Libo, L. Scribonius, 175
Libo, M. Scribonius Drusus, 2, 29, 63, 95–97, 153, 166, 175–78, 181, 187, 199, 202
Livia, 3–4, 13, 43, 47, 54, 56, 58, 61–62, 89, 100, 107–8, 111, 114–15, 125, 128–34, 140, 151, 153, 178, 186, 195–97, 203
Livilla, daughter of Germanicus, 148
Livilla, sister of Germanicus, 90, 108, 112, 160, 185–86, 197, 202
Livy, 93, 99, 163, 191
Lucilius Capito, 54, 89
Lucius Caesar, adopted son of Augustus, 22–23, 45, 60, 69, 81, 83, 107, 118, 150, 179, 186, 195
Ludi Saeculares, 45, 57, 64
Lugdunum, 98–99, 101, 104

Macedonia, 181
Macro, Q. Naevius Cordus Sutorius, 197, 202–5
Maecenas, 161, 169
maiestas, 6, 33, 52, 80, 121, 138, 150, 152, 158, 165, 188, 190, 195, 197, 202, 205, 209
Mamercus Scaurus, 191, 201
Manilius, 95, 142, 144–46, 148
Marcellus, nephew of Augustus, 3, 22–23, 118, 157
Marcellus, Theater of, 115
Marcia, 190
Marcius Philippus, L., 11
Marcomanni, 86–87

Marius, C., 16
Marius, Sextus, 79
Maroboduus, 86
Mars, 38, 40, 47, 49, 51, 63, 85, 108, 125, 128, 144, 176
Mausoleum of Augustus, 14, 59, 97, 105, 108
Messalla Corvinus, M. Valerius, 57, 139
Messalla Volesus, M. Valerius, 168, 182
Messalla, M. Valerius (cos. 3 BC), 45
Messene, 24
Minerva, 155
Misenum, 161
moderatio, 101, 111, 151, 166

Narbo, 42, 192
Nero, emperor, 1, 4, 6, 48, 104, 159, 207
Nero, son of Germanicus, 51, 55, 73, 87, 104, 112, 131, 148, 167, 186, 194–96, 199, 201, 203
Nola, 47, 150
numen, 41–43, 58, 61, 110, 137, 144–45, 155–59, 180, 182

Octavia Maior, 51, 178
Octavia Minor, 156
Otho, emperor, 208
Ovid, 40, 44, 57–58, 61–63, 85, 108, 135–46, 148, 153, 159, 164, 170–71, 176, 187, 199

Palatine mons, 48, 64, 68, 108, 197
Pannonia, 27–28, 41, 81, 86, 113, 121, 128, 139, 185
Parthia, 81, 85, 88, 114, 117, 128, 140, 179
pater patriae, 15, 22, 24, 31, 55, 57, 115, 151, 154, 156–57, 171
pax Augusta, 45, 50, 80, 88, 97, 138, 147–48, 173
Pergamum, 41, 53, 66, 101
Phaedrus, 159–62
Philippi, 45, 155, 189–91
Philo, 89–92, 94
pietas, 12, 40, 59, 102, 111–13, 154, 158
Pisidia, 106
Piso, Cn. Calpurnius, 43, 49, 106, 109–13, 145, 166, 173, 176, 178–82, 187, 192, 198, 202
Plancina, 109–10
Pliny the Elder, 13, 38, 47, 75, 88, 92, 155, 191, 194, 196
Pliny the Younger, 76, 172, 198
Pompeia Macrina, 200
Pompey, 30, 50, 74, 177, 179, 191, 200
Pompey, Sextus, 15
Pompey, Theater of, 74, 178, 186, 190
Pomponius Secundus, Q., 198
Pontifex Maximus, 8, 31, 50, 55, 97
Pontius Pilate, 94
Porticus Liviae, 62

Praetorian Guard, 27–28, 128, 185, 193,
    197–98, 207–8
Prima Porta, statue of Augustus, 13, 114, 118–23
Propertius Celer, 78
providentia, 43–44, 58, 100, 154, 164

Quirinus, 47

radiate crown, 49, 100–1, 115, 129, 132
Raetia, 81, 139
recusatio imperii, 27, 30, 123
Res Gestae, 12–18, 22, 26, 40, 44, 61, 73, 79–80,
    82, 84–85, 97, 101–2, 104–5, 147–48,
    154, 208
Rhescuporis, 88, 181
Rhine, 27, 82–86, 194
Rhodes, 23, 25, 81, 83, 88, 118, 150
Roma, 36–37, 49, 57, 99, 105, 124–25, 128, 131
Romulus, 16, 40, 46–47, 144
Rubrius, 173, 175

Sacrovir, Julius, 81, 86–87, 187
Sallustius Crispus, C., 177
salus, 102, 112–13, 154, 158, 165
Sardinia, 90–91, 93
Saturninus, friend of Tiberius, 91
Saturninus, L. Appuleius, 167
Scorpio, 101, 128
Scribonia, 175, 177
Second Cyrene Edict, 167
Second Triumvirate, 14, 22, 26, 30, 63, 135,
    155, 192
Seius Strabo, L., 185
Sejanus, L. Aelius, 27, 33, 50, 60–61, 63–64, 68,
    79–80, 92, 97–98, 112, 121, 123, 131, 145,
    148, 152–53, 159–62, 167, 185–86,
    188–91, 193–94, 196–205
Sempronius Gracchus, Ti., 204
Senatus Consultum de Pisone patre, 6, 17, 34, 43,
    109–13, 179–82, 187
Senatus Consultum from Larinum, 68–72
Seneca the Elder, 84, 162–64, 168–70, 191, 202
Seneca the Younger, 78, 159, 162, 164, 182,
    184–85, 190–91
servus publicus, 126
Sextius Paconianus, 199, 202
Sibylline Books, 96
Silanus, App., 202
Silanus, C. Junius, 54, 89, 168, 173, 182, 186
Silanus, D. Junius, 136, 180
Silanus, M. Junius, 180
Silius, C., 173, 186–88, 193–94

Smyrna, 54, 89
Sodales Augustales, 47–50, 58, 108, 111, 197
Sosia Galla, 187
Spain, 23, 40, 49, 54–55, 66, 79, 81, 83, 86,
    104, 107, 109, 163, 175, 192, 207
Strabo, 33, 84–86, 93, 145–49, 196, 200
Suillius, P., 188
Sulla, 7, 167, 178
Sword of Tiberius, 125–28, 141
Syria, 81, 107, 179

Tabula Hebana, 41, 68, 106–10, 113
Tabula Siarensis, 58, 85, 106–10, 113, 140
Tacfarinas, 87, 90, 93
Tarius Gratianus, 202
Tarraco, 42, 48, 50, 103, 163
Theophanes, 50, 200
Thrace, 88, 139, 181
Thrasyllus, 94–95, 183, 205
Titius Sabinus, 51, 186, 194–95, 199
Togonius Gallus, 198
Trajan, emperor, 1, 3, 76, 89, 172
Trebellienus Rufus, 202
tribunicia potestas, 1, 8, 15, 20, 25–27, 31, 110,
    171
Tusculum, 203

Valerius Maximus, 78, 110, 135, 142, 152–59,
    189, 191
Varus, P. Quinctilius, 29, 80, 82–86, 127–28,
    139, 145, 177
Velleius Paterculus, 1, 17, 21, 25, 27–28, 33–34,
    43, 45, 50, 52, 69, 81–83, 86, 102, 110,
    135, 139, 142, 147–55, 160, 164, 175, 186,
    189, 191, 196
Vespasian, emperor, 14, 208
Vesta, 64, 100
Vibius Marsus, C., 205
Vibius Serenus, C., 188
Vinicius, M., 148, 153
Vipsania, 83, 117
Virgo, 143–44
Vistilia, 71–72, 90
Vistilius, Sex., 199
Vitellius, emperor, 208
Vitellius, P., 198
Vonones, 179
Votienus Montanus, 162, 192

Waldgirmes, 83
Weber, Max, 4–6, 14, 17–20, 35, 64, 209
Weser, 82–84

www.ingramcontent.com/pod-product-compliance
Ingram Content Group UK Ltd.
Pitfield, Milton Keynes, MK11 3LW, UK
UKHW022039050125
452959UK00008B/55

9 781009 476676